Milestones

HEINLE
CENGAGE Learning

Australia • Brazil • Japan • Korea • Mexico • Singapore • Spain • United Kingdom • United States

HEINLE
CENGAGE Learning™

Milestones C

Contributing Writer: Kerrie Tilney

Editorial Director: Joe Dougherty

Publisher: Sherrise Roehr

Managing Editor: Carmela Fazzino-Farah

Associate Development Editor:
Sarah Sandoski

Editorial Assistant: Jennifer Kuhnberg

Technology Development Editor:
Debie Mirtle

Executive Marketing Manager:
Jim McDonough

Director of Product Marketing:
Amy T. Mabley

Product Marketing Manager: Katie Kelley

Assistant Marketing Manager:
Andrea Bobotas

Director of Content and Media Production:
Michael Burggren

Content Project Manager:
Dawn Marie Elwell

Manufacturing Manager: Marcia Locke

Development Editor: Arley Gray

Composition and Project Management:
Nesbitt Graphics, Inc.

Illustrations/Photography:
see pages 491–493 for credits

Interior Design: Studio Montage

Cover Design: Page 2, LLC

Cover Image:
Joseph Sohm/Visions of America/Corbis

Library of Congress Control Number: 2007940576

ISBN-13: 978-1-4240-0889-6

ISBN-10: 1-4240-0889-1

Heinle Cengage Learning
25 Thomson Place
Boston, Massachusetts 02210
USA

Cengage Learning products are represented in Canada by Nelson Education, Ltd.

Visit Heinle online at **elt.heinle.com**
Visit our corporate website at **www.cengage.com**

Printed in the United States of America
1 2 3 4 5 6 7   12 11 10 09 08

Program Authors

NEIL ANDERSON

Dr. Neil J. Anderson received his Ph.D. from the University of Texas at Austin, where he specialized in research in the teaching of reading. He has done significant work in the area of reading comprehension, reading strategies, and fluency. He has published several books in this area and continues to actively research and publish.

Dr. Anderson has been teaching English and teachers of English for over twenty-five years. He is a professor in the Department of Linguistics and English Language at Brigham Young University in Salt Lake City, Utah. He has received many awards for outstanding teaching and believes that everyone can learn to be a good reader.

Dr. Anderson helped to establish the pedagogical framework of the *Milestones* program with a particular focus on reading strategies and reading fluency.

JILL KOREY O'SULLIVAN

Jill Korey O'Sullivan holds a Masters Degree in Education from Harvard University. Her specific area of research and interest is language and literacy. Ms. Korey O'Sullivan is an experienced author and editor of educational materials with a background in curriculum development and teaching. She has taught and developed materials for students of a broad range of levels and in a variety of educational settings, including kindergarten, middle school, and community college programs.

Ms. Korey O'Sullivan has brought her classroom experience and creativity to the writing of several textbooks and has served as editor on many publications in the field of English language learning.

She helped to establish the pedagogical framework of the *Milestones* program, incorporating the latest in research and pedagogy.

The students she has taught and the students who use her materials serve as her inspiration.

JENNIFER TRUJILLO

Jennifer Trujillo received her Ph.D. in Educational Leadership and Change from Fielding Graduate University, Santa Barbara, CA. Dr. Trujillo grew up in a home where another language besides English was spoken. Her family moved back and forth between her mother's homeland and the United States. Her dedication to reading led her to earn degrees and teaching credentials in English and Reading from the University of Northern Colorado.

She is currently a professor in the Teacher Education Department at Fort Lewis College in Durango, Colorado. Her areas of specialization are reading and writing, ESL, home-school partnerships, professional development, cognitive coaching, differentiated instruction and diversity training.

Dr. Trujillo feels strongly about the importance of culturally responsive and universally relevant readings, with challenging activities, to help all students succeed. To that end, she helped to establish the pedagogical framework of the *Milestones* program and provided valuable feedback on each of the reading selections to ensure culturally responsive instruction for the pre and post reading activities.

Program Advisors

ROBERT J. MARZANO, Ph.D., Vocabulary Advisor

Dr. Robert J. Marzano is president and founder of Marzano & Associates, specializing in long term school reform efforts to enhance student academic achievement. His work guiding teachers to assist students in developing academic language can be found in the books *Building Background Knowledge for Academic Achievement* and *Building Academic Vocabulary*.

Over his 35 years in education, the central theme of his work has been translating research and theory into practical programs and tools for teachers and administrators. He is a Senior Scholar at Mid-continent Research for Education and Learning (McREL) and an Associate Professor at Cardinal Stritch University.

Dr. Marzano received his M.Ed. degree in Reading and Language Arts from Seattle University, and his Ph.D. in Curriculum and Instruction from the University of Washington.

He is the author of more than 20 books, 150 articles, and more than 100 curriculum guides and related materials for teachers and students. His most recent publication is *The Art and Science of Teaching: a Comprehensive Framework for Effective Instruction.*

KEITH LENZ, Ph.D., Differentiated Instruction/Universal Access Advisor

Dr. Keith Lenz specializes in adolescents with learning problems, teacher planning, and strategic instruction for teaching diverse groups. He has degrees in Special Education and Secondary Education from Bradley University and a Ph.D. from the University of Kansas. At the University of Kansas, Dr. Lenz is an Associate Professor, Director of the Institute for Effective Instruction, and Senior Research Scientist at the Center for Research on Learning.

Dr. Lenz is the founder and member of the Board of Trustees at the Strategic Learning Center, Inc., Seattle, WA. He is an adjunct professor at Seattle Pacific University, and a National Trainer of The Strategies Intervention Model.

Dr. Lenz's work with guiding teachers on effective differentiated instruction practices can be found in his co-authored book *Teaching content to all: Inclusive teaching in grades 4–12*, amongst others.

Dr. Lenz taught at Florida Atlantic University and serves as a Project Trainer for the Florida Department of Education.

ANNE KATZ, Ph.D., Assessment Advisor

Dr. Anne Katz has worked for 20 years as a researcher and evaluator for projects connected with the education of linguistically and culturally diverse students. As a teacher educator, she has provided and supported professional development in the areas of curriculum, assessment, and evaluation.

Dr. Katz co-directed a national study of successful leadership strategies to create more harmonious racial and ethnic environments in K–12 schools. She is co-author of *Leading for Diversity: How School Leaders Promote Positive Interethnic Relations* and author of numerous publications on diversity and the development of standards-based assessment systems.

Dr. Katz was instrumental in developing standards for English as a second language with the Teachers of English to Speakers of Other Languages organization, and she has assisted many school districts in developing more authentic assessments of student performance. In all her work, she promotes the links between research and the classroom to support meaningful school change.

Anne Katz holds a doctorate in second language education from Stanford University. She is a lecturer at the School for International Training's graduate teacher education program.

Teacher Reviewers

Sonia Abrew
Orange County Public Schools
Orlando, FL

Ruby Ali
H.L. Watkins Middle School
Palm Beach Gardens, FL

Jean Anderson
Broward County Public Schools
Ft. Lauderdale, FL

Teresa Arvizu
McFarland Unified School District
McFarland, CA

Maridell Bagnal
Fletcher Middle School
Jacksonville Beach, FL

Miriam Barrios-Chacon
Chipman Middle School
Alameda, CA

Cathy Bonner
Bowie High School
El Paso, TX

Irene Borrego
CA State University Bakersfield
Bakersfield, CA

Tanya Castro
Pharr-San Juan-Alamo Independent
School District
Alamo, TX

Nicole Chaput
Metro Nashville Public Schools
Nashville, TN

Vikki Chavez
San Bernardino High School
San Bernardino, CA

Anthony Colonna
Ocala Middle School
San Jose, CA

Catherine Cominio
Howell Watkins Middle School
Palm Beach Gardens, FL

Ayanna Cooper
DeKalb County Schools
DeKalb, GA

James Coplan
Oakland Technical High School
Oakland, CA

Alicia Cron
Austin Middle School
San Juan, TX

Libby Taylor Deleon
Plano ISD
Plano, TX

Farida Doherty
Boston Public Schools
Boston, MA

Mercedes A. Egues
Fort Lauderdale High School
Fort Lauderdale, FL

Karen Ernst
Highland High School
Palmdale, CA

Rafael Estrada
Lake Shore Middle School
Belle Glade, FL

Mary Ford
Pahokee Middle High School
Pahokee, FL

Beverly Franke
Palm Beach County Schools
Greenacres, FL

Helena Gandell
Duval County Public Schools
Jacksonville, FL

Linsey Gannon
Lawrence Cook Middle School
Santa Rosa, CA

Renee Gaudet
New River Elementary School
Wesley Chapel, FL

Nathalie Gillis-Rumowicz
Seminole Middle School
Seminole, FL

Evelyn Gomez
The Academy for New Americans
Middle School
Astoria, NY

Rafael Gonzalez
Wasco Union High School District
Wasco, CA

Sarah Harley
ALBA Elementary School
Milwaukee, WI

Renote Jean-Francois
Boston Public Schools
Boston, MA

Vivian Kahn
I.S. 296 Halsey School
Brooklyn, NY

Tony King
Boston Public Schools
Boston, MA

Christa Kirby
Pinellas Country School District
Largo, FL

Letitia Laberee
Angelo Patri Middle School
Bronx, NY

Gemma Lacanlale
Houston Independent School District
Houston, TX

Arthur Larievy
Boston Public Schools
Boston, MA

Alisa Leckie
Billy Lane Lauffer Middle School
Tucson, AZ

Chad Leith
Boston Public Schools
Boston, MA

Arnulfo Lopez
Delano High School
Delano, CA

Carmen Lopez
Cesar E. Chavez High School
Delano, CA

Lana Lysen
Multicultural, ESOL Education
Fort Lauderdale, FL

Vanessa MacDonna
Andries Huddle Middle School
Brooklyn, NY

Rita Marsh-Birch
Sandalwood High School
Jacksonville, FL

Lorraine Martini
Nova Middle School
Davie, FL

Jean Melby-Mauer
Valley High School
Las Vegas, NV

Patsy Mills
Houston Independent School District
Houston, TX

Amy Mirco
Charlotte-Mecklenburg Schools
Charlotte, NC

Gloria Pelaez
University of Miami
Miami, FL

Maria Pena
Doral Middle School
Doral, FL

Yvonne Perez
Alief Middle School
Houston, TX

Lunine Pierre-Jerome
Boston Public Schools
Boston, MA

Yolanda Pokaski
Boston Public Schools
Boston, MA

Diana Ramlall
School District of Palm Beach County
West Palm Beach, FL

Marlene Roney
New River Middle School
Fort Lauderdale, FL

Cheryl Serrano
Lynn University
Boca Raton, FL

Raynel Shepard
Boston Public Schools
Boston, MA

Michele Spohn
Fort Caroline Middle School
Jacksonville, FL

Ilza Sterling
Falcon Cove Middle School
Weston, FL

John Sullivan
Clark County School
District, East Region
Las Vegas, NV

Teri Suzuki
Lincoln Middle School
Alameda, CA

Daisy Torres
Marion County Schools
Ocala, FL

Matthew Trillo
Maxwell Middle School
Tucson, AZ

Heather Tugwell
Oakland Unified School District
Oakland, CA

Cassandra Vukcevic
Ridgewood High School
New Port Richey, FL

Sheila Weinstein
Deerfield Beach Middle School
Deerfield Beach, FL

MaryLou Whaley
Immigrant Acculturation Center
Tampa, FL

Jill Wood
Dr. John Long Middle School
Wesley Chapel, FL

Veronica Yepez
Washington Middle School
Pasadena, CA

Choices

Page 138

Cultures and Traditions
Page 212

Making a Difference
Page 286

UNIT 5

UNIT 6

Leadership
Page 354

Welcome to *Milestones!* Your Steps to Success

The title of this book is *Milestones*. Milestones are rocks set on a road to show the distance from one place to another. Like milestones on a road, this book will help guide you from one step in your learning to the next. It will provide the support you need every step of the way.

There are four specific skills you will learn and practice in *Milestones*:

Reading Reading is the foundation of learning. This book will help you become a more effective reader in many ways. For example, you will learn important vocabulary words that come from the readings. You will also learn academic vocabulary. These are the words that are used frequently in all subject areas. Learning academic vocabulary will help you understand academic texts and succeed in subject areas. Reading Fluency activities will help you learn to read more fluently. Reading Strategies will teach you specific methods for comprehending readings more effectively.

Listening Effective listening requires you to be focused and attentive. This book will provide you with opportunities to practice and improve your listening skills.

Speaking You will have many opportunities to practice your speaking skills by discussing the readings, performing role plays, and working on projects with your classmates.

Writing This book will help you understand and practice the writing process. You will plan, draft, revise, and edit each of your writing assignments. You will learn how to evaluate your own writing and how to give feedback to your classmates on their writing.

Your teachers will provide important guidance as you work through this book. The assessment material at the end of each chapter and unit will help you and your teacher identify material you have successfully learned and areas where you may need more practice.

However, the most important ingredient for academic success is . . . YOU! You are the one holding the book. You are the one reading these words. You have the power and ability to work towards academic success. As you open this book, open your mind by thinking carefully and critically.

With this book, help from your teacher, and your own determination, you will achieve wonderful academic milestones!

Language

Explore the Theme

1. What kinds of **languages** do you see in the pictures?
2. What **languages** do you read or speak?

Theme Activity

Think about the people you speak with every day, such as your family, friends, and teachers. Do you use the same kind of language with each of them? With a partner, discuss the differences between informal language and formal language. Which do you use with friends? When do you use formal language?

CHAPTER 1

Objectives

Reading Strategy

Relate your own experiences to a reading

Listening and Speaking

Discuss the readings

Grammar

Learn subject-verb agreement in the simple present tense

Writing

Write an autobiographical short story

Academic Vocabulary

relate	analyze
summarize	predict

Academic Content

Learning and appreciating a new language

Words borrowed and words loaned in languages

● **Chapter Focus Question**

Why is it important to feel connected to other people?

Reading 1 **Literature**

Autobiographical short story

Making Connections

by Francisco Jiménez

Reading 2 **Content:** Social Studies

Magazine article (adaptation)

Words Around the World

by Carla Meskill

Making Connections

● **About the Reading**

You are going to read a short story about a young boy named Panchito, who works hard to read and write in a new language: English.

Build Background

Migrant Workers in the 1930s

In the 1930s, migrant workers and their families moved from place to place, picking potatoes, cotton, oranges, and other crops. The work was difficult. Often, the pay was so low that families could not buy food to eat. John Steinbeck wrote about migrant workers in a novel called *The Grapes of Wrath*. In it, he describes the Joads, a family of struggling migrant workers in the 1930s.

Dorothea Lange used her talent as a photographer to document the lives of migrant workers.

1. Look at the photo of a mother and her two children.
2. Describe the expression on the mother's face and the clothing she and her children are wearing.
3. What does the image tell you about the life of migrant workers, like the Joads, in the 1930s?

In "Making Connections," Panchito lives with a family of migrant workers. Like the Joads, Panchito's family once lived under challenging conditions in migrant labor camps. Panchito recalls these experiences in an assignment for English class.

"Migrant Mother" (1936), Dorothea Lange

Use Prior Knowledge

Talk About What You Like to Read

What do you enjoy reading? In "Making Connections," the main character discovers that he does not know how to read for enjoyment. Create a word web to reveal what you like to read. In the center, write a general subject you like a lot. In the smaller rings, identify a few ideas related to your main subject. In the smallest rings, write a more specific topic related to your general subject.

Share your word web with a partner.

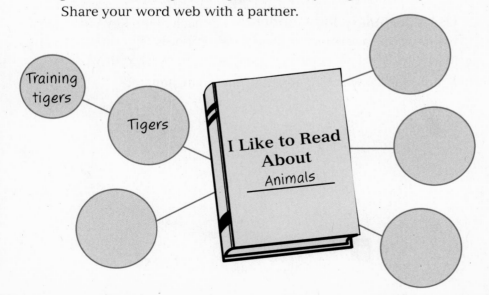

Key Vocabulary

anxious

approach

exhausted

pace

reputation

rupture

● Vocabulary From the Reading
Learn, Practice, and Use Independently

Learn Vocabulary Read each sentence. Look at the **highlighted** word. Think about the context (the words around the highlighted word). Use the context to determine the meaning of the word.

1. Mary felt **anxious** about her exam because she had not studied enough and wasn't prepared.
2. When I **approach** a strange dog, I am careful in case he bites.
3. After walking for hours, Alaina was **exhausted** and needed to take a break.
4. Trevor walked out of the library. When he saw he was late for work, he increased his walking **pace.**
5. I hear that Mrs. Chen's English class is hard. She has a **reputation** for challenging her students.
6. It rained so much that we were afraid the dam in the river would **rupture** and flood the town.

Practice Vocabulary Fill in the blanks with the correct Key Vocabulary words.

1. Slow down as you _____ a busy intersection filled with cars.
2. When Susan arrived at her new job, she felt _____ and a little scared.
3. The _____ puppies slept all morning after playing with the toys.
4. She read at a slow _____ to understand better what she was reading.
5. The _____ in the bag of sugar made a mess on the kitchen shelf.
6. Her father has a _____ for treating his children fairly.

Use Vocabulary Independently For each of the Key Vocabulary words, create a short list of synonyms, or words with similar meanings. Use a dictionary or a thesaurus to check your work.

1. **anxious**   worried, nervous, uncertain, agitated

✓Checkpoint

1. What word means very tired? What word means to break open?
2. Write a sentence using the word **approach.**

Vocabulary Log

Workbook page 29

Independent Practice CD-ROM/Online

● Academic Vocabulary

Vocabulary for the Reading Strategy

Word	Explanation	Sample Sentence	Visual Cue
relate *verb*	to connect	Robby could **relate** to how the losing team felt because he had also lost a game early in the season.	
summarize *verb*	to make a summary, or a brief account of a reading	The student worked hard to **summarize** the long novel.	

Draw a picture and write a sentence for each word.

● Reading Strategy

Relate Your Own Experiences to a Reading

As you read about Panchito's experiences, think about events in your own life. This will help you **relate** to the character and understand him better.

1. Think about how hard Panchito works to succeed in school.
   a. What does Panchito do to succeed in school? What do you do?
   b. Who helps him to succeed? Who helps you to succeed?
   c. What challenges does he face, both in and out of school? What challenges do you face?
   d. What motivates Panchito to do his best? What motivates you?

2. For each question above, create a chart like the one below. You will complete the charts after you read the story.

What does Panchito do to succeed in school?		What do I do to succeed in school?
_____ _____ _____ _____	◄──►	_____ _____ _____ _____

3. When you finish reading, you will **summarize** your responses to show how closely you **relate** to Panchito's experiences.

> ✓ **Checkpoint**
>
> Summarize a story you have read to a partner.

Vocabulary Log

Workbook page 30

Independent Practice CD-ROM/Online

Text Genre

Autobiographical Short Story

"Making Connections" is an **autobiographical short story.** An autobiographical short story is one that comes from the author's experiences. Autobiographical short stories usually include the features below.

Autobiographical Short Story	
characters	people in a story
conflict	a struggle between two opposing forces
plot	events in a story that happen in a certain order
description	vivid details that add interest to the narrative

Meet the Author

Francisco Jiménez was born in Mexico in 1943. At age four, he and his family moved to the United States. There, Jiménez attended an English-speaking school, though he spoke only Spanish. For years, his family lived as migrant workers. They traveled from place to place in order to find good jobs. Eventually, they moved back to Mexico. Jiménez later returned to the United States and discovered a love of literature. Today, he is a college professor, an award-winning novelist, and an author of children's books.

Reading Focus Questions

As you read, think about these questions.

1. How does the reading relate to the theme of "language"?
2. What do you think was the author's purpose in writing "Making Connections"?
3. Is it important for Panchito to **relate** to the people he reads about? Why or why not?

Workbook
page 31

Independent Practice
CD-ROM/Online

Making Connections

by Francisco Jiménez

1   At the end of my **freshman** year, I received good grades in all subjects except English, even though I had worked the hardest in it. Writing was difficult for me. My freshman English teacher told me that my writing was weak. She suggested that I read more, that reading would improve my writing. "At least read the newspaper every day," she told me. "Read for enjoyment." I had little time to read. I read only for information for my classes, and I could barely **keep up**. Besides, we had no reading material at home and we didn't get the newspaper. I never got more free time to read all during high school, but I did learn to read for enjoyment. It happened in my **sophomore** year, in English class.

2   Miss Audrey Bell, my teacher, had a **reputation** for being hard. When she walked into the class the first day and wrote her name on the board, I heard moans from classmates sitting next to me. "I am **sunk**!" one of them said. "Hello, F," another uttered. Now I was even more worried.

Reading Strategy

Relate Your Own Experiences to a Reading Panchito's teacher tells him to read for enjoyment. How does he feel about this? Do you read for enjoyment?

Reading Check

1. **Recall facts** What class is challenging for the narrator?

2. **Recall facts** What is Miss Bell's **reputation**?

3. **Hypothesize** Panchito's teacher tells him that reading for enjoyment will improve his writing. Explain how reading for enjoyment can influence your school work.

---

freshman first year in high school
keep up continue at the same speed as everybody else
sophomore second year of high school
sunk in trouble

3
Miss Bell had a round face, a small turned-up nose, full lips, and lively blue eyes, and she wore wire-rimmed glasses. Her smile never left her, even when she was upset. When she wrote on the board, her upper arm shook like jelly, just like Mamá's arms. The back of her hands were covered with small brown spots the size of raisins, and her shiny nails looked like the wings of red beetles. She teased students and often made comments that made the class laugh. I laughed too, even though sometimes I did not understand her jokes.

4
No one laughed at her homework assignments, though. Every week she gave us vocabulary and spelling lists and a poem to **memorize.** I wrote the poems on note cards and attached them to the broom handle or placed them in my shirt pocket and memorized them as I cleaned the offices after school. I did the same thing with spelling and vocabulary words. I had a harder time with reading and writing. I was a slow reader and often had to read each assignment twice. At times my mind wandered off as I worried about Papá. When we discussed the readings in class, I was surprised to find out that I had not really understood what I had read.

5
Writing was even more difficult for me. Miss Bell asked us to write short compositions analyzing short stories we read for class. I was happy whenever I understood the plot and **summarized** it, but this was not good enough.

Reading Strategy

Relate Your Own Experiences to a Reading Has there ever been a time when other people laughed and you didn't understand why? **Summarize** the event by telling who was there, where you were, and what happened.

---

memorize remember something exactly, learn something by heart

6   "Don't tell me the story," she would say, smiling. "I know it. I want you to analyze it." I thought I knew what she meant, so in my next composition I wrote about the lesson I learned from reading the story. I hoped this was what she wanted. The stories I had heard from Papá and Mamá, Tío Mauricio, and other migrant workers all had a lesson in them about right and wrong, like "**La Llorona**," "The Boy and His Grandfather," or "The Three Brothers."

7   When Miss Bell returned our compositions, I fixed my eye on the stack of papers as she walked around the aisles passing them out, trying to spot mine. My papers always came back looking as though she had poured red ink on them. My heart pounded faster with each step she took toward me. She grinned as she handed me my paper. I quickly grabbed it. It had fewer corrections than my previous papers, but the grade was only a disappointing C. I stuck it in my binder, and for the rest of the class I had a hard time concentrating. During study hall, I took out the paper. She had written "Good progress" at the bottom of it. I felt better. I then went over the corrections carefully to make sure I understood them. I did not want to make the same mistakes in my next writing assignment, which Miss Bell announced the following day.

Reading Strategy

Relate Your Own Experiences to a Reading How did Panchito react when he saw the words "Good progress" on his paper? Have you ever reacted the same way to positive words?

✓ Reading Check

1. **Recall facts** Who told Panchito stories about right and wrong?
2. **Interpret** Why did Miss Bell smile when she handed back Panchito's paper?
3. **Summarize** Tell a story you know that teaches a lesson.

_____

La Llorona the crying woman (Spanish)

Farm labor workers lived in housing that was very simple and basic, which made daily life challenging.

Reading Strategy

Relate Your Own Experiences to a Reading What is Panchito's writing assignment? If you had the same assignment, what would you write about?

8   "Our next unit is on autobiography, the history of a person's life written or told by that person," she explained. "So for your next composition, I want you to write about a personal experience, something that happened to you." I liked the assignment, but it was harder than I expected. I thought of writing about being **deported,** but I did not want my teacher to know that my family had crossed the border illegally and that I was born in Mexico.

9   An idea finally came to me late that evening. As I was sitting at the kitchen table trying to figure out what to write, Trampita entered the room, pulling up his white shorts. "What are you doing?" I asked.

10   "I am getting a glass of water," he responded, half-asleep. His small body cast a thin shadow on the wall. We called him "Trampita," "little tramp," because Mamá had dressed him in baby clothes we found in the city **dump.** As he passed me on his way back to bed, I noticed his **bulging navel,** the size of an egg, that had **ruptured** when he was a few months old.

11   We had been living in a farm labor camp in Santa Rosa. It was winter. Papá and Mamá worked at an apple **cannery** at night and left Roberto to take care of Trampita and me while they were gone. One evening, before leaving for work, Mamá prepared the milk bottle for Trampita and laid him on a wide mattress that was on the dirt floor. After my parents left, Roberto and I sat on the mattress and told ghost stories until we got sleepy. We said our prayers and went to bed next to Trampita. We kept our clothes on because it was freezing cold. At dawn, we woke up, frightened by our parents' screams. "Where's Trampita?" Mamá cried out. "Where is he?" Papá shouted. They had terror in their eyes when they saw Trampita was gone.

---

deported forced to leave a country
dump place where people take their garbage
bulging swelling or sticking out, like a lump
navel belly button
cannery business where food is prepared and put into cans

12   "I don't know, Mamá," Roberto stuttered, shivering from the cold. Papá noticed an opening at the foot of the tent near the mattress. He rushed out. Seconds later he returned with Trampita in his arms. My baby brother was stiff and purple.

13   I decided to write about that experience. I wrote three drafts, making sure I did not make any mistakes. I turned it in, feeling confident. When I got my paper back, I was disappointed to see the red marks again. I had made a few errors. I felt worse when I read Miss Bell's note at the bottom of the paper, asking me to see her after class. *She must be pretty upset with the mistakes I made,* I thought. I half listened to what she said during the rest of the class. When class was over, I waited until everyone had left the room before I **approached** her, folding the paper in half to hide the red marks.

Reading Strategy

Relate **Your Own Experiences to a Reading** Summarize the story of a time when you worked hard on a challenging homework assignment.

✓ **Reading Check**

1. **Recall facts** What sound woke up Panchito and Roberto?

2. **Make an inference** Do you think life at the farm labor camp was comfortable for Panchito? Use examples from the story to support your answer.

3. **Predict** Why do you think Miss Bell wants to see Panchito?

14   "Is what you wrote a true story?" Miss Bell asked.

15   "Yes," I answered, feeling **anxious**.

16   "I thought so," she said, smiling. "It's a very **moving** story. Did your brother die?"

17   "Oh no!" I exclaimed. "He almost did, but God saved him. He rolled off the mattress, landed outside the tent, and cried so much that he hurt his navel."

18   "His **hernia** must have really hurt," she said thoughtfully. "I am sorry." She looked away and cleared her throat. "Now, let's look at your paper." I handed it to her, lowering my head. "You're making a lot of progress," she said. "Your writing shows promise. If you're able to **overcome** the difficulties like the one you describe in your paper and you continue working as hard as you have, you're going to succeed." She gave me back the paper and added, "Here, take it home, make the corrections, and turn it in to me tomorrow after class."

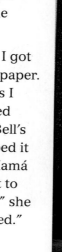

Reading Strategy

Relate **Your Own Experiences to a Reading** Why does Panchito feel lucky to be in Miss Bell's class? Have you ever felt the same way? Explain.

19   "I will. Thank you, Miss Bell." I floated out of the room, thinking about how lucky I was to be in her class. She reminded me of Mr. Lema, my sixth-grade teacher, who had helped with English during the lunch hour.

20   That evening when I got home I worked on the paper. I looked at the mistakes I had made and corrected them, following Miss Bell's suggestions. As I retyped it on the kitchen table, Mamá came over and sat next to me. "It's late, Panchito," she said softly. "Time for bed."

---

moving making you feel a strong emotion
hernia opening in the muscles of the abdomen, often resulting in a lump or bulge
overcome succeed or get through something difficult

21 "I am almost finished."

22 "What are you working on, *mijo*?"

23 "It's a paper I wrote for my English class on Trampita. My teacher liked it," I said proudly.

24 "On Trampita!" she exclaimed.

25 She got up and stood behind me. She placed her hands on my shoulders and asked me to read it. When I finished, I felt her tears on the back of my neck.

26 The next day after class I turned in my revised paper to Miss Bell. She glanced at it, placed it on a pile of papers on her desk, and picked up a book. "Have you read *The Grapes of Wrath*?" she asked. "It's a wonderful novel by John Steinbeck."

27 "No," I said, wondering what the word **wrath** meant.

28 "I'd like for you to read it." She handed it to me. "I think you'll enjoy it. You can read it for your book report."

Reading Strategy

Relate Your Own Experiences to a Reading Why is Panchito so proud of his work? Describe a time when you felt proud of an effort you made.

29 *When am I going to find time to read such a thick book?* I thought, running my fingers along its **spine**. I was planning to read a smaller book for my report. Miss Bell must have noticed the pain in my face because she added, "And you'll get extra credit because it's a long book." I felt better.

30 "Thanks!" I said. "It'll give me a chance to improve my grade." Her gentle smile reminded me of Mamá and the blessing she gave every morning when I left the house.

Reading Check

1. **Recall facts** Why does Panchito stay up late?

2. **Speculate** Why do you think Panchito's mother cries when he finishes his story?

3. **Speculate** Panchito wondered what the word "wrath" meant. How will he figure out its meaning?

---

mijo "my child" or "my son" (Spanish)
wrath anger, hostility
spine part of a book that is bound; the part seen on a bookcase

31   After my last class, I picked up the books and binders I needed from my locker and walked to the public library to study before going to work at five o'clock. I double-checked to make sure I had the novel with me. On the way, I kept thinking about how I was going to get through such a long book. I felt its weight on my shoulders and the back of my neck. I quickened my **pace,** passing students left and right. The honking of car horns from students **cruising** by sounded far away. I rushed into the library and went straight to my table in the left back corner, away from the main desk. I piled my books and binders on the table.

32   I took a deep breath, picked up the novel, and placed it in front of me. I grabbed my worn-out pocket dictionary from the stack and set it next to it. I **muttered** the title, *"The Grapes of Wrath."* The word *grapes* reminded me of working in the vineyards for Mr. Sullivan in Fresno. I looked up the word *wrath* and thought of the anger I felt when I lost my blue notepad, my *librito,* in a fire in Orosi. I began reading. It was difficult; I had to look up many words, but I kept on reading. I wanted to learn more about the Joad family, who had to leave their home in Oklahoma to look for work and a better life in California. I lost track of time. Before I knew it, five o'clock had passed. I was late for work.

Reading Strategy

Relate Your Own Experiences to a Reading Why does Panchito lose track of time? Have you ever lost track of time doing something you enjoy? Explain.

---

cruising driving for pleasure
muttered spoke in a low tone; said quietly

33   When I got home that evening, I continued reading until one o'clock in the morning. That night I dreamed that my family was packing to move to Fresno to pick grapes. "We don't have to move anymore! I have to go to school!" I kept yelling, but Papá and Mamá could not hear me. I woke up **exhausted.**

34   Saturday night I **skipped** the school dance and stayed home to read more of the novel. I kept struggling with the reading, but I could not put it down. I finally understood what Miss Bell meant when she told me to read for enjoyment. I could **relate** to what I was reading. The Joad family was poor and traveled from place to place in an old **jalopy,** looking for work. They picked grapes and cotton and lived in labor camps similar to the ones we lived in, like Tent City in Santa Maria. Ma Joad was like Mamá and Pa Joad was a lot like Papá. Even though they were not Mexican and spoke only English, they had many of the same experiences as my family. I felt for them. I got angry with the growers who mistreated them and was glad when Tom Joad protested and fought for their rights. He reminded me of my friend Don Gabriel, the *bracero* who stood up to Diaz, the **labor contractor,** who tried to force Don Gabriel to pull a plow like an ox.

35   After I finished reading the novel, I could not get it out of my mind. I thought about it for days, even after I had turned in the book report to Miss Bell. She must have liked what I wrote, because she gave me a good grade. My success made me happy, but, this time, the grade seemed less important than what I had learned from reading the book.

The Joad family, a scene from the movie *The Grapes of Wrath*, 1940

skipped didn't go to
jalopy old car that does not run well
bracero laborer (Spanish)
labor contractor person who hires laborers to perform a task

● **Apply the Reading Strategy**

Relate Your Own Experiences to a Reading

Complete the **Reading Strategy** chart.

What does Panchito do to succeed in school?	What do I do to succeed in school?
Panchito works hard every day on homework. He uses tools like dictionaries to improve his language skills.	_____ _____ _____ _____ _____ _____ _____

1. Review the **Reading Strategy** on page 7.
2. Draw a chart for each question.
3. Look back at the reading. Answer the following questions.
   a. What does Panchito do to succeed in school? What do you do?
   b. Who helps him to succeed? Who helps you to succeed?
   c. What challenges does he face, both in and out of school? What challenges do you face?
   d. What motivates Panchito to do his best? What motivates you?
4. When you finish your charts, **summarize** your responses to show how closely you **relate** to Panchito's experiences.

● **Academic Vocabulary**

Vocabulary for the Reading Comprehension Questions

Word	Explanation	Sample Sentence	Visual Cue
analyze *verb*	to examine something to understand what it is and means, or to study	Scientists **analyze** the behavior of animals to learn more about them.	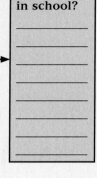
predict *verb*	to say what will happen in the future	Dark clouds help me **predict** that a storm is coming.	

Draw a picture and write a sentence for each word.

✓ **Checkpoint**

1. What things do students **analyze** in science class?
2. Which weather events are difficult to **predict**? Explain your answer.

Vocabulary Log

Reading Comprehension Questions

Think and Discuss

1. **Recall facts** Give two reasons why Panchito has difficulty reading for enjoyment. What does he do to overcome this difficulty?

2. **Identify the main idea** What is the main idea of this story? Provide details and use three Key Vocabulary words to support your answer.

3. **Recognize character traits** Describe Miss Bell. Does she seem like a fair teacher? Why or why not?

4. **Analyze** What is Panchito's conflict, or struggle, in the story? What important lesson does Miss Bell teach Panchito by the end of the story?

5. **Predict** How successful do you think Panchito will be in English class? How do you think he did in English classes later in his life?

6. **Revisit the Reading Focus Questions** Go back to page 8 and discuss the questions.

Workbook
page 32

Independent Practice
CD-ROM/Online

Literary Element

First-Person Narrative

"Making Connections" is a **first-person narrative**. A first-person narrative is a story that is told by the main character who uses the first-person pronoun "I" to refer to him or herself. The narrator of "Making Connections" is Panchito. As the narrator, he tells us his story from his point of view, the first-person point of view. This helps you **relate** to Panchito because you see the events through his eyes.

1. Locate sentences in the first paragraph of "Making Connections" where Panchito refers to himself as "I." Does it sound to you as though the narrator is a young student? How do you know?

2. Look back at paragraphs 31 and 32 on page 16. What is Panchito's point of view?

3. How does this first-person narrative help you to **relate** to Panchito and his experiences?

✓Checkpoint

1. Write a sentence about yourself using the first-person point of view.

2. Write a sentence about someone else using the first-person point of view.

Workbook
page 33

Independent Practice
CD-ROM/Online

Words Around the World

● About the Reading

In "Making Connections," Panchito learns that he can **relate** to the experiences of characters in literature. In the article you are about to read, words around the world connect people to one another.

● Build Background

Loanwords

Languages around the world borrow words from each other. For example, the French word *denim* is a word that English speakers have adopted into their vocabulary. In this way, languages around the world have grown much larger because of loanwords, or words loaned to them from other languages.

Key Vocabulary

export

global

template

● Vocabulary From the Reading

Understand and Use Definitions

Look at the **highlighted** words in the chart below. Read each definition and the sentence that follows. Use the chart to help you understand the article you are about to read.

Word	Definition	Sentence
export	to ship from one country to another	The United States wants to **export** products like denim to many countries around the world.
global	worldwide, or relating to the whole world	English is a **global** language. It is a common second language spoken in many countries around the world.
template	guide with codes, symbols	I filled out the form on my computer using a **template**.

✓Checkpoint

A **global** issue is a topic that affects people around the world. Identify one example of a **global** issue.

Vocabulary Log

Workbook page 34

Independent Practice CD-ROM/Online

Reading Strategy

Relate Your Own Experiences to a Reading

As you read "Words Around the World," think about your own experiences with language. Look for familiar words as you read. Consider any loanwords that you know and use.

1. Write down any loanwords you use and identify where they come from.
2. Describe or define the words.

Text Genre

Informational Text: Magazine Article

An **article** is an **informational text** that presents nonfiction writing about a topic. Articles are often published in magazines, which can appear in paper form or on the Internet. Most articles share the following features. Look for features like these as you read "Words Around the World."

Magazine Article		
Feature	Purpose	Appearance
photographs and illustrations	allow readers to see new or interesting images related to the article	may be color or black and white; may appear anywhere in the article
segments or sections	break the article into parts that relate to topics in the article's subject matter	may begin with a heading or a space that separates it from the section before it

Meet the Author

Carla Meskill is a professor at the University at Albany, State University of New York. She researches how people learn languages, especially how people learn languages with new technologies. Professor Meskill also enjoys writing novels, short stories, and plays.

Reading Focus Questions

As you read, think about these questions.

1. How does the reading relate to the theme of "language"?
2. What do you think was the author's purpose in writing "Words Around the World?"
3. How does this article **relate** to the languages you speak?

Name two features of a magazine article.

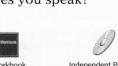

Workbook
pages 35–36

Independent Practice
CD-ROM/Online

Words Around the World

by Carla Meskill

1   Languages are forever growing, shrinking, and disappearing. In short, most languages are always changing. Loanwords are words borrowed from another language. These words travel from one language to another every minute of every day. Sometimes, they replace words that then disappear entirely. Right now, there are about 7,000 languages spoken in the world. Through time, languages disappear because people stop speaking them. **Language historians** guess that the world has already lost thousands of languages, especially those spoken by a country's native people.

2   Many fear that the English language will eventually replace a number of languages, much the way it has replaced thousands of original languages in the United States. The smaller the country, the smaller the number of speakers, and the greater the risk that a more widely used language will replace the native language. Indeed, in most countries of the world, people speak two or more languages. In the United States, however, the majority of people speak only one.

Reading Strategy

Relate Your Own Experiences to a Reading How many languages do you speak? When do you use each one?

The Rosetta Stone is an ancient Egyptian artifact. It is carved with text in three languages.

Language historians experts who study the history of language and how it has changed over the years

The Language of Food

3   The English-speaking world **exports** more than **goods,** movies, and TV shows to other nations. Along with these **exports** go the English words that describe them. For example, the word "sandwich" is understood in most non-English speaking parts of the world. We in the United States also use many non-English words to talk about international foods. Words like **sushi, borscht, hummus,** and **quiche** are loanwords from other nations. Can you think of more examples?

Business in Many Tongues

4   Many different languages are used in the world of **global** business. Business people who speak more than one language have great advantages over those who speak only their native language. English is the most widely used language of business. In fact, you can hear the word "business" used in any number of countries where a word does not exist for it in its native language!

Reading Strategy

Relate **Your Own Experiences to a Reading** When speaking your language, do you use food words from other languages? Give examples.

✓ Reading Check

1. **Recall facts** What language does the word *sandwich* come from?

2. **Recall facts** Which language is the most widely used in the world for conducting business?

3. **Draw a conclusion** Imagine that you are a business person whose native language is French. According to the article, what would you probably have to learn to be able to work internationally?

---

goods products that can be bought or sold
sushi Japanese dish made of rolls of rice, vegetables, and fish
borscht Russian or Polish cabbage soup
hummus thick Middle Eastern spread made with chickpeas, garlic, and lemon
quiche pie made with eggs, cream, and cheese

5 People may never all speak the same language. Luckily, the growth of a **global** society has made it easier for the world's people to communicate.

Loanwords
Words English Has Borrowed

6

giraffe (Arabic)	**guitar** (Spanish)
pajamas (Hindi)	**umbrella** (Italian)
icky (Yiddish)	**cookie** (Dutch)
clique (French)	**icon** (Russian)
denim (French)	

Words Borrowed from English

7

bye-bye (used in China)	**job** (French)
humu ran ("home run" in Japanese)	**brother** (Brazilian Portuguese)
stop (Italian)	**hip-hop** (multiple languages)
weekend (French)	

Reading Strategy

Relate Your Own Experiences to a Reading Do you use any words borrowed from other languages? Which ones?

Technology

8   For a long time, the language of computers was English. In recent years, though, people have come to use computers in their native language as a way of keeping their culture, their identity, and the **mother tongue** alive and in use. Still, words such as "Windows," "click," and "Web site" are often borrowed from English. These loanwords get worked into the everyday languages of other countries.

9   Most computer keyboards have the QWERTY layout. This name comes from the top left row of letters on a keyboard. Speakers of non-Roman alphabet languages, such as Russian or Chinese, can use a QWERTY keyboard. To do so, they can use a keyboard **template**, special software, and the **word processing font** for their language. More often, though, computer companies are making keyboards based on different alphabets. Among them are Cyrillic, the Russian alphabet, and Pinyin for Chinese speakers. Many users buy translation software. This software quickly translates Web pages from one language to another. In this way, Internet users can read sites in different languages.

Reading Strategy

Relate **Your Own Experiences to a Reading** Have you ever sent an e-mail written in a language other than English? How does writing in another language feel different from writing in English?

A QWERTY Keyboard

_____

mother tongue first language one speaks as a child
word processing font kind of type used by computers

Reading Check

1. **Recall facts** What is the name of a typical English-language keyboard?

2. **Recall facts** What does translation software do?

3. **Explain** Why are computer companies making keyboards based on different alphabets?

English Is a Global Language

10   More people speak English, more than any other language, as a second, third, or fourth language. Often, people who don't speak English as their native language use it to communicate with others. This is called English as a Lingua Franca, or "ELF." At one time, people feared that English would replace other languages. Thankfully, the Internet allows more people to use multiple languages to communicate. By doing so, they are keeping their native languages alive.

After Reading 2

● Reading Comprehension Questions

Think and Discuss

1. **Recall facts** According to the article, why do languages disappear?

2. **Recognize cause and effect** What might happen to some of the world's languages if native speakers stopped speaking them?

3. **Apply** Write a paragraph that describes "Words Around the World" and uses the three Key Vocabulary words.

4. **Speculate** Besides computers, what do speakers rely on to keep their languages alive?

5. **Connect** How is language connected to culture?

6. **Revisit the Reading Focus Questions** Go back to page 21 and discuss the questions.

Workbook page 37   Independent Practice CD-ROM/Online

Spelling

Words with the Same Sounds but Different Spellings

Workbook page 38   Independent Practice CD-ROM/Online

Writing Conventions

Punctuation: Quotation Marks to Refer to a Word

Workbook page 39   Independent Practice CD-ROM/Online

 Connect Readings 1 and 2

You have read two readings on the theme of language.

1. With a partner, use this chart to compare the two readings.

Reading title	What is the text genre?	What is a feature of the text genre?	Which selection uses first-person narrative?	Which selection did you prefer? Explain.
Making Connections				
Words Around the World				

2. Read the main ideas from the article "Words Around the World." Then support or explain each statement with examples from "Making Connections." See example below.

   "Words Around the World": In most countries of the world, people speak two or more languages.

   "Making Connections": Panchito understands both English and Spanish.

   a. "Words Around the World": More people speak English as a second, third, or fourth language than any other language.

   "Making Connections":

   b. "Words Around the World": People who speak more than one language have great advantages over those who speak only their native language.

   "Making Connections":

Phrases for Conversation

Expressing Agreement

I agree with you.
That's an interesting idea.
My idea is similar to ____'s idea.
That's correct.

Listening and Speaking

Discuss the Readings

According to the article "Words Around the World," there are about 7,000 different languages spoken today. In "Making Connections," Panchito faces challenges as he learns one of those languages. Explore the theme of language in the two readings.

1. Work with a partner to answer these questions.
   a. What challenges does Panchito face as he learns English?
   b. If you could speak another language, which one would you choose? Why?
   c. Why is it good for people to speak more than one language?
2. Scan (read quickly through) the readings to find support for each of your answers above. Write down any notes that might help you to discuss your responses.
3. With a group, discuss your answers. Use your notes to support your responses as well as the responses of your classmates.
4. Listen to your classmates as they share their responses. Use the **Phrases for Conversation** to give encouragement to each speaker in your group.

Reading Fluency

Reading to Scan

When you scan a text, you move your eyes quickly over the words. Scanning allows you to read for specific information.

Take 40 seconds and scan "Words Around the World" to locate the following key phrases. Write down the meaning of each phrase as you find it in the article. Complete this task in two minutes or less.

Key Phrases	
loanwords	QWERTY
translation software	English as Lingua Franca

● Vocabulary Development

Greek and Latin Root Words

A **root** is the basic part of a word. Many roots come from Greek or Latin. A root carries a specific meaning. Recognizing the root of a word and its meaning can help you understand the meaning of a new word.

The chart below lists some common **Greek** and **Latin roots**, their meanings, and English words based on those roots. Note any changes in spelling, such as in *scrib* and *description*.

Build Your Knowledge

Greek and Latin prefixes and suffixes (word parts added to the beginnings and ends of words) can also be found in the words in the chart. For example, *ion* is a Latin suffix that turns a verb into a noun. *Tele* is a Greek prefix that means "far off."

	Root	Meaning	English Words
Latin root words	scrib	to write	description, transcribe
	gress	to walk	progress, digress
Greek root words	geo	earth	geometry, geography
	phone	sound, voice	telephone, phonetics

1. Underline the root in each of the following words. Then, using a dictionary, write the definition of the word.

Root	Definition
a. di<u>gress</u>	to move away from the main point
b. prescribe	
c. geology	
d. symphony	

2. Write a sentence for each of the words in the chart. Read your sentences to a partner.

When I give a speech, I try not to <u>digress</u> from the main topic.

✓ **Checkpoint**

1. "Attract" and "contract" share a Latin root that means "to pull or draw." Can you guess the root word?

2. Using a dictionary, define the word **contract.** How does the word **relate** to its Latin root?

Vocabulary Log

Workbook page 40

Independent Practice CD-ROM/Online

● **Grammar**

Subject-Verb Agreement in the Simple Present Tense

Use the singular form of a noun to indicate one subject. Use the plural form of a noun to indicate more than one subject.

Subjects and verbs need to agree in number. If a subject is singular, its verb in the present tense will usually end with an **-s**. If the subject is *I, you, we, they,* or plural, its verb usually does not have an **-s** on the end.

Notes

- When the verb ends in **-ss, -sh, -ch, -x,** or **-z**: Add **-es** for the singular.

  miss**es**, brush**es**, search**es**, mix**es**, buzz**es**

- When the verb ends in consonant + **y**: Change **y** to **i** and add **-es** for the singular.

  study ➝ stud**ies**

Subject-Verb Agreement		
	Subject	**Verb**
Singular Subject	The student	sits.
Plural Subject	The students	sit.

Practice the Grammar For each of the following sentences, underline the subject and the verb. Then label each subject as **singular** or **plural**.

  <u>Languages</u> <u>change</u> every day all over the world. *plural*

1. Panchito's classmates work on their assignments.
2. The teacher hands the paper to Panchito.
3. The students try to do well in their classes.
4. Panchito proudly shows his essay to his mother.
5. Miss Bell guesses that the story about Trampita is true.

Use the Grammar Independently Answer the questions. Make sure the nouns and verbs in your answers agree in number.

1. What do you do to get ready for school in the morning?
2. What do your teachers do in class?
3. What do your classmates and you do after school?
4. What does your friend do at dinner time?

Use the simple present tense to talk about things that are generally true or happen often. Notice the subject-verb agreement in the sentences below.

Build Your Knowledge

Some verbs are often misused because they have similar meanings and forms. These include *lie / lay, sit / set,* and *rise / raise*. See page 443 for definitions and sample sentences.

subject   verb

Generally or always true: The **sun** always **rises** in the east.

subject   verb

Happens often: **Motorcycle riders** **wear** safety helmets to protect their heads.

Practice the Grammar Choose the correct present tense verb in each of the following sentences.

1. Words from other languages (moves / move) from one place to another.
2. Speakers often (mix / mixes) foreign words into English.
3. Business words (travel / travels) from language to language in a **global** community.
4. The word *umbrella* (come / comes) from Italy.
5. Speakers (access / accesses) their native language by using the Internet.
6. When people stop using languages, the languages (disappears / disappear).
7. In many countries people (speak / speaks) more than one language.
8. In the United States, we (talk / talks) about international foods with the original words from other languages.

Grammar Expansion

Compound Subjects and Modified Subjects; *Yes/No* Questions and Negative Statements in the Simple Present Tense

Workbook pages 43–44   Independent Practice CD-ROM/Online

Use the Grammar Independently Write a paragraph about the readings. Use the sentence below as the first sentence of your paragraph. Use subjects and verbs in the present tense. Check your work, and make corrections when you finish.

In "Making Connections," Panchito uses his own experiences to write an essay for his class.

✓*Checkpoint*

1. What is the simple present form of the verb **marry** if the subject is **she**?
2. What is the simple present form of the verb **possess** if the subject is **they**?

● Writing Assignment

Write a Personal Narrative

In an **autobiographical short story,** a writer tells a story about a personal experience. The story may include other characters and description. The story may tell the events from beginning to end. The writer usually uses first-person narration because the events happened to him or her.

Writing Prompt

In "Making Connections," Panchito learned a lot about himself. Write a paragraph that tells the story of a time when you learned something about yourself. Tell the events in order. Then describe what you learned about yourself. Include the use of the simple present tense to make the story active.

Write Your Personal Narrative

1. **Read the student model.** In this model, a student tells the story about how he learned to be a good brother. Look for features of an autobiographical short story. For example, notice the characters, the description, and the first-person narration.

Student Model

Writing Cues: Sequence of Events

First . . .
Then . . .
Later . . .
Finally . . .
When it was all over . . .
At last . . .

My Brother and Me

I have a little brother, Ben, who is six years old. I like to teach him new things, like how to ride a bike or how to play a game. One day, Ben helped me to be a better brother. We were in the park, and Ben wanted to climb a tree. We found a good one, and Ben reached up to the first branches. He climbed up, and then he put out his hand for the next branch. Then he started to fall. I caught him before he fell too far. After I put him on the ground, he smiled at me and said, "Thank you! Maybe I shouldn't climb trees anymore." He was right. I learned that day that a good brother does not let a little guy do things he can't do. So sometimes, I say no to Ben. I tell him that he can do more things when he gets bigger. He taught me to watch out for him, and I am a better big brother now.

Workbook
page 45

2. **Prewrite.**
  a. Create a list of people, places, and events that taught you something about yourself. Or, use the word web on page 5 to explore topics for writing.
  b. Explore your topic. Once you have an idea, list the events in order. Be sure to place them in the correct order.

3. **Write your short story.**
  a. Include details to interest the reader.
  b. Tell the reader what you learned about yourself.
  c. Use the **Writing Cues** to tell the events from beginning to end.

4. **Revise.** Reread your short story. Revise your story if any ideas are not clear or complete.

   Use the **editing and proofreading symbols** on page 455 to mark any changes you want to make.

5. **Edit.** Use the **Writing Checklist** to help you find problems and errors.

6. **Read your short story to the class.**

Writing Checklist

1. I revised and edited my work for better organization, grammar, and spelling.

2. I listed all events in my story in order.

3. I included vivid details.

4. I spelled correctly any words with Latin and Greek roots, prefixes and suffixes.

5. I used correct subject-verb agreement, the present tense, and first-person point of view.

 **Writing Support**

Grammar

Capitalization of Proper Nouns and Adjectives

All **proper nouns** need to be capitalized. Proper nouns and adjectives include the names of people, like *Panchito* and *Trampita*, and places, such as *California* and *London*. Some proper nouns, like *January* and *Thursday*, describe time. Some, like *Americans* or *English*, refer to nationality or languages. Names of academic courses are also proper nouns.

Names	Places	Times	People/Languages	Courses
Ben	Victory Park	April	French	English Language Arts
Miss Bell	March School	Thursday	Austrian	Algebra 1
Mamá	Mexico	January	Chinese	American History

Apply Read your autobiographical short story. Do you see any proper nouns that need to be capitalized? Correct any errors in capitalization.

Workbook
pages 46–48

Independent Practice
CD-ROM/Online

Progress Check

MILESTONESTRACKER

How well did you understand this chapter? Try to answer the questions. If necessary, go back to the pages listed for a review.

Skills	Skills Assessment Questions	Pages to Review
Vocabulary From the Readings	What do these words mean?	
	• **anxious, approach, exhausted, pace, reputation, rupture**	6
	• **export, global, template**	20
Academic Vocabulary	What do these academic vocabulary words mean?	
	• **relate, summarize**	7
	• **analyze, predict**	18
Reading Strategy	What does it mean to **relate** your own experiences to a reading? Can you provide an example of a character or moment in the readings that you can **relate** to?	7
Text Genre	What is the text genre of "Making Connections"?	8
	What is the text genre of "Words Around the World"?	21
Reading Comprehension	What is "Making Connections" about?	19
	What is "Words Around the World" about?	27
Literary Element	What is a **first-person narrative**?	19
Spelling	Explain when to use *your/you're* and *its/it's*.	27
Writing Conventions	When do you use quotation marks to refer to a word?	27
Listening and Speaking	**Phrases for Conversation** What phrases can you use to express agreement with a speaker during a discussion?	28
Vocabulary Development	What is a **root**? Can you give examples of words with a **root** of **scrib** or **geo**?	29
Grammar	What does it mean when a **subject** and **verb** agree?	30
Writing Support: Grammar	What is a **proper noun**? Can you write three sentences that include a **proper noun** in each?	33

Assessment Practice

Read this passage. Then answer Questions 1 through 4.

The Language on the Field

1   The baseball season is just starting, and a new player comes late to our first practice. "This is Max," Coach Chin says. "He's a catcher with a great reputation." We need a new catcher because Jaime, our old catcher, moved away. I'm the team's pitcher, and I was anxious to know who the new catcher would be.

2   At the next practice, Max asks me, "Do you know the sign for *strike*?" I say that I don't know any signs. Max explains that each pitch has its own sign. If he holds up one, two, or three fingers, I know what kind of pitch I should throw. Max also tells us that there are signs for the batters, too. Coach Chin will be able to tell us without using words how he wants us to hit the ball.

3   Coach Chin says he likes the idea of using signs, so Max teaches the team what the different signs mean. At the end of our first game, the other team wants to know what our secret signs mean. Thanks to Max, I'm learning a new language. And our team will be the best in the league!

---

1 **What does the word <u>reputation</u> mean in the following sentence?**

> "He's a catcher with a great <u>reputation</u>."

  A nervous
  B speed
  C what everyone knows about you
  D chance

2 **What part of the passage can all students relate to?**
  A winning a championship
  B learning sign language
  C playing baseball
  D learning something new

3 **Which sentence shows that this is a first-person narrative?**
  A Thanks to Max, I'm learning a new language.
  B "This is Max," Coach Chin says.
  C Coach Chin says he likes the idea of using signs, so Max teaches the team what the different signs mean.
  D Max explains that each pitch has its own sign.

4 **What is the text genre of this passage?**
  A autobiographical short story
  B historical fiction
  C poem
  D informational text

Writing on Demand: Autobiographical Short Story

Write an autobiographical short story about learning a new language or skill. Tell how you feel as you learn it and after you learn it. Include important settings, characters, and a problem/solution if possible. **(20 minutes)**

> ## Writing Tip
> Remember to use first-person narrative (*I* and *we*) when you tell an autobiographical short story.

CHAPTER 2

Objectives

Reading Strategies

Recognize textbook features; Read in sentences

Listening and Speaking

Recite a poem

Grammar

Learn noun-pronoun agreement; Learn the simple past tense

Writing

Write a poem about something important to you

Academic Vocabulary

consist	comprehend
restate	context
define	

Academic Content

Fractions and the language of mathematics

Foreign words used in English

● Chapter Focus Question

How do we use other languages to help us learn English?

Reading 1 **Content:** Math

Math textbook
Mathematically Speaking

Reading 2 **Literature**

Poetry
The Mosaic of English

by Jennifer Trujillo

Mathematically Speaking

● About the Reading

In the United States, Egypt, Spain, and everywhere else, adding one and one will always equal two. This is why math is a universal language that the whole world can speak.

● Build Background

The Language of Fractions

A **fraction** is a part of a whole. When you eat one slice of a whole pie, you are eating a **fraction** of it. When you walk halfway to school in the morning, you are walking a **fraction** of the whole distance. Whether you write the words **one half** or the numbers **50%** or **1/2,** it represents the same fraction: **half.**

Write out the fractions for each of the following examples.

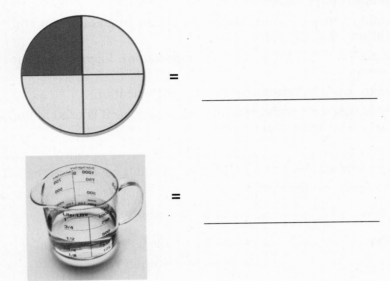

= _____

= _____

● Use Prior Knowledge

Match Signs and Symbols

Math is made up of signs and symbols that are used in the same way in many countries around the world. Can you match the math symbols below to their meanings on the right?

1. +	**a. division** sign
2. =	**b. greater than** sign
3. −	**c. multiplication** sign
4. ÷	**d. subtraction** sign
5. ×	**e. equal** sign
6. >	**f. addition** sign

Now write an equation that uses at least three of these math signs.

Key Vocabulary

- concept
- equation
- equivalent
- notation
- universal

● Vocabulary From the Reading

Learn, Practice, and Use Independently

Learn Vocabulary Read each sentence. Look at the **highlighted** word. Think about the context. Use the context to determine the meaning of the word.

1. Mr. Ortiz taught us about fractions with pieces of pie. It was a **concept** I could understand.
2. Addition and subtraction problems are the first kinds of math **equations** that you learn in school.
3. One mile and 1.61 kilometers are **equivalent**. Each distance is the same.
4. In math, x is a **notation** that means multiplication.
5. Math is called the **universal** language because it is used in the same way all around the world.

Practice Vocabulary Match the Key Vocabulary word on the left to its definition on the right.

1. **equation**   a. found or practiced everywhere

2. **concept**   b. a set of symbols used to represent musical notes, numbers

3. **universal**
                         c. equal, the same
4. **equivalent**
                         d. mathematical statement that two amounts are equal
5. **notation**
                         e. general idea that usually includes other related ideas

Use Vocabulary Independently Write a paragraph that includes each Key Vocabulary word. Share your work with a partner.

✓Checkpoint

1. In your own words, describe what a **concept** is.
2. What is the opposite of unequal?

Vocabulary Log

Workbook page 49

Independent Practice CD-ROM/Online

Academic Vocabulary

Vocabulary for the Reading Strategy

Word	Explanation	Sample Sentence	Visual Cue
consist *verb*	to be made up of; to be composed of	The cake **consists** of flour, eggs, butter, and milk.	
restate *verb*	to say something in a new way	The student tried to **restate** her answer so the teacher could understand her.	
define *verb*	to give the meaning of	The students **define** new words using a dictionary.	

Draw a picture and write a sentence for each word.

Reading Strategy

Recognize Textbook Features

Textbook pages **consist** of special features such as goal lists, charts, diagrams, headings, and subheadings that help readers to understand new material. When you analyze these features, you can learn new information faster and easier.

As you read "Mathematically Speaking," look for special features.

1. Analyze any headings or subheadings you see. How are they similar to each other?

2. As you read, **restate** the information to help you understand. Did the textbook features help you to understand? Explain.

Use the chart below to note textbook features as you read. **Define** each feature in your own words. Explain how each feature helps a reader learn new material. After you read, you will complete the chart.

Feature	What does it look like?	How does it help me?

✓**Checkpoint**

1. Identify one textbook feature on this page and **restate** why it is helpful.

2. **Define** the word **consist**.

Vocabulary Log

Workbook page 50

Independent Practice CD-ROM/Online

● **Text Genre**

Textbook

"Mathematically Speaking" comes from a math textbook. A **textbook** is used in courses to study a specific subject. Look for these features as you read "Mathematically Speaking." What other textbooks do you use that share these same features?

Textbook	
facts	information such as dates, events, and numbers
lessons	information to be learned with activities
visual aids	pictures, drawings, and charts to help you understand what you are reading

● **Reading Focus Questions**

As you read, think about these questions.

1. Do the textbooks you use have features like the ones in this textbook? Which features are used in your textbooks?

2. Look at the samples of textbooks from other countries. How important are visual aids, like photographs and charts, in those textbooks?

This student is using her history textbooks to study for an exam.

Workbook
page 51

Independent Practice
CD-ROM/Online

SECTION 2

Fractions and Tree Diagrams
Mathematically Speaking

IN THIS SECTION **Exploration 1:** Comparing Fractions ○ **Exploration 2** Adding and Subtracting Fractions
Exploration 3: Tree Diagrams and Probability

Setting the Stage

Sprechen Sie Deutsch? (Can you speak German?) Maybe not, but see how much you can understand of this page from a German mathematics book.

13.2. Der Bruch als Teil mehrerer Ganzen

1. Mutter hat 3 Pfannkuchen gebacken und in Viertel geteilt. Heike und Thomas dürfen sich jeder ¾ Pfannkuchen nehmen. Heike will sich von den obersten Kuchen ¾ abnehmen. Thomas kann es einfacher. Er nimmt sich 3 übereinanderliegende Viertel, von jedem Kuchen also ¼, das sind auch ¾ Pfannkuchen.

2. Der Bruch ¾ kann also auf zwei verschiedene Arten entstehen:

a. Ein Pfannkuchen wird in vier gleiche Teile geteilt. 3 Teile davon werden zu einem Bruch zusammengefaßt: ¾ Pfannkuchen.

b. Drei Pfannkuchen werden aufeinandergelegt und geviertelt. Es liegen dann jeweils 3 Viertelstücke aufeinander, das sind: ¾ Pfannkuchen.

Reading Strategy

Recognize Textbook Features Analyze the page. What features help organize the lesson in the German math textbook?

Think About It

1 What mathematics **concept** is presented in the German text? How do you know?

2 Tell a story that could go with the pictures.

✓ Reading Check

1. **Recall facts** Look at the subheading titled **In This Section.** What lesson is the reader going to learn on this page?

2. **Infer** How can you tell that the German lesson is about fractions?

EXPLORATION 1

COMPARING
Fractions

Reading Strategy

Recognize Textbook Features According to the Goal feature, what are the two lessons presented in this section? Restate the goals.

GOAL

LEARN HOW TO...
• write fractions in lowest terms • compare fractions using least common denominators
AS YOU...read a flow chart
KEY TERMS • equivalent fractions • lowest terms least common denominator

✱ As you saw from the page of the German book, mathematical ideas can be communicated without language. Many of the same numerals, diagrams, and symbols are used in different countries. Students all over the world use >, <, and = to compare numbers.

3 Use the circle diagrams to compare the fractions. Replace each __?__ with >, <, or =.

a. $\frac{1}{4}$ __?__ $\frac{1}{8}$ b. $\frac{2}{4}$ __?__ $\frac{4}{8}$ c. $\frac{3}{4}$ __?__ $\frac{7}{8}$

✱ Fractions that represent the same amount are **equivalent** fractions. To write a fraction in lowest terms, you need to find an **equivalent** fraction where the greatest **common factor** of the **numerator** and **denominator** is 1.

4 Which fractions in Question 3 are **equivalent** fractions? Are they in lowest terms? Explain.

5 Use this example from a German mathematics lesson.

a. Find the GCF of 36 and 84.
b. Is $\frac{36}{84}$ in lowest terms? How do you know?
c. Find the GCF of 3 and 7.
d. Is $\frac{3}{7}$ in lowest terms? How do you know?

Beispiel **means "example."**

---

common factor integer, or whole number, that divides two other numbers evenly
numerator number above the line in a common fraction
denominator number below the line in a common fraction

6 Discussion Use the German example $\frac{36}{84} \underset{12}{=} \frac{3}{7}$.

a. Although fraction concepts are **universal**, sometimes a slightly different **notation** is used. Why do you think the number 12 is printed underneath the equals sign in the example?

b. How can the idea of greatest common factor be used to find an **equivalent** fraction in lowest terms?

7 ✓**CHECKPOINT** Write each fraction in lowest terms.

a. $\frac{10}{18}$ **b.** $\frac{12}{27}$

✓ QUESTION 7

..checks that you can write a fraction in lowest terms.

8 How can you use your answers to Question 7 to compare $\frac{10}{18}$ and $\frac{12}{27}$?

✺ **Comparing Fractions** The *flow chart* below appears in a Bulgarian mathematics book in a lesson about comparing fractions.

9 Try This as a Class Look at the examples shown along the left and right sides of the flow chart.

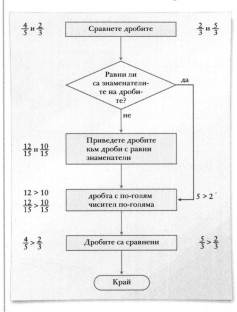

a. What do you think the question in the shaded box is asking?

b. For the example on the right, why do you think the third box of the flow chart is skipped? What do you think are the instructions in the third box?

c. Why are fifteenths used to compare the two fractions on the left side?

d. In the fourth box, what parts of the fractions are compared to find the greater fraction?

> ◀ **Reading Strategy**
>
> **Recognize Textbook Features** Analyze the page. How does the textbook organize the lesson on this page?

> ✓ **Reading Check**
>
> 1. **Recall facts** What heading does the book use for Question 7?
>
> 2. **Deduce** Look at the heading for Question 7 and the question itself. What do you think is the purpose of a **Checkpoint** question?
>
> 3. **Predict** Which feature do you think will come next: Question 10, or an arrow that introduces new material? Refer to the textbook page to support your answer.

✸ One way to compare fractions is by finding the *least common denominator*. The **least common denominator** of two fractions is the least common **multiple** of the denominators.

EXAMPLE

Compare $\frac{5}{8}$ and $\frac{7}{12}$.

SAMPLE RESPONSE

> 24 is the **LCM** of 8 and 12.

First Find a common denominator.

The least common denominator of $\frac{5}{8}$ and $\frac{7}{12}$ is 24.

Next Rename each fraction as an **equivalent** fraction with the common denominator.

$$\frac{5}{8} = \frac{5}{8} \cdot \frac{3}{3} = \frac{15}{24} \quad \text{and} \quad \frac{7}{12} = \frac{7}{12} \cdot \frac{2}{2} = \frac{14}{24}$$

Then Compare the fractions that have the same denominator.

$$\frac{15}{24} > \frac{14}{24}, \text{ so } \frac{5}{8} > \frac{7}{12}$$

---

10 In the Example, two fractions are renamed using the least common denominator. How does this method compare with the Bulgarian method?

11 Create Your Own Create a flow chart of your own for comparing fractions. Include two examples that show how to use your flow chart. In one example, use fractions that have a common denominator. In the other example, use fractions that do not have a common denominator.

Reading Strategy

Recognize Textbook Features Read Question 11, and analyze the picture next to it. **Define** what you think the **Create Your Own** heading means in this math textbook.

12 ✓**CHECKPOINT** Compare each pair of fractions. Replace each ___?___ with >, <, or =.

a. $\frac{3}{5}$ ___?___ $\frac{3}{4}$ **b.** $\frac{2}{5}$ ___?___ $\frac{1}{5}$ **c.** $\frac{2}{3}$ ___?___ $\frac{11}{15}$

d. $\frac{19}{20}$ ___?___ $\frac{54}{60}$ **e.** $\frac{7}{18}$ ___?___ $\frac{5}{12}$ **f.** $\frac{55}{90}$ ___?___ $\frac{11}{18}$

> ✓ QUESTION 12
>
> . . . checks that you can compare

---

multiple number that may be divided by another a certain number of times without any amount being left over
LCM Least Common Multiple

EXPLORATION 2 ADDING and SUBTRACTING Fractions

GOAL

LEARN HOW TO...

- add and subtract fractions with unlike denominators

AS YOU...explore fraction models from other countries

Models for adding and subtracting fractions are also **universal**. See the examples below from an Australian textbook and a Japanese textbook.

Australian textbook:

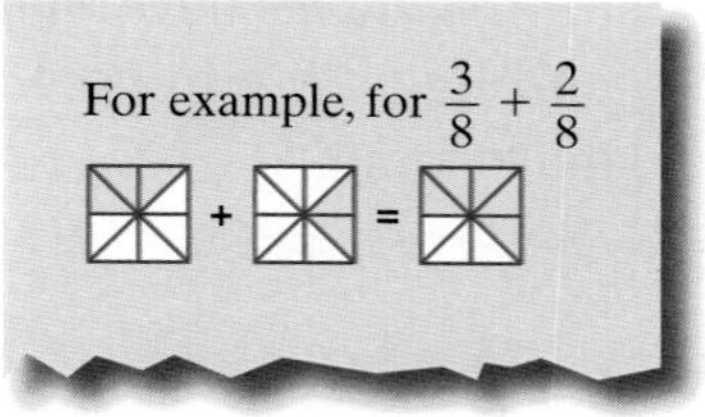
For example, for $\frac{3}{8} + \frac{2}{8}$
+
=

Japanese textbook:

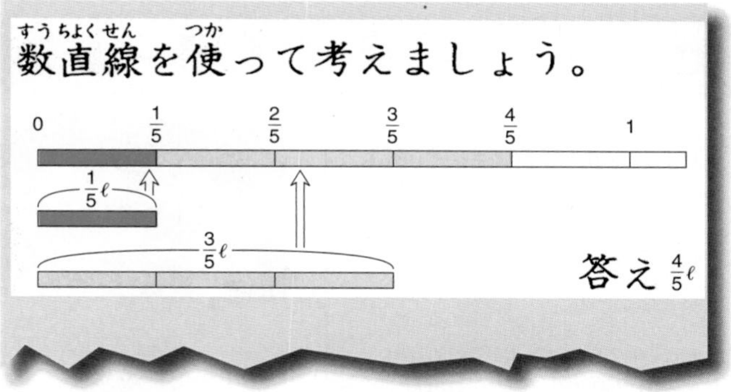
すうちょくせん つか
数直線を使って考えましょう。
0
$\frac{1}{5}$
$\frac{2}{5}$
$\frac{3}{5}$
$\frac{4}{5}$
1
$\frac{1}{5}\ell$
$\frac{3}{5}\ell$
答え $\frac{4}{5}\ell$

13 **a.** Explain what the examples are trying to show.
b. What makes these examples **universal**?
c. Write the **equation** each example represents.

Reading Strategy

Recognize Textbook Features Analyze the Australian and Japanese textbook examples. How does each use textbook features? Which version do you think is clearer? Explain your answer.

Reading Check

1. **Compare** Which country's textbook uses a square version of a pie chart?
2. **Make inferences** Do both examples show how to add fractions? How do you know?

● Apply the Reading Strategy
Recognize Textbook Features

Now complete the Reading Strategy chart.

1. Review the **Reading Strategy** on page 39.
2. Draw the chart on a piece of paper.
3. Look back at the reading. Identify all the textbook features that helped you understand the reading.
4. Write the features in the chart and answer the questions.

Feature	What does it look like?	How does it help me?
Goals	List at the beginning of a section	It introduces new topics and helps me to prepare to learn them.

● Academic Vocabulary
Vocabulary for the Reading Comprehension Questions

Word	Explanation	Sample Sentence	Visual Cue
comprehend *verb*	to understand the meaning of something	Jasmine could not hear the speaker, but she could **comprehend** what the speaker said through sign language.	
context *noun*	the information surrounding a word or phrase that determines exactly how it is meant	In the sentence "She put some dates in the bag," the **context** tells you that "dates" are a fruit, not specific days and times.	

Draw a picture and write a sentence for each word.

✓ Checkpoint

1. How do photographs help you **comprehend** information?
2. How does **context** help you understand a word?

Vocabulary Log

Reading Comprehension Questions

Think and Discuss

Workbook
page 52

Independent Practice
CD-ROM/Online

1. **Recall facts** Identify one kind of text element used in the math textbook.

2. **Apply** Use three Key Vocabulary words to describe **concepts** presented in "Mathematically Speaking."

3. **Describe** Give three examples of how the context of a sentence helps you to understand the meaning of the Key Vocabulary words.

4. **Explain** What is the purpose of presenting math **concepts** in different languages?

5. **Identify** Identify three genres of writing, besides textbooks, that use textbook features.

6. **Make a judgment** Do you think textbook features help students comprehend new information? Explain.

7. **Revisit the Reading Focus Questions** Go back to page 40 and discuss the questions.

Text Element

Visual Aids

Visual aids are text elements that allow readers to understand better a portion of a lesson or an example. Visual aids include photographs, maps, charts, illustrations, and graphs. These learning tools help you visualize the point of a text's lesson.

Imagine that the student sitting next to you is new to your school.

1. Write down the directions he or she would need to go from your school to the school bus stop. Include street names, landmarks, and distances.

2. Next to the directions, draw a map that shows the way to the bus stop.

3. Which kind of direction is easier to follow, the written direction or the map?

4. If the directions were written in a language your partner does not speak, would the map help him or her get to the bus stop?

✓ **Checkpoint**

What kind of **visual aid** helps you find the location of a street in a city?

Workbook
page 53

Independent Practice
CD-ROM/Online

Mosaic of a world map

The Mosaic of English

● About the Reading

"The Mosaic of English" is a poem about the many languages that have influenced English. The poem celebrates our individual identities that, like a mosaic, come together to form a unique American culture.

● Build Background

Mosaics

A mosaic is a picture or design made up of many tiny stones, pieces of glass, or other small items. The tiles or stones are set with glue or a similar substance to keep the mosaic pieces in place. Together, the many pieces create a whole picture or pattern. The finished product is made up of many different parts, and each part is unique and special.

● Vocabulary From the Reading

Use Context Clues to Determine Meaning

To determine a word's meaning, look at the words and phrases that surround it. A word's context can give you clues to its meaning.

Key Vocabulary
evolve
jazz
slim
stroll
trek
vast

1. The English we speak today is different from the English that people spoke one hundred years ago; it has **evolved** over time.
2. The **jazz** musician enjoyed playing his trumpet.
3. A twig is **slim** compared to the thick trunk of a tree.
4. Kelly was **strolling** slowly down the sidewalk when she met Sandra.
5. After their long **trek** through the woods, the hikers were tired.
6. The wide-open field looked **vast** and unending to the cowboy.

✓ Checkpoint

Identify three things in your classroom that are as **slim** as a pencil.

Vocabulary Log

Workbook page 54

Independent Practice CD-ROM/Online

● Reading Strategy

Read Poetry in Sentences

Poets often write poems in lines to enhance the rhythm and rhyme of the poem. However, when you are trying to understand a poem, pausing at the end of every line will interrupt the sentences and make the ideas in the poem hard to **comprehend.** Instead of pausing at the end of each line of poetry, be sure to pause only where there is punctuation. Pausing at the end of each sentence, rather than at the end of each line, will help you to understand the meaning of the poem.

● Text Genre

Poetry: Lyric Poem

Poems have many different shapes, sizes, styles, and purposes. "The Mosaic of English" is an example of a **lyric poem,** a kind of poem that expresses a personal emotion. The chart below lists features of a lyric poem.

Lyric Poem	
stanzas	groups of lines that share a subject or a theme
rhythm	a regular beat within a line of poetry
rhyme	words that end with a similar sound

● Meet the Author

Jennifer Trujillo was born in Denver, Colorado. Her family came from Caracas, Venezuela. She spent part of her childhood there and part of it in Colorado. Traveling between countries made her interested in learning languages. Today, Trujillo teaches at Fort Lewis College in Colorado and on the Navajo Indian Reservation. She says, "The story of English is amazing!"

● Reading Focus Questions

As you read, think about these questions.

1. How does the reading relate to the theme of "language"?
2. What experiences probably helped the author to write this poem?
3. What do you think was the author's purpose in writing "The Mosaic of English"?

Workbook
pages 55–56

Independent Practice
CD-ROM/Online

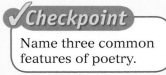

✓Checkpoint

Name three common features of poetry.

The Mosaic of English

by Jennifer Trujillo

1   One day I was walking to the store with my mom,
    speaking Spanish, our language,
    and just **strolling** along,
    when someone drove by in a big, fancy car
    yelling, "Speak English, Kid! Don't you know where you are?"

2   Well, English is hard and I'm trying my best
    to learn all these words and spell all the rest!
    So I wonder, please tell me, in "PIZZA," no "E"?
    What's up with English? It seems crazy to me.

3   See English has traveled on a boat by the sea.
    It's even crossed borders like my mom and me.
    Along the way, it has borrowed a lot.
    New words and meanings have all been **sought.**

4   Italian has given us words like *piano*
    and the opposite of ***alto***, a high-voiced ***soprano.***
    From music to art to food we can taste,
    spaghetti and *pasta* are words we don't waste.

5   Now Spanish has given us some of the most.
    From place names to cowboys, it goes coast to coast.
    Florida means flowered; *Colorado* means red;
    Montana means mountain where
       they **staked homesteads.**
    The cowboys used ***lassos*** and
       ***lariats* galore**
    from *corrals* to ***mesas*** to the **vast**
       Texas shore.

Strategy

Read in Sentences
How many sentences
are in stanza 2? Read
the stanza, following
the punctuation.

---

sought searched for
alto a low, female singing voice
soprano the highest singing voice, often sung by a woman or a boy
staked homesteads took pieces of land and built homes
lassos and ***lariats*** ropes with a loop on the end, for catching cattle
galore in large numbers
mesas hills with flat tops and steep sides (Spanish)

6 But before they came, someone else had these lands;
   Native American tribes had words for these sands.
   Minnesota means "white water"; *Dakota* is a tribe.
   Caribou is an animal and a **toboggan** is a ride.

7 The Dutch gave us **waffle** and *cookie* and **sleigh**,
   while the French gave **corsage**, **baguette** and **café**.
   Germans gave a temperature we call **Fahrenheit**
   and **kindergarten** rooms where kids play with delight.

8 African languages loaned us some too . . .
   from **jazz** to *jukebox*; even sweet **yam** was new.
   Slim and **trek** are also a few.

9 Arabic even got in on the games,
   Giving *algebra*, *candy*, and *caramel* their names.

10 And I bet you could never guess from where
    comes the word that we use to wash our hair!
    Northern India uses Hindi where they gave us
    shampoo. A *jungle*, a **bangle** come from there too.

11 **Bistro** is from Russian and *breeze* is Portuguese.
    There are still many more from Cantonese.
    This is Chinese—the number one language spoken on Earth.
    Just imagine what all these words are worth!
    You might have a *yen* or a deep, long **yearning**
    to find out more and keep on learning.

Reading Strategy

Read in Sentences
How are the first four lines of stanza 11 different from the last two lines?

Reading Check

1. **Infer** Why do you think Native Americans chose the name "Minnesota" for that region?

2. **Analyze** What do you think is the poet's attitude toward all the languages that have contributed words to English?

---

toboggan sled
waffle breakfast food with a square pattern on the surface
sleigh carriage for riding on snow and ice
corsage flowers worn by a woman on special occasions
baguette long, narrow loaf of French bread
café restaurant that serves simple food and drinks
Fahrenheit system of measuring temperature
kindergarten classes children go to the year before first grade
yam type of sweet potato
bangle metal band worn on the wrist as jewelry, a stiff bracelet
Bistro small restaurant
yearning strong desire

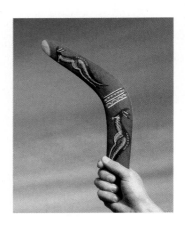

12   Japanese, too, has played a part.
     Origami is a delicate art.

13   From there to Australia we get even more,
     just think how far a *boomerang* can soar . . .
     past *koala* bears and *kangaroos*
     we have so many words to choose.

14   If I want to describe the color blue,
     I have a *palette* of words that will easily do:
     turquoise, *cobalt*, *navy* or *azure*,
     there is one thing of which you can be sure,
     English will always offer you a choice
     Because it's a mosaic, you'll have a voice.

15   As I thought back to the man who yelled from his car,
     I wonder if he knew English came from afar.
     So many cultures **pitched in** to this mix,
     It's no wonder the spelling still has some tricks.
     English has **evolved** and developed anew.
     Now we surf waves and the Internet too.

16   My mom and I arrived at the store as we'd planned;
     She reached back around to grab my hand.
     "*Mi hija*, are you hungry?
     Let's get some bread."
     I thought, "I'd rather have a *croissant*
                                   or *tortilla*
                               or *pita*
                                   instead . . ."

Reading Strategy

Read in Sentences
Does the use of dialogue make it easier to read the poem in sentences? Why or why not?

17   So please be patient as I learn
         this tongue,
     You mastered this mix when you
         were young.
     I'll learn your language given time,
     Just please don't ask me to give
         up mine.

Origami the Japanese art of folding paper into shapes
boomerang flat, curved piece of wood that will return to the person who threw it
koala bears small furry animals from Australia that live in trees
palette flat plate used by artists to mix paints
turquoise, cobalt, navy, azure shades of blue
pitched in added
Mi hija my girl, my daughter (Spanish)
croissant, tortilla, pita various forms of bread

After Reading 2

● Reading Comprehension Questions

Think and Discuss

1. **Recall facts** According to stanza 3, how has English picked up words from other languages?

2. **Identify the main idea** What is the main idea of stanza 14?

3. **Restate** In your own words, **restate** the connection between the English language and a colorful mosaic. Use three Key Vocabulary words from the poem to support your explanation.

4. **Relate to your own experience** How do your experiences with the English language compare with the speaker's? Use examples from the poem in your answer.

5. **Revisit the Reading Focus Questions** Go back to page 49 and discuss the questions.

Workbook page 57   Independent Practice CD-ROM/Online

Spelling

Words with the Same Sounds but Different Spellings

Workbook page 58   Independent Practice CD-ROM/Online

Writing Conventions

Quoting Poetry

Workbook page 59   Independent Practice CD-ROM/Online

Connect Readings 1 and 2

You have read two readings on the theme of language: "Mathematically Speaking" and "The Mosaic of English." Use these activities to make connections between the readings.

1. With a partner, use this chart to compare the two readings.

Reading title	What is the text genre?	What is a feature of the text genre?	Does the selection include languages other than English as part of its main idea?
Mathematically Speaking			
The Mosaic of English			

2. With a partner, ask and answer these questions.
   a. How do both readings rely on visual aids to communicate the main idea?
   b. Which reading is about culture? Which reading is about a language that is present in all cultures?
   c. Which reading was more interesting to you? Explain your answer.

3. **Revisit the Chapter Focus Question** Go back to page 36 and discuss the question.

Phrases for Conversation

Asking and Giving Advice

What should I do
    about . . .?
What would you do?
In my opinion, . . .
Here's something
    to try.

● Listening and Speaking

Recite a Poem

Rehearse and then recite a poem of your choice. Follow these steps to prepare for your recitation.

1. Choose a poem that interests you, or ask others for their recommendations. Look for vivid words and phrases.
2. **Define** any unfamiliar words, and study the poem carefully to make sure you understand all of it.
3. Read your poem. Then listen as your partner reads his or her poem. As a listener, you should:
    a. listen for sentences and for vivid words and phrases.
    b. wait until your partner has finished reciting before giving any feedback.
    c. tell your partner what you liked about the recitation. Then give suggestions for improvement.
4. Finally, use your partner's feedback to improve your recitation. Recite your poem to the class.

Checklist for Reciting Poems

1. Speak clearly and slowly.
2. Speak loudly enough so the entire class can hear you.
3. Use a tone of voice that reflects the meaning of the poem.
4. Look at the audience.
5. Use appropriate posture at the podium or in front of the class.

● Reading Fluency

Repeated Reading

Repeated reading helps you improve your reading rate and builds confidence. Each time you read a passage, your comprehension and understanding improves.

1. Turn to page 50.
    a. Read the first stanza of "The Mosaic of English" three times in 45 seconds.
    b. Did you read the first stanza three times in 45 seconds? If you did, you are reading 150 words per minute.

c. Repeat the process with the second stanza. Read it three times in 45 seconds. If you do this you are reading 150 words per minute.

d. Now, read the third stanza three times in 40 seconds. If you can do this you are reading 175 words per minute.

e. Read the fourth stanza three times in 40 seconds. If you can do this you are reading 160 words per minute.

f. Finally, read the last stanza three times in 1 minute. You are reading 144 words per minute.

● Vocabulary Development

Figurative Language

Figurative language is language that goes beyond the literal meanings of words in order to help the reader see an idea or subject in a new way. For example, in "The Mosaic of English," the speaker tells us that English has traveled by boat and crossed borders. This is an example of a kind of figurative language called **personification**. Personification gives human traits and abilities—such as the ability to travel—to non-human things like the English language.

Find an example of personification in each sentence below. Underline the non-human thing and the human trait or ability. The first one is done for you.

> The <u>flag</u> <u>danced</u> in the breeze.

1. Charlie's car alarm shouted from the street.
2. My shoes looked old and tired after wearing them all summer.
3. The computer came to life when I plugged it in.
4. Leila's skis whistled against the snowy mountain.

Build Your Knowledge

Word choice is very important in poetry. Poets think very carefully about the multiple meanings of words and how some words create an overall feeling better than others.

✓Checkpoint

1. Find an item in your classroom and write a sentence about it using **personification.**

2. "My heart sings when you are near." Does this sentence contain personification? Explain your answer.

Vocabulary Log

Workbook page 60

Independent Practice CD-ROM/Online

● Grammar

Noun-Pronoun Agreement

A **pronoun** is a word that can replace a noun.

Subject Pronouns: replace subject nouns	Object Pronouns: replace object nouns	Possessive Pronouns: replace possessive nouns
I	me	mine
you	you	yours
she	her	hers
he	him	his
it	it	its
we	us	ours
they	them	theirs

Pronouns have to match the nouns that come before them. These nouns are called *antecedents*.

When *Miss Bell* walked in, **she** wrote her name on the board.

I wrote the poems on *note cards* and put **them** in my desk.

Panchito thinks that the Joad family's *experiences* are a lot like **his**.

Practice the Grammar Find the pronoun in each of the following sentences. Then draw an arrow from the pronoun to its antecedent.

1. The man got into his car and started it.
2. My papers always came back with red ink on them.
3. I took the books from my teacher and thanked her.
4. My little sister wants new clothes because she is tired of wearing mine.

Use the Grammar Independently Write a sentence for each of the nouns below. Include a pronoun that follows each antecedent.

basket

She went to the basket and picked it up.

1. Maria   2. horse   3. water   4. Joe   5. gate

Grammar Expansion

Pronouns: Using the Correct Case

Workbook page 63

Independent Practice CD-ROM/Online

✓ Checkpoint

Which pronoun(s) could follow the antecedent **actress**?

Workbook page 61

Independent Practice CD-ROM/Online

Grammar

Simple Past Tense

Use the simple past tense to write or speak about events that have already happened.

Most verbs in the simple past tense end in **–ed**.

visit ⟶ visit**ed**

If a verb ends in **–e**, add **–d** to create the past tense.

amuse ⟶ amus**ed**

If a verb ends in a consonant + **-y**, change the **y** to an **i** and add **–ed**.

carry ⟶ carr**ied**

If a verb ends in a consonant + a vowel + a consonant, double the final consonant and add **–ed**.

stop ⟶ stop**ped**

Singular and plural subjects use the same form of the verb in the simple past tense.

Carlos **played** soccer with his brother yesterday afternoon.
The two girls **played** outside on the swing.

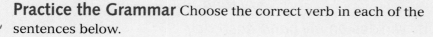

Practice the Grammar Choose the correct verb in each of the sentences below.

1. The airplane (rumbles / rumbled) down the runway before it took off.

2. I (picks / picked) up the ball after I (drop / dropped) it.

3. Green tomatoes (ripened / ripens) in the afternoon sun.

4. Little frogs (jump / jumped) into the water when the dog raced into the stream.

5. A group of students (studied / studies) in the library yesterday.

Use the Grammar Independently Write a paragraph using verbs in the simple past tense. Underline any pronouns you use, and make sure they match their antecedents.

Grammar Expansion

Yes/No Questions and Negative Statements in the Simple Past Tense

Workbook
page 64

Independent Practice
CD-ROM/Online

✓ *Checkpoint*

What are the past tense forms of the verbs **work, dance, worry, mop**?

Workbook
page 62

Independent Practice
CD-ROM/Online

● **Writing Assignment**

Write a Poem About Something Important to You

> **Writing Prompt**
>
> Think of something that is important to you, such as an item that has a significant history. Write a poem about it, using personification and vivid words and phrases to describe the item. Include complete sentences within your poem.

About Poetry A poem can have any or all of the following features: rhythm, rhyme, stanzas, figurative language, and descriptive details. Make your poem your own by choosing from any of those elements to describe the item you are writing about.

Write Your Poem

1. **Read the student model.** You can use this as an example as you make choices about your own poem.

Student Model

My Ring

It twinkles on my hand each day
and dances in the light.
The silver — smooth and rounded —
holds reds, both dark and bright.

My ruby ring, my mother's ring,
my daughter's ring-to-be,
is more than just jewelry.
It's a story about me.

2. Prewrite.

   a. Think about things that are important to you because you worked hard to get them or because they would be difficult to replace. Brainstorm a short list of topics and choose one that seems to be the most important.

   b. Develop your ideas. Think about your subject's color and shape, texture, and size. Think about its unique qualities— what makes it different from all the rest? Think about its personality. In other words, if this item could speak to you, what would it say? What do you do to take care of this item? Write down these ideas.

   c. Outline your poem. Choose ideas you want to include in your poem. If you plan to use stanzas, write about only one major idea in each one.

3. Write your poem. Choose active words that describe your item. Use sentences to communicate clearly to a reader exactly what your item looks and feels like.

4. Revise. Read your poem aloud. Then revise any stanzas or ideas that seem unclear or misplaced.
   Use the **editing and proofreading symbols** on page 455 to mark any changes you want to make.

5. Edit. Use the **Writing Checklist** to help you find problems and errors.

6. Read your poem to the class.

> **Writing Suggestion**
>
> Write down your ideas as quickly as they come to you. Do not stop to edit or rewrite until you have written down all of your ideas. Then go back and organize your ideas.

> **Writing Checklist**
>
> **1.** I chose an item that has some history or importance to me.
>
> **2.** I included personification.
>
> **3.** I included one major idea in each stanza.
>
> **4.** I used some features of poetry.
>
> **5.** I used correct noun-pronoun agreement.

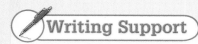

Writing Support

Grammar

Apostrophes and Possessive Nouns, Adjectives, and Pronouns

All nouns can show **possession,** or ownership. For most nouns, add an **apostrophe** and an **-s** to show possession.

   my daughter**'s** ring   the ruby**'s** glow   the silver**'s** gleam

Possessive nouns, adjectives, and possessive pronouns can do the same thing.

   Is this **Roberto's** room? (possessive noun)

   Is this **his** room? (possessive adjective)

   No, **his** is across the hall. (possessive pronoun **his** = **Roberto's room**)

See page 432 for a complete list of possessive pronouns.

Apply Check the possessive nouns, adjectives, and pronouns in your poem.

Progress Check

How well did you understand this chapter? Try to answer the questions. If necessary, go back to the pages listed for a review.

Skills	Skills Assessment Questions	Pages to Review
Vocabulary From the Readings	What do these words mean? • **concept, equation, equivalent, notation, universal** • **evolve, jazz, slim, stroll, trek, vast**	38 48
Academic Vocabulary	What do these academic vocabulary words mean? • **consist, restate, define** • **comprehend, context**	39 46
Reading Strategies	How do textbook features help you understand texts? How does reading poetry in sentences help you understand a poem?	39 49
Text Genre	What is the text genre of "Mathematically Speaking"? What is the text genre of "The Mosaic of English"?	40 49
Reading Comprehension	What is "Mathematically Speaking" about? What is "The Mosaic of English" about?	47 53
Text Element	Name four kinds of visual aids.	47
Spelling	What is the difference between *there, their,* and *they're*?	53
Writing Conventions	What punctuation is inserted between lines of poetry?	53
Listening and Speaking	**Phrases for Conversation** What phrases can you use to ask for or give advice?	54
Vocabulary Development	What is **figurative language**? Explain **personification**.	55
Grammar	Give an example of each type of pronoun. When is the simple past tense used?	56 57
Writing Support: Grammar	Give examples of a possessive noun, a possessive adjective, and a possessive pronoun.	59

Assessment Practice

Read this passage. Then answer Questions 1 through 4.

Math Is Fun

1   Many students think that math concepts like fractions, decimals, and ratios are difficult. Your teacher can help you learn them with games, or teach you tricks to help you solve a certain equation. If you still think you'll never understand how to find a square root, Danica McKellar can help.

2   When McKellar, a television and theater actress, was in middle school, she was scared of going to math class. But once she learned that algebra and geometry can be fun, she decided to study mathematics at the University of California, Los Angeles. To show middle school students, especially girls, that math can be interesting and fun, she wrote a book that includes tips and sample equations. Also, McKellar's book shows students why learning math is important. Math, she says, can help you to understand things like sports averages, cooking recipes, and how to spend your money wisely.

3   McKellar shows that anyone who is scared of math is not alone. She hopes that with her help, all students will be able to score high on their next math quiz.

---

1 **What does the word <u>concepts</u> mean in the following sentence?**

> Many students think that math <u>concepts</u> like fractions, decimals, and ratios are difficult.

  A problem
  B piece
  C number
  D idea

2 **What is the heading of the passage?**
  A Danica McKellar
  B Fractions, decimals, and ratios
  C Math Is Fun
  D Mathematics

3 **According to the passage, how can knowing math help you in everyday life?**
  A It helps you to plan how much money you can spend.
  B It helps you to be on time.
  C It shows you how to eat healthy foods.
  D It helps you to be better at sports.

4 **What is the genre of this passage?**
  A lyric poem
  B novel
  C informational text
  D textbook

Writing on Demand: Paragraph

Write a paragraph about your experience with mathematics. Talk about a particular time when you thought math was fun, or when you thought it was really difficult. How did that experience make you feel?
(20 minutes)

> **Writing Tip**
> Remember to begin your paragraph with a topic sentence. Include several sentences that give details to support the topic. Then write a conclusion.

Objectives

Listening and Speaking
Make a presentation about word origins

Media
Analyze persuasive language in advertisements

Writing
Write a response to literature

Projects

Independent Reading

● Listening and Speaking Workshop
Make a Presentation About Word Origins

> **Topic**
>
> In this unit, you read about loanwords that are borrowed from another language. You will choose a topic and make a presentation about English words related to that topic that come from other languages.

1. **Plan**
   a. Choose a topic that interests you, such as sports, music, or food. Make a list of as many words as you can think of that relate to that topic.
   b. Use a dictionary or the Internet to investigate which words from your list have origins in other languages. For example, the word origin for *song* is 12th century Middle English, which came from the Old English word *sang*.

2. **Prepare for Your Presentation**

   Organize your research about words and their origins on note cards. Determine whether there are connections between any of the words by their languages of origin. Does finding out the origins of words help you to discover other words that are related to the topic?

3. **Make Your Presentation About Word Origins**
   a. Explain your topic and why you chose it.
   b. Share your research about the words related to your topic with your classmates. Use your note cards to help you, but do not read from them.
   c. Clarify your presentation with examples of how these words are used.

4. **Respond to Your Classmates' Presentations**

   Listen carefully as your classmates make their presentations. Take notes. When they finish their presentations, ask them questions about their topic and the words that they discussed.

5. **Evaluate**

   Use the **Speaking Self-Evaluation** to evaluate how well you presented your word origins. Use the **Active Listening Evaluation** to evaluate and discuss your classmates' presentations.

Active Listening Evaluation

1. Your presentation was clear and easy to understand.

2. I understand more about the origins of words related to your topic.

3. The most interesting part of your presentation was _____ .

4. The presentation would have been better if _____ .

Speaking Self-Evaluation

1. I spoke slowly and clearly.

2. I made eye contact with my classmates while speaking.

3. My presentation was well organized.

4. I made good connections between my topic, the words related to it, and the words' origins.

5. I used examples to clarify my presentation.

● Media Workshop

Analyze Persuasive Language in Advertisements

Advertisements often use **persuasive language** to try to convince you to buy a product or to persuade you to do something.

1. Look at various types of advertisements. Keep in mind that advertisements try to persuade you to do something.

   a. Find a magazine in your school library. Go through the magazine and look for advertisements.

   b. Watch a half-hour television program. Pay attention to the advertisements that appear during breaks in the program.

   c. Look at the advertisements that appear along the top and sides of a Web page.

2. Look at or listen to the words and phrases used in the advertisements. Make a chart like the one below to help you evaluate the advertisements you see.

What is the advertisement for?	What is the advertisement trying to persuade me to do?

3. Choose one advertisement. Think about these questions:

   a. What is the advertisement trying to persuade me to do? Is this something I would not do without seeing it?

   b. What words, phrases, or images does the advertisement use?

   c. Did the advertisement persuade me?

4. Present the advertisement to your class. Show it to your classmates or summarize it for them. Discuss whether it is persuasive or not.

5. With your class, make a list of words and phrases that often appear in advertisements.

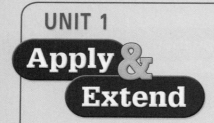

Apply & Extend

● **Writing Workshop**

Write a Response to Literature

In a **response to literature,** you give your reaction to a literary work. Writing about literature is a way for you to share your personal feelings about what you read. A response to literature essay also shows how well you understand the characters and themes of a story.

Writing Prompt

In "Making Connections," you read about a character who discovered a book that was meaningful to him. Write a response to literature essay about a book that is meaningful to you. Write your response to literature essay in the present tense.

PREWRITE

1. Read the student model. It will help you understand how to write a response to literature essay.
2. Make a list of books that have personal meaning to you.
3. Choose the book from your list that is most meaningful to you.
4. Think about the following questions. Take notes on your ideas.
   a. Who are the characters in the book?
   b. What is the plot of the book?
   c. What is the theme of the book?
   d. What do I like about the book?
   e. Why does the book have personal meaning for me?
5. Make an outline of your essay. Your outline should also include details from the book.

WRITE A DRAFT

1. Write the introduction. Give the title and author of the book and explain briefly what it is about. Include a sentence explaining why the book is important to you.
2. The body of your essay should be two or three paragraphs. Each paragraph should focus on a different reason that the book is important to you. Support your reasons with examples from the book and from your own life.
3. Write the conclusion. The conclusion should restate the main idea you expressed in your introduction.

Student Model

Rodrigo Ayala

The Call of the Wild Calls to Me

Main idea of the essay

Introduction

A book that is meaningful to me is The Call of the Wild by Jack London. The novel is about a dog named Buck who is forced to be a sled dog during the Gold Rush in Canada. The Call of the Wild is special to me because it focuses on many themes that have been important in my own life, such as change, survival, and loyalty.

Body

One theme I really understand from The Call of the Wild is the difficulty of adapting to change. Buck is kidnapped from his owner in California, where he had an easy life. He is sold to traders who make money selling dogs to people in search of gold in the Klondike. These people need dogs to pull their sleds across the snow and ice. When Buck becomes part of a dogsled team, his life becomes hard. Not only is he in a challenging new environment, but he also has to adjust to a new life as a sled dog. Buck's struggles remind me of the hard time I had when I moved here with my family from El Salvador.

Personal connection to the book

Even though Buck's new life is hard, he learns how to survive in the Klondike. He defends himself against other dogs, finds food, and stays warm. The Call of the Wild shows that sometimes life can be hard, and we must learn new skills to survive. An important skill I learned in the United States was learning to speak English.

Another theme in The Call of the Wild that I identify with is loyalty. Buck becomes very loyal to his new owner, John Thornton, when Thornton saves the dog from a man named Hal. I understand Buck's loyalty, because when I was struggling, my sixth-grade teacher helped me. I am still grateful for her help, and I have stayed in touch with her.

Main idea restated

Conclusion

The Call of the Wild has a lot of meaning for me because it deals with so many issues that I have dealt with in my own life. The Call of the Wild's themes of change, survival, and loyalty will be familiar themes for anyone who has a hard time adapting to a new situation.

REVISE

1. Read through your essay. Use the **Revising and Editing Checklist** to help you evaluate and revise your draft.
2. Exchange your revised essay with a partner. Ask your partner to use the **Peer Review Checklist** to help you make your draft better.
3. Revise your draft again based on your partner's suggestions.
4. Use the **editing and proofreading symbols** on page 455 to help you mark the changes you want to make.

EDIT

1. Re-evaluate your essay using the **Revising and Editing Checklist.**
2. Fix any errors in grammar, spelling, and punctuation.

Peer Review Checklist

1. The essay includes a brief description of the book's plot.

2. The essay helped me understand why the book is meaningful to the writer.

3. The essay includes examples from the book.

4. The most interesting thing I learned from this essay is _____ .

5. This essay would be better if _____ _____ .

Revising and Editing Checklist

1. My essay includes an introduction.

2. My essay explains why the book is meaningful to me.

3. I gave reasons that explain why the book is important to me.

4. I drew parallels between the book and my own life.

5. I used the present tense and the past tense correctly, and my verbs agree with my subjects.

PUBLISH

1. Write your essay in your best handwriting or use a computer.
2. Read your essay to the class. Read clearly and slowly enough so that everyone can understand you. Change the level of your voice to express the important ideas in your essay.
3. Ask classmates who have also read the book to share their feelings about your essay.

● Projects

Choose one or more of the following projects to explore the theme of language further.

PROJECT 1

Learn About American Sign Language.

American Sign Language (ASL) is a system of hand symbols used by many people who cannot hear. Sign language allows them to communicate.

1. Work with a partner. Use library resources or the Internet to find a guide that shows basic ASL signs.

2. With your partner, practice using some of the signs. Try to use signs to form a simple sentence.

3. Present your sentence to the class. One partner will sign the sentence while the other translates it into spoken English. Try to figure out your classmates' signs before they are translated.

4. Discuss with the class what you think it would be like to use sign language as your main form of communication. Do you or does someone you know use sign language on a regular basis? If so, share your experiences with the class.

SIGN LANGUAGE

Aa Bb Cc Dd Ee Ff Gg
Hh Ii Jj Kk Ll Mm
Nn Oo Pp Qq Rr Ss
Tt Uu Vv Ww Xx Yy Zz

PROJECT 2

Make a Chart About Recent Additions to the English Language.

1. In your classroom, your library, or on the Internet, find a dictionary that includes the year or approximate year that a new word became official. Many word listings use parentheses to identify the year that a word was first recognized.

2. Look for words that were added after 2000.

3. After you identify five words, make a list of your findings. Create a chart that gives the word, its definition, and the year it became official.

4. Present your findings to the class. Discuss why you think each word became official in the year that it did.

PROJECT 3

Interview People About the Languages They Speak.

1. Ask your family, your friends, and your neighbors which languages they speak. How many different languages can you find? How and why did they learn those languages?

2. Write all the languages across the top of a chart. Under each language, list the people who speak that language.

3. Write a paragraph describing what you learned. Did you find out anything new about the people you know?

4. Present your paragraph to the class.

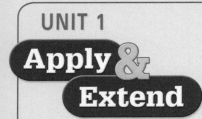
Heinle Reading Library

A Tale of Two Cities by Charles Dickens

In a specially adapted version by Marion Leighton

This famous novel takes place in the cities of London and Paris during the late 18th century. Set against the backdrop of the French Revolution, and filled with spies, angry mobs, and political prisoners, the novel explores the themes of love, friendship, and loyalty. Dickens expertly captures the language of people from different social classes on every page of this classic novel.

● Independent Reading

Explore the theme of language further by reading one or more of these books.

Breaking Through by Francisco Jiménez, Houghton Mifflin Company, 2001.

Fourteen-year-old Francisco and his family are determined to make a living when they arrive in California from Mexico. They struggle to stay together and deal with many challenges, such as prejudice, poverty, and long hours of hard labor. Francisco and his family teach each other English, are encouraged by their teachers, and learn to adapt to their new life in California.

Sweet Words So Brave: The Story of African American Literature by Barbara K. Curry, Zino Press, 1996.

In this book, an elderly man tells his granddaughter some of the inspiring tales behind African-American literature, bringing to life the stories of these authors. A recommended reading list is also provided.

Locomotion by Jacqueline Woodson, Putnam Publishing, 2003.

This book of poems tells the story of an 11-year-old boy named Lonnie. After Lonnie's parents die, he and his sister are separated and sent to live on opposite sides of the city. As Lonnie gets used to a new life with his foster mother, his teacher helps him learn to express his feelings through poems.

The Music of Dolphins by Karen Hesse, Scholastic Inc., 1998.

When four-year-old Mila loses her family in a plane crash over the ocean, a family of dolphins adopts her and cares for her until she is found 13 years later. Once she is living on land again, she must relearn human language and behavior and decide which world she is happiest to live in.

The Ink Drinker by Éric Sanvoisin, Dell Yearling, 1996.

The main character of this novel is a boy who hates to read, but must spend all summer in his father's bookstore. When he sees an unusual customer drinking the words from the books, the adventures of the book vampire begin. Read to find out what the boy learns about the powerful effect a book can have.

Milestones to Achievement

Writing: Revise and Edit

Read this rough draft of a student's lyric poem, which may contain errors. Then answer Questions 1 through 4.

Bilingual Brothers

(1) We are bilingual, my brother and I.
(2) When we buy food with our's mamá
(3) or go to school on the bus,
(4) I speak English without any fuss.
(5) But when we're at home just hanging around,
(6) we speak spanish in voices soft or loud.
(7) And when we're together without much to do,
(8) my brother and I speaks whatever we choose.

1 **How can you correct line 2?**
A Change *our's* to *ours.*
B Change *our's* to *our.*
C Change *our's* to *our is.*
D Change *our's* to *of us.*

2 **How can you improve line 4?**
A Change *I* to *we.*
B Change *I* to *me.*
C Change *I* to *my.*
D Change *I* to *mine.*

3 **How can you correct line 6?**
A Change *we* to *We.*
B Change *speak* to *Speak.*
C Change *spanish* to *Spanish.*
D Change *loud* to *Loud.*

4 **How can you correct line 8?**
A Change *speaks* to *speaking.*
B Change *speaks* to *speaked.*
C Change *speaks* to *spoke.*
D Change *speaks* to *speak.*

Writing on Demand: Lyric Poem

Write a lyric poem about the language or languages you speak. You may want to tell where and when you speak the language(s), and how it feels to speak them. You may want to personify, or give human traits and abilities to, the language(s). Use both the simple present and the simple past tense. **(20 minutes)**

● Reading

Read this informational text. Then answer Questions 1 through 8.

The History of English

1   Languages, like cultures and countries, have histories. The history of a language can be difficult to trace, or find the origin of. Most languages are formed from and influenced by other languages. It is sometimes difficult to tell where one language ends and another begins. English is an example of a language that has a long history. Formed from ancient languages and influenced by modern languages, English is always changing.

2   The native people who lived in what is today Ireland, England, Scotland, and Wales spoke Celtic languages. Around the 5th century, Germanic tribes from northern and central Europe came to this area, and from the mix of Germanic dialects, or types of speech, English was born. The Germanic tribes also introduced many Latin words that they used in their language. Language historians call this Old English.

3   In the 11th century, the Normans, who spoke a dialect of Old French, invaded these countries. They used their language in the courts and government. Common people still spoke Old English. However, the Norman French influenced their vocabulary and the way they formed their verbs and sentences. This time period of the English language is known as Middle English.

4   By the 16th century, Norman French was no longer used. The sentence and verb structures and the pronunciation of the English language became more similar to what they are today.

5   Today, the English language continues to evolve at a fast pace. People all over the world speak English. They take ideas and concepts from the languages that they speak and incorporate them into the English language. English is a universal language, not only because people around the world use it to speak to each other, but because it is influenced by languages everywhere.

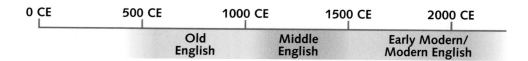

1 What does the word <u>evolve</u> mean in the following sentence?

> Today the English language continues to <u>evolve</u> at a fast pace.

A change

B speak

C break

D write

2 What does the word <u>universal</u> mean in the following sentence?

> English is a <u>universal</u> language, not only because people around the world use it to speak to each other, but because it is influenced by languages everywhere.

A powerful

B used always

C spoken

D existing everywhere

3 What dialects did Old English come from?

A Greek

B French

C Germanic

D Roman

4 Which language influenced Middle English the most?

A German

B Norman French

C Latin

D Greek

5 How is the timeline helpful in understanding the reading?

A It tells you what people spoke before they spoke English.

B It shows you how long people in the United States have been speaking English.

C It gives you a better idea of how long each stage of English lasted.

D It helps you to imagine how much longer in the future English will be spoken.

6 Which statement is true about the verb tenses of paragraph 2?

A All the sentences except the last are in the present tense.

B The last sentence is in the present tense.

C All the sentences except the first are in the present tense.

D The first sentence is in the present tense.

7 Which is an example of personification?

A The native people who lived in what is today Ireland, England, Scotland, and Wales spoke Celtic languages.

B From the mix of Germanic dialects, or types of speech, English was born.

C They used their language in the courts and government.

D People all over the world speak English.

8 Which of the following words from the passage has a Latin root?

A English

B because

C Norman

D described

Transitions

Explore the Theme

1. Based on the images, how would you describe a **transition**?
2. Describe the **transitions** you see in the images.

Theme Activity

With a partner, discuss the many kinds of transitions that people experience in life. Use the chart below to list a few of them.

From	To
summer vacation	first day of school
winter	spring

CHAPTER 1

Objectives

Reading Strategies

Identify main ideas; Identify cause and effect

Listening and Speaking

Tell a story about a time of transition

Grammar

Learn the present and past progressive tenses

Writing

Write a descriptive essay

Academic Vocabulary

support	contrast
deduce	participate

Academic Content

The geography, people, and language of Haiti

The states of matter

● **Chapter Focus Question**

How is a transition a change that happens over time?

Reading 1 **Literature**

Novel (excerpt)
Behind the Mountains
by Edwidge Danticat

Reading 2 **Content:** Science

Informational text: Science Textbook

Changes of state are physical changes

Behind the Mountains

● **About the Reading**

Behind the Mountains is a story about Celiane, a young girl who comes to the United States from Beau Jour, Haiti. Celiane adjusts to her new home and new challenges while holding on to memories of her life in Haiti.

Build Background

Haiti

Haiti is a country that is located on the western side of a large island in the Caribbean Sea. It is a mountainous country with deep forests, beautiful beaches, large cities, and small villages.

The official language of Haiti is French, but most people speak a language called Haitian Creole. It is based on French and various African languages. In *Behind the Mountains,* Celiane and her father use their knowledge of Haitian Creole to help them better understand some of the English words they hear in the United States.

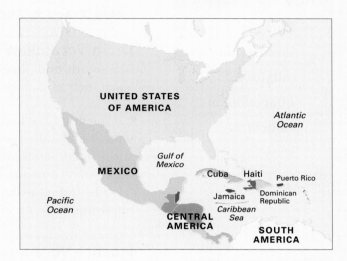

Use Prior Knowledge

Understand Proverbs

Proverbs are sayings that express common truths. These sayings are a little like puzzles: they don't seem to make sense until you apply them to an experience.

Edwidge Danticat uses part of a Haitian proverb in the title of her book *Behind the Mountains.* The proverb is: "Behind the mountains are more mountains." It expresses the idea that life is filled with

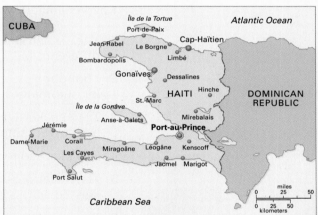

obstacles, or problems—some that you can see in front of you, and some that are beyond those you can see.

With a partner, explain the proverbs below using your own experiences and your understanding of the words in the proverbs.

1. An apple a day keeps the doctor away. (*Clue:* Apples are good for you.)
2. Laughter is the best medicine. (*Clue:* Medicine helps people feel better.)
3. Many hands make light work.
4. No man is an island.

Key Vocabulary

- fluid
- impression
- outshine
- quarrelsome
- reluctantly
- slew

● Vocabulary From the Reading
Learn, Practice, and Use Independently

Learn Vocabulary Read the following paragraph. Use the context (the words and phrases surrounding the **highlighted** words) to learn their meanings.

The first time I met Kim, my **impression** of her was that she wasn't a friendly person. I thought she was **quarrelsome** because she argued about everything. However, her arguments were **fluid**. People saw how intelligent she was. She soon made a **slew** of friends. **Reluctantly,** I became one myself. Now we don't try to **outshine** each other at all. We're best friends!

Practice Vocabulary Complete the sentences with the correct Key Vocabulary words.

1. The _____ friends finally stopped arguing and forgot their differences.
2. I bought a _____ of vegetables at the farmers market, including a lot of tomatoes, broccoli, and carrots.
3. The speaker wanted to make a good _____, so he was careful to use correct English during his speech.
4. She planned to _____ the other girls by creating the best report.
5. The ballet dancer's _____ moves were a pleasure to watch as she danced across the stage.
6. The little boy did not have time to read all his books. He _____ returned the last book to the library.

Use Vocabulary Independently Identify an antonym, or a word or phrase that means the opposite, for each of the Key Vocabulary words. Use a dictionary to check your work.

✓ Checkpoint

1. Describe an experience where your first **impression** of someone was correct.
2. Which would you do **reluctantly**: jump into an icy lake or eat your favorite food?

Vocabulary Log

Workbook page 69

Independent Practice CD-ROM/Online

Academic Vocabulary

Vocabulary for the Reading Strategy

Word	Explanation	Sample Sentence	Visual Cue
support *verb*	to agree with, advocate, or back up with information	The researcher looked for information to **support** his opinion in order to convince the others.	
deduce *verb*	to reach a conclusion by reasoning	The scientist tries to **deduce** a result using information she learned while performing experiments.	

Draw a picture and write a sentence for each word.

Reading Strategy

Identify Main Ideas

The **main idea** of a reading is the most important, or central, idea. **Supporting details** include any information that **supports** the main idea and helps you understand it. In many stories, the author does not state the main idea directly. As a reader, you can **deduce** the main idea first, then examine all the details that the author gives you. After you read, you will use the graphic organizer below to find the main ideas in *Behind the Mountains*.

1. As you read, **deduce** what the main idea of each page is. Write it down in the box on the left.

2. Note details that **support** the main idea. Those will go in the box on the right.

Main ideas:	Supporting details:
_____	_____
_____	_____
_____	_____
_____	_____

✓Checkpoint

1. Identify one argument that **supports** recycling as a good thing for the environment.

2. What can you **deduce** about a friend who tells you that he studied very hard for an exam?

Vocabulary Log

Workbook page 70

 Independent Practice CD-ROM/Online

● Text Genre

Novel

A **novel** is a long work of fiction. In works of fiction, the characters and events are invented by the author. Most novels share the features below.

Novel	
setting	where and when a story takes place
theme	main message or point that an author wants a reader to take from the story
voice	characteristics of the narrator in a story

● Meet the Author

Edwidge Danticat was born in Port-au-Prince, Haiti, in 1969. She moved to Brooklyn, New York, when she was 12. In Haiti, storytelling plays an important role in the local culture, and both storytelling and reading influenced Danticat's growth as a writer. She wrote her first short story at age 9 and has since written a number of novels, produced a film about Haiti, and taught creative writing at New York University and the University of Miami.

● Reading Focus Questions

As you read, think about these questions.

1. How does Celiane's experience relate to the theme of "transitions"?

2. What do you think was the author's purpose for writing this novel?

3. Is Celiane's experience on her first day of school a common experience? Why or why not?

✓ Checkpoint

1. Explain what **theme** means in your own words.

2. What are the characteristics of a narrator called?

Workbook
page 71

Independent Practice
CD-ROM/Online

Behind the Mountains

by Edwidge Danticat

1   The school is in a gray concrete building, facing a **slew** of giant **housing complexes,** which Papa said are called "projects." The projects are so tall that they look like mountains with windows.

2   We went directly to the main office, where teachers and school administrators were sitting behind desks, performing different tasks to prepare for the school day. Papa stood quietly facing the desks, waiting for one of the administrators to look up. Finally, a man walked over to us.

3   Papa's English was not nearly as **fluid** as the man's was. Still, Papa managed to explain why we were there. In his **quick-fire** speech, the man asked about my **vaccination** and medical papers. ("Vaccination" and "medical" are similar words in Creole as in English.) When Papa handed him the papers, the man walked back to his desk and picked up a form. He filled in some of the form, then gave Papa the rest to finish.

4   The man called someone else over, an older woman. The woman looked down at the form and told us in Creole that I had been assigned to Class 8M5. Papa asked what room that was. She said she would take us.

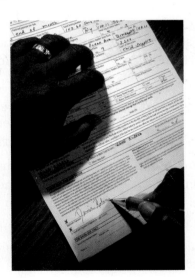

---

housing complexes groups of crowded apartment buildings
quick-fire very fast
vaccination medical treatment, usually an injection, meant to prevent disease

Reading Strategy

Identify Main Ideas
What main idea can you **deduce** from Celiane's feelings in her statement "My knees were shaking..."?

5   My knees were shaking as we followed the woman through the hallway. At times, I fell behind Papa and the woman, my new backpack weighing me down.

6   There was a long buzz and suddenly it was **mayhem**, with students pouring into the halls, some running and knocking into one another as they climbed the staircase around us.

7   My main room, the homeroom, was on the fourth floor in a corner near the stairwell. The students were beginning to arrive, slipping into their seats as we approached the teacher's desk. The woman from the main office introduced the homeroom teacher as Mr. Marius.

8   Mr. Marius was a young man, looking not much more mature than many of his students. The woman from the main office gave him my records. He looked them over, then said, *"Bienvenue,* Celiane."

9   The class was full now and everyone was looking at me. While the lady from the main office was leaving, I tried to keep my back to the other students and concentrate on Mr. Marius.

10   Papa was telling him (too loudly for my taste) what a good student I had been in Beau Jour, how my teacher had always "appreciated" me, how I had often been first in my class.

11   I kept wishing Papa wasn't saying those things. From the silence in the room, I could tell the others were listening, adding Papa's words to their first **impressions** of me.

---

mayhem total confusion
Bienvenue welcome (French)

12   I had already decided that I was no longer going to try to **outshine** everyone in class and Papa was ruining my plans. Being the teacher's favorite was no way to make friends.

13   When it was time for Papa to leave, he handed me a piece of paper with his telephone number at work, our home address, two quarters, and a five-dollar bill for me to take a taxi if I got lost. He told me (again too loudly) that I should not be afraid to call him at work if I needed him. Some of the students were smiling when I waved good-bye to Papa, who looked back one last time before the door closed behind him. I wanted so badly to go with Papa, but I knew this was not possible, so I turned back to the classroom and tried to find a desk.

14   "You are there, Celiane," Mr. Marius said, pointing to an empty desk in the back of the room. Mr. Marius had a chart of small cards lined up in front of him. He explained that this seat would be mine for the rest of the school year, as he handed me a blank card on which to write my name. When I was done, he placed the card on the chart to match where I was sitting.

Reading Strategy

Identify Main Ideas
The main idea of paragraphs 12 and 13 is that Celiane is uncomfortable with her father's behavior. Find details that **support** this main idea.

Reading Check

1. **Recall facts** What did Papa hand to Celiane as he left?

2. **Interpret** Why do you think Celiane wanted to go with Papa when he left?

3. **Speculate** Do you think Celiane was happy to have a seat in the back of the room rather than in the front? Explain.

15   "Celiane," he said, "We have a presentation we make whenever someone new comes to us. Class, let us begin."

16   Each of the students took turns getting up to tell me his or her name and something about the school. The first boy who spoke reminded me of Pouchon. He looked just as serious as Pouchon, too, wearing a crisp white shirt buttoned up all the way to the top.

17   "My name is Faidherbe," he said. "You are now a student at Jackie Robinson Intermediate School."

18   A boy named Gary, with a blue **bandanna** around his head, explained that Jackie Robinson was the first African-American baseball player in something called the major leagues.

19   Once Gary was done talking, Mr. Marius asked him to remove his bandanna, which Mr. Marius said was a **gang** symbol. Gary denied that his bandanna was a gang symbol, but took it off anyway.

20   The next row told me things like where the bathroom and water fountains were, and the best times to go to avoid some of the more **quarrelsome** kids who liked to tease the Haitian students.

Jackie Robinson, the first African-American major league baseball player in the 20th century

---

bandanna colorful scarf worn around the head or neck
gang a group of young people joined together for support and protection (usually used in a negative way)

21   I learned from the third row that the school day was divided into something called "periods" and that we would all be together for six periods—the different teachers would come to us in this room—except for gym class, where we had to do some kind of physical exercise in the gymnasium with students from the rest of the school, and "lunch period," where we would receive a free meal. (Mr. Marius handed me a book of numbered tickets for the free meals at that point.)

22   At the end of the presentations, Mr. Marius added that I should not worry about feeling lost at first, that slowly I would get used to my surroundings.

23   "It was the same for everyone here at first," he said. "Right, class?"

24   The class **reluctantly** answered, "Yes," as if he were forcing them to remember a time they would rather forget.

Reading Strategy

Identify Main Ideas
Celiane learns about what her typical school day will be like. Is this a new experience for her? How do you know? **Support** your answer with details.

Reading Check

1. **Recall facts** How many class periods are in one of Celiane's typical school days?

2. **Make an inference** In your opinion, is Mr. Marius a sensitive teacher? Use details from the reading to **support** your response.

3. **Deduce** What can you **deduce** about the other students' experiences based on the last line of the story?

● **Apply the Reading Strategy**

Identify Main Ideas

Now complete the Reading Strategy graphic organizer.

1. Review the **Reading Strategy** on page 77.
2. Copy the graphic organizer.
3. **Deduce** the main idea of each page. Write it down in the box on the left.
4. List supporting details in the box on the right.

Main ideas:	Supporting details:
1. page 79: Papa's English is very good.	_____ _____ _____

● **Academic Vocabulary**

Vocabulary for the Reading Comprehension Questions

Word	Explanation	Sample Sentence	Visual Cue
contrast *verb*	to compare two things as a way to show their differences	Our assignment was to write a paragraph that **contrasts** city life and country life.	
participate *verb*	to take part or have a role in an activity or event	The players **participate** in all of the practice activities in order to be ready for the game.	

Draw a picture and write a sentence for each word.

✓**Checkpoint**

1. How can you **contrast** winter and summer?
2. Identify two skills you use when you **participate** in a discussion.

Vocabulary Log

Reading Comprehension Questions

Think and Discuss

1. **Recall facts** What is the name of Celiane's new school?

2. **Describe** Using information from the story, describe what Celiane's personality was like at her old school.

3. **Contrast** Tell how Celiane's personality in Beau Jour is different from her attitude at her new school in New York.

4. **State your opinion** Do you think it is helpful to Celiane when the students **participate** in welcoming her to the school? Explain.

5. **Summarize** Summarize Celiane's first morning at school using the Key Vocabulary words from page 76. Then compare your summary to the original text to be sure you have noted all the main ideas in the story.

6. **Revisit the Reading Focus Questions** Go back to page 78 and discuss the questions.

Workbook
page 72

Independent Practice
CD-ROM/Online

Literary Element

Tone

Tone is the author's overall attitude toward the reader or the subject he or she is writing about. Tone can be described as serious or humorous, happy or sad, angry or kind, or any of the feelings that human beings experience. You can figure out the tone of a text by looking at the words the author uses.

1. Read the sentences from *Behind the Mountains*. Then choose an adjective that best describes the tone of each sentence.

   a. "Some of the students were smiling when I waved good-bye to Papa, who looked back one last time before the door closed behind him."

   b. "He told me (again too loudly) that I should not be afraid to call him at work if I needed him."

   c. "... Mr. Marius added that I should not worry about feeling lost at first...."

   d. "The next row told me ... the best times to go to avoid some of the more **quarrelsome** kids who liked to tease the Haitian students."

2. What one adjective best describes the tone of the entire story? Why do you think the author uses this tone?

Checkpoint

1. What does it mean when a writer uses an angry **tone**?

2. Can a story's setting have an effect on the writer's tone? Explain.

Workbook
page 73

Independent Practice
CD-ROM/Online

Changes of state are physical changes

About the Reading

In *Behind the Mountains*, you read about a young girl's transition to her new school. Transitions happen in science and nature, too. In the next reading, you will learn how water and other substances transition from one form to another.

Great Fountain geyser,
Yellowstone National Park

Build Background

What Is Matter?

Objects that take up space and have a mass, or weight, are called **matter.** Everything around you is made up of matter. You, your desk, and even the air you breathe!

Matter can be found in three basic states, or forms: solid, liquid, and gas. A glass of juice is a good example of a solid and a liquid; the glass is the solid, the juice is the liquid. The air you breathe is a gas that contains water and other molecules. Whether one substance, like water, is in a solid, liquid, or gaseous state, it is all the very same original substance.

Vocabulary From the Reading

Use Context Clues to Determine Meaning

Read each sentence below. Then, with a partner, discuss the **highlighted** words to determine their meanings.

1. The books in the library are organized in alphabetical order by the author's last name. This **arrangement** makes it easy for me to find any book I am looking for.

2. After it rained, small **droplets** of water rolled off the tree's leaves.

3. Tiny **particles** of dust floated in the air. They were so small that I could see them only when they drifted into the sunlight.

4. The blue paint at the store came in a **range** of shades, from light blue to dark blue, and every color in between.

5. After the water began to boil, water **vapor** filled the room.

Key Vocabulary

arrangement

droplet

particle

range

vapor

✓ Checkpoint

1. Describe to a partner the **arrangement** of the furniture in your classroom.

2. Look at the picture of the geyser. Where do you see **vapor**?

Vocabulary
Log

Workbook
page 74

Independent Practice
CD-ROM/Online

Reading Strategy

Identify Cause and Effect

A **cause** is an event or action that produces a result, or an **effect.** For example, your stomach making grumbling noises is an effect caused by hunger. Understanding why something happens—the cause—and what happens because of it—the effect—will help you understand what you read.

While you read, note the causes and effects that occur when substances change from one state to another. Then, when you finish reading, you will complete the graphic organizer below.

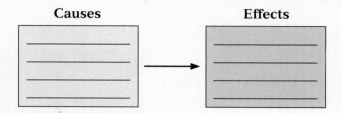

Causes   Effects

Text Genre

Informational Text: Science Textbook

"Changes of State Are Physical Changes" is a reading from a science textbook. Textbooks are used by students in school. They provide factual information on specific subjects. Science texts contain features like the ones below.

Science Textbooks	
vocabulary	a group of words related by subject matter
real-life examples	true experiences that prove a point or provide a model for learning
scientific experiments	tests done to see if something happens or works

Reading Focus Questions

As you read, think about these questions.

1. How is cause and effect a type of transition?
2. What is the purpose of this reading?
3. What examples of cause and effect can you find in nature?

Workbook
pages 75–76

Independent Practice
CD-ROM/Online

✓Checkpoint

1. In your own words, summarize the definitions of **cause** and **effect.**

2. Identify one example of **cause** and **effect** that you might find during a typical day.

2.2 Changes of state are physical changes

1 ▷ NOW, you will learn

- How liquids can become solids, and solids can become liquids
- How liquids can become gases, and gases can become liquids
- How energy is related to changes of state

Matter can change from one state to another.

THINK ABOUT

Where does dew come from?

2 On a cool morning, **droplets** of dew cover the grass. Where does this water come from? You might think it had rained recently. However, dew forms even if it has not rained. Air is made of a mixture of different gases, including water **vapor**. Some of the water **vapor** condenses—or becomes a liquid—on the cool grass and forms drops of liquid water.

3   Matter is commonly found in three states: solid, liquid, and gas. A solid has a fixed volume and a fixed shape. A liquid also has a fixed volume but takes the shape of its container. A gas has neither a **fixed volume** nor a fixed shape. Matter always exists in one of these states, but it can change from one state to another.

4   When matter changes from one state to another, the substance itself does not change. Water, ice, and water **vapor** are all the same basic substance. As water turns into ice or water **vapor**, the water molecules themselves do not change. What changes are the **arrangement** of the molecules and the amount of space between them. Changes in state are physical changes because changes in state do not change the basic substance.

---

fixed specific, rigid
volume amount of space an object or substance occupies

Solids can become liquids, and liquids can become solids.

5   If you leave an ice cube on a kitchen counter, it changes to the liquid form of water. Water changes to the solid form of water, ice, when it is placed in a freezer. In a similar way, if a bar of iron is heated to a high enough temperature, it will become liquid iron. As the liquid iron cools, it becomes solid iron again.

Melting

6   Melting is the process by which a solid becomes a liquid. Different solids melt at different temperatures. The lowest temperature at which a substance begins to melt is called its melting point. Although the melting point of ice is **0°C (32°F)**, iron must be heated to a much higher temperature before it will melt.

7   Remember that **particles** are always in motion, even in a solid. Because the **particles** in a solid are bound together, they do not move from place to place—but they do **vibrate**. As a solid heats up, its **particles** gain energy and vibrate faster. If the vibrations are fast enough, the **particles** break loose and slide past one another. In other words, the solid melts and becomes a liquid.

8   Some substances have a **well-defined** melting point. If you are melting ice, for example, you can predict that when the temperature reaches 0°C, the ice will start to melt. Substances with an **orderly structure** start melting when they reach a specific temperature.

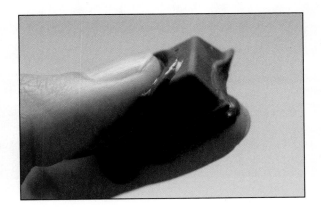

> ### Reading Strategy
>
> **Identify Cause and Effect** What causes iron to change into a liquid state?

> ### ✓ Reading Check
>
> 1. **Recall facts** What is a melting point?
> 2. **Interpret** What happens to the **particles** in a solid when the solid hits its melting point?

0°C (32°F) C, or Celsius, is a temperature scale that sets water's freezing point at 0 degrees and its boiling point at 100 degrees. On a Fahrenheit (F) scale, water freezes at 32 degrees and boils at 212 degrees.
vibrate shake
well-defined specific or clear
orderly structure (in science) **arrangement** of molecules that has a tight and neat pattern

9   Other substances, such as plastic and chocolate, do not have a well-defined melting point. Chocolate becomes soft when the temperature is high enough, but it still retains its shape. Eventually, the chocolate becomes a liquid, but there is no specific temperature at which you can say the change happened. Instead, the melting happens gradually over a **range** of temperatures.

Freezing

10   Freezing is the process by which a liquid becomes a solid. Although you may think of cold temperatures when you hear the word freezing, many substances are solid, or frozen, at room temperature and above. Think about a soda can and a candle. The can and the candle are frozen at temperatures you would find in a classroom.

11   As the temperature of a liquid is lowered, its **particles** lose energy. As a result, the **particles** move more slowly. Eventually, the **particles** move slowly enough that the **attractions** among them cause the liquid to become a solid. The temperature at which a specific liquid becomes a solid is called the freezing point of the substance.

12   The freezing point of a substance is the same as that substance's melting point. At this particular temperature, the substance can exist as either a solid or a liquid. At temperatures below the freezing/melting point, the substance is a solid. At temperatures above the freezing/melting point, the substance is a liquid.

---

attractions forces that pull molecules together as a substance reaches its freezing point

After Reading 2

● Reading Comprehension Questions

Think and Discuss

1. **Recall facts** What are the three states of matter?

2. **Describe** Describe the process of a substance changing from a solid to a liquid.

3. **Describe** Using information you learned in the reading, write a paragraph about matter changing from one state to another using the Key Vocabulary words.

4. **Speculate** What do you think happens to the motion of **particles** in warm water when they are mixed with cold water **particles**?

5. **Hypothesize** Which substance has a higher melting point: ice cream or a plastic cup? Explain your answer.

6. **Revisit the Reading Focus Questions** Go back to page 87 and discuss the questions.

Workbook
page 77

Independent Practice
CD-ROM/Online

Spelling

Regular Past Tense Verbs

Workbook
page 78

Independent Practice
CD-ROM/Online

Writing Conventions

Spelling: Abbreviations of Weights, Measures, and Temperatures

Workbook
page 79

Independent Practice
CD-ROM/Online

⟳ Connect Readings 1 and 2

You have read two readings on the theme of transitions: *Behind the Mountains* and "Changes of State Are Physical Changes." Use these activities to make connections between the readings.

1. With a partner, use this chart to compare the two readings.

Reading title	What is the text genre?	Which reading entertains? Which informs?	Which reading includes facts? Which is fiction?
Behind the Mountains			
Changes of state are physical changes			

2. With a partner, ask and answer these questions.
   a. How is each reading related to the theme of transitions?
   b. What is the main idea of each reading?
   c. Identify one image or fact that you remember from each of the two readings.

3. **Revisit the Chapter Focus Question** How is a transition a change that happens over time? Use examples from *Behind the Mountains* and "Changes of State Are Physical Changes" to answer this question.

● Listening and Speaking

Tell a Story About a Time of Transition

Work with a partner to tell a story about a transition you experienced. Focus on developing a main idea, or theme, for your story. **Support** that main idea with details.

Phrases for Conversation

Transitional Phrases

Then . . .
Next . . .
At first . . .
Finally . . .

1. Begin by brainstorming ideas.
   a. Write down a few important changes in your life, such as your first days in a new school, or moving to a new area or home. Identify a few details for each idea. Consider details from before the transition and after.
   b. Choose one topic that you feel comfortable sharing with a partner.
2. Write down the events, in order, that created the transition. Be sure to identify the people involved in your story.
3. End your story with a lesson that you learned from the change you experienced.
4. Be sure to speak clearly and to use the volume and tone of your voice to add interest to the story. Move around and use gestures and facial expressions to show your story rather than simply tell it.
5. As you listen to your partner, note the main idea in his or her speech and the supporting details.
6. Summarize your partner's story to make sure that you understood the main idea and supporting details in the story.

Reading Fluency

Reading Words in Chunks

Reading words in chunks, or groups of words, can help you to read more quickly and fluently. As your reading skills improve, you will become a more confident and accurate reader.

1. Silently read the paragraph below. Do not read word by word. Instead, read the chunks of words. Pause briefly at every slash, and a little longer at every double slash.

    On a cool morning,/ **droplets** of dew cover the grass.// Where does this water come from?// You might think it had rained recently.// However, dew forms / even if it has not rained.// Air is made of a mixture of different gases,/ including water **vapor.**// Some of the water **vapor** condenses / —or becomes liquid— / on the cool grass and forms drops of liquid.//

2. With a partner, practice reading the paragraph aloud.

3. Reread the paragraph until your reading becomes smoother and more fluent. Discuss with your partner ways to improve your reading.

Vocabulary Development

Words with Multiple Meanings

Often, one word has more than one meaning. For example, the word *state* can mean "a portion of a country that has specific laws in addition to the laws of the country," like the state of California or New York. Or the word *state* can mean "a condition or situation." Water, for example, is in a liquid state.

As you read, use the context of a word to understand which meaning is being used. In other words, think about what the sentence is about. Then use the words that surround a multiple-meaning word to determine its meaning.

Read each sentence below. Use the context to determine the meaning of the underlined words.

1. Maria <u>fixed</u> the broken television. Now it works perfectly.
2. A solid has a <u>fixed</u> shape, but a liquid and a gas do not.
3. José heard his favorite song on the radio. He turned up the <u>volume</u> until his ears hurt.
4. The large measuring cup holds a total <u>volume</u> of 32 ounces.
5. I found the poem in the second <u>volume</u> of the collection of books called *Great Poems*. There were ten books in that collection.

> ### Build Your Knowledge
>
> Words that have the same spelling and pronunciation but different meanings are also called **homographs.** **Homophones** are words that are pronounced the same but have different spellings and meanings, for example, *to, two,* and *too.* See page 449 for more examples.

> ### ✓Checkpoint
>
> 1. How can a reader determine the meaning of a word that has **multiple meanings**?
> 2. Write two sentences using different meanings for the word *light.*

● **Grammar**

The Present Progressive Tense

The **present progressive tense** describes an action that is happening right now.

> I **am practicing** the piano. Diego **is playing** his guitar.
> The students **are taking** an exam.

The present progressive can also be used to describe a longer action in progress, though that action may not be happening at this very moment.

> I **am studying** to become a doctor.
> We **are saving** money for our vacation.

To form the present progressive tense, use the correct form of the auxiliary verb **be** in the present tense. Then add the **present participle**, or **-ing** form, of the verb.

Note: When the verb ends in **–e**, drop the **–e** before adding **–ing**.

Present Progressive Tense		
subject	*be*	**verb + *-ing***
I	**am**	**driving.**
You / We / They	**are**	**studying.**
He / She / It	**is**	**singing.**

Grammar Expansion

Present Progressive for Planned Activities in the Future

Workbook pages 83

Independent Practice CD-ROM/Online

Practice the Grammar Copy the sentences below. Underline the verbs in the present progressive tense.

1. We are walking to the main office.
2. The woman is speaking Creole to us.
3. Papa is filling out school forms.
4. The students are arriving to class.
5. I am learning about my new school.

Use the Grammar Independently Write three sentences using the present progressive tense. Underline the verbs in the present progressive.

Curt <u>is studying</u> for tomorrow's test.

✓**Checkpoint**

Give the present participle of the following verbs: eat, write, draw, cry.

Workbook page 81

Independent Practice CD-ROM/Online

● Grammar

The Past Progressive Tense

The **past progressive tense** describes actions that were in progress at some point in the past. Sometimes this tense indicates actions that were interrupted, or that were happening at the same time as other actions.

Valerie **was eating** dinner when the phone rang. It was her mother, who **was calling** to say hello. Valerie's dinner got cold while she **was speaking** with her mom.

To form the past progressive tense, use the correct form of the auxiliary verb **be** in the simple past tense. Then add the **present participle**, or **-ing** form of the verb.

Past Progressive Tense		
subject	*be*	verb + *-ing*
I	was	driving.
You / We / They	were	studying.
He / She / It	was	singing.

Practice the Grammar Copy the sentences below. Use the verb in parentheses to fill in the blank with the correct past progressive tense.

1. The water on the street _____ (change) into ice because of the freezing temperatures.
2. As the chocolate _____ (melt), it _____ (become) a liquid.
3. We _____ (learn) how a liquid becomes a gas when Jacob asked a question.
4. They _____ (heat) the iron in order to melt it.
5. I _____ (hope) to play in the snow when I saw that it had all melted.

Use the Grammar Independently Write a paragraph about your actions and the actions happening around you last night at 8:00. Include verbs in the past progressive tense. Underline the verbs in the past progressive.

Last night I <u>was watching</u> a movie when the electricity went out.

Workbook
page 82

Independent Practice
CD-ROM/Online

Grammar Expansion

Yes/No Questions and Negative Statements in the Present and Past Progressive

Workbook
pages 84

Independent Practice
CD-ROM/Online

✓Checkpoint

What is the difference between the present progressive and the past progressive?

● **Writing Assignment**

Write a Descriptive Essay

Writing Prompt

Look at the painting on the next page. Write an essay that describes what the painting is about. This will be your thesis statement. Identify details in the painting that **support** your interpretation of the art. Include the present and past progressive verb tenses to say what is going on in the art and what you think was happening before the moment captured in the painting.

Write Your Descriptive Essay

1. **Read the student model.**

Student Model

Thesis Statement

A Family Celebration

Barbacoa para Cumpleaños, by Carmen Lomas Garza, is a painting about a family enjoying a big, back-yard barbecue in celebration of a young girl's birthday.

In the painting, the family is celebrating a birthday. A big cake is sitting on a table, waiting to be eaten. The birthday girl is surrounded by her family. She is trying to hit a piñata—a big, bright star—and hoping that candy and toys fall at her feet. All week long, she was dreaming about the barbecue and about all the good food they would eat. Her uncle is grilling the meat now, and her grandfather is adding charcoal to the grill. It is a lovely day, and her family and friends are looking forward to an evening of smiles and fun.

Barbacoa para Cumpleaños (1993),
Carmen Lomas Garza

Workbook
page 85

2. Prewrite.

a. On a piece of paper, make a list of the details shown in the second painting, called *Sandía/ Watermelon*. Begin with the most prominent detail, and then continue with the details that surround it.

b. From your list, write one sentence that summarizes what you think the painting is about. This statement will become your thesis statement.

3. Write your essay.

a. Begin with your thesis statement.

b. The body of your paragraph will contain all the details that helped you to determine the thesis statement. Do not include anything that does not **support** the thesis statement. Use the present progressive tense to describe what is happening in the art, and use the past progressive to describe the events that led to the moment captured in the art.

4. Revise.
Make sure the thesis statement and the body work together. Use the **Writing Checklist** to help you find problems and errors.

5. Edit.
Use the **editing and proofreading symbols** on page **455** to help you mark the changes you need to make.

6. Read your essay to the class.

Sandía/Watermelon (1986), Carmen Lomas Garza

Writing Checklist

1. I created a thesis statement that I **supported** in the body of my writing.

2. I described what is happening in the painting.

3. I described events leading up to the moment captured in the art.

4. I included present and past progressive verb tenses.

5. I proofread and edited my work.

Writing Support

Mechanics

Hyphens and Dashes

Hyphens and dashes have different uses. **Hyphens** are used to connect words or phrases. They are used in three ways:

- in numbers (twenty-one) and fractions used as adjectives (two-thirds vote)
- with the prefixes *ex-, pro-, self-,* and *anti-* (ex-partner, pro-recycling, self-starter, anti-slavery)
- in compound adjectives before the noun that is modified (after-school meeting, well-planned party)

Dashes are used to indicate a break in thought.

The game was delayed for three days—the playing fields were too muddy for use.

Mother planted cosmos—bright pink and purple flowers—in her flower bed.

Apply Check your essay for places to use hyphens or dashes. Have you used each type of punctuation correctly?

Workbook
pages 86–88

Independent Practice
CD-ROM/Online

Progress Check

MILESTONES TRACKER

How well did you understand this chapter? Try to answer the questions. If necessary, go back to the pages listed for a review.

Skills	Skills Assessment Questions	Pages to Review
Vocabulary From the Readings	What do these words mean?	
	• fluid, impression, outshine, quarrelsome, reluctantly, slew	76
	• arrangement, droplet, particle, range, vapor	86
Academic Vocabulary	What do these academic vocabulary words mean?	
	• support, deduce	77
	• contrast, participate	84
Reading Strategies	What is a **main idea** in a reading selection?	77
	What is a **cause**? What is an **effect**?	87
Text Genre	What is the text genre of *Behind the Mountains*?	78
	What is the text genre of "Changes of State Are Physical Changes"?	87
Reading Comprehension	What is *Behind the Mountains* about?	85
	What is "Changes of State Are Physical Changes" about?	91
Literary Element	Choose an adjective that might describe the **tone** of a story.	85
Spelling	Give the simple past tense of the verbs **shop**, **climb**, and **carry**.	91
Writing Conventions	What is the abbreviation of "ounce"?	91
Listening and Speaking	**Phrases for Conversation** What does a transitional phrase do?	92
Vocabulary Development	How does a reader determine the meaning of a word with multiple meanings?	93
Grammar	How do you form the present progressive tense?	94
	How do you form the past progressive tense?	95
Writing Support: Mechanics	Which punctuation mark is used to interrupt thoughts in writing?	97

Assessment Practice

Read this passage. Then answer Questions 1 through 4.

Going Home Again

1   My family lives in New York City. On weekends, we sometimes explore different neighborhoods. We feel like strangers, but since it is our city, it is still home.

2   My brother and I know what it is like to feel like strangers. Last summer, we went to Mexico, where our grandparents were living. The transition was not very fluid. My grandfather wanted us to speak Spanish with him. The food was very different. But our grandmother took us to a beach that was prettier than any we have seen in New York, and we decided we loved it. Just as we were getting used to life there, it was time to return to New York. My brother said, "I can't believe we are going home already!" Our grandparents reluctantly said goodbye to us at the airport.

3   When we stepped off the plane, we felt like strangers again because we were used to how things are in Mexico. But as soon as I saw my house, it felt like home again!

1 What does the word <u>fluid</u> mean in the following sentence?

> **The transition was not very fluid.**

A scary

B kind

C welcoming

D smooth

2 What is the main idea of the passage?

A New York City is the best place.

B Family is important.

C It takes time to adjust to new surroundings.

D Traveling is tiring.

3 What is the effect of the writer's getting used to life in Mexico?

A He wanted to go back.

B He felt like a stranger in New York.

C His grandparents didn't want to say goodbye.

D He liked the food.

4 What are the two settings of this passage?

A two different neighborhoods of New York

B New York and New Mexico

C school and home

D New York and Mexico

Writing on Demand: Descriptive Essay

Describe your favorite place. Give enough details so that the reader feels like he or she is there. Include in your description the sights and sounds of the place and how it makes you feel.
(20 minutes)

> **Writing Tip**
> Remember to use adjectives and adverbs to make your description more interesting.

CHAPTER 2

Objectives

Reading Strategies

Organize information; Make and revise predictions

Listening and Speaking

Retell a story

Grammar

Learn about adjectives and adverbs; Use adjective and adverb phrases

Writing

Write an expository essay about a problem and a solution

Academic Vocabulary

sequence	solution
influence	trigger

Academic Content

Origins of the United States Constitution

The performing arts

● **Chapter Focus Question**

What qualities does a person need to face an important transition in life?

Reading 1 **Content:** Social Studies

Informational text: Magazine article

CRISIS OF GOVERNMENT

by Gina DeAngelis

Reading 2 **Literature**

Memoir (excerpt)

A Shot at It

by Esmeralda Santiago

CRISIS OF GOVERNMENT

● **About the Reading**

After the Revolutionary War, the young United States turned its attention to creating a new government. The article you are about to read tells the story of the documents that made this government work.

Build Background
A New Way of Governing

In 1777, the Articles of Confederation were created. The Articles were the guidelines by which the United States governed itself following the Revolutionary War. Within ten years, however, it became clear that the Articles had created a government of individual states, not a unified nation. It was difficult for each state to pay off the money it owed to the nation. Tax laws varied from state to state, and this caused confusion and rebellion. The nation needed a new way of governing.

Use Prior Knowledge
Working Together

In the late 1700s, the United States of America did not have a powerful national government, and sometimes the original 13 states could not agree on how to run the new country. "Crisis of Government" shows how cooperation among the states was necessary in order to pass laws, solve problems, and form a central government. This cooperation created a strong nation.

Where do you see examples of cooperation in your own life? What goals are achieved when people work together? Think about the different situations below and provide an example for each.

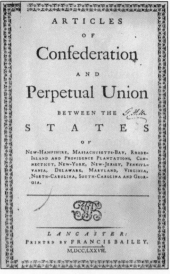

The Articles of Confederation were guidelines for all the existing states in 1777.

Your family	In the classroom	On a sports team	In your community	Public leaders
		winning a game		

Key Vocabulary

- crisis
- debt
- enforce
- framework
- impose
- resolve

H135060708
TRUC092

● Vocabulary From the Reading

Learn, Practice, and Use Independently

Learn Vocabulary Read each sentence. Look at the **highlighted** words. Use the context to learn their meanings.

1. The hurricane tore down houses and trees and devastated our town. During this time of **crisis**, we depended on each other and slowly rebuilt our community.
2. Jorge borrowed fifty dollars from his mother last week; he owes her a **debt** of fifty dollars.
3. The umpires **enforce** the rules in baseball. They decide what is fair play and what is not.
4. Workers were building a new house in the neighborhood. We could see the **framework** of wood boards and beams.
5. My mother **imposed** a new rule: no television until all my homework is done.
6. We can **resolve** conflicts by compromising and seeing each other's point of view.

Practice Vocabulary Read each description below. Then identify the Key Vocabulary word that best fits the description.

1. _____ list of topics that will later become a full speech
2. _____ a police officer writing a ticket for a traffic fine
3. _____ a government creating a new tax that its citizens must pay
4. _____ money borrowed from the bank to buy a new house
5. _____ the lack of clean water, electricity, or food caused by a tornado
6. _____ two friends shaking hands after an argument

Use Vocabulary Independently Write a paragraph that uses each of the Key Vocabulary words.

✓ Checkpoint

1. Which Key Vocabulary word is an antonym, or opposite, of "profit"?
2. Which word is a synonym for, or the same as, "trouble"?

Vocabulary Log

Workbook page 89

Independent Practice CD-ROM/Online

● Academic Vocabulary

Vocabulary for the Reading Strategy

Word	Explanation	Sample Sentence	Visual Cue
sequence *noun*	a connected series of events or items, one following the other	I wake up at 7:00 AM, eat breakfast, then get ready for school. This is the **sequence** I follow every morning.	
influence *verb*	to change someone's mind or have an effect on	The trainer tries to **influence** the dog's performance by offering him treats.	

Draw a picture and write a sentence for each word.

● Reading Strategy

Organize Information

Readers understand more of what they read when they organize the information in a reading. As you read, look for the **sequence** of events and the **influences** on the making of the Constitution. When you finish reading "**Crisis** of Government," you will organize the information into an outline like the one below.

1. Use Roman numerals (I, II, III) to indicate major topics.
2. Use capital letters (A, B, C) to organize information related to those topics.
3. Use numbers (1, 2, 3) to clarify specific information.

I. Documents that existed after the Revolution

   A. Articles of Confederation

      1. Gave power to the states and not to a central government

✓Checkpoint

1. What is the **sequence** of names in a telephone book?

2. Describe a person who has positively **influenced** the lives of others.

Vocabulary Log

Workbook page 90

Independent Practice CD-ROM/Online

● Text Genre

Informational Text: Magazine Article

"**Crisis** of Government" is a magazine article. The purpose of informational texts is to inform the reader about a specific topic. Magazine articles about history share the following features.

Magazine Article: History	
dates	important days, months, and years
events	specific important happenings
chronological order	order in which events take place

● Meet the Author

Gina DeAngelis is the author of many nonfiction books for young readers. She holds advanced degrees in history, and her writing includes biographies and screenplays. DeAngelis is originally from Hershey, Pennsylvania. She currently lives in Virginia with her husband, her daughter, and her pets.

● Reading Focus Questions

As you read, think about these questions.

1. What events in the reading suggest that a transition in the government was about to occur?
2. Why do you think the author chose to write about this event in history?
3. What is the purpose of studying transitional events such as the one in "**Crisis** of Government"?

✓Checkpoint

Name three features of a magazine article about history.

Workbook
page 91

Independent Practice
CD-ROM/Online

CRISIS OF GOVERNMENT

by Gina DeAngelis

Prologue

The Revolutionary War left the United States with a large **debt**. Individual states had the responsibility of raising the money to pay off this **debt,** so each state began to **impose** higher taxes on its citizens. The owners of small farms found it especially hard to pay their taxes. Farmers who could not pay had to sell their farms or hand them over to the state. Shays's Rebellion, a protest of farmers against unfair state taxes, showed the Founders how much the nation needed a **centralized** government.

1   The 55 men who gathered in Philadelphia, Pennsylvania, in May 1787 were prepared to take **drastic** action. They were meeting to address the difficulties facing the nation and a **crisis** surrounding the U.S. government.

Independence Hall in Philadelphia, Pennsylvania, was a meeting place for the Founders.

2   The Articles of Confederation, written in 1777 and **ratified** by the states in 1781, had been the **framework** for the U.S. government following the American Revolutionary War. The writers of the Articles, however, had **resisted** giving their new national government any real power. They were more concerned with protecting individuals' and states' **rights**, and their outline for operating the young government was designed to do just that.

Reading Strategy

Organize Information
What information from paragraph 2 should you include in an outline?

Reading Check

1. **Recall facts** What key event caused the decision to change the government?

2. **Draw conclusions** Where did the power to govern lie in the early days of the U.S. government?

---

centralized under the control of one authority
drastic extreme
ratified formally approved or accepted
resisted refused to allow
rights things that are guaranteed to a person or government by law

3   Under the Articles, the 13 state governments had more lawmaking power than the national government. Each state was allowed to send **representatives,** or delegates, to a national governing **body** called Congress.

4   The state governments, not the individual citizens, chose their delegates and had the authority to **recall** them at any time. No matter how many delegates a state sent to Congress or how many people lived in a state, each state had only one vote. And laws could not be passed unless at least nine of the 13 states agreed.

5   Though Congress was the entire U.S. government under the Articles of Confederation, its powers were limited **severely.** Congress could not raise money by **imposing** taxes, nor could it form an army. And it could not **resolve** disputes among the states. The president of Congress also had very little authority. Perhaps most difficult of all under the Articles was that laws passed by Congress were worthless unless each state government chose to **enforce** them.

6   There were leaders in each state who were aware of the weaknesses in the Articles of Confederation. Many, like James Madison of Virginia and Alexander Hamilton of New York, called for a special meeting to revise the Articles. Other leaders, even some members of Congress, felt there should be no **tinkering** with the framework, and they opposed any meeting.

Reenactment of the signing of the Declaration of Independence at Independence Hall.

---

representatives people who represent the residents of a community
body group of people
recall ask that something be returned, brought back
severely extremely, strictly
tinkering adjusting (in a small way)

7   Shays's Rebellion, however, changed a lot of minds. Droughts and economic problems in the **decade** following the Revolutionary War left many Massachusetts farmers—often former soldiers—unable to pay their **debts**. They watched their farms get **seized** by tax collectors, and some farmers were thrown in jail.

8   In the autumn of 1786, Daniel Shays, a captain during the Revolution, and other leaders led mobs of angry farmers in the closing of several western Massachusetts courthouses. They hoped to prevent—by force, if necessary—the **bankruptcy cases** from being heard. The revolt threatened to spread to other states, and Congress had no authority to stop it.

9   Even though the rebellion was over by the end of February 1787, many people feared the young nation was falling apart. Convinced now that a meeting was **crucial**, delegates from 12 states (Rhode Island did not send anyone) met in Philadelphia in May. They were prepared to make important changes to the Articles of Confederation. But instead of simply revising them, the representatives wrote an entirely new Constitution.

Reading Strategy

Organize Information Should Shays's Rebellion be a part of your outline? Why or why not?

10   In the **Preamble** to the Constitution, the **Framers** clearly explained why a new government structure was needed and what they expected of the central government. The biggest question they needed to answer, however, was how to form a government that represented its people and had enough power to get things done, without allowing it to become **tyrannical**. Certainly, nobody wanted to return to the way things had been under Great Britain's rule.

King George III was the ruler of Great Britain during the American Revolution.

Reading Check

1. **Recall facts** Which two factors made it difficult for farmers to pay their taxes?

2. **Make an inference** Why is it important to know that many small farmers were also former soldiers?

decade ten years
seized taken over
bankruptcy cases trials for small farmers who were too poor to pay their taxes
crucial critical, of extreme importance
Preamble introduction
Framers men who designed and wrote the Constitution
tyrannical having total governing power without limitation

The Matchup

Ever wonder exactly how the Articles of Confederation and the Constitution differed? Here's a comparison of some of the points that show how the Founding Fathers **modified** their ideas about the federal government between 1781 and 1787.

Articles of Confederation	Constitution
Unicameral legislature, called Congress (one house or governing body)	Bicameral legislature, called Congress (two houses or governing bodies)
2–7 members per state, appointed by state legislatures, served for one-year **term**	two senators per state, appointed by state legislatures, serve for six-year terms; representatives determined according to state population, elected by popular vote, serve for two-year terms
members limited to serve three out of every six years	no term limits for members
each state had one vote	each senator and representative has one vote
led by president of Congress	led by vice president in Senate, speaker in House of Representatives
required **unanimous** states' consent for **amendments** to articles	requires consent of three-fourths of states for amendments
state and federal governments shared responsibilities regarding issues of an army, a navy, coining money, and raising taxes	federal government assumes all authority over raising and supporting an army and a navy, coining money, and raising taxes

Reading Strategy

Organize Information
What two positions could politicians hold in the bicameral Congress? Under what heading in your **outline** should this information be placed?

modified changed
term length of time in a political office
unanimous with the agreement of every person
amendments changes or additions

11   The Framers decided to give the national government specific duties, along with the responsibilities necessary to keep the country strong. The state governments then would get control over any tasks not given to the federal government. Also, power had to be separated and balanced among different **branches** of the national government. Congress represented the people and had the power to make laws, but its large body of members made it difficult to respond quickly in an emergency. A chief executive, or president, could do this, but his power had to be **checked** to avoid having rule by a king. Neither the president nor Congress could properly **enforce** laws or **resolve** disputes among the states, so a third **arm** of the government was needed. Thus, three branches were created: the legislative (Congress), the executive (a president and his advisors), and the judicial (the Supreme Court).

12   But should Congress represent the states or the people living in them? In what became known as "the Great **Compromise**," the Framers decided Congress would do both. With a Senate and a House of Representatives, Congress would be bicameral. The Constitution **preserves** the equality of the separate states by giving each, regardless of population size, two members in the Senate. In the House, the size of a state's membership is determined according to its population and ranges from only one representative to as many as 53. Congress was **deemed** so important that the Framers addressed its powers in Article I of the Constitution.

Reading Strategy

Organize Information Which branch of government was the last in the **sequence** to be developed? Be sure to include this branch in your outline.

A view of a modern-day state senate chamber

branches divisions
checked controlled
arm division, branch
Compromise agreement where each side gets some, but not all, of what they wanted
preserves keeps safe
deemed acknowledged to be

Reading Check

1. **Recall facts** What power goes to the state governments?

2. **Make an inference** What do you think the word *judicial* means?

3. **Speculate** Why do you think Article I of the Constitution was important?

● **Apply the Reading Strategy**

Organize Information

Now that you have read "**Crisis** of Government," you are ready to complete the Reading Strategy graphic organizer.

1. Review the **Reading Strategy** on page 103.
2. Copy the beginning of the outline.
3. Look back at the reading. Complete your outline, choosing, organizing, and putting the information you read in the correct **sequence**. Be sure to note the major **influences** that led to the writing of the Constitution.

> **I.** Documents that existed after the Revolution
>
>   **B.** Articles of Confederation
>
>   **1.** Gave power to the states and not to a central government

● **Academic Vocabulary**

Vocabulary for the Reading Comprehension Questions

Word	Explanation	Sample Sentence	Visual Cue
solution *noun*	an answer to a problem, or a way to solve a problem	I am good at figuring out the **solutions** to crossword puzzles.	
trigger *verb*	to cause something to start; start a reaction	The freshly cut grass **triggered** an allergic reaction; it made me sneeze and made my eyes itchy and red.	

Draw a picture and write a sentence for each word.

✓ Checkpoint

1. Provide an example of a problem and a **solution**.
2. What kinds of things might **trigger** sneezing?

Vocabulary
Log

● Reading Comprehension Questions

Think and Discuss

1. **Recall facts** What document was replaced by the Constitution?

2. **Recognize problems and solutions** The Framers of the Constitution did not want a government that could become tyrannical. What solution did they offer to that problem?

3. **Speculate** According to the article, many people worried that the young nation would fall apart after Shays's Rebellion began. How might a small rebellion in Massachusetts trigger the downfall of the nation?

4. **Speculate** Why do you think the writers of the Articles were so concerned about protecting the rights of individuals and states?

5. **State your opinion** Do you think the Constitution was an improvement over the Articles of Confederation? Explain your answer.

6. **Revisit the Reading Focus Questions** Go back to page 104 and discuss the questions.

Workbook
page 92

Independent Practice
CD-ROM/Online

● Text Element

Audience

Every time you read a text, you become the **audience** for the writer of that text. Writers know what their audiences enjoy, and they often write with a specific audience in mind. An audience with an interest in gardening will enjoy reading a book about flowers and trees written by an expert on nature. Likewise, a book about computers will appeal to an audience that likes technology. Gina DeAngelis wrote "**Crisis** of Government" to appeal to an audience that enjoys American history and government.

Read the list of subjects below. Decide what kind of audience would enjoy reading about each subject.

1. Endangered animals

2. Race-car driving

3. Taking care of children

4. The world's greatest inventions

5. Food

Workbook
page 93

Independent Practice
CD-ROM/Online

✓Checkpoint

1. What is an **audience**?

2. How do your interests and hobbies play a part in what you choose to read?

A Shot at It

● About the Reading

In "**Crisis** of Government," you read about a nation struggling through political changes. In "A Shot at It," you will read a memoir about a teenager from Puerto Rico who changes her mind about her future career.

● Build Background

Performing Arts Schools

What do you think these performing arts students are doing?

Performing arts is a broad label that applies to activities that take place on the stage. Usually, it includes acting, singing, dancing, and music. Since the 1930s, there have been special high schools and colleges built just for teaching students with a talent for performing arts. Often, those schools include academic courses, too, such as math and science. Over time, performing arts has grown to include related fields, such as makeup and costume design, technical theater (sound, lighting, and set design), and more.

Key Vocabulary

audition

enunciate

monologue

panel

● Vocabulary From the Reading

Use Context Clues to Determine Meaning

Look at the **highlighted** words in the sentences below. Use the other words of the sentences to determine their meaning.

1. The local theater was holding an **audition** for their next show. I wanted to be in the show, so I prepared for the tryouts.
2. I knew that I should **enunciate** each word clearly so that the people sitting in the back would not think that I was mumbling.
3. At the audition, I stood alone on the stage and acted out my **monologue.**
4. I looked hopefully at the **panel** of six judges, who sat behind a long table and stared back at me.

✓Checkpoint

1. What do you think might be hard about performing a **monologue**?
2. Work with a partner to clearly **enunciate** the Key Vocabulary.

Vocabulary Log

Workbook page 94

Independent Practice CD-ROM/Online

Reading Strategy

Make and Revise Predictions

When you predict, you guess what will happen in the future based on clues in the past or in the present. You revise predictions by changing or adjusting your guess based on new information. Make and revise predictions while you read "A Shot at It" to become a more active reader.

Text Genre

Memoir

A **memoir** is a story from the life of an author. The purpose of a memoir is to share a personal experience with the reader. Sometimes an author uses his or her personal experience to help others. Most memoirs include the following elements.

Memoir	
first-person point of view	narration that is told by one of the characters in the story; the narrator uses the pronoun "I"
dialogue	conversation between characters
internal dialogue	thoughts of the narrator revealed for the reader

Meet the Author

Esmeralda Santiago was born in San Juan, Puerto Rico, and came to the United States when she was 13 years old. She studied dance and drama at New York City's Performing Arts School, and later graduated from Harvard University. Santiago has written numerous memoirs, novels, films, and articles. She has won many prestigious awards and honorary doctorate degrees from three universities for her work.

Reading Focus Questions

As you read, think about these questions.

1. What significant transitions has the author experienced?
2. What might be the purpose of writing a memoir?
3. What famous person's memoir would you like to read? Why?

✓ Checkpoint

1. What information do you use to make a prediction?
2. How do you check your prediction to determine whether it was correct?

Workbook
pages 95–96

Independent Practice
CD-ROM/Online

A Shot at It

by Esmeralda Santiago

1   The first week of high school I was given a series of tests that showed that even though I couldn't speak English very well, I read and wrote it at the tenth-grade level. So they put me in 9-3, with the smart kids.

2   One morning, Mr. Barone, a guidance counselor, called me to his office. He was short, with a big head and large **hazel** eyes under shapely eyebrows. His nose was long and round at the tip. He dressed in browns and yellows and often perched his **tortoiseshell** glasses on his forehead, as if he had another set of eyes up there.

3   "So," he pushed his glasses up, "what do you want to be when you grow up?"

4   "I don't know."

5   He shuffled through some papers. "Let's see here ... you're fourteen, is that right?"

6   "Yes, sir."

7   "And you've never thought about what you want to be?"

8   When I was very young, I wanted to be a *jíbara.* When I was older, I wanted to be a **cartographer,** then a **topographer.** But since we'd come to Brooklyn, I'd not thought about the future much. . . .

9   "I'd like to be a model," I said to Mr. Barone.

10   He stared at me, pulled his glasses down from his forehead, looked at the papers inside the folder with my name on it, and glared. "A model?" His voice was **gruff,** as if he were more comfortable yelling at people than talking to them.

Reading Strategy

Make and Revise Predictions Do you think Mr. Barone will encourage the narrator? What clues help you to make your prediction?

---

hazel brown and green mix
tortoiseshell brown and cream-colored, like a substance made from the shell of a turtle
jíbara person who lives in the country (Spanish)
cartographer maker of maps
topographer maker of a specialized map that shows elevation and surface features
gruff rough or stern

11 "I want to be on television."

12 "Oh, then you want to be an actress," in a tone that said this was only a slight improvement over my first career choice. We stared at one another for a few seconds. He pushed his glasses up to his forehead again and reached for a book on the shelf in back of him. "I only know of one school that trains actresses, but we've never sent them a student from here."

13 Performing Arts, the write-up said, was an academic, **as opposed to vocational,** public school that trained students wishing to pursue a career in theater, music, and dance.

14 "It says here that you have to audition." He stood up and held the book closer to the faint gray light coming through the narrow window high on his wall. "Have you ever performed in front of an audience?"

15 "I was announcer in my school show in Puerto Rico," I said. "And I recite poetry. There, not here."

16 "The **auditions** are in less than a month. You have to learn a **monologue,** which you will perform in front of a **panel.** If you do well, and your grades here are good, you might get into the school. Mr. Gatti, the English teacher," he said, "will coach you. … And Mrs. Johnson will talk to you about what to wear and things like that."

Reading Strategy

Make and Revise Predictions Do you think the narrator will go to the audition? Why do you think this?

Instrument Zoo II (1997), Margie Livingston Campbell

Reading Check

1. **Recall facts** How many of Mr. Barone's students have gone to the performing arts school?

2. **Analyze characters** Do you think the narrator has given much thought to becoming an actress? Explain your answer.

---

as opposed to in contrast to
vocational work-related

Reading Strategy

Make and Revise Predictions Do you think her teachers' questions will help the narrator at her **audition**?

17   Mrs. Johnson, who taught Home Economics, called me to her office.

18   "Is that how you enter a room?" she asked the minute I came in. "Try again, only this time, don't **barge** in. Step in slowly, head up, back straight, a nice smile on your face. That's it." I took a deep breath and waited. "Now sit. No, not like that. Don't just plop down. Float down to the chair with your knees together." She demonstrated, and I copied her. "That's better. What do you do with your hands? No, don't hold your chin like that; it's not ladylike. Put your hands on your lap, and leave them there. Don't use them so much when you talk."

19   I sat stiff as a **cutout** while Mrs. Johnson and Mr. Barone asked me questions they thought the **panel** at Performing Arts would ask.

20   "Where are you from?"

21   "Puerto Rico."

22   "No," Mrs. Johnson said, "Porto Rico. Keep your r's soft. Try again."

23   "Do you have any **hobbies**?" Mr. Barone asked. Now I knew what to answer.

24   "I enjoy dancing and the movies."

25   "Why do you want to come to this school?"

26   Mrs. Johnson and Mr. Barone had worked on my answer if this question should come up.

27   "I would like to study at Performing Arts because of its academic program and so that I may be trained as an actress."

Students reading through their lines for a school play

---

barge enter forcefully or loudly
cutout stiff cardboard or paper doll
hobbies activities used to pass the time

28   "Very good, very good!" Mr. Barone rubbed his hands together, twinkled his eyes at Mrs. Johnson. "I think we have a shot at this."

✳ ✳ ✳

29   Three women sat behind a long table in a classroom where the desks and chairs had been pushed against a wall. As I entered, I held my head up and smiled, and then I floated down to the chair in front of them, clasped my hands on my lap, and smiled some more.

30   The moment I faced these three **impeccably groomed** women, I forgot my English and Mrs. Johnson's lessons on how to behave like a lady. In the **agony** of trying to answer their barely **comprehensible** questions, I **jabbed** my hands here and there, forming words with my fingers because the words refused to leave my mouth.

31   "Why don't you let us hear your **monologue** now?" the woman with the dangling glasses asked softly.

32   I stood up **abruptly**, and my chair clattered onto its side two feet from where I stood. I picked it up, wishing with all my strength that a thunderbolt would strike me dead to ashes on the spot.

33   "It's all right," she said. "Take a breath. We know you're nervous."

34   I closed my eyes and breathed deeply, walked to the middle of the room, and began my **monologue**.

Reading Strategy

Make and Revise Predictions Look back at the prediction you made on page 114. What new information might cause you to revise your prediction about Mr. Barone?

Reading Check

1. **Recall facts** What caused the narrator to forget her English temporarily?

2. **Analyze** How well did the narrator do at the beginning of her **audition**?

3. **Make an inference** Why did the narrator wish a thunderbolt would strike her dead in the middle of her **audition**?

---

impeccably well-dressed, perfectly neat and clean
groomed cared for the appearance of; made neat
agony intense pain (mental)
comprehensible capable of being understood
jabbed quickly poked
abruptly suddenly

35   In spite of Mr. Gatti's reminders that I should speak slowly and **enunciate** every word, even if I didn't understand it, I recited my three-minute **monologue** in one minute flat.

36   The small woman's long lashes seemed to have grown with amazement. The **elegant** woman's **serene** face twitched with controlled laughter. The tall one dressed in **beige** smiled sweetly.

37   The elegant woman stretched her hand out for me to shake. "We will notify your school in a few weeks. It was very nice to meet you."

38   On the way home Mami kept asking what had happened, and I kept mumbling "Nothing. Nothing happened," ashamed that, after all the hours of practice with Mrs. Johnson, Mr. Barone, and Mr. Gatti, after the expense of new clothes and shoes, after Mami had to take a day off from work to take me into Manhattan, after all that, I had failed the **audition** and would never, ever, get out of Brooklyn.

✳ ✳ ✳

39   A decade after my graduation from Performing Arts, I visited the school. I was by then living in Boston, a scholarship student at Harvard University. The tall, elegant woman of my **audition** had become my **mentor** through my three years there.

40   I walked the halls of the school, looking for the room where my life had changed. It was across from the **science lab,** a few doors down from the big bulletin board where someone with neat handwriting still wrote the letters "**P.A.**" followed by the graduating year along the edges of the newspaper clippings featuring famous **alumni.**

41   "P.A. '66," I said to no one in particular. "One of these days."

Reading Strategy

Make and Revise Predictions The narrator predicts that she will someday become a successful actress. Do you share her prediction? On what clues do you base your response?

---

elegant stylish, refined
serene peaceful, calm
beige tan
mentor teacher and advisor
science lab room dedicated for science and research
P.A. abbreviation for Performing Arts
alumni graduates

Reading Comprehension Questions

Think and Discuss

1. **Recall details** What was the narrator's theater experience before auditioning for Performing Arts?

2. **Interpret** Why does Mr. Barone think the narrator has a shot at being accepted to the performing arts school?

3. **Speculate** Why do you think Mrs. Johnson advised the narrator to use her hands less when she spoke and to soften her r's?

4. **Make predictions** Did you think that the narrator would be accepted into the school? What clues helped you make your prediction?

5. **Draw conclusions** Reread the last line of the story on page 118. When the narrator says "One of these days," what is she referring to? What internal dialogue is going on in her mind?

6. **Revisit the Reading Focus Questions** Go back to page 113 and discuss the questions.

Workbook
page 97

Independent Practice
CD-ROM/Online

Spelling

Possessive Nouns Ending
in -s

Workbook
page 98

Independent Practice
CD-ROM/Online

Writing Conventions

Spelling: Heteronyms

Workbook
page 99

Independent Practice
CD-ROM/Online

Connect Readings 1 and 2

You have read two readings on the theme of transitions. Use these activities to make connections between the readings.

1. With a partner, use this chart to compare the two readings.

Reading title	Which reading is a memoir and which is an article?	How does each reading use chronological order?	How does each reading show an example of a transition?
Crisis of Government			
A Shot at It			

2. With a partner, ask and answer these questions.

   a. "A Shot at It" uses the first-person point of view, and because it is a memoir, the events in the story happened in the life of the author. How do these features compare to those in "**Crisis of Government**"?

   b. What kind of audience would be interested in "**Crisis** of Government"? What kind of audience would enjoy "A Shot at It"?

3. **Revisit the Chapter Focus Question** What qualities does a person need to face an important transition in life? Use examples from the two readings to answer this question.

Listening and Speaking

Retell a Story

In "A Shot at It," the narrator moves quickly from her **audition** at Performing Arts to the decade after, when she is a student at Harvard. Imagine an event from that time and tell the story of that event in greater detail. Be sure to note any important characters and details in the setting that would have been a part of the narrator's life.

1. Brainstorm ideas.

   a. Choose one event in the narrator's life. Consider these possibilities:

      * the narrator receiving her acceptance letter to Performing Arts
      * her first day at school
      * her first show
      * graduation
      * her move to Harvard
      * her first performance there

   b. Think about things that might have happened to the narrator. Imagine you are the narrator. Address where these events took place and the narrator's feelings about the events.

2. Tell the story of your event from beginning to end. Use the first-person point of view to match the original text.

3. Share or act out your story with your classmates. Be sure to use facial expressions and gestures that are appropriate for the story. Compare and contrast the details of the stories with the original selection, and discuss these details with the speakers.

Phrases for Conversation

Comparing and Contrasting

It is the same.
It is different.
It is more or less the same.

Expressing Agreement

I agree with. . . .
My idea is similar to . . . 's idea
I think so.
You are right.

● Reading Fluency

Rapid Word Recognition

Rapidly recognizing words helps you to increase your reading rate. The ability to read rapidly is an important characteristic of a fluent and effective reader.

1. With a partner, review the words in the list below.
2. Read the words aloud for one minute. Your partner will time you as you read.
3. How many words did you read in one minute? Count the words and record your results.

famous	breath	members	famous	article
separate	article	breath	separate	members
article	breath	famous	members	article
members	separate	breath	famous	separate
famous	article	members	separate	breath

● Vocabulary Development

Prefix: fore-

A **prefix** is a word part, or a group of letters, added to the beginning of a word to change the word's meaning. For example, the prefix **fore-** means "before, or in front of." Your *forehead* is the front part of your head.

Use the meaning of the prefix **fore-** and the base word to determine the meaning of each of the words below.

1. **a.** father: male parent
   b. forefather: _____
2. **a.** ground: area of earth
   b. foreground: _____
3. **a.** name: what a person is called
   b. forename: _____
4. **a.** see: to spot something with the eyes; to understand clearly
   b. foresee: _____

✓Checkpoint

1. What does the word *forewarn* mean?
2. What does the word *foreword* mean?

Vocabulary Log

Workbook page 100

Independent Practice CD-ROM/Online

● Grammar

Adjectives and Adverbs

Adjectives modify, or describe, nouns. An adjective can describe a noun by telling about the quality or quantity of the noun. Each of the adjectives below modifies the noun *apple*.

a **Granny Smith** apple → the **green** apple → those **five** apples

A **predicate adjective** is separated from the noun it modifies by a linking verb. Each of the predicate adjectives below modifies the noun *apple*.

The apple is **red.** → The apple tasted **good.** → The apple looks **ripe.**

An **adverb** is a word used to describe a verb, an adjective, or another adverb. An adverb can describe by telling how, when, where, or to what extent (how much).

Adverb	What it Modifies	What it Tells
She walks **everywhere.**	verb: *walks*	where she walks (**everywhere**)
She is an **extremely** fast walker.	adjective: *fast*	how fast a walker she is (**extremely** fast)
She walks **very** slowly.	adverb: *slowly*	how slowly she walks (**very** slowly)

Grammar Expansion

Nouns as Adjectives

Workbook page 103   Independent Practice CD-ROM/Online

Practice the Grammar Underline and label the adjectives and adverbs in the paragraph below. Then identify the word that is modified.

   Jason bought a red bike to ride to his new school. He liked to ride quickly down the narrow road. He rode everywhere on his new bike. He never went anywhere without his bike.

Use the Grammar Independently Write a paragraph about the narrator in "A Shot at It." Identify the adjectives and adverbs in your paragraph, and note the words they modify.

✓ Checkpoint

How is an adjective different from an adverb?

Workbook page 101

Grammar

Adjective and Adverb Phrases

Adjective phrases are used in the same way as adjectives—to modify a noun. An adjective phrase is a group of words that indicates what kind or which one. The phrase usually begins with a preposition, such as *in, by, near, with, about, on, over, from, before,* and *down,* and ends with a noun.

> The fireplace provided warmth **from the bitter cold.** (what kind of warmth)

> Every student **in the first row** will give a presentation on Monday. (which students)

Adverb phrases work like adverbs: to modify verbs by telling how, when, where, to what extent, and why. They also begin with a preposition and end with a noun.

> She rehearses **with determination.** (how she rehearses)

> She rehearses **in the morning.** (when she rehearses)

> She rehearses **at the theater.** (where she rehearses)

> She rehearses **for months.** (how long—to what extent—she rehearses)

> She rehearses **for the upcoming show.** (why she rehearses)

Practice the Grammar Underline and label the adjective and adverb phrases in the paragraph below. Identify the word modified by each phrase.

Esmeralda Santiago attended a performing arts school in the city. She studied in the theater department. She left the school of her dreams and moved to another city. Harvard University, in Massachusetts, challenged Santiago. The author wrote in her spare time and became a writer of memoirs and novels.

Use the Grammar Independently Write three sentences containing adjective phrases and three sentences containing adverb phrases. Label each phrase, and identify the word modified by each.

Grammar Expansion

Adverbs of Frequency

Workbook pages 104   Independent Practice CD-ROM/Online

✓Checkpoint

1. What part of speech does an adjective modify?
2. Write a sentence using **in the cafeteria** as an adverb phrase.

Workbook page 102

Independent Practice CD-ROM/Online

● Writing Assignment

Write an Expository Essay About a Problem and a Solution

Writing Prompt

Write a three-paragraph essay that answers this question: What law would you pass today to solve a problem you see in your community? Include an introduction with a thesis statement, a body, and a conclusion. Use adjectives, adverbs, and adjective and adverb phrases in your essay.

Write Your Expository Essay

1. **Read the student model.** In this example, the last sentence in the first paragraph is the **thesis statement**.

Student Model

One of the problems in my community is the number of cars on the streets and highways. I live near a big city, and most of the people who live here have one car for every driver in the house. If there are two parents and two children over 16, then that's four cars on the road. **If I were going to pass a law in my community, I would allow no more than two cars per family and provide tax cuts for anyone who uses public transportation.**

The new law would keep track of every registered car on the road. Drivers would have to sell or donate any extra cars they owned. This law would have positive effects. For example, people would carpool more, which is good for the environment. There would be fewer cars on the road—which means less traffic—allowing people to get to their destinations even faster. People would also get a tax break if they used public transportation, which is good for anyone who pays taxes.

If I could pass a law today, my law would allow no more than two cars per household. The law would benefit both people and the environment, and it would be an easy **solution** to the problem of overcrowded streets.

Workbook
page 105

2. **Brainstorm ideas.**

   a. Consider the kinds of problems you see or hear about in your community every day.

   b. Choose one problem, then brainstorm a few possible **solutions**. Create an outline that identifies the points you want to cover in your essay.

3. **Draft your essay.** Create rough drafts of each of your paragraphs.

   a. Your introduction should identify the problem. Include evidence of the problem and tell how it affects your community. Your last sentence should be the thesis statement. In it, identify the law you would create to solve the problem in your community.

   b. Your body should include your **solution** and the ways your community would improve if your law were passed. Any related benefits of your law can be included here.

   c. Your conclusion should include a restatement of the problem and **solution**—a restatement of your thesis statement. Summarize your **solution**.

4. **Write your essay.** Be sure to include adjectives, adverbs, and adjective and adverb phrases.

5. **Revise.** Check the organization of your essay. Use the **Writing Checklist** to help you find problems and errors. Delete or revise any sentences that seem unclear or misleading.

6. **Edit.** Use the **editing and proofreading symbols** on page 455 to help you mark the changes you need to make.

Writing Checklist

1. I identified a problem and proposed a **solution**.

2. I described ways in which my community is affected by the problem and its **solution**.

3. I included an introduction with a thesis statement, a body, and a conclusion.

4. I proofread my work.

5. I included adjectives and adverbs and adjective and adverb phrases.

Writing Support

Grammar

Comparative and Superlative Adjectives and Adverbs

Adjectives and adverbs that compare a degree of quality are called **comparatives** and **superlatives**.

	Comparative	Superlative
big	**big**ger	**big**gest
young	**young**er	**young**est
cheaply	**more** cheaply	**most** cheaply
happy	**happ**ier	**happi**est
bad	**worse**	**worst**

Apply Check your essay and correct any errors in comparatives and superlatives. If you are uncertain as to how an adjective or adverb changes in these forms, consult your dictionary.

Progress Check

How well did you understand this chapter? Try to answer the questions. If necessary, go back to the pages listed for a review.

Skills	Skills Assessment Questions	Pages to Review
Vocabulary From the Readings	What do these words mean?	
	• crisis, debt, enforce, framework, impose, resolve	102
	• audition, enunciate, monologue, panel	112
Academic Vocabulary	What do these academic vocabulary words mean?	
	• sequence, influence	103
	• solution, trigger	110
Reading Strategies	What is one method of organizing information?	103
	How do readers make predictions?	113
Text Genres	What is the text genre of "**Crisis** of Government"?	104
	What is the text genre of "A Shot at It"?	113
Reading Comprehension	What is "**Crisis** of Government" about?	111
	What is "A Shot at It" about?	119
Text Element	What is the **audience** of a piece of writing?	111
Spelling	How do you make a plural noun ending in -s possessive?	119
Writing Conventions	Give examples of heteronyms, and tell what each word means.	119
Listening and Speaking	**Phrases for Conversation** What phrases can you use to show agreement?	120
Vocabulary Development	What does the prefix **fore-** mean?	121
Grammar	What do adjectives and adverbs modify?	122
	How are adjective and adverb phrases similar to adjectives and adverbs?	123
Writing	Which paragraph usually contains the thesis statement?	124
Writing Support: Grammar	What are the comparative and superlative forms of the word "bad"?	125

Assessment Practice

Read this passage. Then answer Questions 1 through 4.

Additions to the Constitution

1   The Constitution of the United States was signed by our forefathers on September 17, 1787. However, in the next two years, they created 10 amendments, or additions, to the Constitution and called them the Bill of Rights.

2   The writers used the Constitution as a framework for the Bill of Rights. The first 10 amendments were written to protect the individual rights of the American people. They enforce freedom of speech and religion, for example. The later amendments were created to resolve problems that occurred after the Constitution was written. These amendments include ending slavery and giving women the right to vote.

3   Today there are 27 amendments. It is possible that in our time we will see more amendments added to the Constitution.

1 Read this sentence from paragraph 2.

> The later amendments were created to <u>resolve</u> problems that occurred after the Constitution was written.

What does the word <u>resolve</u> mean?

A find a solution to

B write

C create

D make up

2 How is the passage organized?

A by dates

B by time

C in order of importance

D in an outline

3 Based on this article, what can we predict for the future?

A We will never need to add more amendments to the Constitution.

B Someday we will not need the Bill of Rights.

C Some amendments will no longer be necessary.

D In the future there will be a need for more amendments.

4 What is the genre of this text?

A folktale

B informational text

C historical fiction

D persuasive essay

Writing on Demand: Expository Essay
About a Problem and a Solution

Write a three-paragraph essay that tells about a rule in your school or other organization that you think doesn't work. Then suggest a way to improve this rule. What is the present rule? How do you think your new rule would help? **(20 minutes)**

Apply & Extend

Objectives

Listening and Speaking
Respond to literature

Media
Analyze the passing of time in film and television

Writing
Write a short story

Projects

Independent Reading

● Listening and Speaking Workshop
Respond to Literature

> **Topic**
>
> When you respond to literature, you talk about what you have read. In this activity, you will work with a group to discuss a transition you read about in one of the readings in this unit. You will then decide, based on the text, what the author thinks about transitions. Then, as a group, you will share what you learned with the class.

1. **Choose a Selection to Discuss**
   Work in a small group. Decide which reading your group will discuss. You may choose the excerpt from "Behind the Mountains," "**Crisis** of Government," or "A Shot at It."

2. **Brainstorm**
   With your group, discuss the following focus questions. Take notes on your answers.
   a. What is a transition that takes place in the reading you chose?
   b. What were the effects of the change? Were the effects good or bad?
   c. Based on what you read, what conclusions can you draw about the author's opinion of transitions? Are they good or bad? Can they be both?

3. **Plan**
   Choose two or three examples from the reading to support your ideas about the author's view of transitions. Decide how your group will divide up the job of presenting your findings.

4. **Organize Your Presentation**
   On one note card, write down the author's opinion about transitions. On two or three other note cards, write examples that show the author's opinion. Write one example on each note card. You will use the note cards as you are giving your presentation.

5. **Practice, Present, and Evaluate**
   Practice your presentation. Then present it to the class. After you finish, ask for feedback on your presentation and answer your classmates' questions. When listening to your classmates' presentations, what new conclusions are you able to draw about the authors' opinions of transitions? Use the **Speaking Self-Evaluation** to evaluate your presentation. Use the **Active Listening Evaluation** to evaluate and discuss your classmates' presentations.

● Media Workshop

Analyze the Passing of Time in Movies and Television

To make their stories more believable, movies and television shows often need to depict the passing of time. Sometimes a narrator lets the audience know that time has passed. Sometimes there are clues in the dialogue about time passing. Sometimes there are visual cues on the screen, such as the words, "Later that day…"

1. Choose a film or a television show that you like to watch.

2. As you watch, pay attention to how you know that time has passed in the action. Write your answers to the following questions.

   a. What are some ways you know that time has passed?

   b. Is it easy to tell how much time has passed? Why or why not?

   c. How does knowing about the passage of time affect your understanding of the story?

3. Report back to your class on the film or program you watched. Describe how you knew that time had passed.

4. Discuss with your class: Are there other ways of showing time passing that were not covered? Which ways of showing the passage of time are easiest to understand? Which are hardest? Why is it important to understand the timing of events in a story?

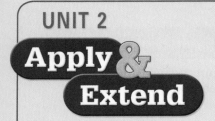

UNIT 2

Apply & Extend

Write a Short Story

A short story has a beginning, a middle, and an end. Usually, a character in the story encounters a problem. The character then tries to solve the problem.

> **Writing Prompt**
>
> Write a short story about someone your age who accepts a new responsibility. How does the person change because of the new responsibility?

PREWRITE

1. Read the student model on the next page. It will help you understand how to write a short story.

2. Choose a situation to write about. Answer the following questions about the situation.

   a. Who are the characters in the story? Who is the main character?

   b. What problem does the main character have to solve?

   c. When does the story happen?

   d. Where does the story happen?

   e. Why does it happen?

   f. How does the main character solve the problem?

3. Make an outline to show which events will happen in the beginning, middle, and end of your story.

WRITE A DRAFT

1. Make sure your story has three parts. In the beginning, introduce the main characters and the setting. Use your answers to the *who, when,* and *where* questions in order to write the beginning of the story.

2. The middle of a short story is when the characters try to solve a problem. Use your answers to the *what* and *why* questions to write the middle of the story.

3. At the end of the story, your character(s) should solve the problem. Use the answer to the *how* question to write the end of your story.

> **Writing Suggestion**
>
> Dialogue is what characters say to each other. Include dialogue to make your story more realistic. Remember to use quotation marks to show when a character is speaking.

Student Model

Hector Cruz

Alba's New Pet

Beginning

One day on her way home from school, Alba saw something moving in a bush. She pulled back the branches and found a small orange kitten.

"I've wanted a pet for so long!" thought Alba. Alba's mom always said she didn't want to clean up after any pets. Alba scratched the kitten behind its ears. "Maybe I can convince Mom to let me keep you," said Alba.

Middle

When Alba got home, she decided to sneak the kitten into her room before her mom saw it. She snuck into the house and into her bedroom. She set the kitten on her bed. Alba went to the kitchen to find her pet some food.

Alba's mother was starting dinner in the kitchen. Alba said, "Hey Mom, I'm looking for some crackers. Do we have any?"

"Dinner will be ready soon," her mom said.

Just then, Alba heard a quiet mewing coming from her room. Alba's mom looked down the hall. "What was that?" she asked. Alba's mother followed the sound to Alba's room. She opened the door just as the kitten ran under the bed.

"Is there something you wanted to tell me, Alba?" Her mother stood with her arms folded in front of her chest.

Alba sighed. "I found him on my way home. I was going to tell you."

"Well," said her mom, "having a pet is a big job. Keeping a secret from me makes me think you can't handle a responsibility like that."

"I know I should have told you right away. I'm sorry."

End

Her mother smiled. "Well, he is a very cute kitten, but we should put up signs in the neighborhood in case he's lost."

"Well, what if he doesn't have an owner?" Alba asked.

"Maybe then you can keep him, Alba. But no more secrets!"

Alba smiled. "No more secrets, I promise."

REVISE

1. Review your short story. Use the **Revising and Editing Checklist** to help you evaluate and revise your draft.
2. Exchange your story with a partner. Ask your partner to use the **Peer Review Checklist** to review your story. Your partner will point out errors and give suggestions for making your draft better.
3. Revise your draft again. Add sentences that help make your story clearer and more interesting. Delete sentences that are not needed.
4. Use the **editing and proofreading symbols** on page 455 to help you mark the changes you need to make.

EDIT

1. Use the **Revising and Editing Checklist** to reevaluate your story.
2. Fix any errors in grammar, spelling, and punctuation.

Peer Review Checklist

1. The story has characters and a setting.

2. The character(s) had a problem to solve.

3. The story uses words that help me picture what is happening.

4. My favorite part of the story was _____ .

5. The story would be better if _____ .

Revising and Editing Checklist

1. My story has a beginning, a middle, and an end.

2. I included details to make my story interesting.

3. I used present and past progressive verb tenses correctly.

4. I used adjectives and adverbs correctly.

5. I used quotation marks to show when a character is speaking.

PUBLISH

1. Write your story in your best handwriting so that it is clear and easy to read. Or use a computer to publish your story. Cut out pictures from magazines to make a cover for your story.
2. Read your story aloud to the class. Read with feeling, changing the level of your voice to express the emotions in your story.
3. Act out your story in front of the class. Show what happens in your story rather than simply tell it.

Projects

Choose one or more of the following projects to explore the theme of transitions further.

PROJECT 1

Compare Two Schools or Places in a Venn Diagram

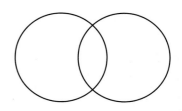

1. Think about a transition in your life, such as changing schools or moving to a new place.
2. Draw a Venn diagram and label each of the two circles. A sample diagram appears here.
3. Fill in the outer parts of the circles with the differences between the two places.
4. Fill in the middle part where the circles overlap with the ways the two places were the same.
5. Write a paragraph in which you describe the transition from the first place to the second place. Was this a good transition for you? Explain why or why not.

PROJECT 2

Interview a Family Member or Friend About Transitions

1. Talk to a family member, friend, or neighbor who is older than you. Ask this person to describe some of the changes he or she has experienced in his or her lifetime. The transition might be a personal one, like getting a new job. Or it might be a way that the world has changed while this person has been alive.
2. Record or take notes about his or her answers to your questions about the transition.
3. Share what you have learned with the class.

PROJECT 3

Make a Poster About a Rite of Passage

A rite of passage is an event that celebrates a person's transition to something new in his or her life. Some examples are a school graduation or a special birthday.

1. Brainstorm rites of passage that you know about. Do a word search using the Internet or use library resources.
2. Choose one that you would like to learn more about, and research it. Use the following questions as a guide: What is celebrated? Who celebrates it? What do people do during the celebration?
3. Make a poster showing four or five events, ideas, or objects that are part of the rite of passage. You can print pictures from Web sites, copy them from books, or cut them out of old magazines. For each picture, write two sentences to explain what is happening.
4. Present your poster to the class and discuss it. Is the rite of passage one you hope to experience yourself?

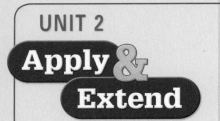

Apply & Extend

● Independent Reading

Explore the theme of transitions further by reading one or more of these books.

Behind the Mountains by Edwidge Danticat, Orchard Books, 2002.

The story opens in October 2000, when political violence forces 13-year-old Celiane, her mother, and her brother to leave Haiti and join her father in New York. There, Celiane keeps a journal about making the transition to a new home and a new life in the United States.

When I Was Puerto Rican: A Memoir by Esmeralda Santiago, Da Capo Press, 2006.

Esmeralda Santiago recalls the tropical beauty of Puerto Rico, where she was born, and also the poverty that her family lived in. When her mother, Mami, decides that the family is moving to New York, Esmeralda must learn a new language and find her way in a new culture.

Johnny Tremain by Esther Forbes, Houghton Mifflin, 1943.

Johnny Tremain is a poor orphan in Boston who, after hurting his hand, becomes a messenger during the American Revolution. His life changes when he becomes a part of exciting events such as the Boston Tea Party and the Battle of Lexington.

Anna of Byzantium by Tracy Barrett, Delacorte Press, 1999.

Anna Comnena is a real princess who will someday rule the Byzantine Empire. Yet as Anna grows up and becomes more independent, her grandmother plans to give the power to Anna's little brother instead. Anna must make the transition from being a respected leader to being forced to leave the kingdom. Read the true story of her fight to take back what is hers.

Flowers for Algernon by Daniel Keyes, Harcourt Brace, 1987.

Charlie Gordon is a man who has been mentally disabled his entire life. As an adult he decides to be a part of an experiment that, if successful, will increase his intelligence. Read about how Charlie's life changes, and find out whether the transition is for good.

Writing: Revise and Edit

MILESTONESTRACKER

Read this rough draft of a student's expository essay about a problem and a solution. It may contain errors. Then answer Questions 1 through 4.

A Difficult Transition

(**1**) The King School is a middle school and high school for students of the performing arts. (**2**) The King School is a wonderful place with excellent teachers. (**3**) It is having only one major problem. (**4**) The transition from middle school to high school is too difficult.

(**5**) In sixth, seventh, and eighth grades, students have about 30 minutes of homework. (**6**) Beginning in ninth grade, students have almost two hours. (**7**) Middle school students audition for two performances each year. (**8**) Yet high school students audition for two performances each season.

(**9**) To solve this problem, middle school and high school teachers need to talk to each other. (**10**) Eighth grade teachers could give more homework and one more performance. (**11**) Or, ninth grade teachers could give less homework and ask for fewer performances. (**12**) Then, students would transition from middle school to high school more easier.

---

1 How can you correct sentence 3?

A Change *is having* to *was having*.

B Change *is having* to *has*.

C Change *is having* to *had*.

D Change *is having* to *have*.

2 Which sentence could you insert before sentence 7?

A In tenth grade, the students have even more homework.

B The number of performances also increases.

C Another problem is how many performances are required.

D Ninth graders can accept more responsibility.

3 What adverb phrase can you add to the end of sentence 5?

A very easy

B lightly and easily

C each night

D about thirty minutes

4 How can you improve sentence 12?

A Change *easier* to *easily*.

B Change *more* to *most*.

C Change *easier* to *easy*.

D Delete *more*.

Writing on Demand: Expository Essay
About a Problem and a Solution

Write a three-paragraph expository essay about a problem at your school. Describe your school and explain the problem. Then give details to support your ideas. Finally, suggest and explain a realistic solution to resolve the problem. (**20 minutes**)

● Reading

Read this memoir. Then answer Questions 1 through 8.

A Season of Changes

1   When I think back to when I first moved to the United States from Vietnam, I remember many different things. I wore different clothes, I had short hair, and I did not speak English very well. With time, things began to change. My English improved as I learned to enunciate new words. I participated in class and made new friends. I was learning to play soccer, joining clubs at school, and reading the same books my classmates were reading—a slew of changes. With all these changes, sometimes I felt like I was a different person.

2   After several months, all of these changes started to become normal. Then one morning I woke up to a new change—snow. The world outside was covered in white. I was amazed. Of course, I had read about snow and heard my friends talking about it. But reading and hearing about snow is very different from seeing it. I quickly dressed in my new coat and boots. I opened the door and noticed that the air had changed, too. It was fresher. I stepped into the snow. I laughed and kicked my feet out in front of me, and there were droplets of snow on my boots. I bent down to touch some snow. It was soft and cold, like the ice drinks they sell in the seaside town in Vietnam where my grandparents still live. The schools were closed that day, and my friends and I spent all day playing in the white snow.

3   We had a lot of fun, but memories of Vietnam were swirling inside my head like snowflakes. It suddenly felt sad and uncomfortable to be caught between two worlds. I was changing so much. Who was I? American or Vietnamese? As I raced to the bus, I realized that I was both.

1 What does the word <u>slew</u> mean in the following sentence from paragraph 1?

> I was learning to play soccer, joining clubs at school, and reading the same books my classmates were reading—a <u>slew</u> of changes.

A cultural

B large amount

C small amount

D natural

2 What does the word <u>droplets</u> mean in the following sentence from paragraph 2?

> There were <u>droplets</u> of snow on my boots.

A small amounts

B large handfuls

C ice

D flakes

3 What is the narrator's problem?

A He no longer likes Vietnam.

B He no longer likes the United States.

C He feels like he lives in two different worlds.

D He feels like he doesn't belong anywhere.

4 What is the narrator's solution?

A He will try to forget Vietnam.

B He will try to leave the United States.

C He will accept both worlds.

D He will find a new place to belong to.

5 What is the tone of the memoir?

A scared

B angry

C joyful

D thoughtful

6 What kind of audience would enjoy this memoir?

A people who like to read scary stories

B people who like to read true, personal stories

C people who like history

D people who like natural science

7 Which sentence from the memoir is in the past progressive tense?

A I was changing so much

B Then one morning I woke up to a new change—snow.

C The world outside was covered in white.

D Of course, I had read about snow and heard my friends talking about it.

8 Which meaning does the writer want for the word <u>change</u> in the following sentence?

> Then one morning I woke up to a new <u>change</u>—snow.

A coins

B something different

C clothes

D a thought

PApEETE, TAHiTi 6371 MiLES

BERLiN 9750 MiLES

NOME 4010 MiLES

SYDNEY 12,944 MiLES

231

SANTA CRUZ, CA

TOKYO 8374 MiLES

526

Choices

Explore the Theme

1. What are some choices you see in the pictures?
2. Is making a choice difficult for you?
3. What are some of the things you think about before making a choice?

Theme Activity

Work in a small group. Tell the group about an easy choice you made today, such as what to wear to school or what to eat for breakfast. Then tell about a more important choice you recently made. Talk with your group about the differences between these kinds of choices.

Italian Prunes $1.99 lb

SWEET FLORIDA AVOCADOS $3.99 EA.

CLEMENTINES $2.99 LB

Objectives

Reading Strategies
Ask questions; Draw conclusions

Listening and Speaking
Tell a story

Grammar
Learn to use conjunctions

Writing
Write a short story

Academic Vocabulary

interact	evidence
tradition	setting

Academic Content

Researching family history
The biological roots of basic math skills

● **Chapter Focus Question**
What kinds of choices are we faced with in our daily lives?

Reading 1 **Literature**
Short story (abridged)
An Hour with Abuelo
by Judith Ortiz Cofer

Reading 2 **Content:** Math
Informational text: Internet article
It's a Math World for Animals
by Emily Sohn

An Hour with Abuelo

● **About the Reading**

You are about to read a short story about a teenager named Arturo, who visits his Puerto Rican grandfather, or *abuelo,* at a nursing home.

● Build Background

Puerto Rican Culture

The island of Puerto Rico is a mix of many different cultures. The Taínos, an indigenous tribe, were living there when Christopher Columbus landed on the island in 1493. Puerto Rico belonged to Spain for more than four centuries, so Spanish is spoken there. Puerto Rican food, music, and literature have strong Spanish roots. In the 1950s, many Puerto Ricans moved to the United States, especially to the New York area.

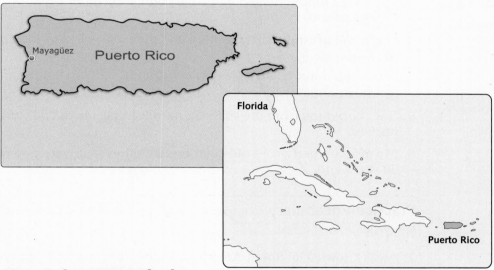

● Use Prior Knowledge

Think About Your Family

In "An Hour with Abuelo," the main character learns about his grandfather, who was born in Puerto Rico. Think about your family members and where they were born. Draw a family tree. Look at the example below. In each square, write a person's name and his or her relationship to you. Also include where they were born.

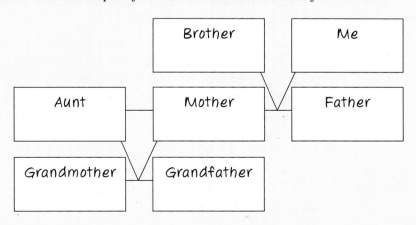

Key Vocabulary

- depressed
- embarrassed
- graduate
- ignorant
- obvious
- old-fashioned

● Vocabulary From the Reading

Learn, Practice, and Use Independently

Learn Vocabulary Read each sentence. Look at the **highlighted** word. Think about the context (the words around the highlighted word). Use the context to determine the meaning of the word.

1. I often feel **depressed** in the winter because it is dark, cold, and rainy.
2. Carlos felt **embarrassed** when his younger brother screamed in the restaurant.
3. Leigh will **graduate** from school and then she will start looking for a job.
4. Now that I have taken a class in geography, I am no longer **ignorant** about the locations of countries around the world.
5. It was **obvious** from the smile on her face that Tanya had passed her test.
6. My grandfather wears **old-fashioned** clothes that were popular 50 years ago.

Practice Vocabulary Complete the sentences with the correct Key Vocabulary word.

1. Alma knows a lot about American history, but she is _____ about Puerto Rican history.
2. Dale was _____ when his best friend moved away.
3. The furniture in my grandparents' house is _____ because it's from the 1950s.
4. Ivan feels very proud that he will _____ from school in June.
5. Sometimes people's faces turn red when they feel _____.
6. It is _____ that the twins were playing outdoors because their clothes are muddy and torn.

Use Vocabulary Independently Write your own words or phrases to explain the meanings of the Key Vocabulary words. Then use a dictionary or thesaurus to check your work.

embarrassed: ashamed, self-conscious, ill at ease, uncomfortable

✓ Checkpoint

1. What word means the opposite of *modern*? What word means the opposite of *informed*?
2. Write a sentence using the word **embarrassed**.

Vocabulary Log

Workbook page 109

Independent Practice CD-ROM/Online

● Academic Vocabulary

Vocabulary for the Reading Strategy

Word	Explanation	Sample Sentence	Visual Cue
interact *verb*	to communicate with someone through words or actions	A mother and child **interact** when they play together.	
tradition *noun*	a custom or belief that is passed on from one generation to another	Pablo's family has a **tradition** of playing music at family gatherings. Every year they play the same songs.	

Draw a picture and write a sentence for each word.

● Reading Strategy

Ask Questions

Asking questions before, while, and after you read will help you to understand the story, its characters, their **traditions**, and how they **interact**.

As you read "An Hour with Abuelo," pause whenever you have a question. Write your question in the first column of the chart. Continue reading. You will answer these questions once you have finished the reading.

My Question	The Answer I Found

✓Checkpoint

1. What special **traditions** does your family have during holidays?

2. How do you **interact** differently with your classmates and with your teacher?

● Text Genre

Short Story

"An Hour with Abuelo" is a **short story**. A short story is a work of fiction—a story that is not true. A short story usually focuses on one character or one main event. Short stories are usually read for enjoyment. Most short stories have a **plot**. The plot is the sequence of events in the story. As you read "An Hour with Abuelo," look for these plot elements.

Short Story	
introduction	presents the characters, the setting, and the main problem in the story
rising action	the events that lead up to the climax
climax	the turning point of the story
resolution	the conclusion or final result of the story

● Meet the Author

Judith Ortiz Cofer was born in Puerto Rico in 1952. Because her father was in the U.S. Navy, her family moved to the United States. But they moved back to Puerto Rico several times. As the author grew up, her mother worked hard to help her hold on to her Puerto Rican roots. Today, the author writes poems, novels, and short stories. She often writes about her experiences growing up between two cultures.

● Reading Focus Questions

As you read, think about these questions.

1. How does the story connect to the theme of "choices"?
2. What do you think was the author's purpose in writing "An Hour with Abuelo"?
3. Is it important to work to make your dreams come true? Why?

✓ Checkpoint

1. Explain what a **short story** is in your own words.
2. Which **plot** element is the turning point of a story?

Workbook
page 111

Independent Practice
CD-ROM/Online

An Hour with Abuelo

by Judith Ortiz Cofer

1 "Just one hour, *una hora,* is all I'm asking of you, son." My grandfather is in a **nursing home** in Brooklyn, and my mother wants me to spend some time with him, since the doctors say that he doesn't have too long to go now. I don't have much time left of my summer vacation, and there's a stack of books next to my bed I've got to read if I'm going to get into the AP English class I want. I'm going stupid in some of my classes, and Mr. Williams, the principal at Central, said that if I passed some reading tests, he'd let me move up.

2 Besides, I hate the place, the old people's home, especially the way it smells like industrial-strength **ammonia** and other stuff I won't mention, since it **turns my stomach.** And really the abuelo always has a lot of relatives visiting him, so I've gotten out of going there except at Christmas, when a whole vanload of grandchildren are herded over there to give him gifts and a hug. We all make it quick and spend the rest of the time in the recreation area, where they play checkers and stuff with some of the old people's games, and I catch up on back issues of *Modern Maturity.* I'm not picky, I'll read almost anything.

3 Anyway, after my mother **nags** me for about a week, I let her drive me to Golden Years. She drops me off in front. She squeezes my hand and says, *"Gracias, hijo,"* in a choked-up voice like I'm doing her a big favor.

nursing home place where sick or elderly people live and are cared for
ammonia strong smelling gas that when mixed with water is used for cleaning
turns my stomach makes me sick
nags bothers or annoys by asking several times
Gracias, hijo Thank you, son (Spanish)

Reading Strategy

Ask Questions Ask a question about paragraph 1. As you continue to read, think about a possible answer.

✓ Reading Check

1. **Recall facts** How does Arturo describe the nursing home?

2. **Recall facts** How did Arturo spend his time in past visits to the nursing home?

3. **Generalize** Are you surprised that Arturo's mom wants him to visit his grandfather? Why or why not?

4   I get **depressed** the minute I walk into the place. They line up the old people in wheelchairs in the hallway as if they were about to be raced to the finish line by **orderlies** who don't even look at them when they push them here and there. I walk fast to room 10, Abuelo's "suite." He is sitting up in his bed writing with a pencil in one of those **old-fashioned** black hardback notebooks. It has the **outline** of the island of Puerto Rico on it. Since I'm supposed to talk to him, I say, "What are you doing, Abuelo, writing the story of your life?"

5   It's supposed to be a joke, but he answers, "Sí, how did you know, Arturo?"

6   His name is Arturo too. I was named after him. I don't really know my grandfather. His children, including my mother, came to New York and New Jersey (where I was born) and he stayed on the Island until my grandmother died. Then he got sick, and they brought him to this nursing home in Brooklyn. My mother tells me that **Don** Arturo had once been a teacher back in Puerto Rico, but had lost his job after the war. Then he became a farmer. She's always saying in a sad voice, "*Ay, bendito!* What a waste of a fine mind." Then she usually shrugs her shoulders and says, "*Así es la vida.*" That's the way life is. It sometimes makes me mad that the adults I know just accept whatever is thrown at them because "that's the way things are." Not for me. I go after what I want.

---

orderlies workers who clean and do other chores in a hospital or a nursing home
outline outer shape of something
Don a term of respect used with male elders
Ay, bendito! Oh my gosh! (Spanish)

7   Since I like stories, I decide I may as well ask him if he'll read me what he wrote. I look at my watch: I've already used up twenty minutes of the hour I promised my mother.

8   Abuelo starts talking in his slow way. "It is a short story, Arturo. The story of my life. It will not take very much time to read it."

9   "I have time, Abuelo." I'm a little **embarrassed** that he saw me looking at my watch.

10   Abuelo reads: "I loved words from the beginning of my life. In the *campo* where I was born one of seven sons, there were few books. My mother read them to us over and over: the Bible, stories of Spanish **conquistadors** and of pirates that she had read as a child and brought with her from the city of Mayagüez; that was before she married my father, a coffee bean farmer. She taught each of us how to write on **slate** with **chalks** that she ordered by mail every year. We used those chalks until they were so small that you lost them between your fingers.

> **Reading Strategy**
>
> **Ask Questions** Ask a question about paragraph 10. As you continue to read, think about a possible answer.

An old-fashioned slate

---

campo countryside (Spanish)
conquistadors leaders of the Spanish conquest of the Americas
slate a tablet to write on made from a gray rock cut into smooth flat pieces
chalks sticks made of soft white rock used for writing and marking

> ✓ **Reading Check**
>
> 1. **Recall facts** What was Abuelo's job in Puerto Rico?
> 2. **Recall details** How did Abuelo learn to read and write?
> 3. **Analyze character** How does Arturo react when his mother talks about *"la vida"* or life?

Reading Strategy

Ask Questions Ask a question about paragraph 12. As you continue to read, think about a possible answer.

11   "I always wanted to be a writer and teacher. With my heart and my soul I knew that I wanted to be around books all of my life. And so, against the wishes of my father, who wanted all his sons to help him on the land, she sent me to high school in Mayagüez. I **boarded** with a couple she knew. I paid my rent in **labor**, and ate vegetables I grew myself. But I **graduated** at the top of my class! My whole family came to see me that day.

12   "In those days you could teach in a country school with a high school **diploma**. So I went back to my mountain village and got a job teaching all grades in a little classroom built by the parents of my students.

13   "I had books sent to me by the government. I felt like a rich man although the pay was very small. I had books. All the books I wanted! I taught my students how to read poetry and plays, and how to write them. We made up songs and put on shows for the parents. It was a beautiful time for me.

"We made up songs and put on shows for the parents."

---

boarded paid rent to live and have meals in a private home
labor hard work
diploma official paper stating that one has completed a course of study

14   "Then the war came, and the American President said that all Puerto Rican men would be **drafted.** I wrote to our governor and explained that I was the only teacher in the mountain village. I told him the children would go back to the fields and grow up **ignorant** if I could not teach them their letters. I said that I thought I was a better teacher than a soldier. The governor did not answer my letter. I went into the U.S. Army.

15   "I told my sergeant that I could be a teacher in the army. I could teach all the farm boys their letters so that they could read the instructions on the **ammunition** boxes and not blow themselves up. The sergeant said I was too smart for my own good, and gave me a job cleaning **latrines.** He said to me there is reading material for you there, scholar. Read the writing on the walls. I spent the war mopping floors and cleaning toilets.

16   "When I came back to the Island, things had changed. You had to have a **college degree** to teach school, even the lower grades. My parents were sick, two of my brothers had been killed in the war, and the others had stayed in Nueva York. I was the only one left to help the old people. I became a farmer. I married a good woman who gave me many good children. I taught them all how to read and write before they started school."

17   Abuelo then puts the notebook down on his lap and closes his eyes.

18   "*Así es la vida* is the title of my book," he says in a whisper, almost to himself. Maybe he's forgotten that I'm here.

Reading Strategy

Ask Questions Ask a question about paragraph 16. As you continue to read, think about a possible answer.

drafted required to serve in the military
ammunition bullets that can be fired from a gun or objects made to explode
latrines toilets, especially in the military
college degree title from a college or university indicating completion of a course of study

Reading Check

1. **Recall facts** What did Abuelo have to do to get a high school education?

2. **Recall details** How did his sergeant react when Abuelo asked to teach the other soldiers?

3. **Analyze character** How did Abuelo feel about teaching?

Reading Strategy

Ask Questions Ask a question about paragraph 20. As you continue to read, think about a possible answer.

19   For a long time he doesn't say anything else. I think that he's sleeping, but then I see that he's watching me through half-closed **lids,** maybe waiting for my opinion of his writing. I'm trying to think of something nice to say. I liked it and all, but not the title. And I think that he could've been a teacher if he had wanted to bad enough. Nobody is going to stop me from doing what I want with my life. I'm not going to let *la vida* get in my way.

20   I want to discuss this with him, but the words are not coming into my head in Spanish just yet. I'm about to ask him why he didn't keep fighting to make his dream come true, when an old lady in hot-pink running shoes sort of appears at the door. She calls out to my grandfather in a **flirty** voice, "Yoo-hoo, Arturo, remember what day this is? It's poetry-reading day in the **rec room**! You promised us you'd read your new one today."

21   I see my abuelo **perking up** almost immediately. He points to his wheelchair, which is hanging like a huge metal bat in the open closet. He makes it **obvious** that he wants me to get it. I put it together and with Mrs. Pink Running Shoes's help, we get him in it. Then he says in a strong deep voice I hardly recognize, "Arturo, get that notebook from the table, please."

---

lids eyelids, the folds of skin over a person's eyes
flirty inviting romantic interest
rec room an area for social activities
perking up becoming lively or happy

22   I hand him another map-of-the-Island notebook—this one is red. On it in big letters it says, **POEMAS DE ARTURO.**

23   I start to push him toward the rec room, but he shakes his finger at me.

24   "Arturo, look at your watch now. I believe your time is over." He gives me a **wicked** smile.

Reading Strategy

Ask Questions Ask a question about paragraph 24. As you continue to read, think about a possible answer.

25   Then with her pushing the wheelchair—maybe a little too fast— they roll down the hall. He is already reading from his notebook, and she's making bird noises. I look at my watch and the hour is up, to the minute. I can't help but think that Abuelo has been timing me. It **cracks me up.** I walk slowly down the hall toward the sign. I want my mother to have to wait a little. I don't want her to think that I'm in a hurry or anything.

Reading Check

1. **Recall facts** What makes Abuelo cheer up?

2. **Analyze** What does Arturo think of Abuelo's life story?

3. **Analyze character** Why does Arturo laugh at the end of the story?

Poemas de Arturo Arturo's Poems (Spanish)
wicked mischievous or playful
cracks me up makes me laugh

● Apply the Reading Strategy

Ask Questions

Now that you have read "An Hour with Abuelo," you are ready to complete the Reading Strategy chart.

1. Review the **Reading Strategy** on page 143.
2. Look at the list of questions that you wrote down in the My Question column of the chart.
3. Now, answer the questions in the column "The Answer I Found" using what you remember about the story.

My Question	The Answer I Found
Is Arturo's grandfather looking forward to his visit?	

● Academic Vocabulary

Vocabulary for the Reading Comprehension Questions

Word	Explanation	Sample Sentence	Visual Cue
evidence *noun*	words, objects, or facts that help someone find the truth	Criminals often leave behind fingerprint **evidence** at the scene of a crime.	
setting *noun*	the time and place where the events of a story take place	The **setting** of the Robin Hood stories is Sherwood Forest.	

Draw a picture and write a sentence for each word.

✓ Checkpoint

1. Explain in your own words what **evidence** means.
2. What is the **setting** of "An Hour with Abuelo"?

Vocabulary
Log

● Reading Comprehension Questions

Think and Discuss

Workbook
page 112

Independent Practice
CD-ROM/Online

1. **Recall facts** What does Arturo's mother want him to do?

2. **Understand** setting Use Key Vocabulary words to describe the setting of the story. Why doesn't Arturo want to go there?

3. **Recall details** What events lead to Abuelo becoming a farmer? Write them in order.

4. **Describe** Tell what the main problem, or conflict, in the story is. Then tell how it is resolved. Use Key Vocabulary words.

5. **Evaluate** evidence Do you think Abuelo fails or succeeds in achieving his goals?

6. **Analyze character** How does Arturo's attitude change from the beginning to the end of this story?

7. **Revisit the Reading Focus Questions** Go back to page 144 and discuss the questions.

● Literary Element

Plot

The **plot** is made up of the **introduction,** the **rising action,** the **climax,** and the **resolution.** Go back to page 144 to reread the description of each plot element.

Copy this diagram into your notebook. Look at the reading again with a partner. Read the following sentences from the story. Place these events in the correct box of the diagram.

a. Since I like stories, I decide I may as well ask him if he'll read me what he wrote. … Abuelo starts talking in his slow way. "It is a short story, Arturo. The story of my life."

b. "Yoo-hoo, Arturo, remember what day this is? It's poetry-reading day in the rec room!"

c. My grandfather is in a nursing home in Brooklyn, and my mother wants me to spend some time with him.

d. I look at my watch and the hour is up, to the minute. I can't help but think that Abuelo has been timing me. It cracks me up.

Discuss these events with your partner. Try to identify the **introduction,** the **rising action,** the **climax,** and the **resolution** of "An Hour with Abuelo."

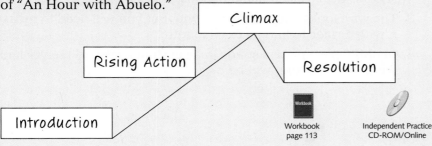

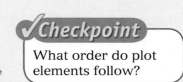

Workbook
page 113

Independent Practice
CD-ROM/Online

✓Checkpoint

What order do plot elements follow?

It's a Math World for Animals

● About the Reading

In "An Hour with Abuelo," Arturo learns about the choices that his grandfather made in his life. In the article you are about to read, you will learn that animals can make some surprising choices of their own.

● Build Background

Behavior

Why do babies cry? Why do dogs dig? Crying and digging are behaviors. Scientists usually divide behaviors into two types. Behaviors that seem to be automatic, or don't have to be learned, are instinctive behaviors. Behaviors that change as a result of experience are learned behaviors.

Babies don't have to learn to cry. Dogs don't have to learn to dig. These behaviors are part of a baby's and a dog's instinct. They are "built into" their nervous systems. Just as a computer does certain tasks automatically, humans and animals do some things automatically, too.

Other behaviors are learned by people and animals. You were not born knowing how to read or write. These skills come to us after we practice and repeat them many times.

Can you think of some other examples of humans' instinctive and learned behaviors?

● Vocabulary From the Reading

Use Context Clues to Determine Meaning

Read each sentence below. Then, with a partner, use the context clues to determine the meaning of each **highlighted** word.

1. We did an **experiment** with plant seeds. We planted one seed in the dark and one in the sun. We learned that the seed in the sun grew better than the one in the dark.

2. The three-year-old child has an **innate** ability to play the piano; she has never taken piano lessons, but she plays perfectly.

3. The wire looks about 3 inches long, but you will need to **measure** it with a ruler to find its exact length.

4. My MP3 player plays songs in a **random** order, so I never know what the next song will be.

Key Vocabulary

experiment

innate

measure

random

 Checkpoint

Think of newborn babies. Make a list of their **innate** behaviors.

 Vocabulary Log

 Workbook page 114

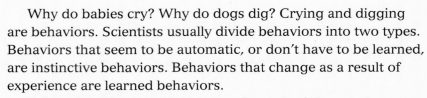 Independent Practice CD-ROM/Online

Reading Strategy

Draw Conclusions

You can draw conclusions from the clues given in a reading and from your own experiences. For example, if a character in a story is wearing gloves and a scarf, you can conclude from your own experience that the weather is probably very cold. Drawing conclusions helps you to gather information as you read and to better understand the author's purpose.

1. Read "It's a Math World for Animals." After each section of the story, think about the clues that the author has given you.

2. Ask yourself whether any of these clues, together with your own knowledge and experience, can help you to draw any conclusions about the topic.

Text Genre

Informational Text: Internet Article

Like most articles, an **Internet article** can address a single topic and often develops that idea using one or more of the features identified below.

Internet Article	
interviews	conversations in which one person asks questions, and another person answers
quotes	exact statements made by a person, enclosed by quotation marks
supporting material	**evidence** that proves statements are correct

Meet the Author

Emily Sohn writes news stories about science. Her stories have appeared in many newspapers and magazines. In college, she assisted with research on seals, led other students on backpacking trips, and studied coral reefs.

Reading Focus Questions

As you read, think about these questions.

1. How does this reading connect to the theme of "choices"?

2. What do you think was the author's purpose in writing about animals and math?

3. How do you think animals are helped by math concepts?

✓Checkpoint

How does drawing conclusions help you to understand a reading better?

Workbook
pages 115–116

Independent Practice
CD-ROM/Online

It's a Math World for Animals

by Emily Sohn

1   Birds do it. Dogs do it. Even **salamanders** do it.

2   The ability to solve math problems is showing up in all sorts of unlikely creatures. From monkeys who know the difference between 2 and 3 to dogs who can **calculate** the fastest **route**, animal **mathematicians** are teaching scientists a few things about numbers.

3   A growing body of research suggests that nature probably discovered math long before people did. Studies of animal mathematicians might help explain how people learn to add, subtract, and multiply and indicate what types of math people can do without going to class. Watching animals solve problems could also make math more fun for people who say they don't like the subject.

A Fetching Dog

4   Mathematician Tim Pennings, for instance, was at the beach when he discovered that his dog Elvis could do a type of math called **calculus.**

5   "I would throw a ball into the water," Pennings says. "I noticed he'd run along the beach and then jump into the water and swim at an angle toward the ball."

---

salamanders a kind of lizard
calculate determine an answer by using mathematical processes
route path
mathematicians those who are skilled at using mathematics
calculus method of mathematical analysis

6   That's a good strategy. Swimming is slow compared with running, so swimming all the way to the ball would take longer even if the route is more direct. On the other hand, running along the beach adds to the total distance Elvis must go to get to the ball. The best bet is a compromise between the two—running a certain distance along the beach before **plunging** into the water.

7   Pennings wondered if Elvis was instinctively taking the fastest possible route to the ball. First, he **measured** how fast Elvis runs and swims. Then, he threw a tennis ball into the water and let the little **Welsh corgi** go.

8   "I ran after Elvis with a screwdriver," says Pennings, who works at Hope College in Holland, Michigan. "Where he turned toward the water, I **drove** a screwdriver into the sand. While he was swimming to the ball, I ran and grabbed a **tape measure** and beat him to the ball."

9   Man and dog ran back and forth like this for more than 3 hours. After throwing out **trials** with bad tosses or high waves, Pennings had 35 sets of measurements. Then, he went home and did some calculations, using calculus to find the fastest route.

Reading Strategy

Draw Conclusions
Why were there so many sets of measurements made? Explain your answer.

A Welsh corgi

Reading Check

1. **Recall facts** What kind of math does Tim Pennings think his dog can do?

2. **Predict** Will Pennings find out that Elvis performed almost perfectly, pretty well, or not well at all? Check your prediction on the next page.

---

plunging forcefully jumping or falling into something (usually water)
Welsh corgi breed of dog with a long body, short legs, and a fox-like head
drove forced something in
tape measure long, flexible ruler made of cloth or metal and used for measuring
trials experiments, attempts

10   "I did all the math," Pennings says, "and I figured out that where Elvis jumps in is pretty much perfect. He kind of naturally knows the right spot to jump in."

11   It took the grown man about an hour to come up with the same solution that the 3-year-old dog could figure out in a **fraction** of a second. But is the dog really doing the math?

12   "Elvis is doing calculus in the sense that he somehow knows how to find the **minimum** time to get to the ball," Pennings says.

13   One interesting follow-up study would be to do a similar **experiment** with people of different ages, Pennings says. Results might show an **innate** ability to do math that gets better or worse as people grow up and go to school.

Number Sense

14   Studying math skills in dogs to understand math in people might not be such a **far-fetched** idea. In fact, some research is showing that babies and animals actually have a lot in common when it comes to numbers.

---

fraction section or part of a complete unit
minimum least amount needed
far-fetched foolish or unlikely to occur

15   Most animal math research has focused on **primates**. To test whether a monkey can tell the difference between numbers of objects, scientists **measure** how long an animal looks at things. A monkey will look longer at something that doesn't match what it expects to see.

16   Using this technique, researchers have shown that monkeys can add and subtract small numbers of objects. If they are shown one apple slice and then another, for example, they know there should be a total of two. They will then look for a longer time at a pile of three or one than at a pile of two.

17   Likewise, 12-month-old babies look longer at a bigger pile of sugar cookies. Even though they can't talk or count, the babies seem to know how to go for more.

18   Most interesting of all, says **cognitive** scientist Claudia Uller, is that those skills fall apart at about the same number in both monkeys and babies.

19   "It's so incredible," says Uller, who is at the University of Louisiana at Lafayette. "It breaks down at around four. If you give babies two or three, they'll go for three. At three versus four, their choices are **random**. At four versus six, they're **random**." The same is true for monkeys and **tamarins**.

_____

primates mammals such as gorillas, chimpanzees, and monkeys
cognitive related to brain activity, such as thinking, reasoning, or remembering
tamarins small monkeys that are found in South America

> **Reading Strategy**

Draw Conclusions
Why would a 12-month-old baby look longer at a bigger pile of sugar cookies?

✓
Reading Check

1. **Recall facts** How long did it take Pennings to come up with the solution? How long did it take Elvis to do this?

2. **Explain** When the researcher says that "it breaks down at around four," what does she mean?

3. **Make inferences** Why does the author provide information about human babies in an article about animals?

Uller wanted to try the same **experiment** with a completely different kind of animal: salamanders. Amazingly, she found the same results.

21 When shown **test tubes** holding different numbers of live fruit flies, red-backed salamanders looked at the tube that held more. But only up to a certain point. Just as in babies and monkeys, the system seemed to break down around four. Uller published her results recently in the **journal** *Animal Cognition*.

22 Her study is the first example that an animal other than a primate might be able to distinguish between more and less. Another scientist is now looking for the same **phenomenon** in fruit flies, Uller says. Further research could help explain the **biology** behind basic math skills.

23 A widespread use of math in nature makes sense, experts say, considering the **challenges** to survival in the wild. By recognizing which bush offers more berries, for instance, or which pack of lions is more fearsome, an animal might improve its own chances of survival. The same was probably true for our **ancestors.**

24 So, maybe math is more than just a grade on your report card. At some point, your life might depend on it!

> ## Reading Strategy
>
> **Draw Conclusions**
> How could Claudia Uller's research be helpful to scientists studying fruit flies?

A red-backed salamander

---

test tubes hollow cylinders made of glass or plastic used for experiments
journal publication made up of articles, usually with a scholarly or academic focus
phenomenon an occurrence that is often not easily understood
biology science of living things and how they work
challenges difficulties or obstacles
ancestors relatives or forbears from an earlier time

After Reading 2

● Reading Comprehension Questions

Think and Discuss

1. **Recall facts** Claudia Uller's research on primates and salamanders has led to similar studies on what insects?

2. **Draw conclusions** Why do scientists find out how long animals look at things? Use a Key Vocabulary term in your answer.

3. **Evaluate** Do the research findings presented convince you that animals and other creatures may have mathematic skills? Explain your answer with examples from the reading.

4. **Summarize** Choose Tim Pennings or Claudia Uller and describe how he or she studied animal behavior and mathematic skills.

5. **Revisit the Reading Focus Questions** Go back to page 155 and discuss the questions.

Workbook page 117

Independent Practice CD-ROM/Online

Spelling

Present Participles

Workbook page 118

Independent Practice CD-ROM/Online

Writing Conventions

Punctuation: Commas

Workbook page 119

Independent Practice CD-ROM/Online

Connect Readings 1 and 2

You have read two readings on the theme of choices. Use these activities to make connections between the readings.

1. With a partner, use this chart to compare the two readings.

Reading title	What is the text genre?	Is it fiction or nonfiction?	Which reading uses plot elements?	Which reading was more interesting to you? Why?
An Hour with Abuelo				
It's a Math World for Animals				

2. With a partner, ask and answer these questions.

   a. In "It's a Math World for Animals," animals make mathematically influenced choices. In "An Hour with Abuelo," characters make choices about their education and jobs. Think of examples of each kind of choice. Compare the reasons for each. How are they alike and different?

   b. Compare the use of numbers in the two readings. Are exact numbers equally important in both? Explain.

3. Revisit the Chapter Focus Question What kinds of choices are we faced with in our daily lives? Use examples from the two readings to answer this question.

Phrases for Conversation

Reacting to a Story

That part of your story isn't clear to me.

Try moving that part to . . . (the beginnng, the middle, the end).

Maybe you could add some detail about . . . (the person, the **setting**, your feelings).

Do you think this part is . . . (too long, not necessary)?

I think your story is a little too . . . (long, short).

● Listening and Speaking

Tell a Story

The main character in "An Hour with Abuelo" learns something about himself when he spends time with his grandfather. Has another person ever taught you something about yourself? Tell a story about it. Work with a partner to practice telling your story.

1. Think of a time when a person taught you something about yourself.

2. Write the answers to these questions on note cards.
   a. Who was the person?
   b. What did the person teach you?
   c. How did you feel when you learned something new about yourself?

3. Use your note cards to help you tell your story to your partner. As listeners, you each should:
   a. listen carefully to your partner's story
   b. make inferences about what your partner learned, and ask questions to understand better what happens in your partner's story
   c. tell your partner what you like about the story. Then give suggestions about how your partner might improve the story.

4. Use your partner's feedback to improve your story. Tell your story to the class.

● Reading Fluency

Read Aloud with Emotion

Identifying emotions in a text and reading aloud with appropriate expression helps you to read more naturally and fluently.

1. First, read silently Abuelo's words from his notebook on page 148.

2. Your teacher will give you a copy of this section of the reading.
   a. Underline the words and phrases that express emotion.
   b. Pay attention to punctuation. Take note of places where the writer uses an exclamation mark (!) to show strong emotion.

3. Practice your reading.
   a. Think about the emotions that your underlined words express.
   b. To show emotion, you may need to make your voice louder or softer.

4. Then, read the selection aloud to a partner. Take turns.

   a. Use your voice and your body movements to express emotion.

   b. Discuss with your partner whether you read with appropriate expression and ask him or her to evaluate your fluency.

5. Record your progress in your workbook. How did you do on this passage in comparison to other readings? Are you becoming a more fluent reader?

● Vocabulary Development

Idioms

An **idiom** is a phrase, or group of words, that does not have the same meaning as its individual words. Idioms help people to explain themselves in interesting, colorful, and sometimes funny ways. Look at these idioms from "An Hour with Abuelo" and their meanings.

Idiom	Meaning
". . . it smells like industrial-strength ammonia and other stuff I won't mention, since it **turns my stomach**."	makes me feel sick
"I can't help but think that Abuelo has been timing me. It **cracks me up**."	makes me laugh

Copy the chart. Read the sentences. Using clues from the sentences, try to guess the meaning of each idiom and write it in the column on the right.

	Meaning of Idiom
1. I can't do this alone. Can you <u>lend me a hand</u>?	
2. She is an <u>early bird</u>. She wakes up at 6:00 A.M. and arrives at school before 8:00 A.M.	
3. I got the wrong answer, so it's back to <u>square one</u>.	
4. I don't want to go to school. I'm feeling <u>under the weather</u>.	
5. She found out about the surprise party! Who <u>let the cat out of the bag</u>?	

Vocabulary Log

Workbook page 120

Independent Practice CD-ROM/Online

✓Checkpoint

1. What is an **idiom**? Explain in your own words.

2. Think of another English idiom you know and use it in a sentence of your own.

● **Grammar**

Conjunctions

A **conjunction** is a part of speech. It can connect words, groups of words, or independent clauses (clauses that can stand alone as a sentence). Some common conjunctions are *and, but, or,* and *so (that)*.

Conjunction	What It Does	Example
and	connects similar ideas	I always wanted to be a writer **and** a teacher.
but	shows contrast	Abuelo wanted to be a teacher, **but** he became a farmer instead.
or	gives two or more choices	Researchers can learn about people's math skills by studying the math skills of monkeys **or** dogs.
so (that)	gives a reason	The dog jumped into the water **so (that)** he could get the ball.

Practice the Grammar Complete the paragraphs with *and, but, or,* or *so that*.

Arturo goes to the nursing home (**1**) _____ he can visit his grandfather. He does not really want to go, (**2**) _____ he knows it will make his mother happy. When Arturo arrives, his grandfather is sitting up in bed, (**3**) _____ he is writing his life story. Abuelo says that his father wanted him to be a farmer, (**4**) _____ Abuelo wanted to be a teacher instead. He taught his students to make up songs (**5**) _____ to put on shows for their parents.

When the war came, Abuelo hoped that he could either stay in his village (**6**) _____ become a teacher in the army. He wrote to the governor, (**7**) _____ the governor did not write back. Abuelo told his sergeant that he could teach the soldiers to read, (**8**) _____ the sergeant made Abuelo mop floors instead.

Use the Grammar Independently Write a sentence for each of the conjunctions below. Share your sentences with a partner.

1. and   **3.** or
2. but   **4.** so (that)

Conjunctions in Compound Sentences

When a conjunction combines two independent clauses, it forms a **compound sentence.** Some conjunctions that are often used in compound sentences are *and, but,* and *or.* Look at the chart. See how conjunctions are used to combine simple sentences to create compound sentences.

Note that a comma is placed *after* the independent clause and *before* the conjunction.

Simple Sentences	Compound Sentence
He threw the ball into the water. The dog swam after it.	He threw the ball into the water, **and** the dog swam after it.
I start to push him toward the rec room. He shakes his finger at me.	I start to push him toward the rec room, **but** he shakes his finger at me.
Arturo told his mom to come back in an hour. He would take the bus home.	Arturo told his mom to come back in an hour, **or** he would take the bus home.

Practice the Grammar Read each pair of sentences. Combine the sentences using one of these conjunctions: *and, but,* or *or.*

1. People do not usually think that animals can do math. Some animals seem to solve math problems by using their instincts.
2. Tom Pennings noticed that his dog would run on the beach before entering the water. He wondered if his dog was taking the fastest route.
3. Elvis jumped into the water. Pennings drove a screwdriver into the ground to mark where Elvis jumped.
4. Do monkeys choose which pile of apple slices to take randomly? Do they choose based on math?
5. Babies will look at a pile of two cookies and a pile of three. They will look at the pile of three cookies longer.
6. I wasn't surprised that the primates could count. I was surprised that the salamanders could count.
7. Do you prefer "An Hour with Abuelo"? Do you prefer "It's a Math World for Animals"?

Use the Grammar Independently Write a paragraph about your favorite hobby. Use at least three compound sentences.

Grammar Expansion

Compound Conjunctions and Transition Words and Expressions

Workbook
pages 123–124

Independent Practice
CD-ROM/Online

✓Checkpoint

1. What do **conjunctions** connect?
2. Give an example of a **compound sentence.**

Workbook
pages 121–122

Independent Practice
CD-ROM/Online

● Writing Assignment

Write a Short Story

> **Writing Prompt**
>
> Write a short story about a character who must make a choice about something. Your story should have an introduction, rising action, a climax, and a resolution. Include conjunctions and compound sentences in your story.

Write Your Short Story

1. **Read the student model.** A character in the following story made a choice that he was later sorry about.

Student Model

> **Writing Suggestion**
>
> When writing a narrative in the simple past tense, remember that you can use the simple present tense in the characters' dialogue.

Just Tell the Truth

Charlie asked his friend Pete to go see a movie about baseball on Saturday. Pete said, "Yes!"

Later that day, Charlie's father said, "My boss gave me two tickets for the baseball game on Saturday. Let's go!" Charlie said, "Great!" Then he remembered he had promised to see a movie with Pete the same day. "What should I do?" he thought.

Charlie had to make a choice; he decided to go to the baseball game and tell Pete that he had to do homework on Saturday. Pete said, "I understand." Charlie didn't feel good about lying to Pete.

At the baseball game on Saturday, Charlie saw Pete and his father walking toward them. Charlie wanted to disappear! Charlie said, "Pete, let's talk."

Charlie said, "I'm sorry. I lied to you. This is what happened: My father got tickets to the game, and I really wanted to go. I made the wrong choice. Please forgive me." Pete said, "I understand, but next time, just tell me the truth. And of course I forgive you."

Charlie smiled and said, "Thanks, Pete. But...why are you here?" Pete said, "Well, my dad got two tickets from his boss yesterday. So here we are!" "Great," said Charlie. "Let's go watch the game!"

Workbook
page 125

2. **Brainstorm ideas.**

    a. Think about choices that you could write a story about. Select a choice.

    b. Think about characters. How many do you need? Who are they? Remember that you could be a character in your short story.

3. **Write your short story.** Introduce your characters. Write about the choice that a character must make and what happens.

4. **Revise your short story.**

    Use the **editing and proofreading symbols** on page 455 to mark any changes you want to make.

5. **Edit.** Use the **Writing Checklist** to help you find problems and errors in your story.

Writing Checklist

1. One of the characters in my story had to make a choice.

2. My story had an introduction, rising action, a climax, and a resolution.

3. I used several sentences with conjunctions.

4. I used compound sentences.

5. I used correct spelling, grammar and punctuation.

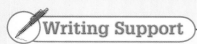 **Writing Support**

Mechanics

Semicolon and Colon

A **semicolon** allows a writer to connect two independent clauses to form one sentence. A **colon** starts a list at the end of a sentence.

- A semicolon can take the place of a period between what would otherwise be two separate sentences.

  Example (as two sentences): It was a very hot day. My friends and I went to the pool.

  Example (with a semicolon): It was a very hot day; my friends and I went to the pool.

- A semicolon can be used instead of a conjunction such as *and* in a compound sentence.

  Example (as a compound sentence): It was a powerful storm, and there was a lot of thunder and lightning.

  Example (with a semicolon): It was a powerful storm; there was a lot of thunder and lightning.

- A colon alerts the reader to an upcoming list of terms.

  Example: I have family living in four states: New York, Florida, Ohio, and New Mexico.

- A colon can also follow introductory terms such as *the following*.

  Example: The following months have 30 days: April, June, September, and November.

Apply Look through your short story to try to find places where you might want to use a semicolon or a colon.

Workbook
pages 126–128

Independent Practice
CD-ROM/Online

Progress Check

How well did you understand this chapter? Try to answer the questions. If necessary, go back to the pages listed for a review.

Skills	Skills Assessment Questions	Pages to Review
Vocabulary From the Readings	What do these words mean?	
	• **depressed, embarrassed, graduate, ignorant, obvious, old-fashioned**	142
	• **experiment, innate, measure, random**	154
Academic Vocabulary	What do these academic vocabulary words mean?	
	• **interact, tradition**	143
	• **evidence, setting**	152
Reading Strategies	Why is it important to ask questions when reading?	143
	How do you draw conclusions?	155
Text Genres	What is the text genre of "An Hour with Abuelo"?	144
	What is the text genre of "It's a Math World for Animals"?	155
Reading Comprehension	What is "An Hour with Abuelo" about?	153
	What is "It's a Math World for Animals" about?	161
Literary Element	What four elements make up the **plot** of a story?	153
Spelling	How do you usually create present participles?	161
Writing Conventions	Name three uses of commas.	161
Listening and Speaking	**Phrases for Conversation** What phrases could you use to react to a story?	162
Vocabulary Development	What makes an **idiom** different from other phrases?	163
Grammar	What is a **conjunction**, and what does it do?	164
Writing Support: Mechanics	What is the difference between a **colon** and a **semicolon**?	167

Assessment Practice

Read this passage. Then answer Questions 1 through 4.

Community Reading

1   Before I graduate, I have to complete a community service project. I like projects, but I am nervous about going to a new place and doing something unfamiliar.

2   Today is the first day of my project: reading books aloud at a retirement home. I can't believe I am following a nurse down a hallway toward the room of someone I have never met. I grip the book that I brought tightly in my hand. I have butterflies in my stomach; I think about stopping and turning around, but it's too late. We walk into the room. There are two men playing a card game. They stop when they see me.

3   I stumble into a chair. One of the men smiles and looks at the book. "*The Pearl* by John Steinbeck is one of my favorites, too. I can't wait to hear you read it." His voice is kind and gentle. I smile; I don't feel embarrassed to be there anymore. I open the book and begin reading.

---

1 What does the word <u>embarrassed</u> mean in the following sentence?

> I smile; I don't feel <u>embarrassed</u> to be there anymore.

  A self-conscious

  B excited

  C upset

  D scared

2 What conclusion can you draw about the narrator?

  A He won't go back to the retirement home.

  B He is a poor reader.

  C He is a senior citizen.

  D He will enjoy doing his project.

3 What is the climax of the passage?

  A The writer is assigned a community service project.

  B The writer arrives at the retirement home.

  C The elderly man speaks to the writer for the first time.

  D The writer begins to read.

4 What is the genre of this passage?

  A poem

  B persuasive essay

  C textbook excerpt

  D short story

Writing on Demand: Short Story

Write a short story about a young person who was nervous about doing something but chose to do it anyway. What was the character nervous about? What decision did he or she make? What was the effect of his or her decision? When writing, keep in mind the four plot elements. **(20 minutes)**

> **Writing Tip**
> Be sure your story has a strong beginning, middle, and end.

CHAPTER 2

Objectives

Reading Strategies
Analyze the author's purpose; Recognize elements of poetry

Listening and Speaking
Describe the characteristics of different forms of poetry

Grammar
Use complex and compound–complex sentences

Writing
Write an expository essay

Academic Vocabulary

process	conclusion
valid	identify

Academic Content

The history of slavery in the U.S.

Poetry about culture and choices

● **Chapter Focus Question**

How do the choices we make affect our present and future?

Reading 1 **Content: Social Studies**

Historical nonfiction
THE DRED SCOTT DECISION
by Brendan January

Reading 2 **Literature**

Poetry
The Road Not Taken
by Robert Frost
Saying Yes
by Diana Chang

THE DRED SCOTT DECISION

● **About the Reading**

You are going to read about a slave named Dred Scott, who tried to win his freedom through the courts in the mid-1800s. The Supreme Court's choice in this case led to a conflict between the North and the South, and moved the nation closer to civil war.

● Build Background

Slavery in the United States

Slavery began to divide the United States in the early 1800s. States in the North did not support slavery. In the South, white people believed that they needed slaves.

At the time, there were several territories that were not part of the United States. Northerners and Southerners argued over whether slavery should be allowed in these territories. In 1820 and 1821, Congress divided the territories into two sections. Congress did away with slavery in the northern section and allowed slavery in the southern section. The agreement also made Missouri a state where slavery was allowed. This agreement was called the Missouri Compromise, and most people agreed with it for many years.

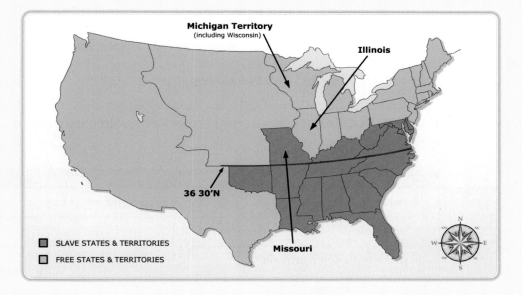

● Use Prior Knowledge

Tell About a Difficult Decision You Made

In *The Dred Scott Decision,* the Supreme Court has to make a very difficult decision. Think of a time you had to make a difficult decision. Answer these questions.

1. What was the decision you had to make?
2. What were your choices?
3. What decision did you make? Why did you make this decision?

Key Vocabulary

- argument
- ban
- convince
- guarantee
- intention
- possess
- violate

● Vocabulary From the Reading
Learn, Practice, and Use Independently

Learn Vocabulary Read each sentence. Look at the **highlighted word.** Use the context to determine the meaning of the word.

1. The lawyer made an **argument** to prove to the jury that he was right.
2. So many students were using cell phones during class that the teacher had to **ban** them.
3. I wanted to **convince** my brother to read the book, so I told him that it was my favorite.
4. The people are happy with their country's new law because it **guarantees** that all children can go to school.
5. Tim told his mother that he would clean his room, but he had no **intention** of doing it and continued watching TV.
6. The twins **possess** many good qualities like intelligence and kindness.
7. If you drive too fast, you **violate** traffic laws.

Practice Vocabulary Match the correct Key Vocabulary word to each definition below.

Definition	Word
1. debate by lawyers in court	argument
2. persuade	
3. promise to do or provide	
4. not allow or make illegal	
5. idea or plan	
6. break a law or rule	
7. own or have	

Use Vocabulary Independently Make a flashcard for each Key Vocabulary word. Ask a partner to show each word to you. Tell your partner the definition of each word you see.

ban

✓Checkpoint

1. Complete this sentence with a Key Vocabulary word: She studied science because she had the _____ of becoming a scientist.
2. Write a sentence using the word **ban.**

Vocabulary Log

Workbook page 129

Independent Practice CD-ROM/Online

Academic Vocabulary

Vocabulary for the Reading Strategy

Word	Explanation	Sample Sentence	Visual Cue
process *noun*	a series of actions taken to get a result	Neil took the first step in the **process** of learning how to swim; he tried getting used to the water.	
valid *adjective*	based on sensible reasoning	When Amy explained that she was late because of the snowstorm, her teacher thought it was a **valid** excuse.	

Draw a picture and write a sentence for each word.

Reading Strategy

Analyze the Author's Purpose

As you read about Dred Scott, think about the author's purpose. To figure out the author's purpose, consider his thought **process**. When you analyze an author's purpose, you try to understand why the author wrote the text. Did the author want to inform, entertain, or persuade?

1. As you read *The Dred Scott Decision*, choose details from the readings to analyze. Write these details in your chart.
2. For each detail, consider how the author wanted readers to react.
   a. Will the readers become informed?
   b. Will the readers be entertained?
   c. Will the readers be persuaded to agree with a certain opinion?
3. When you finish reading, determine the author's purpose for writing. Did the author want to inform, entertain, or persuade readers? Explain your answer. Is your reasoning **valid**?

Detail from Text	Author's Purpose
He was born into slavery in Virginia sometime around 1800.	

✓ **Checkpoint**

Why is it important to learn English? Think of **valid** reasons and discuss them with a partner.

Vocabulary Log

Workbook page 130

Independent Practice CD-ROM/Online

● **Text Genre**

Historical Nonfiction

The Dred Scott Decision is **historical nonfiction.** Historical nonfiction is about real events that happened in the past. Historical nonfiction usually includes the following features.

Historical Nonfiction	
events	what happened
dates	when the events happened
characters	real people in history who appear in the reading

● **Meet the Author**

Brendan January has written more than forty nonfiction books for young readers. January has been interested in U.S. history for a long time. He studied history and English at Haverford College. He also studied journalism at Columbia University. January's book *Genocide* was named one of the top ten nonfiction books for young readers in 2006 by a group called *Voice of Youth Advocacy.* January lives in Maplewood, New Jersey.

● **Reading Focus Questions**

As you read, think about these questions.

1. How does the reading connect to the theme of "choices"?
2. What do you think was the author's main purpose in writing *The Dred Scott Decision*?
3. Is it important to learn about Dred Scott? Explain your answer.

✓ Checkpoint

1. Who are the characters in historical nonfiction? Explain your answer to a partner.
2. Explain the word *event* in your own words.

Workbook
page 131

Independent Practice
CD-ROM/Online

THE DRED SCOTT DECISION

by Brendan January

Prologue

1   Dred Scott's journey to the **Supreme Court** was long and complicated. He was born into **slavery** in Virginia sometime around 1800. In 1830, Dred Scott and his owner, Peter Blow, settled in Missouri. Soon after, either Blow or his daughter sold Dred to a U.S. army doctor named John Emerson. Scott lived with Dr. Emerson in St. Louis, Missouri, until 1834, when Emerson moved to Fort Armstrong in Illinois. Dred went to Fort Armstrong with Dr. Emerson. For two years, they lived a quiet life in the fort. Emerson, however, grew tired of the **post**.

2   In 1836, the War Department transferred Emerson to Fort Snelling in the Wisconsin **Territory**. Scott accompanied him. After only a year in the Wisconsin Territory, Emerson complained of poor health and asked to leave.

3   In 1837, after sending several letters of complaint to the War Department, Emerson was transferred to a fort in Louisiana. There, Emerson met and married Eliza Sanford. Soon after, Dr. Emerson, Eliza, and Dred Scott returned to Fort Snelling in the Wisconsin Territory. In 1842, Emerson finally decided to settle in St. Louis, where he died on December 29, 1843. In his **will**, Emerson left Dred and Dred's wife, Harriet, to Eliza Emerson.

Dred Scott

Supreme Court the highest court in the U.S. system of justice
slavery system by which people are property of other people
post military station with permanent buildings
Territory area of the country that was not a state
will document in which a person says what to do with his or her property upon dying

> ## Reading Strategy
>
> **Analyze the Author's Purpose** Why does the author mention Dr. Emerson's marriage to Eliza Sanford?

> ## ✓ Reading Check
>
> 1. **Recall details** When did Emerson move to Fort Armstrong?
> 2. **Recall details** Where is Fort Snelling?
> 3. **Make inferences** Why do you think Emerson was transferred to a fort in Louisiana?

4   Almost three years later, on April 6, 1846, Dred and Harriet Scott petitioned, or asked, a Missouri court for their freedom. Scott claimed that he should be free because he had lived for two years in Illinois, a **free state**. Scott pointed out that he had also lived in the Wisconsin Territory, where slavery was **banned** by the 1820 Missouri Compromise.

5   The Missouri state court accepted Scott's request for a **hearing** and set a date for the **trial**, which began on June 30, 1847. In 1850, after more than two years of complicated **arguments**, the jury hearing the Scotts' **case** awarded them their freedom. Mrs. Emerson appealed the decision (asked that the case be reheard in a higher court). In 1852, the case was heard in the highest court in Missouri. The judge **overturned** the first court's decision. Dred and Harriet's quest for freedom had been **crushed**.

6   Soon after, Dred Scott was contacted by Roswell M. Field, a Vermonter who had settled in St. Louis. Field hated slavery and he hoped to use the Scotts' case to attack the laws that protected it. Dred, however, was no longer owned by Eliza Emerson. She had given Dred to her brother, John Sanford, who lived in New York.

7   Field told Dred Scott that John Sanford could be **sued** because New York was a free state. Cases between citizens of different states were heard in United States federal courts. Since Eliza Emerson and Dred Scott both lived in Missouri, Dred's case could only be heard in Missouri courts. But now that the citizens of two different states (Scott of Missouri and Sanford of New York) were involved, Roswell Field believed that Scott could win his case in the **federal** court.

Reading Strategy

Analyze the Author's Purpose Why did Eliza Emerson appeal the Missouri court's ruling? What is the author's purpose for including this information?

1800(?): Dred Scott is born into slavery in Virginia.
1830:   Dred settles in St. Louis, Missouri, with owner, Peter Blow.
1832:   Dred is sold to John Emerson.
1834:   Dred goes to Fort Armstrong, Illinois, with Emerson.
1836:   Dred moves to Fort Snelling, Wisconsin Territory, with Emerson.
1837:   Dred stays at Fort Snelling while Emerson goes to Louisiana.
1838:   Emerson returns to Fort Snelling.
1840:   Dred goes back to St. Louis with Eliza Emerson; John Emerson travels to Florida.
1842:   Emerson returns to St. Louis.
1843:   Emerson dies; Eliza becomes Dred's owner.

---

free state any one of the U.S. states that outlawed slavery before the Civil War
hearing appointment in the trial of a case in a court of law
trial formal examination of the facts and law before a court of law
case (in law) a good cause or reason for an action
overturned reversed a previous decision
crushed badly defeated
sued brought to court for violation of his rights
federal relating to the central government

An abolitionist group from the mid-1800s

8   On November 2, 1853, Roswell Field **filed suit** in a U.S. federal court for Dred Scott's freedom. The fact that Scott's case would be heard in a federal court increased its importance. Decisions made in federal courts affect every state in the Union.

9   The first trial was unsuccessful. The court declared that Scott was still a slave by Missouri law. The unfavorable decision left Scott with one last chance—the Supreme Court of the United States. Field wrote to Montgomery Blair, a prominent Republican lawyer in Washington, D.C. Blair had experience arguing in front of the Supreme Court, and he agreed to take Dred's case. Sanford hired a tough pro-slavery lawyer, Henry Geyer, to argue his side of the case. The case was accepted as *Dred Scott v. Sandford* (the court reporter misspelled Sanford's name and it was never corrected).

10   The U.S. Supreme Court was led by **Chief Justice** Roger B. Taney. He viewed the anti-slavery movement with fear and alarm, and he believed **abolitionists** were dangerous **radicals** intent on destroying the rights of Southerners. Taney hoped to use the Dred Scott case to strengthen slavery. Most of the other eight justices on the court shared Taney's beliefs.

Reading Strategy

Analyze the Author's Purpose What does the author tell readers about decisions made in federal court? What is the author's purpose for including this information?

Reading Check

1. **Recall details** Who filed Dred Scott's case in federal court?

2. **Recall details** Who did Sanford hire to argue his side of the case before the Supreme Court?

3. **Recognize order of events** When did Field write to Montgomery Blair?

---

filed suit asked that a case be brought to a law court
Chief Justice judge who presides over the Supreme Court
abolitionists people in the 18th and 19th centuries who spoke out against slavery
radicals people with extreme views on political or social issues

The courtroom where Dred Scott's case was heard

Reading Strategy

Analyze the Author's Purpose Why do you think the author provides a definition of the word *citizen*?

11   Dred Scott's case was scheduled to begin on February 11, 1856, in the Supreme Court in Washington, D.C. The nine justices, clothed in long black robes, sat in a row behind a long table at the head of the courtroom.

12   As the **arguments** began, important questions emerged: What does it mean to be a citizen? A citizen is a member of a country or state. A citizen can testify in court and is protected by the law. Can a slave be a citizen? Blair argued that Dred Scott was a citizen, so he had rights **guaranteed** by the Constitution. Geyer responded that slaves were not citizens, and that Scott had no right to be in the Supreme Court.

13   When the **arguments** were completed, the justices debated the details of the case in their private **chambers.** Finally, on May 12, 1856, the justices decided to hear the **arguments** again on December 15. The case had attracted the attention of several groups throughout the country. The **arguments** over Dred Scott's future were also at the center of heated debates between Northerners and Southerners. Republicans, slaveholders, and abolitionists all understood that the Court's decision would have a serious impact on slavery and its future in the United States.

---

chambers judges' private offices for discussing cases

14   On December 15, 1856, reporters and politicians crowded into the **courtroom** to hear the **arguments**. Again, the question of whether Dred Scott was a citizen arose. Montgomery Blair continued to argue that Scott was a citizen. Although black people had no rights in many states, some states (such as Massachusetts) gave free black people rights as citizens. If the state of Massachusetts recognized blacks as citizens, so should the United States government.

15   In Henry Geyer's response to Blair, Geyer stated that Dred Scott, as a black person, was not a citizen. Non-citizens did not have the full protection of the law because the law was for white people only. Black people could not sue another person in court, nor could they argue against a white person in court.

Reading Strategy

Analyze the Author's Purpose What state gave free black people rights as citizens? Why does the author include this detail?

Montgomery Blair argued Dred Scott's case.

Reading Check

1. **Recall details** Who went to the courtroom to hear the **arguments**?

2. **Recall facts** Why did Geyer say that Dred Scott was not a citizen?

3. **Explain** Do you think black people were treated fairly? Use examples from the reading to support your answer.

_____

courtroom room used for holding a trial

Analyze the Author's Purpose In this paragraph the author describes the reasoning behind both lawyers' **arguments**. Why does he do this?

16   In response to Geyer's **argument**, Blair decided to change **tactics**. He reminded the justices that Dred had lived in Illinois for two years. So, Blair asked, how could Dred Scott be a slave in a place where there was no slavery? Geyer replied that Dr. Emerson and Scott had simply traveled through Illinois because Emerson had no **intention** of living there. Blair reminded the Court that Scott had also spent three years living in the Wisconsin Territory. As a result, Scott and his family should be free because the Missouri Compromise **banned** slavery from the Wisconsin Territory.

17   At that moment, Henry Geyer made a **fateful** decision. He decided to argue that Scott was not free in the Wisconsin Territory because the Missouri Compromise **violated** the Constitution. Geyer argued that the U.S. **Congress** had no right to **restrict** slavery from the territories. Geyer's **argument** changed the case. Instead of simply ruling on one slave's freedom, the Supreme Court could decide the future of slavery in all of the territories. In his reply to Geyer, Blair pointed out that Congress had **banned** slavery in other territories, and no one had declared that decision **unconstitutional**. The **arguments** lasted for four days before they ended on December 19, 1856. Dred Scott, the lawyers, and the **spectators** would have to wait until the justices made a decision.

Henry Geyer argued against setting Dred Scott free.

tactics methods for achieving a goal
fateful having an important and often bad effect on future events
Congress national lawmaking body of the United States
restrict limit
unconstitutional against the principles set down in a nation's written constitution
spectators people who watch an event take place

18   For three months, the nation waited while the nine justices argued among themselves. Was Dred Scott a citizen? Was the Missouri Compromise unconstitutional? Chief Justice Taney hoped to write a decision that would be supported by all of the justices on the Court. (Cases are decided by a majority vote.) Justice Taney **convinced** most of the justices to support his view of the case. With these justices in agreement, Taney wrote the Court's decision.

19   On March 6, 1857, the small courtroom was packed with reporters and spectators. Dred Scott, Montgomery Blair, and Henry Geyer stood silently as the justices entered the room and sat down. Exhausted from long hours of writing, Chief Justice Taney read the **opinion** in a weak and whispery voice. It took him more than two hours to read the fifty-five-page decision.

Reading Strategy

Analyze the Author's Purpose Why do you think the author mentions that cases are decided by a majority vote?

Spectators in the courtroom hear the arguments in *Dred Scott v. Sandford.*

Reading Check

1. **Recall details** How long did the Supreme Court justices argue among themselves before making a decision?

2. **Make inferences** Why did Taney read the decision in a weak and whispery voice?

3. **Speculate** How do you think Dred Scott felt right before Chief Justice Taney read the opinion?

_____

opinion written decision in a court case in which one or more judges have the same view

20　　Taney **addressed** the first question: Was Dred Scott a citizen? No, he answered. Taney explained that black people did not have the same rights as white people. The writers of the **Declaration of Independence** did not intend to include black people when they wrote "all men are created equal."

21　　Taney addressed the next question: Was Dred Scott free because he lived in a territory where slavery was **banned** by the Missouri Compromise? No, Taney ruled, because the Missouri Compromise was a violation of the Constitution. Taney declared that Congress in 1820 had no right to establish the Missouri Compromise. Taney reasoned that slaves were property, and the right to own property is **guaranteed** by the Constitution. Congress could not deny slave owners the right to take their slaves with them wherever they went.

Reading Strategy

Analyze the Author's Purpose Why does the author present Taney's view that slaves were property?

22　　Finally, Taney answered one last question: Was Dred Scott free because he lived in the free state of Illinois? No. Taney explained that Scott spent only a brief amount of time in Illinois. Since the state laws of Illinois did not apply in the state of Missouri, Scott became a slave again as soon as he returned to Missouri.

ROGER B. TANEY
CHIEF JUSTICE OF U.S. SUPREME COURT

Chief Justice Roger Taney wrote the Supreme Court's opinion that Dred Scott was not a citizen.

---

addressed dealt with
Declaration of Independence written statement adopted by Congress in 1776 stating that the 13 North American colonies would govern themselves

23   Not all of the justices agreed with Taney's decision. Justice Benjamin Curtis wrote a separate decision, called a **dissenting** opinion. The next day (March 7), Justice Curtis read his opinion to the Court. He first argued that black people in several states in the Union **possessed** the rights of free citizens. Therefore, Taney's statement that black people were not citizens of the United States was wrong. Curtis then questioned Taney's decision that Congress could not **ban** slavery from the territories. Curtis argued that Congress had **banned** slavery from territories in the past. The Constitution gave Congress the right to make the laws within territories. Therefore, Curtis reasoned, the Missouri Compromise did not **violate** the Constitution. Dred Scott, Curtis concluded, should be free.

24   Justice Curtis's opinion, however, could not **outweigh** the other justices who supported Taney. Within weeks, Taney's opinion was printed in newspapers across the country. In the South, slave owners were thrilled that the Missouri Compromise no longer legally existed. The *Louisville* (KY) *Democrat* declared, "the decision is right, and the **argument** unanswerable." The *Constitutionalist* bragged, "Southern opinion upon the subject of slavery … is now the law of the land." Other newspapers stated that resistance to the Dred Scott decision is "rebellion, treason, and revolution."

---

dissenting disagreeing with the beliefs or opinions of a majority
outweigh be more important or have greater value than something else

Notice of a public meeting to talk about the Dred Scott decision

Reading Strategy

Analyze the Author's Purpose What is the author's purpose for telling about the effects of the Dred Scott decision?

25   The Dred Scott decision did not receive the same reaction in the North. Cries of outrage filled the northern newspapers. Horace Greeley, editor of the *New York Tribune*, described the decision as "atrocious, wicked, and abominable." The *Chicago Democratic-Press* expressed a "feeling of shame and loathing." The *Chicago Tribune* was at a loss for words: "We scarcely know how to express our [disgust]."

26   Northern Republicans claimed that a southern **conspiracy** existed to make slavery legal throughout the country. In Ohio, the state **legislature** declared that any slave who entered Ohio would be freed immediately. Justice Curtis was so disappointed with Taney's opinion that he resigned from the Supreme Court.

27   The Dred Scott decision did not achieve Taney's aim to preserve slavery. Instead, Taney drew ferocious criticism. Many Northerners believed the decision was a step toward making slavery legal throughout the United States. Anti-slavery feeling throughout the North increased dramatically, and thousands of Northerners joined the Republican Party. The reputation of the U.S. Supreme Court was shattered. The slavery issue remained unresolved, and the country drifted closer to civil war.

---

conspiracy plan between two or more people to do something illegal
legislature elected body of people with the power to make or change laws

28   After the Civil War began in April 1861, President Abraham Lincoln and Republican members of Congress treated the Supreme Court as if it didn't exist. Ignoring Taney's **feeble** protests, the Republicans abolished slavery from all of the western territories in 1862. Later that year, President Lincoln made a decision that surprised even his closest supporters—he issued the Emancipation Proclamation, which freed slaves in most states. By that time, however, it was too late to help Dred Scott.

29   In May 1858, Taylor Blow, a **descendant** of Dred Scott's original owner, Peter Blow, took possession of Scott and his family and set them free. The **courageous** slave who had fought so long and so hard for his freedom was finally free. Dred, however, could enjoy his freedom for only a short time. He died on September 17, 1858.

> **Reading Strategy**
>
> **Analyze the Author's Purpose** What is the author's purpose for telling about the Emancipation Proclamation?

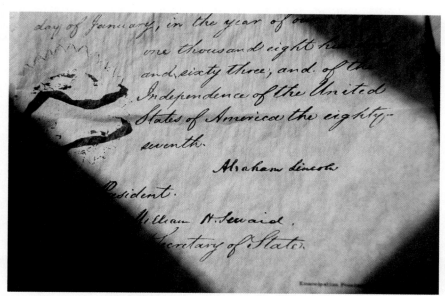

The Emancipation Proclamation signed by Abraham Lincoln

✓ Reading Check

1. **Recall facts** How did President Abraham Lincoln and Republican members of Congress treat the Supreme Court after the Civil War began?

2. **Make inferences** How did Taylor Blow most likely feel about slavery?

---

feeble weak
descendant person related to someone who lived in the past
courageous brave

● **Apply the Reading Strategy**

Analyze the Author's Purpose

Now complete the Reading Strategy graphic organizer.

1. Review the **Reading Strategy** on page 173 and copy the chart.

2. Fill in the chart with details from the reading. Consider the author's thought **process**. How did he want readers to react?

3. When you finish your chart, determine the author's purpose for writing. Explain why your reasoning is **valid**.

Detail from Text	Author's Purpose
He was born into slavery in Virginia sometime around 1800.	To inform readers of important background information to help them understand the court case.

● **Academic Vocabulary**

Vocabulary for the Reading Comprehension Questions

Word	Explanation	Sample Sentence	Visual Cue
conclusion *noun*	something you decide is true after thinking about it carefully	Every time I see Cheng, he is reading a different book. I have come to the **conclusion** that he loves to read.	
identify *verb*	to recognize something and be able to say what it is	I can **identify** 10 different kinds of trees.	

Draw a picture and write a sentence for each word.

✓Checkpoint

1. Look at how the people in your class are dressed today. What **conclusion** can you draw about the weather based on their clothes?

2. **Identify** three buildings in your town.

Vocabulary Log

Reading Comprehension Questions

Think and Discuss

1. **Explain** Why did Dred Scott say he should be free?
2. **Describe** Describe Chief Justice Taney's view of abolitionists.
3. **Identify main ideas** What are the main ideas of this reading? Use three Key Vocabulary words in your answer.
4. **Draw conclusions** Where in the country do you think African Americans were treated more fairly? Why?
5. **Compare and contrast** Compare and contrast the reaction to Chief Justice Taney's opinion in the North and in the South.
6. **Revisit the Reading Focus Questions** Go back to page 174 and discuss the questions.

Workbook
page 132

Independent Practice
CD-ROM/Online

Text Element

Chronological Order

Chronological order is the order in which events happen. Knowing the chronological order can help you find information in a text and remember what you read. You can make a timeline to show the order of events in a text.

Review the events in the Dred Scott court case, starting with when Dred Scott first filed a petition (April 6, 1846).

1. List major events in the Dred Scott case in chronological order.
2. On a blank sheet of paper, draw a horizontal line.
3. List each event in chronological order on the timeline from left to right.

April 6, 1846:
Dred Scott petitions
for his freedom

1850:
Missouri state court
awards the Scotts
their freedom

✓Checkpoint

1. How can listing events in chronological order help you understand a text?
2. Create a timeline showing the major events of your life in **chronological order**.

Workbook
page 133

Independent Practice
CD-ROM/Online

The Road Not Taken
Saying Yes

● About the Reading

Reading 2 includes two poems. "The Road Not Taken" is a poem about choices we make as we move through life. "Saying Yes" is a poem about an American's desire to not be asked to choose between her Chinese heritage and her American heritage.

● Build Background
New England Countryside

The poet Robert Frost lived for many years in New England, a group of six states in the northeastern part of the United States. Frost's poetry often paints pictures of the New England countryside.

Much of New England is covered with woods, or large areas covered with tall trees. Each year, in September and October, the green leaves of many trees change to bright red, orange, and yellow. In Frost's time, there were many simple dirt roads through these wooded areas.

● Vocabulary From the Reading
Use Context Clues to Determine Meaning

Read each sentence. Look at the **highlighted** word. Use the context to determine the meaning of the word.

1. The **age** when kings ruled most countries ended long ago.

2. It will not make a **difference** whether you choose pink or red.

3. Mr. Simmons treats all his students **equally**.

4. Sam would **rather** stay home than go to the mall.

Key Vocabulary

age

difference

equally

rather

✓Checkpoint

Write a sentence using the word **difference** and another sentence using the word **equally**.

Vocabulary Log

Workbook page 134

Independent Practice CD-ROM/Online

● Reading Strategy
Recognize Symbols

Poems often contain **symbols** that make the writing rich. A **symbol** is an object that represents something else. For instance, a dove is often used as a symbol for peace. Notice how the authors of the poems use symbols in their writing.

● Text Genre
Poetry

"The Road Not Taken" is an example of **rhyming poetry.** Rhyming poetry uses words that rhyme, or have the same sound at the end of the lines. Each line usually is about the same length. Each stanza, or group of lines, often has the same number of lines.

In **free verse poetry,** such as "Saying Yes," the lines usually do not rhyme. Lines may have different numbers of words. Often each stanza has a different number of lines.

Poetry		
element	rhyming poetry	free verse poetry
rhyming words at the ends of lines	yes	not usually
lines of about the same number of syllables	yes	no
stanzas with the same number of lines	usually	not always

● Meet the Authors

Robert Frost was born in San Francisco, California, in 1874. He wrote his first poems as a high school student. In October 1900, he moved to New Hampshire. Frost died in 1963.

Diana Chang's work reflects her cultural heritage. She is Chinese-American and was born in New York City. She spent most of her childhood in China but returned to New York.

● Reading Focus Questions

As you read, think about these questions.

1. How do these poems relate to the theme of "choices"?

2. What were the authors' purposes in writing the poems?

✓ Checkpoint

1. Why do poets use **symbols**?

2. What is an element of **rhyming poetry**?

The Road Not Taken
by Robert Frost

Reading Strategy

Recognize Symbols
Do you think that the two roads are a symbol for something else? If so, what?

1   Two roads **diverged** in a yellow wood,

And sorry I could not travel both

And be one traveler, long I stood

And looked down one as far as I could

To where it bent in the **undergrowth**;

2   Then took the other, as just as **fair**,

And having perhaps the better **claim**,

Because it was grassy and wanted **wear**;

Though as for that the passing there

Had worn them really about the same,

---

diverged separated and went in different directions
undergrowth tangled plants growing under trees
fair pleasant
claim reason to take it
wear use for a long period of time

³   And both that morning **equally** lay

In leaves no step had **trodden** black.

Oh, I kept the first for another day!

Yet knowing how way leads on to way,

I doubted if I should ever come back.

⁴   I shall be telling this with a sigh

Somewhere **ages** and **ages hence:**

Two roads diverged in a wood, and I—

I took the one less traveled by,

And that has made all the **difference**.

> **Reading Strategy**
>
> **Recognize Symbols**
> What does the road "less traveled by" represent?

✓ **Reading Check**

1. **Recall details** How many roads does the author talk about in this poem?

2. **Use context** What does the word *diverge* mean in this poem?

3. **Make inferences** What does the author mean by "ages and ages"?

***

trodden stepped on
hence later from the present time; the future

Saying Yes
by Diana Chang

1   "Are you Chinese?"

"Yes."

2   "American?"

"Yes."

3   "*Really* Chinese?"

"No . . . not quite."

4   "*Really* American?"

"Well, actually, you see . . ."

5   But I would **rather** say

yes.

Not neither-nor,

not maybe,

but both, and not only

6   The homes I've had,

the ways I am

7   I'd **rather** say it

twice,

yes.

Reading Strategy

Recognize Symbols
What does the word "homes" in stanza 6 represent?

Reading Comprehension Questions

Think and Discuss

1. **Recall facts** What are the two cultures of the narrator in the Diana Chang poem?

2. **Identify themes** What is the theme of "The Road Not Taken"?

3. **Interpret** How do you think the narrator of "Saying Yes" would describe her identity?

4. **Understand author's purpose** What purpose did the authors have in writing these poems?

5. **Compare your experiences** Describe an experience you have had that you can compare to Diana Chang's experiences.

6. **Revisit the Reading Focus Questions** Go back to page 189 and discuss the questions.

Workbook
page 137

Independent Practice
CD-ROM/Online

Spelling

Silent Letters: **k, gh, h, l, b**

Workbook
page 138

Independent Practice
CD-ROM/Online

Writing Conventions

Punctuation: Colons

Workbook
page 139

Independent Practice
CD-ROM/Online

Connect Readings 1 and 2

You have read two readings on the theme of choices. Use these activities to make connections between the readings.

1. With a partner, use this chart to compare the two readings.

Reading title	What is the text genre?	Which reading uses chronological order and which uses symbols?	What is the author's purpose—to inform, to persuade, or to entertain?	How does each reading present the concept of choices?
THE DRED SCOTT DECISION				
The Road Not Taken Saying Yes				

2. With a partner, ask and answer these questions.

   a. What kinds of choices do the authors of these readings describe? How are these choices alike or different?

   b. Imagine that Dred Scott is reading one of the two poems. What do you think he would say about it?

   c. Which image from one of the poems did you relate to the most? Which **argument** in *The Dred Scott Decision* did you find most persuasive?

3. **Revisit the Chapter Focus Question** How do choices that we make affect our present and future? Use examples from "The Road Not Taken," "Saying Yes," and *The Dred Scott Decision* to answer this question.

Phrases for Conversation

Discussing a Poem

This poem is written in free verse.

This poem has _____ stanzas.

I think the author meant . . .

Lines _____ and _____ of this poem rhyme.

The main idea of the poem is . . .

● Listening and Speaking

Describe Poetry

Describing the characteristics of a poem's form can help you understand the poem. Work with a partner to describe one of the poems from the chapter.

1. With your partner, write down some of the characteristics of poetry you learned about in the chapter. Answer the following questions.
   a. What is a stanza?
   b. What is the **difference** between a free verse poem and a rhyming poem?
2. Choose one of the poems from this chapter.
   a. One partner should read the poem aloud.
   b. What are some of the sounds you hear in the poem? Do you hear rhythm or rhyme?
   c. Take notes on what you hear in the poem.
3. Describe the poem you chose.
   a. Take turns with your partner making statements that describe your poem. For example, one statement might be "'Saying Yes' is written in free verse."
   b. Discuss each statement with your partner. Why do you think the author chose to use the form he or she did?
   c. Write down three of the statements about your poem. For each statement, write down what you think it reveals about the meaning of the poem.
4. Present your statements to the class.
   a. Take turns with your partner speaking to the class.
   b. Tell the class about the characteristics you identified in the poem and what you feel they reveal about the poem.

● Reading Fluency

Reading Poetry Aloud

When you read a poem aloud, you can use pacing, expression, and intonation to help listeners understand the poem better. Pacing describes the speed at which you read. Expression is the feeling you put into your voice while reading. Intonation is the level and sound of your voice.

1. Choose one of the poems from the chapter.
   a. Practice reading the poem aloud with expression.
   b. Make sure you vary your pacing and intonation, the rise and fall of your voice.
2. Recite your poem to a partner.
   a. Your partner will listen and give feedback about what was good about the reading and what could be improved.
   b. Take your partner's suggestions to improve your reading.
3. Perform your poetry reading for the class.

● Vocabulary Development

Denotative and Connotative Meanings

The **denotative meaning** of a word is its actual meaning. The **connotative meaning** of a word is the images or feelings we attach to the word.

1. Read the words taken from the poems and their denotative and connotative meanings below.

Word	Denotative Meaning	Connotative Meaning
road	a path used for traveling	life, journey
morning	the time of day from sunrise to noon	new beginnings, birth

2. Copy the chart. Then, with a partner, read the denotative and connotative meanings to come up with the missing words.

Denotative Meaning	Connotative Meaning	Word
1. a large African cat	strength, courage	lion
2. the house you live in	a place where you feel comfortable	
3. the color of a clear sky	cold, ice	
4. energy you get when you strike a match	anger, passion	

✓ Checkpoint

1. If you were to look up a word in the dictionary, would you find the word's **denotative** or **connotative** meaning?

2. Choose a word from the chart. Write a sentence using the word with its denotative meaning. Then write another sentence using the word with its connotative meaning.

Vocabulary Log

Workbook page 140

Independent Practice CD-ROM/Online

● Grammar

Complex Sentences

A **complex sentence** is one or more **dependent clauses** joined to an independent clause by a **subordinating conjunction**. A dependent clause cannot stand alone as a sentence. Some subordinating conjunctions are *after, before, when, because, although,* and *if.*

Subordinating Conjunction	What it Shows	Examples
after, before, when	time	**After** he visited his grandfather, Arturo understood him better. Arturo didn't know much about his grandfather **before** he visited him at the nursing home. I'm about to ask him why he didn't keep fighting to make his dream come true **when** an old lady appears at the door.
because	reason	**Because** the experiment was successful, he tried the experiment with salamanders.
although	contrast	I felt like a rich man **although** the pay was very small.
if	condition	**If** you give babies two or three, they'll go for three.

When the independent clause comes first, do not put a comma between the two clauses.

I felt like a rich man **although the pay was very small.**

When the dependent clause comes first, put a comma between the two clauses.

Although the pay was very small, I felt like a rich man.

Practice the Grammar Copy and combine the sentences using the conjunction in parentheses.

1. Arturo passes some reading tests. He will be happy. (if)
2. He was angry. His mother asked him to visit his grandfather. (when)
3. He doesn't want to go there. He has a lot of school work. (because)
4. Abuelo was a farmer. He wanted to be a teacher. (although)

Use the Grammar Independently What did you do **before** you came to school? What will you do **after** you leave school? Write two sentences for each question.

Compound-Complex Sentences

A **compound-complex sentence** has one or more dependent clauses and two or more independent clauses. Notice the position of the clauses and the punctuation in these examples.

Dependent Clause	Independent Clause (1)	Independent Clause (2)
Because the first experiment didn't work,	the scientists wanted to try it again;	but once again it failed.

Notice the punctuation: There is a **comma** after the dependent clause; a **semicolon** after the first independent clause; a **period** after the second independent clause.

Independent Clause (1)	Dependent Clause	Independent Clause (2)
The scientists wanted to try the experiment again	because it didn't work the first time;	but once again it failed.

Notice the punctuation: There is a **semicolon** after the dependent clause. There is a **period** after the second independent clause.

Practice the Grammar Use these independent and dependent clauses to make compound-complex sentences.

1. he was unhappy / but he went there to please his mother / because he didn't want to go to the nursing home
2. and he became a teacher / although his father wanted him to stay on the farm / he went to high school
3. but he had to go to war anyway / he wrote to the governor / when the war came
4. he may agree to go / but he may have too much school work / if his mother asks him to go to the nursing home next week

---

Use the Grammar Independently Write three compound-complex sentences about someone in your family.

Grammar Expansion

Showing Contrast and Cause, and Linking Ideas

Workbook pages 143–144 Independent Practice CD-ROM/Online

✓*Checkpoint*

1. Give an example of a subordinating conjunction to show each of the following: time, reason, contrast, and condition.

2. How many independent clauses does a complex-compound sentence have?

Workbook pages 141–142 Independent Practice CD-ROM/Online

● Writing Assignment

Write an Expository Essay

Writing Prompt

Write an essay in which you describe the qualities of the two different styles of poetry in this chapter. Give examples of each style. Use examples from the poems in this chapter and examples that you make up yourself. Use complex sentences and at least one compound-complex sentence.

Write Your Expository Essay

1. **Read the student model.** This essay explains the **difference** between two other types of poems: a limerick and a haiku.

Student Model

How can you tell the **difference** between a limerick and a haiku? Although these forms of poetry have specific qualities, the structure of each poem shows its purpose. A limerick is short, funny, and has a very strong rhythm and a particular way of rhyming. Read these two lines from a limerick:

> Let me tell you about my pet possum.
>
> Her name is Lorraine and she's awesome!

They tell the reader that the poem will not be a serious one. A limerick always has five lines. The first two lines and the last line rhyme. The third and fourth lines also rhyme.

A haiku is shorter than a limerick; is only three lines long; and most haiku poems have 17 syllables—five in the first line, seven in the second line, and five in the third line. Unlike a limerick, haiku are not usually meant to be funny. Instead, haiku describe nature and the seasons. For example, the lines

> Bright winter starlight
>
> Shining on the new white snow

are meant to help you imagine a scene. A good haiku can help you picture a scene with very few words.

Workbook
page 145

2. **Brainstorm ideas.**
   a. Identify rhyming poetry and find examples of rhymes in the reading.
   b. Write a few lines of a poem with rhymes.
   c. Identify free verse poems, and notice how the lines in the reading do not rhyme.
   d. Write a few lines of a poem that do not rhyme.

3. **Make an outline.** Decide which of the two types of poetry you want to describe first. Explain what it is like, and use examples from your reading. Then explain what the other type of poetry is like, and give examples.

4. **Write your expository essay.** Use the details in your outline to help you arrange your thoughts into paragraphs. Be sure to use transitional words and phrases to connect your paragraphs.

5. **Revise your essay.** Use the **editing and proofreading symbols** on page 455 to mark any changes you want to make.

6. **Edit.** Use the **Writing Checklist** to help you find problems and errors.

Writing Support

Grammar

Varying Sentences for Style

When you write, it is important to use different types of sentences. This can help you connect your ideas together better, and it can also help you hold the interest of the reader.

Simple sentences can help you state your main idea clearly or make a strong point. For example:

In "An Hour with Abuelo," a young man discovers his grandfather's life experience.

Compound sentences can help you give information.

The babies in the experiment could understand the idea of three cookies, but they couldn't understand the idea of four.

Complex sentences can help you make logical connections in your writing through the use of conjunctions such as *because, although, when,* and *after.*

Although the experiment was a success, we decided that we should do it again with more subjects.

Compound-Complex sentences work like complex sentences, but by adding extra independent clauses, you can put additional information into your sentence.

Because all of the subjects in the experiment were about the same age, we did it again with older people; but we were pleased that the results were not the same.

UNIT 3 · CHAPTER 2
Progress Check

How well did you understand this chapter? Try to answer the
questions. If necessary, go back to the pages listed for a review.

Skills	Skills Assessment Questions	Pages to Review
Vocabulary From the Readings	What do these words mean? • **argument, ban, convince, guarantee, intention, possess, violate** • **age, difference, equally, rather**	172 188
Academic Vocabulary	What do these academic vocabulary words mean? • **process, valid** • **conclusion, identify**	173 186
Reading Strategies	How can you determine an author's purpose? Give an example of a symbol and what it stands for.	173 189
Text Genres	What is the text genre of *The Dred Scott Decision*? What is the text genre of "The Road Not Taken" and "Saying Yes"?	174 189
Reading Comprehension	What is *The Dred Scott Decision* about? What are "The Road Not Taken" and "Saying Yes" about?	187 193
Text Element	What does it mean to put events in **chronological order**?	187
Spelling	Name three examples of words with silent letters.	193
Writing Conventions	Give two new uses for colons.	193
Listening and Speaking	**Phrases for Conversation** What are some phrases to use when discussing a poem?	194
Vocabulary Development	Explain what **denotative** and **connotative** mean.	195
Grammar	How is a complex sentence formed? How is a compound-complex sentence formed?	196 197
Writing Support: Mechanics	Why is it important to use different types of sentences?	199

Assessment Practice

Read this passage. Then answer Questions 1 through 4.

Brown v. Board of Education

1   After slaves were given their freedom, many African Americans were segregated, or separated, from white people. Segregation meant that African Americans could not attend the same schools as white people, could not sit in the same restaurants as white people, and could only ride in the backs of buses. In 1954 a court case known as *Brown v. Board of Education* changed the way people thought about segregation.

2   Oliver L. Brown wanted his daughter Linda to go to the school near their home in Topeka, Kansas, instead of another school farther away that was for African-American students. However, the law allowed the government to segregate the schools. Brown and 12 other parents went to court. After a long battle, they convinced the Supreme Court that separate schools were not equal.

3   The schools were desegregated and children could go to their neighborhood schools, no matter what race they were. Although African Americans and their supporters would have to fight 10 more years to ban segregation in other public places, the changes had begun with *Brown v. Board of Education*.

1 Read this sentence from paragraph 2.

> After a long battle, they <u>convinced</u> the Supreme Court that separate schools were not equal.

What does the word <u>convinced</u> mean?

A   talked about   B   fought

C   persuaded   D   violated

2 What is the author's purpose?

A   to entertain   B   to inform

C   to persuade   D   to share personal thoughts

3 Which of the following statements about the reading is false?

A   Oliver L. Brown was the only parent involved in the court cases.

B   Desegregation began in 1954.

C   Blacks and whites had to sit separately in buses.

D   The Supreme Court decided that separate schools were not equal.

4 What is the genre of this text?

A   folktale   B   poem

C   historical nonfiction   D   persuasive essay

Writing on Demand: Expository Essay

Write a three-paragraph essay that compares this text to *The Dred Scott Decision*. How are the texts similar? How are the court cases similar? How are they different? Also use any information you had already learned about the case. **(20 minutes)**

> **Writing Tip**
> Remember to use examples from both texts to support your arguments. This shows you have understood and correctly interpreted the texts.

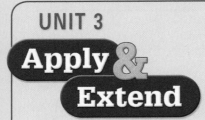

Objectives

Listening and Speaking
Deliver a problem/solution presentation

Media
Identify persuasive techniques in TV advertisements

Writing
Write a persuasive essay

Projects

Independent Reading

● Listening and Speaking Workshop
Deliver a Problem/Solution Presentation

> ### Topic
> In a problem/solution presentation, you identify a problem, tell why it is a problem, and suggest one or more solutions to the problem.

1. **Brainstorm**

   Think about these focus questions and take notes on your ideas.
   a. What are some problems that exist in your community or school?
   b. Why is each a problem?
   c. What are some things people could do to solve each problem?

2. **Choose a Topic**

   Look at your notes. Choose a problem you feel strongly about. Create a list of questions in order to find out more information on your topic. Use library and Internet resources to research the problem and possible solutions.

3. **Organize Your Presentation**

   Write your ideas on note cards. Use the steps below to help you.
   a. Tell what the problem is.
   b. Explain why you think it is a problem.
   c. Describe the causes and the effects of the problem.
   d. Propose one or more possible solutions to the problem.
   e. Tell what you think is the best solution to the problem and why.

4. **Practice, Present, and Evaluate**

   a. Use your note cards to practice your presentation.
   b. Give your problem/solution presentation to the class.
   c. Ask the class for feedback. Use the **Speaking Self-Evaluation** to evaluate your presentation. Use the **Active Listening Evaluation** to evaluate and discuss your classmates' presentations.
   d. Based on your classmates' presentations, make inferences on what could be the community's most urgent problem.

Speaking Self-Evaluation	Active Listening Evaluation
1. I clearly identified a problem and told why it is a problem.	1. I understood the purpose of the presentation.
2. I described the causes and effects of the problem.	2. The presentation helped me understand the problem and a possible solution.
3. I explained the solution(s) to the problem.	3. I agree/disagree with your solution to the problem because _____ .
4. I spoke clearly and loudly enough for people to hear me.	4. I think your presentation needed more information about _____ .
5. I looked at the audience while I spoke.	5. From the information in your presentation, I can conclude that _____ .

● Media Workshop

Identify Persuasive Techniques in TV Advertisements

Television advertisements are designed to persuade or convince people to buy a product or a service. Sometimes advertisements contain **persuasive techniques.** The purpose of these techniques is to convince you to buy what is being advertised.

1. View five advertisements on television.

2. Think about the following questions as you watch each advertisement. Write down your answers.

   a. What product is advertised?

   b. Who is the advertisement aimed at: adults? men? women? teenagers? young children?

   c. What kinds of promises or claims does the advertisement make about the product? Could the claims be proven true or false?

   d. How do graphics, sound, or digital technology affect the message the advertisement is trying to communicate?

3. Decide whether any of the following techniques are being used.

   a. Celebrity endorsement: Is a famous person selling the product in the ad? If so, who? Why do you think this celebrity was chosen?

   b. Emotional appeal: Does the ad try to affect your feelings instead of giving facts and evidence?

   c. Hyperbole: Does the ad exaggerate in any way? If so, how?

4. Tell a small group about the television advertisements you watched. Discuss the different persuasive techniques used and any false or misleading claims the advertisements made.

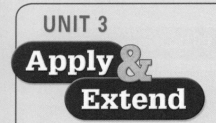

Apply & Extend

Use compound, complex, and compound-complex sentences in your essay. Try to combine some of your sentences with semicolons and the conjunctions *and*, *but*, *or*, and *so that*.

● Writing Workshop

Write a Persuasive Essay

In a persuasive essay, you attempt to convince the reader to agree with your position on a topic. A persuasive essay looks at evidence, considers the alternative position, and presents reasons why the reader should agree with that position.

> **Writing Prompt**
>
> Many schools have dress codes. They set rules for what students are allowed to wear. Do you think a dress code is a good or bad idea for your school? Write a persuasive essay to convince readers to agree with your position.

PREWRITE

1. Read the student model on the next page. It will help you understand how to write a persuasive essay.
2. Decide whether you are in favor of a dress code for your school or opposed to it.
3. Make a list of reasons for and against your position.
4. Try to find evidence that supports your position. Interview a student and a teacher as secondary sources to get opinions. Use the Internet or your school library as primary sources to find news stories about school dress codes.
5. If you find opinions or evidence that do not support your position, take notes on these. Think of how you will respond to opposing views.
6. Use an outline to organize your information in a logical sequence. Consider how much time you will spend on each reason. Make sure you have supporting details for each main point of your argument.

WRITE A DRAFT

1. Write the introduction. The introduction briefly presents the topic and states your position.
2. Write the body of your essay. The body should include at least three paragraphs.
   a. The first paragraph should summarize the arguments others might make against your position.
   b. In the following paragraphs, give reasons for your opinion using ideas you gathered from your sources. Be sure to cite these sources. Give details to support each reason. Be sure to address all the arguments that you summarized in the first paragraph of the body.
3. Write the conclusion. The conclusion should restate your position and briefly summarize the reasons supporting your position.

Student Model

This student wrote a persuasive essay answering the following question: People in the United States depend on computers more now than ever. Do you think this is a good thing or a bad thing?

Margarita Torres

<u>Computers Are a Good Thing</u>

Introduction

In the United States, computers are used for many different things. Although some people think we depend too much on computers, I think using computers is a good thing.

Body

Most people agree that computers are useful, but some say we are letting them take over our lives too much. They think we spend too much time playing with computers and not enough time interacting with other people. Some argue that people spend too much time in front of the computer screen and not enough time with family and friends. They also say that kids spend too much time playing computer games and not enough time getting fresh air and exercise.

I disagree with those arguments. First, computers do not keep us from interacting with other people. E-mail actually helps us stay in touch with family and friends. Computers also allow people to shop and pay bills online. This helps people save time. The extra time can be spent doing things they like to do. Second, I disagree that computers keep kids from fresh air and exercise. Many kids I know like to use computers but also play on sports teams. Computers can even help kids find out about outdoor activities in their area.

There are many additional advantages to using computers. For example, you can use them to find information without making a trip to the library. In school, computers help students learn. Computers even make it possible for students to take online classes from home.

Conclusion

I do not see any disadvantages to using computers. They help us maintain our connection to friends and family and find information right from our own homes. Computers help make our lives easier and better. For these reasons, I think computers are a good thing.

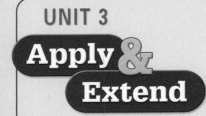
REVISE

1. Exchange your essay with a partner. Ask your partner to use the **Peer Review Checklist** to give you feedback on your essay.

2. Revise your draft. As you revise, consider whether you have enough reasons and explanations supporting the ideas in your essay. Add support to your argument if necessary.

3. Do your arguments make sense? Are they likely to persuade the reader? Take out any weak arguments that are unlikely to persuade. If you have thought of new arguments, add them.

4. Make sure your essay addresses the main arguments against your position.

5. Use the **editing and proofreading symbols** on page 455 to help you mark the changes you need to make.

EDIT

1. Use the **Revising and Editing Checklist** to evaluate your essay.

2. Fix any errors in grammar, spelling, capitalization, and punctuation.

Peer Review Checklist

1. I understood the writer's position on the topic.

2. The writer's arguments persuaded me.

3. The writer supported his or her arguments with reasons and examples.

4. The best argument for the writer's position was _____ .

Revising and Editing Checklist

1. I stated my position clearly and supported it with reasons and examples.

2. I stated the most important arguments of the opposing position and addressed them in my essay.

3. I restated my position at the end of the essay.

4. I used conjunctions to combine some of my sentences. I used compound, complex, and compound-complex sentences.

5. I checked my essay for punctuation and spelling.

PUBLISH

1. If you are writing your essay by hand, use neat handwriting. If you are using a computer, use a spell check and a grammar check.

2. Read your essay to the class. Speak slowly and clearly, and remember to make eye contact. Include gestures to emphasize important points.

● Projects

Choose one or more of the following projects to explore the theme of choices further.

PROJECT 1
Research a Product.

1. Think of a product you want to buy, for example, a new pair of sneakers, a shampoo, or a cell phone.
2. Research the different brands available. Find ads for each brand. Then use print and online resources to find out if each advertiser's claims about the product are true.
3. Based on what you learned, choose the best brand to buy.
4. Present your findings and your choice to the class.

PROJECT 2
Choose a Civil Rights Leader to Research.

1. Go online and access an Internet search engine.
2. Use keywords such as "slavery," "equal rights," and "civil rights leaders" to find information about civil rights leaders such as Dred Scott.
3. Choose one civil rights leader to research further. Ask specific questions about his or her life. Gather information about this person. Be sure to use the bibliographies of other sources to locate books and articles that can help you. Describe the choices they made in order to become a leader for civil rights.
4. Present the information in writing.

PROJECT 3
Find a Song or Poem About Choices.

1. Go to the library or look online for songs or poems that tell the story of someone making a choice.
2. Choose a song or poem. What is the choice made in it?
3. Write a narrative that tells a story of the choice or choices the person or people in the song or poem made. Then act it out in front of the class.

PROJECT 4
Write a Persuasive Letter.

1. Write a letter or an e-mail in which you try to persuade a friend to make a choice.
2. In your first paragraph, state the choice you think your friend should make. Then state possible concerns your friend may have, and reasons that support why you think they should make the choice.

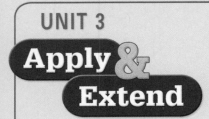

UNIT 3
Apply & Extend

Heinle Reading Library

Frankenstein by Mary Shelley

In a specially adapted version by Malvina G. Vogel

Victor Frankenstein is a university student who is fascinated with the idea of creating life. He builds a creature out of body parts, and it comes alive. However, when Frankenstein realizes he can't take care of his creation, he abandons the creature. Read to find out what happens when the "monster" returns to Frankenstein's life.

● Independent Reading

Explore the theme of choices further by reading one or more of these books.

An Island Like You: Stories of the Barrio by Judith Ortiz Cofer, Puffin Books, 1996.

This collection of short stories tells about a group of teenagers of Puerto Rican heritage living in the same New Jersey neighborhood. Each story focuses on a different teenager. The characters move in and out of each other's stories, playing major and minor roles in each other's lives.

The Dred Scott Decision by Brendan January, Children's Press, 1998.

This book gives a clear, detailed account of one of the most important legal cases in U.S. history. It includes photographs and portraits of the important people involved in the case.

The Poetry of Robert Frost, Thomson Learning, 1979.

This book is a collection of Robert Frost's published poetry. It contains all of his original works, from 1913 to 1962.

Ties That Bind, Ties That Break: A Novel by Lensey Namioka, Delacorte Press, 1999.

When Ailin is young, she refuses to have her feet bound like other Chinese girls her age. This decision changes her life. When her father dies, her uncle forbids her from going to school, and it seems that Ailin has few choices in life. However, she is determined to take control of her own life and create her own destiny.

Tug of War by Joan Lingard, Lodestar Books, 1990.

In 1944, Russian forces are advancing through Latvia. Fourteen-year-old Astra and her family decide to leave the country, but Astra's brother, Hugo, becomes separated from the family. When the war ends, Hugo is faced with a difficult decision. Will he rejoin his family and make a new life in Canada, or will he stay in Germany?

Milestones to Achievement

Writing: Revise and Edit

Read this rough draft of a student's short story, which may contain errors. Then answer Questions 1 through 4.

One or the Other

(**1**) Patricia's face was bright with excitement. (**2**) The first school dance was next week. (**3**) When she arrived home, she brought her things into the kitchen. (**4**) "Next Friday is my first school dance," she sang. (**5**) "It's next Friday? October 20?" her mother asked Patricia.

(**6**) October 20 was her father's 40th birthday party. (**7**) Patricia felt her throat tighten. (**8**) She marched out of the kitchen. (**9**) She walked out of the apartment.

(**10**) She was angry at her mother for planning the party on the same day as the dance. (**11**) She was mad at herself for almost crying about a silly dance. (**12**) Then she thought about her father. (**13**) She thought of all the Sundays that her dad came to her soccer games, and how he helps her with her homework every night. (**14**) Suddenly, Patricia felt depressed for feeling so angry at everyone. (**15**) Although she would have liked to go, she knew there would be other school dances; her father, however, would only turn 40 years old once.

---

1 What punctuation can combine sentences 1 and 2?

A semicolon   B hyphen

C colon   D comma

2 How can you combine sentences 8 and 9?

A She marched out of the kitchen, she walked out of the apartment.

B She marched out of the kitchen and she walked out of the apartment.

C She marched out of the kitchen, and walked out of the apartment.

D She marched, and walked out of the kitchen and the apartment.

3 Which of these is a complex sentence?

A Patricia's face was bright with excitement.

B She was mad at herself for almost crying about a school dance.

C She had never been to a school dance before, and she couldn't wait to go.

D When she arrived home, she brought her things into the kitchen.

4 In sentence 14, which word is a better choice for <u>depressed</u>?

A confused   B hurt

C embarrassed   D sad

Writing on Demand: Short Story

Write a short story about a character who has made a bad decision and tries to fix it. What were the effects of this decision? **(20 minutes)**

Read this informational text. Then answer Questions 1 through 8.

Protecting the Habitats of Chimpanzees

1   Chimpanzees are not only social animals that live in communities and work together, but they are smart in many different ways. For over 40 years, people have been studying chimps both in the wild and in captivity. One thing they have learned is that chimpanzees and their natural habitat— or where they live in the wild—need to be protected.

2   In 1960, a researcher named Jane Goodall began to live with and study wild chimpanzees in Africa. She learned that they are highly intelligent animals that communicate with gestures and physical contact. They make tools to find food, they possess innate decision-making skills, and they make choices about which groups to join and what foods to eat. Chimps cooperate to hunt and often share the food they have caught. In captivity, where they live in zoos and science centers, they can be taught American Sign Language so that they can communicate with their hands. There have even been experiments that show that a few chimpanzees have learned to use computers and to play games! Some scientists argue that chimpanzees can show emotions such as happiness or sadness.

3   Although chimpanzees are impressive and intelligent animals, their safety is in danger every day. In the wild, they can be found in 21 different African countries, living in forests. Chimpanzees are able to adapt to changes in their environment. They can move to a new place, make new nests, and find new sources of food. Yet people are destroying their natural habitats. By cutting down trees for firewood and using the space to build houses, humans leave chimpanzees with smaller areas to live in. Chimpanzees are in danger, and all eyes should be on them. Fortunately, many organizations and researchers have started to take steps to protect them. Everyone should be aware of their work and how important it is to help these amazing animals.

1 What does the word <u>possess</u> mean in the following sentence from paragraph 2?

> They make tools to find food, they <u>possess</u> innate decision-making skills, and they make choices about which groups to join and what foods to eat.

A have

B natural

C learn

D choose

2 What does the word <u>experiments</u> mean in the following sentence from paragraph 2?

> There have even been <u>experiments</u> that show that a few chimpanzees have learned to use computers and to play games!

A games

B tests

C grades

D scientists

3 How do chimpanzees communicate in their natural habitat?

A with American Sign Language

B with tools

C with computers

D with gestures and physical contact

4 According to the passage, why should people help chimpanzees?

A Because they need to learn sign language.

B Because they are losing their natural habitats.

C Because they need to learn how to use a computer.

D Because they are running out of food.

5 What is the writer trying to convince the reader of?

A All humans should protect chimpanzees and their habitats.

B We should stop observing chimpanzees in the wild.

C People need to start giving chimpanzees more food.

D More chimpanzee protection groups should be created.

6 Which sentence does not include a conjunction?

A In the wild, they can be found in 21 different African countries, living in forests.

B Some scientists argue that chimpanzees can show emotions such as happiness or sadness.

C In 1960, a researcher named Jane Goodall began to live with and study wild chimpanzees in Africa.

D In captivity, they can be taught American Sign Language so that they can communicate with their hands.

7 In paragraph 3, what does the idiom "all eyes should be on them" mean?

A Humans need to give chimpanzees something.

B We should go to zoos to see chimpanzees.

C It's time to think about protecting chimpanzees and their habitats.

D We can learn a lesson from chimpanzees.

8 What is the denotative meaning of the word <u>wild</u>?

A intelligent

B uncontrollable

C simple

D in a natural state

Cultures and Traditions

Explore the Theme

1. Do you recognize any of the **cultural traditions** shown in these pictures? Which ones?
2. What **cultural traditions** do you or the people you know take part in?

Theme Activity

Work with a partner. Write a paragraph describing your favorite cultural tradition. Exchange your paragraph with your partner and read your partner's description. Compare and contrast each other's traditions by discussing the similarities and differences.

CHAPTER 1

Objectives

Reading Strategies

Make inferences;
Visualize

Listening and Speaking

Give a demonstration
speech

Grammar

Learn about
prepositional phrases;
Recognize appositives

Writing

Write a short story

Academic Vocabulary

infer	indicate
assume	challenge

Academic Content

Cultural traditions about
food

Learning mathematics
through origami

● Chapter Focus Question

What can we learn by studying the customs and
traditions of other people?

Reading 1 **Literature**

Short story (abridged)

THE ALL-AMERICAN SLURP
by Lensey Namioka

Reading 2 **Content:** Math

Expository text

Mathematics & Origami
by Theoni Pappas

THE ALL-AMERICAN SLURP

● About the Reading

You are going to read a short story. It is about a
Chinese-American family that learns about the dining
customs of the United States.

● Build Background

Chinese Dining Customs

China is a very large country in Asia. Many Chinese people have immigrated to the United States, and they have brought their cooking and dining traditions with them.

Dining traditions in China are different from the traditions in the United States. In a Chinese meal, every person has a bowl for rice, and plates of vegetables and meat are put in the middle of the table. Each person uses chopsticks to take small pieces of vegetables or meat. They eat this with some of the rice. Then they take another piece. In the United States, everyone has a plate, and they put everything they want to eat on it at the beginning of the meal.

A Chinese-style meal

An American-style meal

● Use Prior Knowledge

Think About Your Eating Traditions

In "The All-American Slurp," a family from China tries to learn how to eat the way people in the United States do. How do people eat in your culture? Draw a chart like the one below. Think of several things that people in your culture eat at home. How do you eat these things? With a fork? With a spoon? With chopsticks? With your fingers? With something else?

food	how we eat it
taco	fingers

Key Vocabulary

- disgrace
- etiquette
- progress
- promotion
- spectacle
- stalk

● **Vocabulary From the Reading**
Learn, Practice, and Use Independently

Learn Vocabulary Read each sentence. Look at the **highlighted** word. Use the context to determine the meaning of the word.

1. Tom's bad behavior at the restaurant **disgraced** his family; embarrassed and upset, they left before finishing their meal.

2. André behaves properly at the dinner table—he has good **etiquette.**

3. She practiced swimming every day, and as time passed she could tell she was making **progress** because her swimming was improving.

4. My father got a **promotion** at work; now he makes more money and has more responsibility.

5. Ian felt embarrassed because he made a **spectacle** of himself when he fell down in the middle of the school play.

6. We planted bean seeds in the garden, and soon a bean **stalk** grew out of the ground.

Practice Vocabulary Match the correct Key Vocabulary word to its explanation on the right.

1. **disgrace**
2. **etiquette**
3. **progress**
4. **promotion**
5. **spectacle**
6. **stalk**

a. correct or polite behavior
b. move from one job to a higher-level one in the same company
c. bring shame to
d. stem of a plant
e. strange or amazing sight
f. process of improving or moving toward a goal

Build Your Knowledge

"Shades of meaning" describes the small differences in meaning in related words or synonyms.

Use Vocabulary Independently Use a dictionary or a thesaurus to identify a synonym (a word or phrase with the same meaning as another word) for three of the Key Vocabulary words. Then explain their shades of meaning.

1. **disgrace:** dishonor

Disgrace can mean to cause others to look unfavorably upon you.

Dishonor can mean to damage a reputation.

✓ Checkpoint

Write a sentence using the words **progress** and **promotion**.

Vocabulary Log

Workbook page 149

Independent Practice CD-ROM/Online

● Academic Vocabulary

Vocabulary for the Reading Strategy

Word	Explanation	Sample Sentence	Visual Cue
infer *verb*	to make a guess about something that is unknown using some information that is known	What can you **infer** about the girl's feelings from the expression on her face?	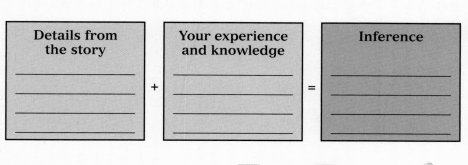
assume *verb*	to believe something is true without knowing for sure	I **assumed** that they were not home when no one answered the phone.	

Draw a picture and write a sentence for each word.

● Reading Strategy

Make Inferences

Authors do not always state everything directly in the text. When you **infer**, you connect clues provided in the reading with your experiences and knowledge. This helps you determine the author's meaning.

As you read "The All-American Slurp," follow these steps to make inferences.

1. Look for details and clues in the text.
2. Think about your own related experiences and knowledge.
3. Put the text details and your knowledge together. Make a logical or reasonable guess. What can you **assume** about the main characters and the story events?
4. Look at the chart. After you read, you will complete the chart.

Details from the story		Your experience and knowledge		Inference
_____ _____ _____	**+**	_____ _____ _____	**=**	_____ _____ _____

✓**Checkpoint**

1. Explain the meaning of the word **assume** to a partner.
2. Think of a situation in which you used clues to **infer** something.

Vocabulary Log

Workbook page 150

Independent Practice CD-ROM/Online

● **Text Genre**

Short Story

"The All-American Slurp" is a short story. A short story is fiction, a story that the author creates from his or her imagination. Short stories can include the following features.

Short Story	
characters	people in a story
setting	when and where the events take place
figurative language	language that goes beyond the literal meaning of words in order to help the reader see an idea or subject in a new way

● **Meet the Author**

Lensey Namioka was born in Beijing, China, in 1929. She and her family moved to the United States in 1938. Her father was a Chinese language specialist. He helped to develop the system for writing Chinese using the same alphabet we use to write in English. Namioka moved around a lot during her childhood. Because of her own experiences, she writes sensitively about the Chinese-American immigrant experience. She also has a sense of humor about the misunderstandings that can occur between the two cultures.

● **Reading Focus Questions**

As you read, think about these questions.

1. How do the narrator's experiences with food relate to the theme of "cultures and traditions"?

2. What do you think was the author's purpose for writing "The All-American Slurp"?

3. How does the use of setting make this story more interesting?

Explain what **figurative language** is in your own words.

Workbook
page 151

Independent Practice
CD-ROM/Online

THE ALL-AMERICAN SLURP

by Lensey Namioka

1   The first time our family was invited out to dinner in America, we **disgraced** ourselves while eating celery. We had **emigrated** to this country from China, and during our early days here we had a hard time with American **table manners.**

2   In China we never ate celery raw, or any other kind of vegetable raw. We always had to **disinfect** the vegetables in boiling water first. When we were presented with our first **relish tray,** the raw celery caught us unprepared.

3   We had been invited to dinner by our neighbors, the Gleasons. After arriving at the house, we shook hands with our hosts and packed ourselves into a sofa. As our family of four sat stiffly in a row, my younger brother and I stole glances at our parents for a clue as to what to do next.

4   Mrs. Gleason offered the relish tray to Mother. The tray looked pretty with its tiny red radishes, curly sticks of carrots, and long, slender **stalks** of pale green celery. "Do try some of the celery, Mrs. Lin," she said. "It's from a local farmer, and it's sweet."

5   Mother picked up one of the green **stalks,** and Father **followed suit.** Then I picked up a **stalk,** and my brother did too. So there we sat, each with a **stalk** of celery in our right hand.

Reading Strategy

Make Inferences Why do you think the Lins sat stiffly in a row? What details in the text help you answer?

Reading Check

1. **Recall facts** Where is the Lin family from originally?

2. **Recall details** What do the Lins normally do with vegetables?

3. **Analyze character** How does Mrs. Gleason act toward her Chinese guests? How does this affect the story?

---

emigrated left one's country to live in another
table manners polite behavior that is expected of people while eating
disinfect clean by killing germs or bacteria
relish tray dish of foods, often raw vegetables, eaten before a meal
followed suit did the same thing (as someone else)

6   Mrs. Gleason kept smiling. "Would you like to try some of the dip, Mrs. Lin? It's my own recipe: sour cream and onion flakes, with a dash of Tabasco sauce."

7   Most Chinese don't care for dairy products, and in those days I wasn't even ready to drink fresh milk. Sour cream sounded perfectly **revolting.** Our family shook our heads **in unison.**

8   Mrs. Gleason went off with the relish tray to the other guests, and we carefully watched to see what they did. Everyone seemed to eat the raw vegetables quite happily.

Celery stalks and carrots with dip

9   Mother took a bite of her celery. *Crunch.* "It's not bad!" she whispered.

10 Father took a bite of his celery. *Crunch.* "Yes, it *is* good," he said, looking surprised.

11 I took a bite, and then my brother. *Crunch, crunch.* It was more than good; it was delicious. Raw celery has a slight sparkle, a **zingy** taste that you don't get in cooked celery. When Mrs. Gleason came around with the relish tray, we each took another **stalk** of celery, except my brother. He took two.

12 There was only one problem: long strings ran through the length of the **stalk,** and they got caught in my teeth. When I help my mother in the kitchen, I always pull the strings out before slicing celery.

---

revolting unpleasant enough to make one sick
in unison at the same time
zingy lively

13   I pulled the strings out of my **stalk**. *Z-z-zip, z-z-zip.* My brother followed suit. *Z-z-zip, z-z-zip, z-z-zip.* To my left, my parents were taking care of their own **stalks**. *Z-z-zip, z-z-zip, z-z-zip.*

14   Suddenly I realized that there was dead silence except for our zipping. Looking up, I saw the eyes of everyone in the room were on our family. Mr. and Mrs. Gleason, their daughter Meg, who was my friend, and their neighbors the Badels—they were all staring at us as we busily pulled the strings of our celery.

15   That wasn't the end of it. Mrs. Gleason announced that dinner was served and invited us to the dining table. It was **lavishly** covered with **platters** of food, but we couldn't see any chairs around the table. So we helpfully carried over some dining chairs and sat down. All the other guests just stood there.

16   Mrs. Gleason bent down and whispered to us, "This is a **buffet dinner.** You help yourselves to some food and eat it in the living room."

17   Our family **beat a retreat** back to the sofa as if chased by enemy soldiers. For the rest of the evening, too **mortified** to go back to the dining table, I **nursed** a bit of potato salad on my plate.

> **Reading Strategy**
>
> **Make Inferences** Why do you think the Gleason family and their neighbors were staring at the Lin family?

What foods do you recognize on this buffet table?

lavishly generously, as if to impress
platters large flat dishes for serving food
buffet dinner meal in which food is placed on a table for people to serve themselves
beat a retreat went away very quickly
mortified deeply embarrassed or ashamed
nursed slowly ate

✓ **Reading Check**

1. **Recall details** Why don't the Lins take any of the special dip?

2. **Recall facts** How does the buffet table look?

3. **Predict** The next day, the narrator and Meg will meet. How do you think Meg will react to the narrator?

18   Next day Meg and I got on the school bus together. I wasn't sure how she would feel about me after the **spectacle** our family made at the party. But she was just the same as usual, and the only reference she made to the party was, "Hope you and your folks got enough to eat last night. You certainly didn't take very much. Mom never tries to figure out how much food to prepare. She just puts everything on the table and hopes for the best."

19   I began to relax. The Gleasons' dinner party wasn't so different from a Chinese meal after all. My mother also puts everything on the table and hopes for the best.

✳ ✳ ✳

20   Then came our dinner at the Lakeview restaurant.

21   The Lakeview was an expensive restaurant, one of those places where a **headwaiter** dressed in **tails** conducted you to your seat, and the only light came from candles and flaming desserts. In one corner of the room a lady harpist played tinkling melodies.

Reading Strategy

Make Inferences
What can you **infer** about Mr. Lin's training?

22   Father wanted to celebrate, because he had just been promoted. He worked for an electronics company, and after his English started improving, his superiors decided to appoint him to a position more suited to his training. The **promotion** not only brought a higher salary but was also a tremendous boost to his pride.

23   Up to then we had eaten only in Chinese restaurants. Although my brother and I were becoming fond of hamburgers, my parents didn't care much for western food, other than **chow mein**.

---

headwaiter person in charge of a restaurant's dining room
tails a formal jacket with two long pieces hanging down at the back, usually worn by men
chow mein westernized Chinese dish containing stir-fried noodles, meat, and vegetables

24   But this was a special occasion, and Father asked his coworkers to recommend a really **elegant** restaurant. So there we were at the Lakeview, stumbling after the headwaiter in the **murky** dining room.

25   At our table we were handed our menus, and they were so big that to read mine I almost had to stand up again. But why bother? It was mostly in French, anyway.

26   Father, being an engineer, was always **systematic.** He took out a pocket French dictionary. "They told me that most of the items would be in French, so I came prepared." He even had a pocket flashlight, the size of a marking pen. While Mother held the flashlight over the menu, he looked up the items that were in French.

27   "*Pâté en croûte,*" he muttered. "Let's see … *pâté* is paste … *croûte* is crust … hmm … a paste in crust."

28   The waiter stood looking patient. I **squirmed** and died at least fifty times.

29   At long last Father gave up. "Why don't we just order four complete dinners at random?" he suggested.

30   "Isn't that **risky**?" asked Mother. "The French eat some rather peculiar things, I've heard."

31   "A Chinese can eat anything a Frenchman can eat," Father declared.

Reading Strategy

Make Inferences Why does the narrator say she "squirmed and died at least fifty times"? Use details from the text and your own experiences learning a new language to help you make an inference.

✓ Reading Check

1. **Recall facts** What does the Lakeview restaurant look like?

2. **Author's purpose** Why do you think the author writes about the family dining in two different settings?

---

elegant tasteful, refined, attractive
murky unclear and dark
systematic based on a system; regular, orderly
pâté en croûte finely ground meat served in a pastry crust (French)
squirmed moved body from side to side from feeling embarrassed or nervous
risky dangerous

32   The soup arrived in a plate. How do you get soup up from a plate? I glanced at the other diners, but the ones at the nearby tables were not on their soup course, while the more distant ones were invisible in the darkness.

33   Fortunately my parents had studied books on western **etiquette** before they came to America. "**Tilt** your plate," whispered my mother. "It's easier to spoon the soup up that way."

34   She was right. Tilting the plate did the trick. But the **etiquette** book didn't say anything about what you did after the soup reached your lips. As any respectable Chinese knows, the correct way to eat your soup is to **slurp.** This helps to cool the liquid and prevent you from burning your lips. It also shows your **appreciation.**

35   We showed our appreciation. *Shloop*, went my father. *Shloop*, went my mother. *Shloop, shloop*, went my brother, who was the hungriest.

36   The lady harpist stopped playing to take a rest. And in the silence, our family's **consumption** of soup suddenly seemed unnaturally loud. You know how it sounds on a rocky beach when the tide goes out and the water drains from all those little pools? They go *shloop, shloop, shloop*. That was the Lin family, eating soup.

37   At the next table a waiter was pouring wine. When a large *shloop* reached him, he froze. The bottle continued to pour, and red wine flooded the tabletop and into the lap of a customer. Even the customer didn't notice anything at first, being also **hypnotized** by the *shloop, shloop, shloop*.

38   It was too much. "I need to go to the toilet," I mumbled, jumping to my feet. A waiter, sensing my **urgency,** quickly directed me to the ladies' room.

Reading Strategy

Make Inferences Why does the narrator leave so quickly from the table? How does your own experience help you to **infer** this?

---

tilt tip at an angle
slurp make loud sucking noises while eating or drinking
appreciation thankfulness or gratitude
consumption process of eating, drinking, or using things
hypnotized put into a sleep-like state where the mind is open to suggestions
urgency strong need that cannot wait

39   I splashed cold water on my burning face, and as I dried myself with a paper towel, I stared into the mirror. In this **perfumed** ladies' room, with its pink-and-silver wallpaper and **marbled** sinks, I looked completely out of place. What was I doing here? What was our family doing in the Lakeview restaurant? In America?

40   The door to the ladies' room opened. A woman came in and glanced curiously at me. I retreated into one of the toilet **cubicles** and latched the door.

41   Time passed—maybe half an hour, maybe an hour. Then I heard the door open again, and my mother's voice. "Are you in there? You're not sick, are you?"

42   There was real concern in her voice. A girl can't leave her family just because they slurp their soup. Besides, the toilet cubicle had a few drawbacks as a permanent **residence.** "I'm all right," I said, undoing the latch.

43   Mother didn't tell me how the rest of the dinner went, and I didn't want to know. In the weeks following, I managed to push the whole thing into the back of my mind, where it jumped out at me only a few times a day. Even now, I turn hot all over when I think of the Lakeview restaurant.

Reading Strategy

Make Inferences Why does the narrator feel she "looked completely out of place"? Why does the girl finally return? Use details from the paragraph and what you know to answer.

✓ **Reading Check**

1. **Recall facts** Why does the Lin family slurp their soup?

2. **Describe** What does the ladies' room at the restaurant look like?

3. **Identify cause and effect** Why does the narrator "turn hot all over" when she remembers the Lakeview restaurant?

---

perfumed with a pleasant, attractive smell; fragranced
marbled made of polished decorative stone
cubicles small areas with walls on three sides and a door
residence place where one lives

Reading Strategy

Make Inferences Why do you think the narrator's mother put on her first pair of high heels for the PTA meeting? Use details from the text and what you know to answer.

44   But by the time we had been in this country for three months, our family was definitely making **progress** toward becoming **Americanized**. I remember my parents' first **PTA** meeting. Father wore a neat suit and tie, and Mother put on her first pair of **high heels.** She stumbled only once. They met my homeroom teacher and beamed as she told them that I would make honor roll soon at the rate I was going. Of course Chinese **etiquette** forced Father to say that I was a very stupid girl and Mother to protest that the teacher was showing **favoritism** toward me. But I could tell they were both very proud.

45   The day came when my parents announced that they wanted to give a dinner party. We had invited Chinese friends to eat with us before, but this dinner was going to be different. In addition to a Chinese-American family, we were going to invite the Gleasons.

46   "Gee, I can hardly wait to have dinner at your house," Meg said to me. "I just *love* Chinese food."

47   That was a relief. Mother was a good cook, but I wasn't sure if people who ate sour cream would also eat chicken **gizzards** stewed in soy sauce.

48   Mother decided not to take a chance with chicken gizzards. Since we had western guests, she set a table with large dinner plates, which we never used in Chinese meals. In fact we didn't use the individual plates at all, but picked up food from the platters in the middle of the table and brought it directly to our rice bowls. Following the practice of Chinese-American restaurants, Mother also placed large serving spoons on the platters.

Americanized like people in the United States in appearance or character
PTA an organization of teachers and the parents of their students
high heels shoes with a high back part worn by women
favoritism unfair special treatment
gizzards the second stomach of a bird where food is broken up

49   The dinner started well. Mrs. Gleason exclaimed at the beautifully arranged dishes of food: the colorful candied fruit in the sweet-and-sour pork dish, the noodle-thin shreds of chicken meat **stir-fried** with tiny peas, and the **glistening** pink **prawns** in a ginger sauce.

50   At first I was too busy enjoying my food to notice how the guests were doing. But soon I remembered my duties. Sometimes guests were too polite to help themselves, and you had to serve them with more food.

51   I glanced at Meg, to see if she needed more food, and my eyes nearly popped out at the sight of her plate. It was piled with food: the sweet-and-sour meat pushed right against the chicken shreds, and the chicken sauce ran into the prawns. She had been taking food from a second dish before she finished eating her helping from the first!

Reading Strategy

Make Inferences
What did the narrator think when she saw Meg's plate of food? What details from the paragraph help you answer?

A sampling of Chinese dishes

Reading Check

1. **Recall details** What details suggest the Lin family is becoming more Americanized?

2. **Recall facts** What foods does the narrator's mother prepare for the dinner party?

3. **Analyze character** What are the duties of a proper hostess according to the narrator?

---

stir-fried cooked quickly over a high heat; a common way of cooking in Asia
glistening shining brightly, usually from wetness
prawns shellfish similar to shrimp but larger

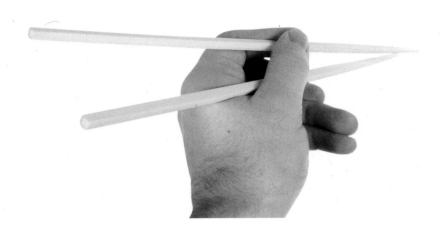

Reading
Strategy

Make Inferences
Why is the narrator surprised at Mr. Gleason's behavior? Use details from the text and what you know to answer.

52   Horrified, I turned to look at Mrs. Gleason. She was dumping rice out of her bowl and putting it on her dinner plate. Then she **ladled** prawns and gravy on top of the rice and mixed everything together, the way you mix sand, gravel, and cement to make **concrete**.

53   I couldn't bear to look any longer, and I turned to Mr. Gleason. He was chasing a pea around on his plate. Several times he got it to the edge, but when he tried to pick it up with his chopsticks, it rolled back toward the center of the plate again. Finally he put down the chopsticks and picked up the pea with his fingers. He really did! A grown man!

54   All of us, our family and Chinese guests, stopped eating to watch the activities of the Gleasons. I wanted to giggle. Then I caught my mother's eyes on me. She frowned and shook her head slightly, and I understood the message: the Gleasons were not used to Chinese ways, and they were just **coping** the best they could. For some reason I thought of celery strings.

55   When the main courses were finished, Mother brought out a platter of fruit. "I hope you weren't expecting a sweet dessert," she said. "Since the Chinese don't eat dessert, I didn't think to prepare any."

---

ladled served using a deep spoon (used for serving liquids)
concrete building material made from cement, sand, and small rocks
coping facing difficulties and trying to overcome them

56   "Oh, I couldn't possibly eat dessert!" cried Mrs. Gleason. "I'm simply **stuffed**!"

57   Meg had different ideas. When the table was cleared, she announced that she and I were going for a walk. "I don't know about you, but I feel like dessert," she told me, when we were outside. "Come on, there's a Dairy Queen down the street. I could use a big chocolate milk shake!"

58   Although I didn't really want anything more to eat, I insisted on paying for the milk shakes. After all, I was still **hostess.**

59   Meg got her large chocolate milk shake, and I had a small one. Even so, she was finishing hers while I was only half done. Toward the end she pulled hard on her straws and went *shloop, shloop*.

60   "Do you always slurp when you eat a milk shake?" I asked, before I could stop myself.

61   Meg **grinned.** "Sure. All Americans slurp."

◄ **Reading Strategy**

Make Inferences Why does the narrator ask Meg about the sound she makes drinking her milk shake? Use details from the text and what you know to answer.

✔ *Reading Check*

1. **Recall details** Did Mrs. Lin prepare a dessert?

2. **Recall details** Where do the narrator and Meg go after the meal?

3. **Analyze theme** How does the last line of the story sum up the theme of the story?

---

stuffed the feeling of being too full from eating too much
hostess female person in charge of a social event
grinned gave a big smile

After Reading 1

● Apply the Reading Strategy

Make Inferences

Complete the Reading Strategy graphic organizer.

1. Review the **Reading Strategy** on page 217.
2. Copy the graphic organizer.
3. Look at each page of the reading. List details and clues that you can use to make inferences in the first box.
4. Write information you know from your experience in the second box.
5. What can you **assume** about the characters and events based on details from the story and your own experience? Write what you **infer** in the third box.

Details from the story		Your experience and knowledge		Inference
At the party, the Lins try to be helpful by bringing chairs to the table.	+	A buffet table is meant for self-service at parties with many guests.	=	_____

● Academic Vocabulary

Vocabulary for the Reading Comprehension Questions

Word	Explanation	Sample Sentence	Visual Cue
indicate *verb*	to show or suggest that something else is true	Dark clouds **indicate** that it is going to rain very soon.	
challenge *noun*	a difficult task	Tina found art class to be a **challenge** because she was not good at drawing.	

Draw a picture and write a sentence for each word.

✓**Checkpoint**

1. What do good grades **indicate** about a person?
2. What is a **challenge** you have faced?

230   Unit 4 • Chapter 1

Independent Practice
CD-ROM/Online

Reading Comprehension Questions

Think and Discuss

Independent Practice CD-ROM/Online

1. **Recall details** What happens when the Lin family tries eating raw celery? Use Key Vocabulary words in your answer.

2. **Describe** Describe what happens at the Lakeview restaurant. Use Key Vocabulary words in your answer.

3. **Recognize cause and effect** What do the Gleasons do that surprises the Lins? How does the Lin family react?

4. **Relate to your own experiences** The author describes the Lin family's first PTA meeting. How would you feel if your parents responded as the main character's parents did? Why do you think the author included this event in the story?

5. **Analyze character** How does Mr. Lin deal with the **challenge** of eating in a French restaurant? What does this **indicate** to you about his character? How does this affect the story?

6. **Revisit the Reading Focus Questions** Go back to page 218 and discuss the questions.

Literary Element

Figurative Language

Figurative language is language that helps the reader see things in new, interesting ways. Figurative language is imaginative. It is not meant to be read as literal. Literal means keeping the exact meaning of a word or phrase.

These are some different types of figurative language.

simile: a comparison of two different things that uses the words *like* or *as*; Example: The Lakeview Restaurant was murky and dark like a cave.

metaphor: a direct comparison of two different things; Example: Learning to eat differently was a bridge the Lin family had to cross.

hyperbole: a figure of speech which is an exaggeration; Example: I squirmed and died at least fifty times.

onomatopoeia: the use of a word whose sound imitates its meaning; Example: Mother took a bite of her celery. Crunch.

Read the following sentences. Identify the figurative language in each, and determine which kind of figurative language it is.

1. It was so cold, Julia said icicles were forming on her eyelashes.

2. The cold air felt like pins and needles on her skin.

3. The snow was a blanket that covered the lawn.

4. Julia zipped up her coat and put on her gloves.

✓ Checkpoint

Name and explain two kinds of **figurative language.**

Independent Practice CD-ROM/Online

Mathematics & Origami

● About the Reading

In "The All-American Slurp," you read a short story about a Chinese family learning the customs and traditions of the United States. Now you will read an expository text about the mathematics of the traditional Japanese art form of origami, or paper folding.

An origami butterfly

● Build Background

Origami, a Japanese Art Form

Origami is the Japanese art of paper folding. To make an origami figure, you take a piece of paper and fold it in special ways to make, for example, a boat or a crane (a kind of bird). You can also make beautiful geometric shapes.

Origami originated in China and then traveled to Japan. Today, origami is an important art form in Japan.

● Vocabulary From the Reading

Use Context Clues to Determine Meaning

Read each sentence. Look at the **highlighted** word and use the context to determine the meaning of the word. Discuss the meanings with a small group.

1. My parents came to my graduation **ceremony** and saw me get my diploma.
2. The last question on the math test was the most difficult. Susan said she could not answer it because of its **complexity**.
3. The marathon runner used great **determination** to finish the race in four hours.
4. This soup doesn't have much flavor. If you add more spices, you might **enhance** the flavor.
5. Before hearing the firefighter speak at our school, we did not know much about fire safety. His talk was so **enlightening** that now we understand exactly what to do if there is a fire.
6. After two kids were hurt by bicycles, the school made a **restriction** against people riding bicycles on the sidewalk.
7. If you pull out the weeds and plant flowers, you can **transform** your backyard into a beautiful garden.

Key Vocabulary

- ceremony
- complexity
- determination
- enhance
- enlightening
- restriction
- transform

✓**Checkpoint**

1. Describe an event that can **transform** someone's life.
2. Which word means "to improve"?

Vocabulary Log

Workbook page 154

Independent Practice CD-ROM/Online

Reading Strategy

Visualize

When you visualize, you form images in your mind. This helps you understand what you are reading.

As you read "Mathematics & Origami," try to visualize what the author is describing.

1. After you read each paragraph, close your eyes. Try to imagine the things that the author is describing.
2. Draw or write what you visualized while reading.
3. Read the paragraph again. Look for the words that helped you visualize the concepts in the paragraph.

Text Genre

Expository Text

"Mathematics & Origami" is an **expository text.** In an expository text, the author's goal is to inform or to explain something. Expository text gives facts about a topic. It usually covers many aspects of the subject.

Look for these features as you read "Mathematics & Origami."

Expository Text	
formal style	serious tone
facts	information that can be proven

Meet the Author

Theoni Pappas taught mathematics to high school and college students for almost 20 years. Then she began to write books that made math fun and easy to understand. Now she has over 18 books and calendars that have been translated into many languages.

Reading Focus Questions

As you read, think about these questions.

1. How does this reading connect with the theme of "cultures and traditions"?
2. What do you think was the author's purpose for writing this?
3. What is the relationship between origami and math?

Workbook
pages 155–156

Independent Practice
CD-ROM/Online

✓Checkpoint

1. How does visualizing help your reading?
2. What is one feature of an **expository text**?

Mathematics & Origami

by Theoni Pappas

1
A square is **transformed** into a box.
A square is **transformed** into a bird.
A square is **transformed** into a snake.
A square is **transformed** into an elephant.

2   Origami is an art form that dates back to 583 AD when Buddhist monks brought paper into Japan from China through Korea. Since the manufacturing of paper at that time was costly, people used it with care, and origami became an **integral** part of certain **ceremonies.** The art of origami has been shared and passed on from **generation** to generation. Animals, flowers, boats, and people have all been created with origami. (The word origami is derived from *ori—to fold* and *gami—paper*.) Origami has delighted and frustrated **enthusiasts** over the centuries. In fact, today there are many international origami societies established in Britain, Belgium, France, Italy, Japan, the Netherlands, New Zealand, Peru, Spain, and the United States.

**Reading
Strategy**

Visualize Picture the enthusiasts at an international origami meeting. How do they feel? Why do you think they feel this way? What words from the reading help you imagine this?

A family making origami figures

---

integral necessary or essential
generation people born at about the same time; an age level in a family such as grandparents, parents, children
enthusiasts people who are eager or excited about a hobby or activity

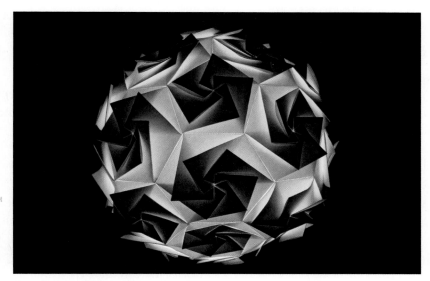

An origami ceiling light

3   In creating an origami figure, the origamist begins with a square sheet of paper and **transforms** it into any shape limited only by his or her imagination, skill, and **determination.**

4   A square was probably chosen as the original starting unit of origami because it possesses four lines of **symmetry,** unlike the rectangle or other **quadrilaterals.** Although some other regular **polygons** and circles have more lines of symmetry, they lack the **right angles** of the square, and would have been more difficult to manufacture. Sometimes origamists do begin with other units, but the **purists** work with squares without using glue or scissors.

Reading Strategy

Visualize How does visualizing these shapes help you to understand this paragraph?

Reading Check

1. **Recall facts** What did Buddhist monks bring to Japan?

2. **Recall facts** What forms can be made with the folded paper in origami?

3. **Explain** Why was the square chosen as the starting unit for origami?

---

symmetry the property of having two sides that are mirror images of each other
quadrilaterals flat figures having four straight sides
polygons closed flat figures such as triangles, rectangles, or hexagons
right angles angles formed by two straight lines coming together at 90°
purists people who do something strictly by the rules

A study of the **creases impressed** on the square sheet of paper, after an origami object has been created, reveals a wealth of **geometric** objects and properties.

Studying the progression of an origami creation is very **enlightening**. One begins with a square (a **2-dimensional** object), and then **manipulates** the square to form a figure (a **3-dimensional** object). If it is a new creation, the origamist will unfold the figure and study the creases impressed on the square. This process involves moving between dimensions. The creases represent the object's 2-dimensional **projection** onto a flat **plane**, namely the square. A transformation of a 2-D object to a 3-D object and back is related to the field of projective geometry.

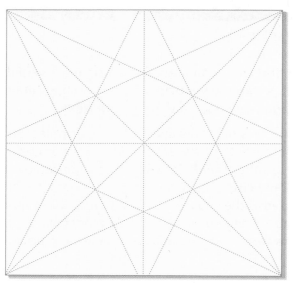

This diagram shows the creases that were impressed when a square was folded into a flying bird.

Reading Strategy

Visualize Visualize the 2-dimensional and 3-dimensional objects described in paragraph 6. How does visualizing help you understand this paragraph?

---

creases lines or marks made by folding
impressed marked by pressing or stamping
geometric related to the mathematical study of angles, lines, and shapes
2-dimensional flat, able to be measured in length and width only
manipulates handles or changes the position of something
3-dimensional not flat, having depth (or height) as well as length and width
projection shining an image onto a surface
plane in mathematics, a surface that is completely flat

7 In the book *Folding the Universe*, author Peter Engel, a master of the art and science of origami, reveals his years of work, unique discoveries, and creations in origami. Engel has taken origami to a whole new **plateau,** which emphasizes the strong connection between origami, mathematics, and nature by drawing **analogies** to **minimization** problems, **fractals,** and the **chaos theory.** An origami creation begins with a **finite** amount of material (e.g., a square of fixed dimensions) and evolves into a desired form, not unlike the restrictions placed upon nature in the formation of natural forms, such as bubbles.

8 Origami is experiencing a **renaissance.** It has come a long way from the foundations developed by early paper-folders. The complexity of the figures folded by today's masters are truly amazing. Their skill in transforming a square sheet of paper, without the use of scissors or glue, is incredible. The completed forms are not simple boxes or flowers, but **anatomically** accurate animals, realistic lifelike paper sculptures—squid, spiders, snakes, dancers, furniture. To achieve such proficiency and creativity takes years of work, experience, and study—it is **analogous** to the years which artists like M.C. Escher devoted to developing the art of **tessellation.** The mathematics, whether identified as such by origamists, is there. Like tessellation art, the understanding of mathematics enhances one's ability and creativity.

An origami horse

plateau level of achievement
analogies situations or stories similar to others that help one to understand
minimization simplifying to the lowest possible level
fractals irregular shapes made up of a large number of smaller shapes identical to each other
chaos theory explanation of the underlying order in seemingly random data or information
finite limited in number
renaissance period of energetic artistic and intellectual activity
anatomically relating to the structure of the bodies of people or animals
analogous similar, nearly the same
tessellation shape that is repeated over and over again without gaps or overlaps

Follow these directions to make an origami cat.

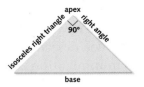

1 Begin with a triangle, yellow side up.

2 Fold one point up to the dot to make an ear.

3 Repeat with the other point.

> ### Reading Strategy
>
> **Visualize** Look at step 4 of the origami cat instructions. How does the folded paper remind you of a tulip?

4 Now it looks like a tulip.

5 Fold the top point down to make another triangle.

6 It looks like this.

7 Turn over. Meow! Draw a face and whiskers.

After Reading 2

● **Reading Comprehension Questions**

Think and Discuss

1. **Recall facts** What is the shape of paper used most often in making origami figures?

2. **Describe** Describe how an origami artist creates an origami figure.

3. **Identify main ideas** What are the author's main ideas? Use Key Vocabulary words in your answer.

4. **Express an opinion** What do you think are the skills you would need to become really good at origami?

5. **Compare your experience** Have you ever done origami? Did you enjoy it? Why or why not? If you have never tried origami, would you like to? Why or why not?

6. **Revisit the Reading Focus Questions** Go back to page 233 and discuss the questions.

 Workbook
page 157

 Independent Practice
CD-ROM/Online

 Spelling

Frequently Confused Words

 Workbook
page 158   Independent Practice
CD-ROM/Online

Writing Conventions

Spelling: The Suffix -y

 Workbook
page 159   Independent Practice
CD-ROM/Online

🔄 **Connect Readings 1 and 2**

You have read two readings on the theme of cultures and traditions. Use these activities to make connections between them.

1. With a partner, use this chart to compare the readings.

Reading title	What is the text genre?	Which reading uses figurative language? Which one is an expository text?	What was the author's purpose: to entertain, persuade, or inform?	Which reading did you prefer?
THE ALL-AMERICAN SLURP				
Mathematics & Origami				

2. With a partner, ask and answer these questions.

a. Look at the article on origami. Suppose the narrator in "The All-American Slurp" was reading this article. What part of the article do you think the narrator or her friend Meg Gleason might find familiar? What part of the article might be unfamiliar to both of them? Use details from the article to support your answer.

b. What is one example of figurative language that you remember from "The All-American Slurp"? What makes it so memorable? What is one factual detail that stands out in your mind from "Mathematics & Origami"? Why?

3. Revisit the Chapter Focus Question What can we learn by studying the customs and traditions of other people?

Phrases for Conversation

Giving Instructions

I'd like to tell you how to . . .

To do this, you will need . . .

Follow these steps: . . .

Be careful to . . .

Be careful not to . . .

● Listening and Speaking

Give a Demonstration Speech

In "The All-American Slurp" and "Mathematics & Origami," you read about people learning how to do something. Demonstration speeches, or how-to speeches, tell how to do something.

1. Think of an activity that you like to do. It could be a sport you play, a recipe you like to make, or a craft you know how to make.

   a. The purpose of your speech is to tell other students from your point of view the steps involved in doing this activity.

   b. Make a list of the most important steps you follow when you do the activity. Use note cards. Write one step on each card.

   c. Think about your audience, or the people you will be speaking to. Will the steps you wrote down tell them what they need to know to do this activity? What tone should you use when speaking?

   d. Think about bringing in props, or objects that you can use to demonstrate the steps in your speech.

2. Practice your speech with a partner.

   a. Use your note cards to help you practice your speech.

   b. Explain each step to your partner. Use gestures to show how each step is done.

   c. Then listen to your partner's speech.

3. Partners should use these questions to help each other improve their speeches.

   a. Does the speech explain how to do something?

   b. After hearing my partner's speech, do I feel like I could do the activity he or she described? Based on your conclusions, does the activity seem fun? Does it seem difficult?

   c. Do I still have questions about how to do the activity? Are there steps that my partner left out? Are there steps that my partner could explain more clearly? Ask your partner to clarify if there is something specific you do not understand.

4. Use your partner's suggestions to improve your speech. Then give your demonstration speech to your class.

5. Choose an activity from another student's speech and try to do it. Did the student's speech tell you everything you needed to know?

● Reading Fluency

Adjust Your Reading Rate to Scan for Information

When you adjust your reading rate, you read faster or slower. There are several reasons to adjust your reading rate. One is when you want to scan for information. When you scan a text for information, you are reading faster to find the information you need quickly.

1. Adjust your reading rate in order to scan "Mathematics & Origami." Glance quickly at the text in order to find key words to answer the following questions.

   a. When did origami begin?

   b. Why was the square chosen as the original unit of origami?

   c. Who is Peter Engel?

2. Work with a partner. Write three questions based on the reading. Answer your partner's questions by scanning the text for key words.

● Vocabulary Development

Words and Phrases From Mythology

There are many English words and phrases that are derived, or come from, words and phrases from ancient Greek, Latin, and Anglo-Saxon mythology.

A mythology is a group of well-known stories from a country or culture. People use the stories to explain events, religious beliefs, and social traditions. The importance of these stories leads to the use of words from them.

Look at the words and phrases and where they are derived from below. Copy the chart and use a dictionary to find their definitions.

Word	Definition	Derived from
1. cornucopia	a large number of different things	a Greek myth about a goat's horn, a cornucopia, that filled with whatever the owner wished for
2. Achilles' heel		a Greek warrior named Achilles, whose heel was the only place he could be wounded
3. volcano		the name of the Roman/Latin god of fire, Vulcan
4. thunder		the name of the Anglo-Saxon god of thunder, Thunor

Checkpoint

What does it mean to say a word was "derived" from mythology?

Vocabulary Log

Workbook page 160

Independent Practice CD-ROM/Online

● **Grammar**

Prepositional Phrases

When you want to tell when, where, or how something happens, you can use a **prepositional phrase.** A prepositional phrase is made up of a **preposition** and an **object.** Some prepositions are: *about, at, down, for, from, in, on, out of, to, with.* Each of the following sentences contains a prepositional phrase.

The soup arrived **in a plate.**

I turned to look **at Mrs. Gleason.**

We had emigrated **from China.**

Prepositional Phrases		
	preposition	**object**
The soup arrived	**in**	**a plate.**
I turned to look	**at**	**Mrs. Gleason.**
We had emigrated	**from**	**China.**

Grammar Expansion

Phrasal Verbs

Workbook page 163   Independent Practice CD-ROM/Online

Practice the Grammar For each sentence, write the preposition and the object in a chart like the one above.

1. We **disgraced** ourselves the first time we were invited to dinner.
2. Most people do not eat celery raw in China.
3. The relish tray was covered with vegetables.
4. The celery was from a farmer.
5. We pulled the strings out of our celery.
6. The next day, Meg and I got on the school bus.
7. I wasn't sure how Meg would feel about me.

✓ Checkpoint

1. When do you use a **prepositional phrase**?
2. Write a sentence with a prepositional phrase. Underline the prepositional phrase.

Use the Grammar Independently Answer each question with a sentence that has a prepositional phrase.

1. When do you usually eat lunch?
2. Where do you live?
3. How do you get to school every day?

Workbook page 161

Grammar

Appositives

When you want to add more information about a noun or pronoun, you can use an **appositive**. An **appositive** is a noun or phrase that is placed next to another noun to help explain it. For example,

Anna's sister, that woman with the red hair, is having a party Saturday.

The appositive in this sentence is *that woman with the red hair* because it describes Anna's sister.

Sentences with Appositives		
noun	**appositive**	
Quentin,	**my brother,**	flew in an airplane for the first time yesterday.
Stan,	**the school's bus driver,**	is moving to Nebraska.
My teacher,	**Ms. Moran,**	is going to have a talk with my mother.

Practice the Grammar For each sentence, write the appositive and the noun it is describing in a chart.

1. We were invited to dinner by our neighbors, the Gleasons.

2. Mr. and Mrs. Gleason and Meg, their daughter, were staring at us.

3. Their neighbors, the Badels, were also staring at us as we busily pulled the strings of our celery.

4. The Lakeview was an expensive restaurant, one of those places where a headwaiter dressed in tails conducted you to your seat, and the only light came from candles and flaming desserts.

5. The origami societies, groups of people who share a common interest in origami, have an annual conference.

6. The origamist, an expert from Japan, showed us how to make cranes.

Use the Grammar Independently Write five sentences, each with an appositive. Underline the appositive in each sentence. Circle each noun the appositive is describing or explaining.

I saw (my history teacher,) Mrs. Rosa, at the mall yesterday.

Grammar Expansion

Nonrestrictive Clauses with *which, who, whom,* and *whose*

Workbook
page 164

Independent Practice
CD-ROM/Online

✓ **Checkpoint**

1. When do you use an **appositive**?

2. Give an example of a sentence with an **appositive**.

Workbook
page 162

Independent Practice
CD-ROM/Online

● Writing Assignment

Write a Short Story

> **Writing Prompt**
>
>   Write a short story about a funny event from your own life. Use each of these three literary features: *onomatopoeia* (a word that sounds like the sound it makes), *metaphor* (a form of comparison), and *hyperbole* (intentional exaggeration). Also, use at least one prepositional phrase and one appositive.

Write Your Short Story

1. **Read the student model.** It will help you understand the assignment.

Student Model

My Terrible Audition

Trying out for the school play was a big mountain for me to climb. I was frightened of acting in front of people, but I was determined to try.

The audition was after school, and I was so nervous I felt butterflies in my stomach. Every minute that passed felt like an hour. When the director, Mr. Lee, asked me what part I wanted, I peeped, "Mimi," in my scared-to-death voice.

Mr. Lee told me that I was too graceful for the part of Mimi. He then asked me to read from three different scenes in the play. I took a deep breath and suddenly found that reading from a script wasn't so hard. I breezed through the lines.

Then as I walked off the stage, I tripped over a chair. Crash! The chair fell off the stage and the metal legs clattered on the floor.

I got the part of Mimi in the play after all. Mr. Lee said I was perfect! I guess I showed I can be just as clumsy as Mimi!

Workbook
page 165

2. Brainstorm ideas.

   a. Brainstorm ideas about an event in your life that was funny.

   b. Think about examples of onomatopoeia. Some examples are *boom, screech, crunch, snap,* and *slam.* Be sure to use at least one example in your story.

   c. Make a list of metaphors. Some examples are "my room is a junkyard" or "my bicycle is a dream." Include one example in your story.

   d. Consider an example of when you would use hyperbole. For example, you might write, "I ran so fast I was flying."

3. Write your short story.
Establish a plot, setting, and point of view that are appropriate for the story. Be sure to use at least one example of onomatopoeia, metaphor, and hyperbole. Describe the setting, and make sure to include the four plot elements.

4. Revise.
Reread your story. Revise your story if any ideas are not clear. Make sure there are clear transitions between paragraphs.

    Use the **editing and proofreading symbols** on page 455 to mark any changes you want to make.

5. Edit.
Use the **Writing Checklist** to help you find problems and errors.

> ### Writing Checklist
>
> **1.** I told a story using onomatopoeia, metaphor, and hyperbole.
>
> **2.** I used at least one prepositional phrase at the beginning of a sentence.
>
> **3.** I used at least one appositive.
>
> **4.** I used correct spelling, grammar, and punctuation.

 **Writing Support**

Grammar

Interjections

An **interjection** expresses strong emotion. It is usually followed by an exclamation point (!).

- An interjection is often used before another sentence that offers some additional explanation.

    Example: **Wow!** The storm last night was really strong!

- An interjection can also be used as a form of command.

    Example: **Look!** The dog just got free from his leash and is running away!

- An interjection can also come before a comma at the beginning of a sentence.

    Example: **Oops,** I didn't mean to spell your name wrong.

Apply Look for places in your story where you can include interjections to express a strong emotion.

Progress Check

MILESTONESTRACKER

How well did you understand this chapter? Try to answer the questions. If necessary, go back to the pages listed for a review.

Skills	Skills Assessment Questions	Pages to Review
Vocabulary From the Readings	What do these words mean? • **disgrace, etiquette, progress, promotion, spectacle, stalk**	216
	• **ceremony, complexity, determination, enhance, enlightening, restriction, transform**	232
Academic Vocabulary	What do these academic vocabulary words mean? • **assume, infer**	217
	• **challenge, indicate**	230
Reading Strategies	How do you make an inference?	217
	What do you do when you visualize a reading?	233
Text Genres	What is the text genre of "The All-American Slurp"?	218
	What is the text genre of "Mathematics & Origami"?	233
Reading Comprehension	What is "The All-American Slurp" about?	231
	What is "Mathematics & Origami" about?	239
Literary Element	What is a **metaphor**? Use a metaphor in a sentence.	231
Spelling	What word is frequently confused with *tail*? What word is frequently confused with *plane*?	239
Writing Conventions	Write these nouns as adjectives using the sufffix **-y**: soup, craze, rain, flake.	239
Listening and Speaking	**Phrases for Conversation** Name a phrase that you can use in a demonstration speech.	240
Vocabulary Development	What are some English words that come from Greek, Latin, and Anglo-Saxon mythology?	241
Grammar	What is an example of a **prepositional phrase**?	242
	What does an **appositive** do?	243
Writing Support: Grammar	What is an **interjection**?	245

Assessment Practice

Read this passage. Then answer Questions 1 through 4.

A Special Dish

1   When Abuela, my grandmother, turned 70 years old, I decided to make one of her favorite dishes for the party we were giving her. It was a recipe for tamales she had been making since she was a teenager in El Salvador. Because it was a surprise, I didn't tell anyone about my plan to make it.

2   I knew what foods to buy because I have seen her make this dish many times. The only problem was that the recipe was so old I couldn't read the writing. The ink was so light it looked like it had been written hundreds of years ago! The words were Greek to me. I tried to follow the instructions but I only made a mess. I finally asked my mother to read the instructions to me.

3   With my mother's help, it transformed into a beautiful meal. At the party, everyone thought it was delicious—especially Abuela.

1 What does <u>transformed</u> mean in this sentence from paragraph 3?

> It <u>transformed</u> into a beautiful meal.

A created

B changed

C cooked

D appeared

2 What inference can you make about the narrator?

A She has a large family.

B This is her first time making this meal.

C She makes everyone's favorite meals for their birthdays.

D Cooking is her favorite activity.

3 Which sentence from the passage is a metaphor?

A The only problem was that the recipe was so old I couldn't read the writing.

B At the party, everyone thought it was delicious.

C The words were Greek to me.

D The ink was so light it looked like it had been written hundreds of years ago!

4 What is the text genre for this passage?

A poem

B persuasive essay

C textbook excerpt

D short story

Writing on Demand: Short Story

Write a short story about a time when you were determined to do something. Use each of these three literary features: onomatopoeia, metaphor, and hyperbole. **(20 minutes)**

> **Writing Tip**
> Try using prepositional phrases to help the reader visualize where and when the action is taking place.

CHAPTER 2

Objectives

Reading Strategies

Tell fact from opinion; Ask questions

Listening and Speaking

Give a presentation with visual aids

Grammar

Learn about indefinite pronouns; Classifying sentences by purpose

Writing

Write an informative essay

Academic Vocabulary

fact	classify
opinion	
proof	

Academic Content

The Mexican holiday Cinco de Mayo

The Chippewa legend of the dreamcatcher

● Chapter Focus Question

How do the stories we tell reflect our cultures?

Reading 1 **Content:** Social Studies

Expository text
Celebrating Cinco de Mayo
by James Garcia

Reading 2 **Literature**

Legend
Legend of the Dreamcatcher

Celebrating Cinco de Mayo

● About the Reading

Cinco de Mayo is a holiday that celebrates Mexico's victory at the Battle of Puebla on May 5, 1862. "Celebrating Cinco de Mayo" describes how people in the United States celebrate this holiday and what it means to them.

● Build Background

Cinco de Mayo

Mexico is a large country to the south of the United States. Many Mexican people have come to live in the United States. For many Mexican Americans, Cinco de Mayo is an opportunity to celebrate Mexican history and culture. In cities near the U.S.-Mexico border, many people, not just Mexican Americans, enjoy this holiday.

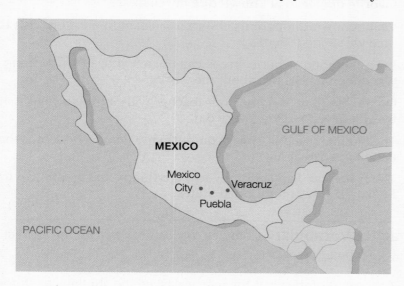

● Use Prior Knowledge

Describe a Holiday You Celebrate

Every culture has special days when people celebrate important occasions. Think of a holiday you have celebrated. Create a word web to show the holiday and some ways it is celebrated. Put the name of the holiday in the center circle. Use the questions below to help you think of ideas to write in the surrounding circles.

1. What does the holiday celebrate?
2. Are there special foods for the holiday? What are they?
3. Do people wear special clothing on the holiday? What do they wear?
4. Is there music or another kind of entertainment? What kind?

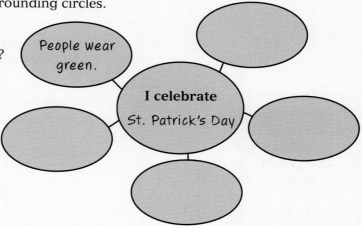

Key Vocabulary

acknowledge

cherish

enrich

establish

reflect

symbolize

● Vocabulary From the Reading
Learn, Practice, and Use Independently

Learn Vocabulary Read each sentence. Look at the **highlighted** word. Use the context to determine the meaning of the word.

1. Because I got an "A" in science class, my mother made my favorite dinner to **acknowledge** my success.

2. Visiting my grandparents is very important to me. I **cherish** the time we spend together.

3. Learning about other cultures can **enrich** your life by helping you understand more about the world.

4. On the first day of school, our teacher will **establish** rules that we will have to follow every day.

5. The old man liked to **reflect** on the many wonderful things that had happened in his life.

6. The American flag and fireworks are things that **symbolize** the Fourth of July in the United States.

Practice Vocabulary Complete the sentences with the correct Key Vocabulary words.

1. At the end of the year, the teacher asked the students to sit for a moment and _____ on what they had learned that year.

2. Young children often _____ a favorite stuffed animal and take it wherever they go.

3. When I think of the start of school, I think of pencils, notebooks, and desks. These things _____ the start of school for me.

4. I'm a pretty good soccer player, but I _____ that Maria is even better.

5. You can learn a lot of new words from books. Reading is one way to _____ your vocabulary.

6. There was no place to buy fresh fruit and vegetables in this town, so the people decided to _____ a farmers' market.

Use Vocabulary Independently Write a paragraph that includes each Key Vocabulary word. Share your work with a partner.

✓ Checkpoint

1. What are some things that **symbolize** summer for you?

2. Make a list of three things you **cherish**.

Vocabulary Log

Workbook page 169

Independent Practice CD-ROM/Online

Academic Vocabulary

Vocabulary for the Reading Strategy

Word	Explanation	Sample Sentence	Visual Cue
fact *noun*	something that can be proven	It is a **fact** that the moon moves around the earth.	True
opinion *noun*	a personal view or idea	In your **opinion**, what is the most delicious fruit?	I think the orange is the most delicious fruit. For me, the apple is the most delicious fruit.
proof *noun*	evidence that shows something is true	If you want to return that hat to the store, you have to provide **proof** that you bought it there.	"I'd like to return this hat, please. Here's my receipt."

Draw a picture and write a sentence for each word.

Reading Strategy

Tell Fact from Opinion

    Facts can be proven. You can use **proof** to show that they are true. An **opinion** is a personal belief. Telling **facts** from **opinions** will help you better understand what you read.

    As you read, look for **facts** and **opinions**.

Fact	Opinion

1. A **fact** is a statement that is true. "The Battle of Puebla happened in 1862" is a **fact**.

2. **Opinions** often use words like "believe," "feel," and "think." "I believe everyone should celebrate Cinco de Mayo" is an **opinion**.

3. Look at the chart. After you read, you will look at the reading again. Then you will complete the chart.

✓*Checkpoint*

1. Write one **fact** about yourself and one **opinion**.

2. What is the **proof** for the **fact** you wrote down?

● Text Genre

Expository Text

"Celebrating Cinco de Mayo" is an example of **expository text**. The purpose of expository text is to inform the reader about a topic. Expository text gives **facts** about a subject. Sometimes it also tells about people's **opinions**.

An expository text has the features below. Look for these features as you read "Celebrating Cinco de Mayo."

Expository Text	
expert opinion	the **opinion**, or belief, of a person who knows a lot about the subject
place names	names of locations where important events happened

● Meet the Author

James Garcia was born in Chicago, Illinois. His father and mother have roots in Mexico, and he still has family there. He teaches writing and ethnic studies at Arizona State University. In addition to teaching, Garcia writes and produces plays. About a dozen of his plays have been produced in Arizona and Texas, including *Voices of Valor*, a play based on the oral histories of Hispanic World War II veterans and their families. "Celebrating Cinco de Mayo" comes from *Cinco de Mayo: A Mexican Holiday about Unity and Pride*, the first book Garcia wrote. He wrote about Cinco de Mayo because he believes the holiday, while well-known, is often misunderstood.

● Reading Focus Questions

As you read, think about these questions.

1. How does the reading connect to the theme of "cultures and traditions"?
2. What do you think was the author's purpose in writing "Celebrating Cinco de Mayo"?
3. In your **opinion**, why are holidays important to people?

Checkpoint

1. What is the purpose of **expository text**?
2. What is **expert opinion** in expository text?

Workbook
page 171

Independent Practice
CD-ROM/Online

Celebrating Cinco de Mayo

by James Garcia

1   In Mexico, Cinco de Mayo is celebrated with events organized by the Mexican government. Soldiers march in parades. Serious ceremonies honor the soldiers who gave their lives at the Battle of Puebla. People dress up like 19th-century soldiers and **reenact** the famous battle. Some of the events are like those held in the United States on Veterans Day and Memorial Day, which honor soldiers who fought in America's wars.

2   More than 20 million people in the United States were born in Mexico or have ancestors who came from Mexico. They like to celebrate Cinco de Mayo, too. Mexican Americans celebrate Cinco de Mayo differently from people in Mexico. The partying is often more lively and fun in the United States. There are noisy, colorful festivals with lots of Mexican foods, folk dancing, and music. A Cinco de Mayo festival in America often includes Latin music bands and theater, many children's activities, and even carnival rides.

Reading Strategy

Tell Fact from Opinion
Is the first sentence in paragraph 2 a **fact** or an **opinion**? How do you know?

A Cinco de Mayo parade with a man dressed in a 19th-century uniform

Reading Check

1. **Recall facts** What are some ways people celebrate Cinco de Mayo in Mexico?

2. **Compare and contrast** How are Cinco de Mayo celebrations in the United States different from those in Mexico?

3. **Analyze** Why is Cinco de Mayo a popular holiday in the United States?

---

reenact act out or role-play events that occurred before

3   Until recently, only Mexicans and Mexican Americans celebrated Cinco de Mayo. But the growing popularity of Latino food and culture across the country has meant that many others are also enjoying the holiday. Cinco de Mayo festivals in cities such as Los Angeles, Houston, Chicago, and San Antonio attract large and **diverse** crowds, just as St. Patrick's Day is celebrated by many people with no link to Ireland.

4   The popularity of Cinco de Mayo in the United States is expected to grow. Most immigrants to the United States in the past ten years have come from Mexico. Meanwhile, many more Americans have begun to enjoy and celebrate Latino culture.

5   States with large Mexican populations, such as Texas, New Mexico, Arizona, California, Colorado, and Illinois, hold the largest Cinco de Mayo celebrations in the United States. In Texas and California, about one out of every five people is of Mexican origin. More and more Mexicans are living in such states as Florida, Nevada, North Carolina, Georgia, Indiana, and Ohio. Cinco de Mayo fiestas are now held in many cities throughout the United States.

Reading Strategy

Tell Fact from Opinion
How many facts can you find in paragraph 6?

Celebration in Los Angeles

6   The largest Cinco de Mayo celebration in the United States is held in Los Angeles, California. More than 500,000 people participate in the **festivities** there every year. Almost half of the people who live in Los Angeles County are Hispanic. Los Angeles has more Mexicans and Mexican Americans than any other city in the United States.

---

diverse made up of a wide variety
festivities events organized to celebrate something

7   The city of Los Angeles has several Cinco de Mayo celebrations. The biggest and best-known fiesta takes place on Olvera Street, which is in the oldest part of the city. More than 200 years ago, Spanish settlers **established** the city of Los Angeles right on what is now Olvera Street. Today, the street is home to 27 historic buildings, a traditional Mexican plaza, and a church that was built in 1784. Cinco de Mayo on Olvera Street features a parade, live music and dance performances, and mounds of wonderful Mexican food. Thousands of people of all backgrounds come to Olvera Street every Cinco de Mayo. The colorful festival has become an American tradition.

8   Cinco de Mayo is also celebrated at schools and parks across the United States. Many schools provide *baile folklórico* (folk dancing) performances, and cafeterias offer a Mexican menu for the holiday. All people who celebrate this wonderful holiday will find that it has even more meaning when they understand its history.

The Meaning of Cinco de Mayo

9   Cinco de Mayo has become so popular across the country, it is even celebrated at the White House. On May 5, 2001, President George W. Bush and his wife, Laura, hosted the first-ever Cinco de Mayo fiesta on the South Lawn of the White House. It was a **star-studded** event with about 300 guests. The White House celebration included a traditional mariachi band, a colorfully dressed Mexican folkloric dance group, and pop singer Thalia.

Olvera Street in Los Angeles during Cinco de Mayo

---

star-studded including a large number of famous people

Reading Strategy

Tell Fact **from** Opinion
Look at the last sentence in paragraph 8. Is it a **fact** or an **opinion**?

Reading Check

1. **Recall details** What is *baile folklórico*?

2. **Explain** What happens at the Cinco de Mayo celebration on Olvera Street?

3. **Understand author's purpose** Why do you think the author includes information about the Cinco de Mayo celebration at the White House?

10   President Bush delivered a special speech for Cinco de Mayo in English and Spanish—another first for a U.S. president. He said: "May fifth marks the triumph of the spirit of freedom for the people of Mexico. The victory of General Ignacio Zaragoza [the leader of the Mexican force fighting at Puebla] and his Mexican troops over the superior French forces at the Battle of Puebla served as a **stirring** reminder of the determination to win the fight for Mexico's freedom from **foreign intervention.** The Cinco de Mayo display of courage and purpose is a source of pride for all freedom-loving people.

11   "We Americans **cherish** our deep historical, cultural, economic, and, in many cases, family ties with Mexico and Latin America. Cinco de Mayo celebrations remind us how much Hispanics have influenced and **enriched** the United States."

12   Cinco de Mayo has meaning to all kinds of people, not only to Mexicans. The holiday is about more than just a historical event in which the Mexicans defeated the French in a battle at Puebla. For many it is about living life with pride and courage. It is about the importance of standing together to achieve goals.

Reading Strategy

Tell Fact from Opinion
Is the last sentence in paragraph 10 a fact or an opinion? How can you tell?

Statue of General Ignacio Zaragoza

---

stirring causing strong emotion
foreign intervention when one country gets involved in events in another country

Different Meanings to Different People

13   Writer Victor Garcia believes, "Cinco de Mayo **symbolizes** the struggle for **sovereignty**, **self-determination**, and commitment to fight even when the odds seem **insurmountable.**"

14   Roberto Vargas, a parent in California, sees Cinco de Mayo in much the same way. He also believes the celebration represents a duty to fight for what is right. He explains that Mexican-American college students during the 1970s began celebrating Cinco de Mayo as "a popular community event, using it to teach the importance of continuing to fight for justice, despite the obstacles."

15   Gabriel Buelna, a college professor, says Cinco de Mayo is viewed by many people as the anniversary of an event that showed that "Mexico could **hold its own** against other better-armed enemies."

16   Author Robert Con Davis-Undiano believes Cinco de Mayo simply means, "I'm still standing—**don't count me out.**"

The Battle of Puebla, 5 May 1862, 19th century

---

sovereignty the power of a country to govern itself; independence
self-determination the power to make up one's own mind about what to think or do
insurmountable impossible to overcome
hold its own be able to resist someone who is attacking or opposing it
don't count me out don't think that I will quit

17   Asked to describe what Cinco de Mayo means to him, sixth-grader Peter Robledo says, "It shows it doesn't matter if you're outnumbered. You can still win."

18   Fidel Montoya, a parent in Colorado, sums it up as follows: "It's a day to **acknowledge** our cultural and historical ties to Mexico. It's a day to **reflect** about Mexico's glorious past and its hope for the future. It's also a day when we as Americans can appreciate the cultural and historical contributions of significance made by Mexico. Cinco de Mayo is a day to enjoy and celebrate."

Celebrate Cinco de Mayo

Reading Strategy

Tell Fact from Opinion
Look at paragraph 19. What opinion does the author give in this section?

19   How about having a really special Cinco de Mayo this year? You can go to a big fiesta or invite friends over for your own party at home. Make tacos, listen to mariachi music, and hand out sombreros. But while you're having fun, be sure to remember the heroic soldiers who lost their lives at the Battle of Puebla defending Mexico from foreign invaders. Think of all the times people have had to fight to remain free, in Mexico, in the United States, and around the world.

A mariachi band

²⁰ Timeline

1806: Benito Juárez is born on March 21 in the Oaxaca village of San Pablo Guelatao.

1810: Mexico **launches** its 11-year war for independence against Spain.

1821: Mexico wins independence from Spain. For many years afterwards various groups in Mexico battle against each other for control of the country.

1836: Texas wins independence from Mexico.

1846: War breaks out between the United States and Mexico.

1858: Benito Juárez becomes president of Mexico.

1861: The U.S. Civil War begins. France, Spain, and Britain send troops to Mexico to collect on **outstanding debts.** Spain and Britain change their minds and send their troops home. France decides to stay and take over the country.

1862: Mexico's army defeats French invasion on May 5 at the Battle of Puebla, but cannot prevent the French from taking over the country. President Juárez flees to northern Mexico to avoid capture by French troops.

1864: France's emperor, Napoléon III, appoints Austrian archduke Ferdinand Maximilian to serve as emperor of Mexico. Maximilian and his wife, Carlota, rule for three years.

1865: The U.S. Civil War ends. American troops join the Mexican army in its war for independence from France.

1867: Mexican army defeats the French. Benito Juárez regains the presidency of Mexico.

1872: Benito Juárez dies on July 18.

2001: First Cinco de Mayo celebration is held at the White House.

Benito Juárez

> ✔ **Reading Check**
>
> 1. **Recall facts** When did the U.S. Civil War begin?
> 2. **Recall facts** In what year did Benito Juárez regain the presidency of Mexico?
> 3. **Analyze cause and effect** Why did France, Spain, and Britain send troops to Mexico?

---

launches starts
outstanding debts money that is owed to someone

● Apply the Reading Strategy

Tell Fact from Opinion

Now that you have read "Celebrating Cinco de Mayo," you are ready to complete the Reading Strategy graphic organizer.

1. Review the **Reading Strategy** on page 251.
2. Copy the chart.
3. Look back at the reading. Find **facts** and **opinions**.
4. Write the **facts** and **opinions** in the chart.

Fact	Opinion
In Mexico, Cinco de Mayo is celebrated with events organized by the Mexican government.	The Cinco de Mayo display of courage and purpose is a source of pride for all freedom-loving people.

● Academic Vocabulary

Vocabulary for the Reading Comprehension Questions

Word	Explanation	Sample Sentence	Visual Cue
classify *verb*	to divide things into groups so that similar things are in the same group	I like to **classify** my movies by genre.	

Draw a picture and write a sentence for the word.

✓ Checkpoint

What does **classify** mean? Explain in your own words.

Vocabulary Log

Reading Comprehension Questions

Think and Discuss

1. **Recall facts** What historical event does Cinco de Mayo celebrate?

2. **Describe** Describe how people celebrate this event using at least two Key Vocabulary words.

3. **Classify** Some Cinco de Mayo celebrations are serious ceremonies, but others are more like parties. What kind of celebration is the one that takes place on Olvera Street?

4. **Identify main ideas** Reread the part of the text under the heading "Different Meanings to Different People." What is the main idea?

5. **Compare to your experience** Have you ever participated in a Cinco de Mayo celebration? What was it like? If you have not celebrated Cinco de Mayo before, what is the most similar celebration you have taken part in?

6. **Revisit the Reading Focus Questions** Go back to page 252 and discuss the questions.

Workbook page 172

Independent Practice CD-ROM/Online

Text Element

Author's Perspective

Every author has **opinions** and attitudes about the subjects he or she writes about. These **opinions** and attitudes are the **author's perspective.** When you read, ask the following questions to discover the author's perspective.

1. Does the author describe his or her feelings about the subject? What are they?

2. What do you know about the author's background? Why do you think the author chose to write about the subject?

3. What kinds of words does the author use? What can the author's words tell you about his or her perspective?

Scan the reading. Find sentences that show the author's **opinions** and attitudes about Cinco de Mayo and write them in a chart like the one below. What does each sentence tell you about the author's perspective? Record your answers in the chart.

Sentence	Author's Perspective
All people who celebrate this wonderful holiday will find that it has even more meaning when they understand its history.	The author thinks Cinco de Mayo is a wonderful, meaningful holiday. He seems to feel that people should learn more about it.

✓ Checkpoint

1. What is **author's perspective**?

2. How can you discover the author's perspective in a text?

Workbook page 173

Independent Practice CD-ROM/Online

Legend of the Dreamcatcher

● About the Reading

In "Celebrating Cinco de Mayo," you read about how a Mexican holiday is celebrated in the United States. The story you are about to read is a legend from another culture, the Chippewa Native Americans. A dreamcatcher is an object made by the Chippewa. "Legend of the Dreamcatcher" tells where the dreamcatcher comes from.

● Build Background

The Chippewa

The Chippewa were once one of the largest groups of Native Americans in North America. They lived in the Great Lakes area of what is now the United States and Canada. The traditional way of life of the Chippewa included hunting and fishing. They also farmed corn, beans, and squash and gathered wild rice. Today, some Chippewa live in cities, while others still earn money hunting, fishing, and making traditional arts and crafts.

● Vocabulary From the Reading

Use Context to Determine Meaning

Look at the **highlighted** words in the sentences below. Use the context to help you find the meaning of each word.

1. The insect became **entangled** in the spider's web and could not escape.
2. The dewdrops **glisten** on the grass when the sun hits them. They sparkle like little pieces of glass.
3. Even though she didn't know the words to the song, she was able to **hum** the melody.
4. They ran through the meadow trying to **snare** butterflies in their nets.
5. I could hear my brother **stomp** his feet to try to get the mud off his boots.

Key Vocabulary

- entangled
- glisten
- hum
- snare
- stomp

✓Checkpoint

1. Which two Key Vocabulary words have similar meanings? Explain the differences in their meanings.
2. Which two words are onomatopoeias?

Vocabulary Log

Workbook page 174

Independent Practice CD-ROM/Online

● Reading Strategy

Ask Questions

Asking questions will help you understand what happens in a story. You should ask questions before, while, and after reading.

1. Preview the story you are about to read. Look at the title and the pictures. What questions do you have?

2. As you read, stop after every paragraph. Ask questions about what you have read, and look for answers.

3. When you are finished, ask further questions about the reading.

● Text Genre

Legend: Native American Legend

A **legend** is a story that has been passed down from generation to generation. Legends often include some real events and some events that are made up. Many cultures have legends. "Legend of the Dreamcatcher" comes from the Chippewa Native Americans.

Native American legends often have the features below.

Native American Legend	
personification of animals	animal characters who speak and act like people
moral	lesson based on ideas about what is right or wrong

● Reading Focus Questions

As you read, think about these questions.

1. How does the reading relate to the theme of "cultures and traditions"?

2. Why do the Chippewa people pass down this legend from generation to generation?

3. What is the purpose of the dreamcatcher? Why is it a useful gift?

✓**Checkpoint**

1. How does asking questions help you understand a reading?

2. What is a **legend**?

Workbook
pages 175–176

Independent Practice
CD-ROM/Online

Reading Strategy

Ask Questions
Look at the title of this reading. Ask a question about the reading based on the title.

Legend of the Dreamcatcher

1   A spider was quietly spinning his web in his own space. It was beside the sleeping space of Nokomis, the grandmother. Each day, Nokomis watched the spider at work, quietly spinning away. One day as she was watching him, her grandson came in. "Nokomis-iya!" he shouted, glancing at the spider. He **stomped** over to the spider, picked up a shoe, and went to hit it.

2   "No-keegwa," the old lady whispered, "don't hurt him."

3   "Nokomis, why do you protect the spider?" asked the little boy.

4   The old lady smiled, but did not answer. When the boy left, the spider went to the old woman and thanked her for saving his life. He said to her, "For many days you have watched me spin and weave my web. You have admired my work. In return for saving my life, I will give you a gift."

5   He smiled his special spider smile and moved away, spinning as he went.

A Chippewa woman

A spider's web

6   Soon the moon **glistened** on a magical silvery web moving gently in the window. "See how I spin?" he said. "See and learn, for each web will **snare** bad dreams. Only good dreams will go through the small hole. This is my gift to you. Use it so that only good dreams will be remembered. The bad dreams will become hopelessly **entangled** in the web."

7   Sleep well sweet child
     Don't **worry your head**
     Your dreamcatcher is **humming**
     Above your bed

8   Listen so softly
     I know you can hear
     The tone of beyond
     Close to your ear

9   Love is alive
     And living in you
     Beyond all your troubles
     Where good dreams are true

Reading Strategy

Ask Questions Ask a question about the text on this page.

Reading Check

1. **Recall facts** What is the spider's gift to Nokomis?
2. **Recall facts** How do good dreams get through the dreamcatcher?
3. **Identify literary elements** What features of poetry can you identify in the spider's poem? How is tone or meaning conveyed through these elements?

---

worry your head worry

Dreamcatchers

10   An ancient Chippewa tradition
      The dream net has been made
      For many generations
      Where spirit dreams have played.

11   Hung above the **cradle board,**
      Or in the **lodge** up high,
      The dream net catches bad dreams,
      While good dreams slip on by.

12   Bad dreams become entangled
      Among the **sinew thread.**
      Good dreams slip through the center hole,
      While you dream upon your bed.

13   This is an ancient legend,
      Since dreams will never cease,
      Hang this dream net above your bed,
      Dream on, and be at peace.

Reading Strategy

Ask Questions When you finish reading, ask a question about what you have read.

---

cradle board baby carrier used by some Native Americans
lodge a kind of house where some Native Americans lived
sinew thread thread made out of the material that connects an animal's muscle to its bone

After Reading 2

● Reading Comprehension Questions

Think and Discuss

1. **Recall** facts What does the dreamcatcher do to bad dreams?

2. **Summarize** Summarize what happens in the story. Use at least three Key Vocabulary words.

3. **Analyze** What is the moral, or lesson, of the story?

4. **Speculate** Why do you think Nokomis protects the spider?

5. **State your** opinion Do you think Nokomis does the right thing when she saves the spider? Why or why not?

6. **Revisit the Reading Focus Questions** Go back to page 263 and discuss the questions.

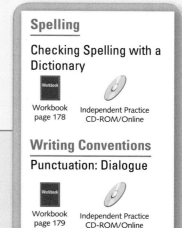

Workbook page 177   Independent Practice CD-ROM/Online

Spelling

Checking Spelling with a Dictionary

Workbook page 178   Independent Practice CD-ROM/Online

Writing Conventions

Punctuation: Dialogue

Workbook page 179   Independent Practice CD-ROM/Online

🔄 Connect Readings 1 and 2

You have read two readings on the theme of cultures and traditions: "Celebrating Cinco de Mayo" and "Legend of the Dreamcatcher." Use these activities to make connections between the readings.

1. With a partner, use this chart to compare the two readings.

Reading title	What is the text genre?	What is the reading about?	Which reading includes facts? Which includes figurative language?	What was the most interesting part of the reading? Why?
Celebrating Cinco de Mayo				
Legend of the Dreamcatcher				

2. With a partner, ask and answer these questions.

   a. How is the spider in "Legend of the Dreamcatcher" similar to the Mexican forces at the Battle of Puebla?

   b. Which selection did you like better? Why?

3. Revisit the Chapter Focus Question How do the stories people tell **reflect** their cultures? Use examples from "Celebrating Cinco de Mayo" and "Legend of the Dreamcatcher" to answer this question.

Listening and Speaking

Give a Presentation with Visual Aids

In "Legend of the Dreamcatcher," you learned about a story told by Chippewa Native Americans. Work with a small group to identify and learn about a Native American group. Then present what you learned using visual aids. Visual aids are pictures or objects that help people understand your presentation.

1. Work with a small group. As a group, decide which Native American group you want to research.

    a. Each person in the group should choose a different part of that nation's culture to learn about. For example, you can choose among food, traditions, where they lived before reservations, or clothing.

    b. Ask questions about what you want to research and use classroom resources and the Internet to learn about the part of the Native American culture that you chose. To make sure you understand the information, take notes in your own words.

    c. As you do your research, think about images or objects that might make good visual aids.

2. Each person in the group will present his or her information to the class.

    a. Choose a main idea to focus on.

    b. Note important details from your research. Use note cards to write down important points you want to make.

    c. Choose at least one visual aid to show what in your opinion is the most interesting thing you have learned. It could be an object, a picture from a book, or a poster you make yourself. It should show the information in detail.

3. Practice your presentation with other members of your group.

    a. Listen to other members of the group present their ideas.

    b. Tell other group members what you liked about their presentations and ways they could improve them.

4. Present to the class.

    a. As a group, decide who will present first, second, third, etc.

    b. Listen to the presentations of other groups.

5. Discuss the following questions as a class:

    a. Did visual aids help you understand the presentations better? How?

    b. What were some of the visual aids you liked best?

    c. What were some other visual aids that groups could have used?

Phrases for Conversation

Directing Attention to Visual Aids

You can see in this photo that . . .

This chart helps us understand that . . .

With this slide, I'd like to make the point that . . .

If you compare these two photos, you will see that . . .

Reading Fluency
Echo Reading

Echo reading helps you learn to read with expression.

1. Listen as your teacher reads a line from the poem at the end of "Legend of the Dreamcatcher."
   a. Follow along as your teacher reads.
   b. Pay attention to the expression in your teacher's voice.
2. Read the same line back. Try to read the line with the same expression your teacher used. Be sure to read it accurately as well.
3. Continue through the poem, repeating each line after your teacher.

Vocabulary Development
Foreign Words and Phrases

The English language uses many foreign words, or words that come from other languages. For example, many cooking words come from French, such as *sauté* (lightly fry over high heat) and *purée* (crush).

In "Celebrating Cinco de Mayo," you read some words that were borrowed from the Spanish language. They are defined in the chart below.

Spanish Word	Definition
mariachi	a Mexican music band
sombrero	a high hat with a wide brim
fiesta	a party, feast, or celebration

The words and phrases below were borrowed from other languages. Work with a partner to guess which definition goes with each numbered word or phrase.

1. sushi (Japanese)
2. pizza (Italian)
3. boutique (French)
4. kindergarten (German)
5. skunk (Abnaki-Native American)

a. flat bread dough covered with cheese, tomato sauce, and herbs
b. a small animal that sprays a bad-smelling liquid when frightened
c. school for young children
d. small shop
e. rice with pieces of seafood and vegetables

✓**Checkpoint**

1. What does it mean to say a word is "foreign"?
2. Use one or two of the borrowed Spanish words in a sentence.

Vocabulary Log

Workbook page 180

Independent Practice CD-ROM/Online

● Grammar

Indefinite Pronouns

Indefinite pronouns refer to unspecified people or things. Most indefinite pronouns are singular and take singular verbs.

another	either	much	one
anybody	everybody	neither	other
anyone	everyone	nobody	somebody
anything	everything	no one	someone
each	little	nothing	something

Everyone has a chance to go.

Each of the men wants to win.

Nobody hears the door slam.

Some indefinite pronouns are plural and take plural verbs. These include: **both, few, many, others, several.**

Both seem like good choices.

Many of the students are in the classroom.

Some indefinite pronouns are either singular or plural and take either singular or plural verbs, depending on what the indefinite pronoun refers to. These include: **all, any, most, none, some.**

All of the snow has melted.

All of the students are reading.

Some of the guests eat with chopsticks.

Some of the food is on the table.

Grammar Expansion

Using Indefinite Pronouns: Avoiding Double Negatives

Workbook page 183

Independent Practice CD-ROM/Online

✓ Checkpoint

1. Which of the following is not a singular pronoun? **each, somebody, several, no one**

2. Give two examples of a pronoun that can be either singular or plural depending on the phrase that follows.

Practice the Grammar Look at the indefinite pronoun in each sentence. Then choose the correct singular or plural verb.

1. Most of the Cinco de Mayo festivals in America (include / includes) Latin music bands and theater.

2. There are many people in the U.S. with Mexican heritage. Some of them (live / lives) in Los Angeles.

3. But not all of them (does / do).

4. Both of the poems (is / are) about the dreamcatcher.

Use the Grammar Independently Write three sentences using three different indefinite pronouns from the list above.

Workbook page 181

Independent Practice CD-ROM/Online

● Grammar

Classifying Sentences by Purpose

Each sentence you speak or write has a purpose. It is either to make a statement (**declarative**), to ask a question (**interrogative**), to express strong feeling (**exclamatory**), or to give an order (**imperative**). Note the punctuation that is used for each of these four sentence types.

Sentence	Purpose	Examples
declarative	to make a statement	The decision angered her parents.
interrogative	to ask a question	Was he right after all?
exclamatory	to express a strong feeling	Oh, I just made it!
imperative	to give an order	Come with me.

Practice the Grammar Read each sentence. Decide what the purpose of the sentence is, then tell if it is interrogative, declarative, exclamatory, or imperative.

1. Nokomis, why do you protect the spider?
2. Write a poem that tells about your culture.
3. He smiled his special spider smile and moved away.
4. See how I spin?
5. I had a bad dream!
6. Use it so that only good dreams will be remembered.
7. The dreamcatcher is so pretty!

Use the Grammar Independently Each of the following sentence beginnings corresponds to a specific kind of sentence. Complete each according to the type of sentence it is. Remember to add the correct punctuation.

1. Don't . . .
2. I think that . . .
3. What a . . .
4. Why did he . . .

Grammar Expansion

Tag Questions

Workbook page 184   Independent Practice CD-ROM/Online

✓ **Checkpoint**

1. How is a **declarative** sentence different from an **exclamatory** sentence?

2. What kind of sentence asks a question?

Writing Assignment
Write an Informative Essay

Writing Prompt

Think about a holiday that you celebrate and research information about it. Then write a three-paragraph essay about the holiday. Make sure to include information such as *who* celebrates the holiday, *what* event is being celebrated, *where* the holiday is observed, *when* the holiday takes place, *why* you celebrate the holiday, and *how long* the celebration lasts. Your essay should include indefinite pronouns and at least two of the four sentence types.

Write Your Essay

1. **Read the student model.** This will help you understand how to write your informative essay.

Student Model

Patriots' Day

Do you know what Patriots' Day is? Each year on the third Monday in April, this holiday commemorates the first battles of the Revolutionary War, which took place on April 19, 1775. While the Fourth of July is a national holiday in the United States, Patriots' Day is celebrated mainly in Massachusetts.

On this day in April 1775, many British soldiers marched toward Concord, Massachusetts to arrest revolutionaries and take supplies. Along the way, they met resistance from soldiers who were known as the Minutemen and were forced to retreat. The first shot of the Revolution is widely known as the "Shot Heard 'Round the World."

On Patriots' Day in Boston, the schools are closed and the Boston Marathon takes place. It can be very exciting! I celebrate this special day because it reminds me, and everyone in Massachusetts, of the part our state played in the American Revolution.

Workbook
page 185

Independent Practice
CD-ROM/Online

2. Brainstorm ideas.

a. Think of the holiday you want to write about.

b. Make a list of the answers to the *who, what, where, when, why,* and *how long* questions in the writing prompt.

3. Write your essay.
First, state the purpose of your essay. In addition to the answers to the questions from the prompt, be sure to use different types of sentences in your essay. Also use descriptive nouns, adjectives, and verbs to give the reader a visual image of the event. End your essay with a conclusion that summarizes the most important ideas in your essay.

4. Revise.
Reread your essay. Revise your essay if any ideas are not clear or complete.

Use the **editing and proofreading symbols** on page 455 to mark any changes you want to make.

5. Edit.
Use the **Writing Checklist** to help you find problems and errors.

Writing Checklist

1. I identified a holiday that I celebrate.

2. I answered the *who, what, where, when, why,* and *how long* questions.

3. I used indefinite pronouns in my essay.

4. I used at least two of the four sentence types.

5. I used correct spelling, grammar, and punctuation.

Writing Support

Mechanics

Sentence Punctuation

- Use a period at the end of declarative statements.

    Example: It is my favorite holiday.

- Use an exclamation point at the end of exclamatory sentences.

    Example: I can't believe it's already here!

- Use a question mark at the end of interrogative sentences.

    Example: When is that holiday celebrated?

- You may use a period or an exclamation point at the end of imperative sentences, depending on how much emotion is being used.

    Example: Don't forget to decorate.

    Example: Open your present now!

Apply Check the punctuation at the end of the sentences in your essay. Did you punctuate them correctly?

Workbook
pages 186–188

Independent Practice
CD-ROM/Online

Progress Check

How well did you understand this chapter? Try to answer the questions. If necessary, go back to the pages listed for a review.

Skills	Skills Assessment Questions	Pages to Review
Vocabulary From the Readings	What do these words mean? • **acknowledge, cherish, enrich, establish, reflect, symbolize**	250
	• **entangled, glisten, hum, snare, stomp**	262
Academic Vocabulary	What do these academic vocabulary words mean? • fact, opinion, proof	251
	• classify	260
Reading Strategies	What is the difference between fact and opinion?	251
	How will asking questions help you while reading?	263
Text Genres	What is the text genre of "Celebrating Cinco de Mayo"?	252
	What is the text genre of "Legend of the Dreamcatcher"?	263
Reading Comprehension	What is "Celebrating Cinco de Mayo" about?	261
	What is "Legend of the Dreamcatcher" about?	267
Text Element	What is **author's perspective**? What questions can you ask yourself to figure out the author's perspective?	261
Spelling	Use a dictionary to correct the spelling of these words: simpal, jeneral, dout.	267
Writing Conventions	What punctuation is missing from this sentence? "See you tomorrow he said with a grin.	267
Listening and Speaking	**Phrases for Conversation** What phrases would you use to direct your audience's attention to visual aids?	268
Vocabulary Development	Choose three foreign words or phrases you learned and use each of them in a sentence.	269
Grammar	What is an **indefinite pronoun**?	270
	What are the four sentences classified by purpose?	271
Writing Support: Mechanics	Punctuate this sentence: When is Thanksgiving	273

Assessment Practice

Read this passage. Then answer Questions 1 through 4.

Celebrating Chinese New Year

1   Many countries celebrate the New Year on January 1. The Chinese New Year is different; it begins on the first full moon of the year and lasts for 15 days. The Chinese New Year is a very interesting and unique celebration. It combines many traditional foods, decorations, and beliefs.

2   There is a special dinner on the day before the celebration begins, and families often prepare fish. Fish symbolizes abundance—it shows that everyone will have more than enough food for the year. This dinner is also an occasion for families to spend time together. Many people decorate their homes with flowers, oranges, trays of delicious dried fruit, and red paper that has short poems to welcome the New Year. One belief is that a house must be cleaned *before* the New Year. If you use a broom on New Year's Day, you may sweep away good luck.

3   For many Chinese people, the New Year is the most important holiday of the year. Chinese communities all over the world cherish the tradition.

1 What does <u>cherish</u> mean in this sentence?

> **Chinese communities all over the world <u>cherish</u> the tradition.**

A   value   B   dislike

C   accept   D   make

2 What is an example of an opinion in this passage?

A   It shows that everyone will have more than enough food for the year.

B   It begins on the first full moon of the year and lasts for 15 days.

C   One belief is that a house must be cleaned before the New Year.

D   The Chinese New Year is a very interesting and unique celebration that combines many traditional foods, decorations, and beliefs.

3 What is the author's perspective?

A   Chinese New Year is a boring holiday.

B   Chinese New Year is special because it is different from other celebrations.

C   More people should celebrate Chinese New Year.

D   People should eat fish to bring good luck.

4 What is the genre of this text?

A   folktale

B   poem

C   historical nonfiction

D   expository essay

Writing on Demand: Informative Essay

Write a three-paragraph essay about a style of music that you know. Include information about how it sounds, how it is performed, and what makes it different from other styles. **(20 minutes)**

Apply & Extend

Objectives

Listening and Speaking
Deliver an informative presentation

Media
Evaluate an editorial

Writing
Write an autobiographical narrative

Projects

Independent Reading

● Listening and Speaking Workshop
Deliver an Informative Presentation

> **Topic**
>
> When you give an **informative presentation,** you give your audience facts about a topic and explain these facts using details and examples. You will deliver an informative presentation about how one culture celebrates the start of a new year.

1. **Brainstorm**
   a. Think about some cultures you would like to learn more about. Make a list.
   b. Look at your list. Choose one culture to focus on.

2. **Plan**
   a. Start by writing questions about new year traditions. What do you want to know about how people of the culture you chose celebrate the new year? Write each question on a separate note card.
   b. Research answers to the questions you wrote. Use reference materials in your school library, such as books, magazines, and encyclopedias. Search online sources such as Web sites and online encyclopedias for further information. Use note cards to take notes on the information you find.

3. **Organize**

   Put your note cards in the order in which you want to present the information. If possible, include visual aids to make the presentation more interesting. For example, you may wish to include photographs or drawings of traditional new year ceremonies, clothing, or foods. Look in magazines and online for your visual aids.

4. **Practice, Present, and Evaluate**
   a. Use your note cards and visual aids to practice your presentation.
   b. Give your presentation to the class. Maintain eye contact with your listeners. Speak slowly and clearly.
   c. Ask the class for feedback. Use the **Speaking Self-Evaluation** to evaluate your presentation. Use the **Active Listening Evaluation** to evaluate and discuss your classmates' presentations.

Speaking Self-Evaluation

1. I identified the culture and explained its new year traditions.

2. I included important facts and details in my presentation.

3. I used visual aids to make my presentation more interesting.

4. I spoke clearly and loudly enough for people to hear me.

5. I looked at the audience throughout my presentation.

Active Listening Evaluation

1. Your presentation was well organized.

2. The presentation clearly explained how the culture celebrates the new year.

3. The most interesting thing I learned from your presentation was _____ .

4. I think your presentation needed more information about _____ .

Media Workshop

Evaluate an Editorial

A newspaper editorial is an article in a newspaper that gives the writer's opinion about a current event or issue.

1. Find a few different newspapers in your library. Look for an editorial in each newspaper. Choose an editorial on a topic that interests you.

2. Answer the following questions to evaluate the editorial.

   a. What is the subject of the editorial?

   b. What opinion does the writer express?

   c. What reasons does the writer give for his or her opinion?

   d. Does the writer give enough evidence to support this opinion? Why or why not? Identify any unsupported inferences or fallacious (incorrect) reasoning.

   e. Were you persuaded by the editorial? Why or why not?

3. Present your evaluation of the editorial to the class.

UNIT 4

Apply & Extend

Writing Suggestion

Try to use prepositional phrases and appositives in your writing.

Use independent and dependent clauses in your narrative.

● Writing Workshop

Write an Autobiographical Narrative

In an **autobiographical narrative,** you describe events that took place in your own life. You tell about what happened and how you felt about it. Autobiographical narratives often include descriptions and details that help the reader understand what happened.

Writing Prompt

In this unit, you read about people discovering customs from other cultures. Write an autobiographical narrative about a time you experienced a custom from another culture. Or, write about a time you participated in a custom from your own culture, such as the celebration of a holiday or a key life event.

PREWRITE

1. Read the student model on the next page. It will help you understand how to write an autobiographical narrative.
2. Think of a time when you experienced a custom from another culture. Alternatively, think about a time you participated in a custom from your own culture, such as a holiday celebration.
3. Answer the following questions. Take notes on your answers.
   a. What custom did you participate in?
   b. What culture does the custom come from?
   c. What is the significance of the custom?
   d. How did you feel about participating in the custom?

WRITE A DRAFT

1. Write the introduction. The purpose of the introduction is to give your readers a general idea of the story you are going to tell. Try to write an introduction that will draw the readers in and make them want to read your story.
2. The next few paragraphs will tell your story. Include sensory details and concrete language (words that refer to objects we see, hear, taste, touch, or smell) in your descriptions of what happened and how you felt as these events took place.
3. Write the conclusion. Tell whether participating in this custom was a positive or negative experience and why.

Student Model

An autobiographical narrative uses the first person.

Jia Yuan

My First Visit to the Medhas' Home

When I was in sixth grade, I became friends with a new girl in our class. Her name was Amala Medha, and her family had just moved here from India. We did lots of things together after school, but we had never been to each other's homes.

Introduction

The beginning of your narrative should draw the reader in.

A month after school started, our parents met at our school's open house. When my parents came home that evening, they told me that Mr. and Mrs. Medha had invited our family to their home for dinner the next Saturday.

In an autobiographical narrative, you tell about your thoughts and feelings.

I was excited and nervous at the same time. I knew that Amala's family ate different kinds of food than our family did. I wondered what the food would taste like because I had never had Indian food before. After giving it some thought, I decided to think of it as an adventure. It would be fun to try something new!

On Saturday evening we arrived at Amala's home. The entire family greeted us at the door. Mrs. Medha invited us to sit down on three wooden chairs near the front door. I thought it was odd that we weren't invited to sit in the living room, which is what I am used to doing. But I took my seat next to my mother and father.

Amala's sister, Nila, disappeared for a minute. When she came back, she was carrying a big bowl of water and three small towels. First she washed and dried each of our hands. That didn't seem too strange. But when she bent down and started to remove my father's shoes, we were really surprised! Nila then washed and dried his feet. Next she did the same for my mother and me. I wondered if the Medhas thought we weren't clean enough to enter their home.

Mrs. Medha must have realized our confusion, so she explained their custom as we put our shoes back on. She said that when guests come to visit, they get a lot of respect and attention. The washing is a custom that honors guests.

We then ate a delicious dinner. After we got home, my parents said they thought it was nice to be treated as honored guests in the Medhas' home. I agreed completely!

REVISE

1. Read through your draft. Check to make sure your story is well organized. Did you remember to describe events in the order in which they occurred?

2. Exchange your narrative with a partner. Your partner will use the **Peer Review Checklist** to review your narrative.

3. Revise your draft. Use the **Revising and Editing Checklist.** Remove any details that do not fit in the story. Add information where it is needed.

4. Use the **editing and proofreading symbols** on page 455 to help you mark the changes you need to make.

EDIT

1. Use the **Revising and Editing Checklist** to reevaluate your essay.

2. Fix any errors in grammar, spelling, capitalization, and punctuation.

Peer Review Checklist

1. The writer's description of the custom that he or she participated in was clear and easy to understand.

2. The beginning of the narrative was interesting and made me want to read more.

3. The writer included details that helped me visualize what happened in the story.

4. My favorite part of the story was _____ .

5. One part of the story that could be improved was _____ .

Revising and Editing Checklist

1. I described the events that took place in chronological order.

2. I included all events that were important to the story.

3. I described how the events made me feel.

4. I used prepositional phrases and appositives.

5. I used independent and dependent clauses.

PUBLISH

1. Write your narrative in your best handwriting or use a computer.

2. Read your narrative to the class. As you tell your story, think about how the tone and pitch of your voice affect the feeling of your story.

Projects

Choose one or more of the following projects to explore the theme of cultures and traditions further.

PROJECT 1

Write a Recipe for a Traditional Dish.

1. Choose a traditional dish from your culture. If you need help, ask relatives which dishes are traditional in your culture.

2. Write a recipe for the traditional dish. Be sure to list the ingredients and write detailed instructions for each step in the recipe.

3. Trade recipes with another student. With the help of a parent or guardian, try to cook the other student's recipe at home.

PROJECT 2

Read and Discuss a Play.

1. Go to your school or local library and look for Lensey Namioka's play *Herbal Nightmare*.

2. Read it and take notes about the characters, plot, and setting.

3. Discuss the play with a partner. Point out the similarities and differences between *Herbal Nightmare* and "The All-American Slurp."

PROJECT 3

Research and Write About a Famous Native American Person.

1. Choose a person who played an important role in the history of a Native American nation.

2. Research the person's life using resources in your library and on the Internet. What was the person like? What contributions did he or she make?

3. Write a poem, a descriptive paragraph, or a scene from a play about the person. Make your decision based on how you think you can best portray the person. Write about an important event that the person took part in.

4. Present your poem to the class, or act out your scene with other students.

PROJECT 4

Compare Body Language in Different Cultures.

1. Interview classmates from two different cultures. Ask them questions about gestures and body language in each culture. Think of questions about eye contact, personal space, and the meanings of gestures.

2. Be sure to take notes during the interviews.

3. After the interviews, organize your information using a chart, outline, Venn diagram, or idea web.

4. Write a paragraph that compares and contrasts gestures and body language in different cultures.

Apply & Extend

● Independent Reading

Explore the theme of cultures and traditions further by reading one or more of these books.

Cinco de Mayo: A Mexican Holiday about Unity and Pride by James Garcia, Child's World, 2003.

This book tells about how people celebrate the Mexican holiday Cinco de Mayo. The author includes descriptions of how the holiday is celebrated and an explanation of the holiday's history and importance.

Motherland: A Novel by Vineeta Vijayaraghavan, Soho Press, 2001.

Fifteen-year-old Maya's mother sends her back to India to spend the summer. At first she feels out of place. As time passes, she grows close to her grandmother. Maya realizes she must come to terms with her feelings about India, the United States, and her own identity.

Ashanti to Zulu: African Traditions by Margaret Musgrove, Dutton Books, 1992.

This book describes 26 African tribes—one for each letter of the alphabet—and their customs. Illustrations show the people in typical dress, as well as their land, animals, and homes. The book also includes a map of the African continent showing where each tribe lives.

Celebrating a Quinceañera: A Latina's 15th Birthday Celebration by Diane Hoyt-Goldsmith, Holiday House, 2002.

Ten-year-old Ariana helps her cousin Cynthia prepare for her upcoming quinceañera. The book takes a photo-essay approach to telling how this tradition is celebrated. The author explains the importance of the quinceañera and gives translations of Spanish words used in the text.

Rio Grande Stories by Carolyn Meyer, Harcourt, 2001.

As part of a fundraising project for their school, a group of seventh graders from Native American, Hispanic, African, and Anglo cultures in Albuquerque, New Mexico, write a book of stories about their individual cultures and traditions. In the process, they learn more about their heritage.

● Writing: Revise and Edit

MILESTONES TRACKER

Read this rough draft of a student's version of a Native American legend, which may contain errors. Then answer Questions 1 through 4.

How Mole Lost His Sight

(1) In the beginning of the world, people and animals got along well and spent every day together by the river. (2) Everyone respected and enjoyed each other's company, everyone except Mole. (3) He would stay in his hole all day long and build tunnels or look for worms and other bugs to eat.

(4) Many times, when everyone went to sleep in the evening, Mole would wake up. (5) Sometimes he would go to the river. (6) Or he would make more holes. (7) Mole cherished building holes.

(8) Anyone began to wonder why Mole never wanted to spend time with them during the day. (9) One afternoon they asked, "Will Mole ever come out to see us during the day?" (10) They all stood around his hole and called to Mole. (11) Mole poked his head out of his hole. (12) He had never seen the afternoon sun. (13) He cried, "The sun is too bright." (14) At the time, Mole could see quite well, just like everyone else. (15) But because he was not used to the sun, his eyes shrank until they were very small. (16) Today, Mole's eyes are still very small; he can only see changes in light, and not much else.

---

1 **What type of sentence is sentence 1?**

A interrogative   B declarative

C exclamatory   D imperative

2 **How can you combine sentences 5 and 6?**

A Sometimes he would go to the river or made more holes.

B Sometimes he would go to the river to make more holes.

C Sometimes he would go to make more holes.

D Sometimes he would go to and make more holes.

3 **How can you correct sentence 8?**

A Change *anyone* to *no one*.

B Change the period to a question mark.

C Change *anyone* to *everyone*.

D Change the period to a semicolon.

4 **How can you improve sentence 13?**

A Change the period to an exclamation point.

B Change "He cried" to "He said."

C Change the period to a question mark.

D Change "He cried" to "He cried!"

⏱ Writing on Demand: Short Story

Write a short story that is a legend explaining a part of nature. You may want to explain why an animal looks the way it does, or why something occurs. Vary the types of sentences you use. **(20 minutes)**

● Reading

Read this expository text. Then answer Questions 1 through 8.

Independence Day Celebrations

1   Many countries around the world have special days when they celebrate their independence from another country. July 4 is a very important day in the United States; it is when we recognize our independence from England. Many people think that Cinco de Mayo is when Mexico celebrates its independence from Spain. However, Mexican independence is actually celebrated on September 16.

2   Each year on September 16, the Mexican government recognizes the day that the struggle to be independent from Spain began. On this day in 1810, Miguel Hidalgo, a priest in a small community, spoke against the government to a large audience. Hidalgo was of Spanish descent, but grew up in a hacienda, or a large estate, where there were many workers and people of different social classes. Because he could speak several native languages, he was able to communicate with many different people who helped him in gathering support. He asked the community to join him in breaking away from the Mexican government, which was controlled by Spain. At that time, Mexico was a Spanish colony. There was a new king in Spain, and people in Mexico took this opportunity to try to win their independence. Many of the people born in Mexico, even those of Spanish descent, fought against the Spaniards who lived there because they wanted their freedom. Hidalgo led an army and fought in the beginning of the war, but was caught by the Spanish and killed on July 30, 1811. Mexico finally won the war in 1821, 11 years after it began. Mexico was the first of all the Spanish-speaking countries in the Americas to establish political freedom.

3   September 16 is acknowledged and celebrated every year in Mexico. The night before the celebration, the president of Mexico rings the bell and shouts the same words Miguel Hidalgo did in 1810. The next day, the ceremony includes a parade in Mexico City.

1 What does the word <u>acknowledged</u> mean in this sentence from paragraph 3?

> September 16 is <u>acknowledged</u> and celebrated every year in Mexico.

A recognized

B talked about

C symbolized

D summarized

2 Read the following sentence from paragraph 3. What does the word <u>ceremony</u> mean?

> The next day, the <u>ceremony</u> includes a parade in Mexico City.

A election

B independence

C game

D event

3 Why is Miguel Hidalgo remembered?

A He was the president of Mexico.

B He fought in the war's last battle.

C He said the important words that started the war.

D He was sent from Spain to fight Mexico.

4 According to the text, what event motivated the people of Mexico to fight for their independence?

A They wanted more Spaniards in the government.

B There was a new king in Spain.

C Miguel Hidalgo wanted to be king.

D The people wanted to have a bigger army.

5 In paragraph 1, what is the author's perspective on celebrating a country's independence?

A The parades are often fun.

B It is something that should be celebrated more often.

C Every country should have an Independence Day.

D These are important days for the people of the country.

6 Based on what you know about the events of the reading, what language does the word <u>hacienda</u> in paragraph 2 come from?

A Portuguese

B English

C Spanish

D Greek

7 Which of the following sentences includes an example of an appositive?

A Miguel Hidalgo, a priest in a small community, spoke against the government to a large audience.

B Mexico was the first of all the Spanish-speaking countries in the Americas to establish political freedom.

C However, Mexican independence is actually celebrated on September 16.

D At that time, Mexico was a Spanish colony.

8 Who does the possessive pronoun <u>their</u> refer to in this sentence from paragraph 2?

> People in Mexico took this opportunity to try to win <u>their</u> independence.

A everyone fighting for independence

B the people of Spain

C people in Mexico

D Miguel Hidalgo's community

Making a Difference

Explore the Theme

1. **Making a difference** means doing something positive for another person or other people. How do the people in the images show they are **making a difference**? Describe what is happening in each of the pictures.
2. What do you do in your life to **make a difference** in the lives of others?

Theme Activity

With a partner, think of some services that your school offers. Then brainstorm ideas for new services that could be offered to students and to people in the community. Complete the chart below, then share your ideas with your classmates.

Service to Students	Service to Community

CHAPTER 1

Objectives

Reading Strategies
Describe mental images; Analyze text evidence

Listening and Speaking
Have a discussion

Grammar
Use present, past, and future perfect tenses

Writing
Write a business letter

Academic Vocabulary

image	attitude
	reveal

Academic Content

Navajo code talkers in World War II

Community service in the United States

Chapter Focus Questions

What kind of reward do you get when you help someone in need? Is the reward worth the effort?

Reading 1 **Literature**
Novel (excerpt)
CODE TALKER
by Joseph Bruchac

Reading 2 **Content:** Social Studies
Brochure
CITY YEAR

CODE TALKER

About the Reading

Many languages were spoken on the battlefields during World War II, including English, French, and Russian. In this excerpt from a novel you will learn how a Native American language, Navajo, played an important part in helping the Allies win the war.

A Navajo woman and girl in Monument Valley, Arizona

Build Background

Navajo Language

The narrator of *Code Talker* is a Navajo man who grew up speaking Navajo, a Native American language. The Navajo are the largest Native American tribe in the United States. Today there are approximately 150,000 speakers of Navajo; many speak English as well. The Navajo language is very complex. Many words have different meanings depending on the tones of the different parts of the word.

To the right is a photo of a code talker, one of the many Navajos who made a difference by serving in the Marine Corps during World War II and using the Navajo language to help win the war.

Dr. Samuel Billison speaking about his experience as a code talker

Use Prior Knowledge

Try to Break a Code

A code is a kind of system that changes a word or message into a form that cannot be easily understood. Codes come in all kinds of forms. Morse code, for example, is a system of dots and dashes that allows a telegraph machine, like the one shown here, to send and receive messages from far away. You can build or break a code by using your knowledge of language and numbers.

Look at the chart below. Can you use the alphabet and numbers from 0 to 9 to break the code and translate the phrases?

A	B	C	D	E	F	G	H	I	J	K	L	M	N	O	P	Q	R	S	T	U	V	W	X	Y	Z
0			3	4		6	7	8				b	c		e	f			B	C	D	E	F		H	

1. C78B c4BB064
2. 8B FA8CC4d
3. 8d 0d 40BH
4. 2e34 Ce 1A40a.

● Vocabulary From the Reading
Learn, Practice, and Use Independently

Key Vocabulary

accomplish

destination

emphasize

escort

stunned

Learn Vocabulary Use the context to determine the meaning of each Key Vocabulary word.

Graduating from high school was an important goal for me to **accomplish.** My next **destination** was college. When I went to visit one university, they had an **escort** give me a tour of the campus. I was **stunned** to see the size of the school! The counselor **emphasized** the importance of grades. I knew this would not be a problem for me; I study all the time.

Practice Vocabulary Match each Key Vocabulary word to the correct definition.

1. escort
2. stunned
3. destination
4. emphasize
5. accomplish

a. surprised or shocked; made speechless

b. place importance on

c. one who goes along with someone as a guide or companion

d. finish or achieve

e. place where someone is going or being sent

Use Vocabulary Independently Write a paragraph that uses each of the Key Vocabulary words.

✓ Checkpoint

1. If you could go on a vacation today, what **destination** would you choose?
2. What do you need to **accomplish** this week?

Vocabulary Log

Workbook page 189

Independent Practice CD-ROM/Online

Academic Vocabulary

Vocabulary for the Reading Strategy

Word	Explanation	Sample Sentence	Visual Cue
image *noun*	a mental picture of someone or something	When I think of my grandfather, the **image** of his kind and caring face comes to mind.	

Draw a picture and write a sentence for the word.

Reading Strategy

Describe Mental Images

Many stories include words that help you to make mental pictures as you read. When you create an **image** of the details you read about, it helps you to understand and remember what you have read.

Creating mental **images** allows readers to use all their senses to imagine the details in a story. You can create an **image** of how something sounds, smells, feels, or even tastes.

As you read, note the vivid details in the story. Use all your senses to create those details in your mind. When you finish, you will describe those **images** in the chart shown here.

Detail From the Story	Image

✓Checkpoint

1. What is an **image**?
2. How can a reader create mental **images** while reading?

● Text Genre

Novel

A **novel** is a long work of fiction. The characters and events in a novel are usually created by the author. Most novels share the features below.

Novel	
narrator	character or voice that tells a story
setting	where and when a story takes place
dialogue	the words that the characters speak; the words are in quotation marks (". . .")

● Meet the Author

Joseph Bruchac is a writer and a professional storyteller. He has written novels, nonfiction books, and picture books for his youngest audience. As a storyteller, Bruchac combines his knowledge of his own Native American culture with traditional tales and music, using flutes and drums in presentations across the United States. This award-winning author lives with his wife in the Adirondack Mountains of New York.

● Reading Focus Questions

As you read, think about these questions.

1. How does this reading connect to the theme of "making a difference"? Explain.
2. Why do you think Bruchac wrote about the code talkers?
3. Do you think it is important to read and listen to stories about historical events? Why or why not?

Checkpoint

1. What is a **novel**?
2. In a novel, who tells the story?

Workbook
page 191

Independent Practice
CD-ROM/Online

CODE TALKER

by Joseph Bruchac

1   "297th. Pack your gear. You're **shipping out**."

2   That is what the **sergeant** barked into our **barracks** the day after our graduation photo was taken.

3   That was the last thing we had expected. It was Sunday. All of the non-Indian Marines who had been in **boot camp** with us were leaving on **furloughs**. They were laughing and joking with each other as they headed for the gate to see friends and family or just go into town and have fun. But not us Navajos.

4   Some of those lucky guys, like my friend Georgia Boy, waved to us as our bus roared through the gate. I smiled and waved back at him, but my smile was an uncertain one. Why were we sixty-seven Indians being sent out this way, to some **destination** no one would tell us about? Were we finally going to begin that important but secret task only we Navajos would **accomplish**? Or was this some kind of punishment?

> **Reading Strategy**
>
> **Describe Mental Images** Visualize the barracks the Marines lived in. Describe the **image** that comes to mind.

---

shipping out leaving; being sent to another location
sergeant lower-level officer in the Marines
barracks buildings where soldiers live and train
boot camp a military training facility for new recruits
furloughs military vacations

> ✔ **Reading Check**
>
> 1. **Recall facts** Who is Georgia Boy?
> 2. **Make inferences** Why was the narrator's smile an uncertain one?
> 3. **Identify** Identify three facts about the narrator.

Reading Strategy

Describe Mental Images The narrator speaks directly to his grandchildren as he tells his story. Describe the image that comes to mind when you think about this moment.

5   Our trip wasn't long at all. They took us to Camp Elliott, a little north of San Diego. We were checked into our new barracks without a word of explanation about what we were going to do there. I didn't sleep well at all that night. At 7:00 the next morning, several non-coms, who were to be our **escorts**, arrived at our barracks. In military language, grandchildren, a "non-com" is a non-commissioned officer, anyone above the rank of a **private**, but no higher than a sergeant. We were lined up, put through **roll call**, and then marched off to breakfast. I could hardly eat and a lot of the other guys were just as nervous as I was, picking at their food. As soon as we had finished, we were **rounded up** again and **quick-marched** to a building with bars on all the windows and a strong door that our **escorts** unlocked and opened.

6   "Inside," the **escort** sergeant barked.

7   "Ah, they are taking us to jail," Henry Bahe whispered to me just before we went through the door.

8   He meant it as a joke, but I didn't laugh. My heart was beating faster. What was happening?

9   As soon as we were all inside, the **escort** sergeant shut the barred door and locked it behind him, leaving the rest of the Marines who had **escorted** us outside on guard. Then he led us down a long hall to another locked door.

---

private enlisted person with the lowest rank in the Marines
roll call calling out the list of names to determine who is present and absent
rounded up gathered
quick-marched made to march or walk quickly

10   It opened to a classroom, much like the ones I had sat in for endless hours at Indian **boarding school.** The blackboards, the rough wooden floor, the uncomfortable-looking chairs were almost exactly the same. Our escort—who had not set foot into the room—shut the door and once again I heard the sound of a lock clicking.

11   All that had happened to that point was strange, grandchildren, but it was not as strange as the words I then heard spoken to us from the front of the classroom.

12   "Be quiet. Be seated."

13   All of us Navajos turned immediately to look. Those words had been spoken in our native language! There, at the front of the class stood two Navajo men wearing the uniforms of Marines. One of them I recognized at once. It was Johnny Manuelito.

14   "This is Corporal Johnny Manuelito. I am Corporal John Benally," said the second Navajo man who stood in front of us, speaking in English. "We will be your instructors."

15   I was **stunned.** The idea of a Navajo being a teacher was new to me. Yes, grandchildren, I know that many of your teachers are Navajos now. But it was different back then.

> **Reading Strategy**

Describe Mental Images What image comes to mind when you visualize the classroom?

✓
Reading Check

1. **Recall facts** What were the first words that the narrator heard in the top-secret classroom?

2. **Explain** Why were those first words so surprising to the narrator?

3. **Make inferences** Why did it surprise the narrator to find Navajo teachers in the classroom?

boarding school school where students live for the academic year

Johnny Manuelito and John Benally passed out pencils and blank sheets of paper and then went to the front of the room by the blackboards. I was so amazed by all that was happening that I do not recall being handed a pencil and paper, but somehow I found them in my hands.

17   "Follow our instructions exactly," Johnny Manuelito said. "We will speak words in Navajo. You must write down those same words on your paper in English." He turned toward John Benally, who held a piece of chalk in one hand and an eraser in the other.

18

"Wóláchíí," Johnny Manuelito said. I looked up in surprise as he said it, then realized he was not looking my way and using my **nickname.** He was just speaking the word for ant.

19   In large block letters, John Benally printed the word ANT on the blackboard. As soon as everyone had seen it, he erased it.

20   "Now it is your turn," Johnny Manuelito said. "We speak in Navajo. You write in English, just as Corporal Benally just did. Be sure to print in block letters." He paused, looked out at all of us, then nodded.

21   *"Wóláchíí,"* he said.

22   *"Shash,"* said John Benally.

23   *"Mósí."*

24   *"Bįįh ."*

Reading Strategy

Describe Mental Images According to this paragraph, the narrator's nickname is Ant. Visualize the narrator, and explain why you think he has this nickname.

nickname *informal name given to a person*

25   *"Dzeh."*

26   *"Ma'ii."*

27   ANT, BEAR, CAT, DEER, ELK, FOX. I put those words down on the paper. But they were speaking so fast that I missed the next few words and could only try to catch up as they continued on.

28   *"Dibé yázhí."*

29   *"Na'ats' ǫǫsi."*

30   *"Neeshch'íí."*

31   *"Ná'áshjaa'."*

32   LAMB, MOUSE, NUT, OWL, I printed. By the time they stopped talking I had printed sixteen words. But I still didn't know what this was all about. I glanced around the room. From the looks on the faces of my other **platoon** mates, they were all confused. Henry Bahe looked as if he was angry. Jimmy King, who was one of the hardest workers of all of us, was shaking his head.

33   Johnny Manuelito and John Benally went around the room collecting the papers. They looked quickly through the **stack** and then carefully placed them in a box at the front of the room.

34   "You have done well," Johnny Manuelito said. "But you must learn to be perfect if you wish to become a code talker."

Reading Strategy

Describe Mental Images Imagine looking around the room as the men are writing. What **image** comes to mind? What sounds might you hear?

Reading Check

1. **Recall facts** What is *dibé yázhí* in English?

2. **Analyze** Why did the platoon find the exercise so difficult?

3. **Make predictions** How do you think the narrator will feel about becoming a code talker?

---

platoon division of a military group
stack group of objects placed one on top of the other

Reading Strategy

Describe Mental Images Imagine the narrator's reaction. What expression do you think he has on his face as the teachers describe the job of a Navajo code talker?

35   Code talker. It was the first time I had ever heard that name, but it sounded good to me. Then our two Navajo instructors began to explain our **duties** to us. The more they said, the better it sounded. Our job was to learn a new **top-secret** code based on the Navajo language. We would also be trained to be expert in every form of communication used by the Marine Corps, from radios to Morse code. Using our code, we could send **battlefield messages** that no one but another Navajo code talker could understand.

36   I realized right away that our job was a really important one. In order to win battles, Marines needed to communicate fast at long distances. In those days before computers, that meant using radio. However, anyone, including the Japanese, could listen to our radio messages. To keep messages secret, the Marines sent them in code. But the Japanese broke every code our American forces used. A new kind of code had to be created.

37   During World War One, our country had used other Indians, Cherokees and Chickasaws, to send messages in their own language to confuse the enemy. After the war, the Japanese had decided to be prepared for something like that if they had to fight America. They sent people to America to learn not only how to speak English fluently, but also to learn our American Indian languages.

A Marine Corps unit comprised of Navajo American Indians sits on the grass in uniform in Peleliu, November 1944.

---

duties responsibilities, assignments
top-secret very important and kept from others
battlefield messages messages sent to or from the front line, with strategic information valuable to enemy forces

Navajo, though, had never been studied. It was one of the hardest of all American Indian languages to learn. Only we Navajos could speak it with complete fluency. Also, because there were so many of us, including hundreds of young Navajo men who had learned to speak English in the boarding schools—our language was chosen for making that unbreakable code.

38   Where did the idea of using Navajo come from? There was a white man named Philip Johnson who was the son of a white trader on the **reservation** and so he could speak "Trader Navajo." He liked our people and had Navajo friends. When the Japanese attacked Pearl Harbor, he brought some of his Navajo friends to the Marines in San Diego to demonstrate how our language could be used to send messages.

39   An important Marine had already been thinking about making an Indian code. His name was Major General Clinton Vogel, commanding general of the **amphibious** division of the Pacific Task Force. He knew that the U.S. Army was already using Comanches in Europe to send messages in their own language. After hearing of Philip Johnson's demonstration, General Vogel authorized the **recruitment** of that first class of twenty-nine Navajo Marines. Just like us, they were brought to Camp Elliott, where they were locked in this same classroom and told to develop an unbreakable code.

> **Reading Strategy**
>
> **Describe Mental Images** What details do you see when you visualize Major General Vogel?

A photo of the Japanese bombing of Pearl Harbor, Dec. 7, 1941

✓ **Reading Check**

1. **Recall facts** At the time, who were the only people able to speak Navajo fluently?

2. **Recall facts** What World War II event drew attention to the Navajo language?

3. **Make inferences** Why was the first class of Navajo marines "locked in" the classroom?

---

reservation land in the United States for tribes of Native Americans to live on as designated by the U.S. government
amphibious operating on land and water
recruitment act of seeking new members for a group or organization

40   Those Navajos did it all by themselves. Some have said that Philip Johnson developed the code and taught it to the Navajos. This is not true. He did not know our **sacred** language well enough to do this. He was nowhere near Camp Elliott during the summer of 1942 when the code was being created by Navajos. Later on, Philip Johnson came to work at Camp Elliott. His job, with the rank of sergeant, was to be an **administrator** for the school, help things run well, and write reports. He could not speak the code and never taught it to anyone.

* * *

41   The first day in class, Johnny Manuelito **emphasized** to us how important our jobs as code talkers would be.

42   "The lives of many men," he said, "will depend on your messages. You have to get it right the first time. Every time."

43   Because of its great value, no one was ever to be told about the code. Nothing I wrote down in that room could ever be taken from the room. It all had to be kept stored in only one place: in my head. That was why everything put on the blackboards was quickly erased. Every scrap of paper we wrote on was collected at the end of each day. If I breathed a word about the very existence of the code to an outsider, even to another Navajo Marine who was not a code talker, I could be placed in the **brig** for the rest of the war.

Reading Strategy

Describe Mental Images Imagine Johnny Manuelito's voice as he says, "The lives of many men will depend on your messages." What do you think his voice sounds like?

Two Navajo Marines use a portable radio set to communicate during World War II, December 1943.

---

sacred spiritually important
administrator a person who supervises or manages; a director
brig military prison

44   I have heard it said that we Navajos carried code books with us. That is not so. Some code books were printed up, but they were kept closely guarded. The only two places in the whole world where they were used were our training areas at Pearl Harbor and Camp Elliott. The code went with us everywhere, but only in our memories.

45   "If you are captured in battle," John Benally said, "die before telling the enemy anything about the code! Even if they beat you, even if **bamboo splinters** are shoved under your fingernails, you must keep quiet about our secret."

46   *I will never tell the enemy.* I wrote these words down on my paper and underlined them twice.

47   John Benally's warning did not frighten me. It made me proud that our secret language was so important to America. It felt good to know that we were the only ones who could do this useful thing. We swore that we would protect the code with our lives, and kept our word. I am not sure how many of us became Navajo code talkers during World War Two, but I know that it was close to four hundred men. While it remained **classified,** not one of us ever told about the code, not even to our families. We kept it secret throughout the war and long after.

Reading Strategy

Describe Mental Images What image comes to mind when you visualize a top-secret code book?

These code talkers used Navajo, their native language, to send secret messages during the war.

✓
Reading Check

1. **Recall facts** What words did the narrator write down and underline?

2. **Analyze** When the narrator says, "We kept it secret," who is "we" referring to?

3. **Speculate** Why do you think the military kept the Navajo codes a secret even after the war?

---

bamboo splinters very fine slivers of bamboo wood
classified top secret, or protected

● Apply the Reading Strategy

Describe Mental Images

Now that you have read *Code Talker,* complete the Reading Strategy chart.

1. Review the **Reading Strategy** on page 291.
2. Copy the chart.
3. Look back at the reading. In the first column of the chart, write the vivid details you noted as you read.
4. Then describe the **image** that the detail helps you to visualize.

Detail From the Story	Image
The sergeant barked into our barracks.	large man in uniform, straight-backed, tall, yelling, frowning

● Academic Vocabulary

Vocabulary for the Reading Comprehension Questions

Word	Explanation	Sample Sentence	Visual Cue
attitude *noun*	an opinion or way of thinking	Alejandro has many friends because people like his positive **attitude**.	
reveal *verb*	to uncover something that is hidden or secret	The girl opened the wrapped box to **reveal** her birthday present inside.	

Draw a picture and write a sentence for each word.

✓ Checkpoint

1. Describe your **attitude** toward your culture.
2. What do our **attitudes reveal** about us?

Vocabulary Log

● Reading Comprehension Questions

Think and Discuss

1. **Recall facts** Where are the Navajo Marines taken?
2. **Apply** Use the Key Vocabulary words to briefly summarize *Code Talker*.
3. **Understand author's point of view** How does the author's heritage connect to this selection? What do you think his **attitude** is toward the story of the code talkers?
4. **Make inferences** How old do you think the narrator is? Identify two clues that **reveal** information about the narrator's age.
5. **Analyze setting** How is the World War II setting important to the story of the code talkers?
6. **Speculate** Why do you think the author included an audience of children in this selection? What purpose does storytelling have in many cultures?
7. **Revisit the Reading Focus Questions** Go back to page 292 and discuss the questions.

Workbook
page 192

Independent Practice
CD-ROM/Online

● Literary Element

Idiom

An **idiom** is an expression or phrase that does not have the same meaning as its individual words. In an idiom, the words have a different meaning.

In *Code Talker*, the narrator says he would never "breathe a word" about the code. In this case, the idiom *not breathe a word* means "not **reveal** a secret."

Use the context of the idioms in the sentences below to determine their meaning.

1. The soldiers did not **set foot in** enemy territory. Instead, they served their country from the safety of Camp Elliott in San Diego.
2. Though it was their first time using the code, their performance was **top drawer.** The corporals knew the men would be excellent code talkers.
3. After a long and stressful day, the men were ready to go back to their barracks and **hit the sack.** They needed their rest for another hard day in the classroom.
4. The code was so difficult to understand that the enemy would not be able to make **heads nor tails** of it.

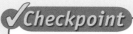

✓**Checkpoint**
1. What is an **idiom?**
2. Tell and explain an idiom from your first language.

Workbook
page 193

Independent Practice
CD-ROM/Online

CITY YEAR

● About the Reading

All over the United States, there are people in need of a helping hand. City Year is a service organization dedicated to helping others in need. You will read their brochure to learn more about this community of volunteers.

● Build Background

Volunteering

A volunteer is a person who does something of his or her own free will, usually without being paid, to help another person or an organization. Volunteerism in the United States dates back to when the country was still young and communities worked together to survive. During the 20th century, many volunteer organizations were created to help people in need, protect national forest lands, and promote world peace. City Year was founded in 1988 and has grown to be a leader in the national volunteerism movement.

● Vocabulary From the Reading

Use Context Clues to Determine Meaning

Use the context of the sentences to determine the meaning of each Key Vocabulary word.

1. Members of the **corps** work together to teach farmers how to grow more crops. The group is small, but very highly skilled.

2. The children **engage** in fun activities, such as singing songs and dancing.

3. We **invested** a lot of time in our garden, and now we have rows of beautiful flowers.

4. Our company **mission** is to serve people in need.

5. When Amy won an award for her service, she set the **standard** for all volunteers. Now everyone tries to be as good a volunteer as she is.

Key Vocabulary

- corps
- engage
- invest
- mission
- standard

✓ Checkpoint

1. Think of a service organization you know. What is its **mission**?

2. Why do you **invest** time in your school work?

Vocabulary Log

Workbook page 194

Independent Practice CD-ROM/Online

Reading Strategy

Analyze Text Evidence

When you analyze text evidence, you look within the reading for evidence, or proof, that supports a point. Text evidence can be in the form of facts, details, quotes, or even pictures. Often, text evidence answers questions that come up as you read.

As you read, note the major points that the City Year brochure makes about its program. When you finish reading, complete the organizer to note the text evidence that supports each point.

Point or Message:		Text Evidence:
_____	→	1. _____
_____		2. _____

Text Genre

Informational Text: Brochure

Brochures are brief documents that describe or advertise a company or product. Brochures use special text elements to help readers understand the information in the brochure.

Brochure	
bullets	dots or small symbols used to create a list
headings	boldfaced words or phrases used to introduce sections of material
testimonials	direct quotes from people who share positive experiences with the company or product

Meet the Founders

Michael Brown and **Alan Khazei** founded City Year in 1988. They knew that young people had the ability to make positive changes in the world. From that idea came City Year, which has expanded to 16 sites across America and to Johannesburg, South Africa.

City Year founders
Michael Brown (top) and
Alan Khazei

Reading Focus Questions

As you read, think about these questions.

1. How does this reading connect to the theme of "making a difference"?

2. Why do you think City Year created a brochure?

3. Is this type of service organization important? Why?

✓**Checkpoint**

1. What is a **brochure**?

2. What are **headings** used for?

CITY YEAR

Explore

Reading Strategy

Analyze Text Evidence
Does this evidence prove that City Year is improving the lives of others? Explain.

1   City Year releases the power of young people. It is more than a service program; City Year is a social change organization. The leadership skills **corps** members learn stay with them. A survey of City Year **alumni** found that:

2   ■ 95% indicated that they made an important difference in someone's life while at City Year

3   ■ 88% indicated that they often worked with people from different backgrounds while at City Year

4   ■ As one City Year graduate put it, "What I like most about City Year is that it is impossible not to learn something useful while you are part of the organization…. Everybody loves that they do something here. What you do with it is entirely up to you."

---

alumni graduates of a program

Why City Year?

5   *Founded in Boston in 1988, City Year now sets the **standard** for national service with over 1,000 **corps** members serving at 16 sites across the country. **Corps** members can serve in their own hometowns, in other cities of their choosing, or wherever the need is greatest.*

6   City Year is a proud member of **AmeriCorps** and was, in fact, a model for AmeriCorps. City Year works to build stronger communities, a stronger country, and a better world through service. Every small task at City Year is part of this **ambitious mission**.

7   City Year brings together young adults from diverse backgrounds for a demanding year of full-time community service, leadership development, and civic engagement. United in their desire to serve, these young leaders **invest** their talents and energy to solve real problems in their communities, **engage** volunteers, and make a positive difference in others' lives.

8   As a leader in the national service **movement**, City Year has helped to inspire **corporate** America. Numerous local and national **sponsors** even give **annual** cash awards, gifts, and scholarships to graduating City Year **corps** members and alumni.

9   City Year has earned the respect of America's leaders, and **corps** members have been honored by governors, senators, and presidents.

Reading Strategy

Analyze Text Evidence
What evidence on this page proves that City Year has inspired businesses in America?

✔ Reading Check

1. **Recall facts**
   How long does a volunteer work with City Year?

2. **Identify evidence**
   How do you know City Year is respected by America's leaders?

AmeriCorps a network, or connection, of over 2,000 service organizations (including City Year)
ambitious high-reaching, enthusiastic
movement political or social cause
corporate business
sponsors groups or individuals that help pay for something
annual yearly

Is City Year Right for You?

10 *City Year's service, culture, and daily operations are **rooted** in diversity, teamwork, and leadership. As a **corps** member, you will be challenged to live these **ideals** every day.*

11 **DIVERSITY** City Year's diverse teams are unifying forces that **foster** understanding and hope in the communities they serve.

Reading Strategy

Analyze Text Evidence
What idea about City Year do these testimonials suggest?

12 *"I've learned that community service is a powerful meeting place for different people and institutions to come together to find common ground … and achieve a positive change."*
—Chris Forbes-Nicotera, '99

13 **TEAMWORK** City Year forms teams because common goals are the hardest to achieve.

14 *"Being part of such a network strengthens my belief in the power of my generation and inspires me to do my small part to help make our mark on humanity."*
—Marcie Kasek, '03

15 **LEADERSHIP** City Year believes that young people have the idealism and energy to be natural leaders.

16 *"When I was a child it was easy to dream of all the things in this world I could change. At City Year I have found the courage to be that little kid who dares to dream. City Year has given me a place to stand so I can change the world."*
—Aaron J. Marquez, '03, '04

---

rooted based on; come from
ideals goals, concepts of how things should be
foster bring about or develop

After Reading 2

● **Reading Comprehension Questions**

Think and Discuss

1. **Recall facts** What national service program used City Year as a model for the kinds of organizations it includes?

2. **Analyze text features** How does each heading on page 308—Diversity, Teamwork, and Leadership—relate to the testimonials that follow?

3. **Compare features** What text feature does "City Year" use on page 306 to create a list? What is used to make the list on page 308?

4. **Summarize** Use each of the Key Vocabulary words on page 304 to summarize the work that City Year does.

5. **Take a stand** Does it sound like City Year provides an important service? Why or why not?

6. **Revisit the Reading Focus Questions** Go back to page 305 and discuss the questions.

Workbook
page 197

Independent Practice
CD-ROM/Online

Spelling

The Combination *ph*

Workbook
page 198

Independent Practice
CD-ROM/Online

Writing Conventions

Punctuation: Using Bulleted Lists

Workbook
page 199

Independent Practice
CD-ROM/Online

Connect Readings 1 and 2

You have read two readings on the theme of making a difference: *Code Talker* and "City Year." Use these activities to make connections between the readings.

1. With a partner, use this chart to compare the two readings.

Reading title	What service does each selection describe?	How do the services differ from each other?	Which way of making a difference is more interesting to you? Why?
CODE TALKER			
CITY YEAR			

2. With a partner, ask and answer these questions.
   a. In what way does each selection show people making a difference?
   b. Do you think the narrator in *Code Talker* would approve of the work done by City Year? Why or why not?
   c. How do young people play an important part in each of the readings?

3. **Revisit the Chapter Focus Questions** What kind of reward do you get when you help someone in need? Is the reward worth the effort? Use examples from *Code Talker* and "City Year" to answer these questions.

Phrases for Conversation

Expressing Disagreement

We do not agree.
I see it a different way.
I don't think so.

Reporting a Group's Ideas

We agreed that …
We decided that …

● Listening and Speaking

Discuss Idioms and Hyperbole

The English language is made rich and colorful by the use of idioms and figurative language, such as hyperbole (exaggeration used for emphasis or effect). With a partner, discuss the phrases below.

1. Discuss the possible meanings of each idiom below.
    a. to pull the wool over someone's eyes
    b. to jump in without looking
    c. to stretch a dollar

2. Then discuss the possible meanings of the examples of hyperbole below.
    a. The rain came down in buckets.
    b. I nearly died of embarrassment.
    c. He is hungry enough to eat a horse.

3. When you finish the list, check your interpretations with another group.

4. Share your final interpretations with the class.

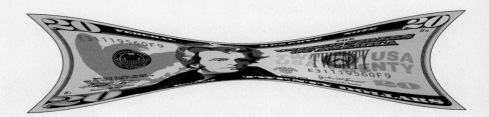

● Reading Fluency

Rapid Word Recognition

Rapidly recognizing words helps you to increase your reading rate. Rapid reading is an important characteristic of a fluent and effective reader.

1. With a partner, review the list of words.

2. Read the words from left to right aloud for one minute. Use appropriate pacing. Do not read so fast that you cannot pronounce the words correctly. When you finish the list, start again at the beginning. Your partner can time you as you read.

3. How many words did you read in one minute? Record your results.

4. Compare your results to the results you had on page 121. Are you recognizing words more quickly?

expected	perfect	fluent	energy	honored
diverse	energy	expected	perfect	fluent
expected	honored	perfect	diverse	honored
diverse	expected	fluent	honored	perfect
energy	diverse	fluent	expected	honored

● Vocabulary Development

Using a Dictionary and a Thesaurus

A **dictionary** provides definitions of words; most dictionaries also provide other information, such as a word's part of speech and etymology (word origin). A **thesaurus** provides synonyms, or words that are the same or similar in meaning. Together, these tools can help you to choose the most effective words for your speaking and writing.

Look at this dictionary entry.

academy / ə **kæd** ə mi / *n.,* pl. -ies **1** a school, or place of study or training [Gk Akademos the Greek mythological hero]

The chart below shows the information included in the entry.

Word	Pronunciation	Part of Speech	Plural Form	Definition	Etymology
academy	ə **kæd** ə mi	noun	academies	a school, or place of study or training	Greek, from Greek mythology

Look at this entry from a thesaurus.

academy (noun) school, college, university, boarding school, institute

The entry includes the word, part of speech, and a list of possible synonyms.

1. For each of the following words, use a dictionary to complete a chart like the one above.

   a. code   **b.** mentor   **c.** communicate

2. Use a thesaurus to find three synonyms each for the words *mentor* and *communicate*.

✓Checkpoint

1. What kinds of words can you find in a **thesaurus**?

2. What is a word's etymology?

Vocabulary Log

Workbook page 200

Independent Practice CD-ROM/Online

● Grammar

Present Perfect Tense

You can use the **present perfect tense** to describe an action that occurred in the past and continues to occur in the present.

She **has lived** here for many years.

It also describes an action that occurred at an unspecified time in the past.

I **have visited** Europe.

Form the present perfect tense by adding the auxiliary verb **have** or **has** before the main verb.

Present Perfect Tense			
subject	auxiliary verb	main verb	
I / You / We / They	have	lived	here for one year.
He / She / It	has		

Past Perfect Tense

Use the **past perfect tense** to describe an action that was completed in the past before another action.

I remembered that I **had read** the book already.
After I **had finished** the job, I asked for my pay.

Form the past perfect tense by adding the auxiliary verb **had** before the main verb.

Past Perfect Tense			
subject	auxiliary verb	main verb	
I / You / We / They	had	worked	for the company for two years when we met.
He / She / It	had		

Future Perfect Tense

Use the **future perfect tense** to describe an action that will take place in the future before another event occurs.

I **will have finished** the project by 8 o'clock tonight.

Form the future perfect tense by adding the auxiliary verb **will have** before the main verb.

Future Perfect Tense			
subject	**auxiliary verb**	**main verb**	
I / You / We / They	**will have**	graduated	high school by next summer.
He / She / It	**will have**		

Practice the Grammar Copy the following sentences and underline the past, present, or future perfect tense in each. Then identify the verb tense you underlined.

The narrator had spoken fluent Navajo long before he learned the code. past perfect

1. He studied English after he had decided to learn a new language.
2. He will have learned a new way to speak Navajo when the code is completed.
3. His grandchildren have listened to his stories with great enthusiasm.
4. The narrator has been a storyteller for many years.
5. The men in the unit will have kept the secret for twenty years before it is finally **revealed**.
6. The grandchildren will have heard this story a million times before they grow up.

Use the Grammar Independently Write three sentences about City Year. Include one sentence that uses the present perfect, one that uses the past perfect, and one that uses the future perfect tense.

Grammar Expansion

Yes/No Questions and Negative Statements in the Present, Past, and Future Perfect Tenses

Workbook pages 203–204   Independent Practice CD-ROM/Online

✓**Checkpoint**

1. Which auxiliary verb is used for the past perfect tense?
2. What type of action does a **present perfect** verb describe?

Workbook pages 201–202

Independent Practice CD-ROM/Online

● Writing Assignment

Write a Business Letter

Writing Prompt

Write a business letter to City Year asking the organization for more information about their programs. Include information about yourself and the kind of work you would like to do in your community. Use a business letter format, with the student model as your guide. Include present, past, or future perfect tenses in your letter.

Write Your Business Letter

1. Read the student model.

Student Model

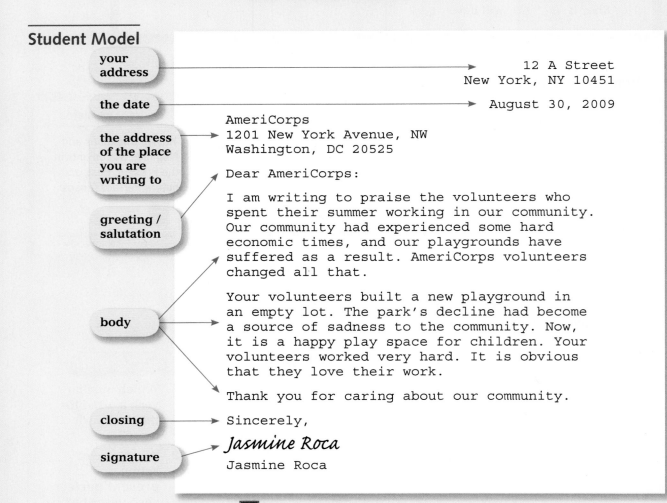

your address → 12 A Street
New York, NY 10451

the date → August 30, 2009

the address of the place you are writing to → AmeriCorps
1201 New York Avenue, NW
Washington, DC 20525

greeting / salutation → Dear AmeriCorps:

body →
I am writing to praise the volunteers who spent their summer working in our community. Our community had experienced some hard economic times, and our playgrounds have suffered as a result. AmeriCorps volunteers changed all that.

Your volunteers built a new playground in an empty lot. The park's decline had become a source of sadness to the community. Now, it is a happy play space for children. Your volunteers worked very hard. It is obvious that they love their work.

Thank you for caring about our community.

closing → Sincerely,

signature → *Jasmine Roca*
Jasmine Roca

Workbook
Workbook
page 205

2. Prewrite.

a. Make a brief list of the information you want to include in your letter. Consider identifying the needs of your community, the kind of work you might enjoy, and any experience you have had with that kind of work. Consider also what you would like from City Year—a brochure, a phone call from someone who can answer your questions, or to arrange a visit to the City Year office.

b. Organize your list. Put the information about yourself in one paragraph and your request for information in a separate paragraph.

3. Write your business letter.

a. Follow the form in the student model. Use the Internet to find the address of City Year's offices. Include this address in your letter.

b. Make sure your letter includes two paragraphs.

4. Revise.
Read your letter aloud. Then revise any sentences or paragraphs that seem unclear.

Use the **editing and proofreading symbols** on page 455 to mark any changes you want to make.

5. Edit.
Use the **Writing Checklist** to help you find any problems and errors.

6. Read your letter to the class.

Writing Checklist

1. I followed the business letter style in the student model.

2. I included two paragraphs.

3. I used a colon after the greeting.

4. I used the present, past, or future perfect tense.

5. I proofread and edited my work.

Build Your Knowledge

One option is to ask City Year for an application to be a volunteer. Looking through the application now and seeing the kinds of information it requires (name, contact information, questions about your interests, and recommendation letters from teachers and other adults) will help you to prepare for filling out applications in the future.

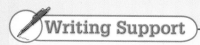

Writing Support

Grammar

Irregular Verbs

An **irregular verb** forms its past tense in a different way than a regular verb. Sometimes the spelling of the verb changes. Other times, the verb does not change at all in the past tense.

Infinitive	Past Tense	Infinitive	Past Tense
(to) write	wrote	(to) swim	swam
(to) catch	caught	(to) bite	bit
(to) know	knew	(to) sit	sat
(to) set	set	(to) speak	spoke

Apply Check the verbs in your letter. Are the past tense verbs in the correct form? If you are not sure whether a verb changes form in the past tense, check your dictionary.

Progress Check

How well did you understand this chapter? Try to answer the questions. If necessary, go back to the pages listed for a review.

Skills	Skills Assessment Questions	Pages to Review
Vocabulary From the Readings	What do these words mean? • **accomplish, destination, emphasize, escort, stunned** • **corps, engage, invest, mission, standard**	290 304
Academic Vocabulary	What do these academic vocabulary words mean? • image • attitude, reveal	291 302
Reading Strategies	What do readers do when they describe mental images? What does text evidence provide?	291 305
Text Genres	What is the text genre of *Code Talker*? What is the text genre of "City Year"?	292 305
Reading Comprehension	What is *Code Talker* about? What is "City Year" about?	303 309
Literary Element	What is an **idiom**?	303
Spelling	Name three words that use the combination *ph*.	309
Writing Conventions	What does a bulleted list help you to do?	309
Listening and Speaking	**Phrases for Conversation** Name two phrases that express disagreement during a discussion.	310
Vocabulary Development	What kinds of information do most dictionaries provide?	311
Grammar	How do you form the present perfect tense? What kinds of actions do the past and future perfect tenses describe?	312–313
Writing Support: Grammar	How is an **irregular verb** different from a regular verb?	315

Assessment Practice

Read this passage. Then answer Questions 1 through 4.

A Year in the City

1   After graduating from high school, I wasn't sure what I wanted to do. I thought I would try something different. I wanted to go out in the world and help people. After reading the City Year brochure and meeting some City Year workers, I knew it was for me.

2   I jumped in headfirst. I became an after-school mentor for elementary school children. We planted gardens, painted murals, and wrote letters to city council members about important issues.

3   When I wasn't working with the children, I was involved in engaging the community on social issues. We emphasized diversity and service. It may sound like I gave a lot of myself that year. However, I really gained so much more than I gave. City Year changed me so that, even today, I still work to improve my community.

1 What does the word <u>emphasized</u> mean in the following sentence?

> We <u>emphasized</u> diversity and service.

A did

B stressed

C revealed

D invested

2 What details help you visualize the children's activities?

A I jumped in headfirst.

B I became an after-school mentor for elementary school children.

C We planted gardens, painted murals, and wrote letters to city council members about important issues.

D It may sound like I gave a lot of myself that year.

3 Which sentence contains an idiom?

A After graduating from high school, I wasn't sure what I wanted to do.

B I jumped in headfirst.

C When I wasn't working with the children, I was involved in engaging the community on social issues.

D City Year changed me so that, even today, I still live to change my community.

4 What is the text genre for this passage?

A poem

B persuasive essay

C textbook excerpt

D autobiographical short story

Writing on Demand: Business Letter

Write a business letter to a local organization that helps others; for example, a soup kitchen, an after-school program, or a nursing home. Ask what they do and how you can volunteer. **(20 minutes)**

> **Writing Tip**
> Remember to use formal, polite language.

CHAPTER 2

Objectives

Reading Strategies
Analyze text structure; Recognize author's style

Listening and Speaking
Give a persuasive speech

Grammar
Use verbals

Writing
Write a response to literature

Academic Vocabulary

structure	promote
propose	outcome
logical	

Academic Content

Inventions
Presidential inauguration

● Chapter Focus Question

When you do something good for another person, are you also doing something good for yourself?

Reading 1 **Content:** Science

Magazine article
COMMUNITY SERVICE
by Chris Jozefowicz

Reading 2 **Literature**

Speech (abridged)
INAUGURAL ADDRESS
by John F. Kennedy

COMMUNITY SERVICE

● About the Reading

Do you think you could invent something that could make a difference in the world? In "Community Service," you will read about how some teenagers worked together to invent a device that makes a difference in the lives of others.

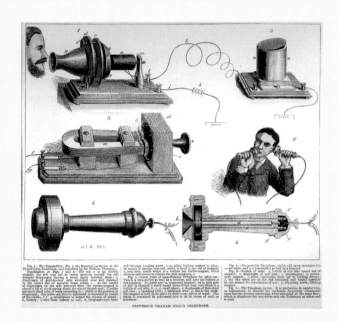

PROFESSOR GRAHAM BELL'S TELEPHONE.

● Build Background

Inventions

What is an invention? It is a new device developed from study and experimentation. Think of the cellular phone, the Internet, and the MP3 music player. These are fairly recent inventions. Other inventions are very old, like the wheel. A person who creates an invention is an *inventor*.

Inventions can solve a problem, or they can make life easier or more enjoyable for people.

Some inventions help people with disabilities, for example, people who can't walk or hear or see well. These inventions can make a big difference in people's lives.

● Use Prior Knowledge

Choose the Best Invention

With a partner, decide on and make a list of the ten best inventions of all time. How did each invention make a difference in the world? Then choose the best one on your list and share your choice with your classmates. Finally, as a class, vote for the best invention.

Invention	What difference did it make?	Best Invention (check one)
telephone	improved speed of communication	

Key Vocabulary

- device
- fine-tune
- garbled
- incident
- launch
- motivate

● Vocabulary From the Reading
Learn, Practice, and Use Independently

Learn Vocabulary Use the context, or the information that appears around the **highlighted** word, to determine its meaning.

For years, Alexander Graham Bell tried to **fine-tune** a machine called a telegraph, that could send signals by wire. He knew the telegraph was a great communication **device**, but he wanted the machine to do even more. At one point, Bell heard noises over his new instrument, but the sounds were **garbled** and difficult to understand. This **incident** had a significant impact on Bell. That small success **motivated** him to keep trying. Eventually, he **launched** a new, exciting way of communicating, and he called it a telephone.

Alexander Graham Bell invented the telephone.

Practice Vocabulary Match the Key Vocabulary word to the situation on the right that best reflects the meaning of the word. Look for clues in the words in **bold**.

1. **device**
2. **fine-tune**
3. **garbled**
4. **incident**
5. **launch**
6. **motivate**

a. The broken speakers made his words **hard to understand.**

b. Rockets **take off** from the Florida coast.

c. Falling down on the stage was the most embarrassing **experience** of her life.

d. He handed me a **special tool** for fixing my bicycle.

e. Good teachers **inspire** me to study more.

f. He **makes many little adjustments** to make the car run better.

Use Vocabulary Independently For each Key Vocabulary word, identify one synonym, or word that means nearly the same thing.

✓ Checkpoint

1. What kinds of things can a cook do to **fine-tune** a recipe?

2. What reward might **motivate** you to complete a difficult task?

Vocabulary Log

Workbook page 209

Independent Practice CD-ROM/Online

Academic Vocabulary

Vocabulary for the Reading Strategy

Word	Explanation	Sample Sentence	Visual Cue
structure *noun*	the way that parts are put together or organized	The most basic sentence **structure** is the simple sentence, which has a subject and a verb.	
propose *verb*	to suggest or recommend	We weren't sure what to order. The waiter **proposed** that we try the chef's special dish.	
logical *adjective*	showing good sense or reason	The friends wanted to enter the old abandoned house but decided not to because they knew it would not be safe. This was a **logical** conclusion.	

Draw a picture and write a sentence for each word.

Reading Strategy

Analyze Text Structure

Text **structure** is the way an author organizes his or her ideas. Analyzing the **structure** of a reading will help you better understand its purpose.

The article "Community Service" has a problem/solution **structure**. In this kind of text, a problem is identified and a **logical** solution is **proposed**.

As you read, note the problems presented in the article. When you finish, create a flow chart like the one here.

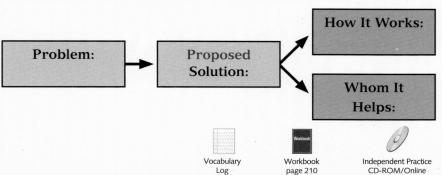

✓**Checkpoint**

1. Describe the basic **structure** of this textbook.

2. Is it **logical** to say that everything great has already been invented? Explain your response.

Vocabulary Log

Workbook page 210

Independent Practice CD-ROM/Online

Text Genre

Informational Text: Magazine Article

A **magazine article** is an informational text that presents nonfiction writing. Magazine articles can be about almost any topic you can imagine. Most articles share the following features.

Magazine Article	
organization	order, or **structure**, of the material presented in the article
coherence	clarity of order; having every sentence, paragraph, and section in an order that helps a reader to understand the subject
unity	the sense that all of the material in an article is related or connected in some way

Meet the Author

Chris Jozefowicz was born in Detroit, Michigan. As a child he was fascinated by the natural world and animals, particularly insects. He studied biology and did laboratory research in evolutionary biology. After five years of working in a lab, he decided he liked learning about all kinds of science, not just biology. He became a science journalist and has been writing and learning about science ever since. Chris Jozefowicz lives with his wife and daughter.

Reading Focus Questions

As you read, think about these questions.

1. How does this article connect to the theme of "making a difference"?
2. What was the author's purpose in writing this article?
3. How can the inventions described in the article help people around the world?

✓ Checkpoint

1. What kind of writing does a **magazine article** present?
2. In your own words, describe what it means for an article to have **unity**.

Workbook
page 211

Independent Practice
CD-ROM/Online

COMMUNITY SERVICE

by Chris Jozefowicz

1   Several years ago, Ashley LaRose's grandmother had to get out of bed one night. Unable to reach the bedside lamp, she got up in the dark, accidentally tripped, and broke her hip.

2   Though the broken hip was a **hardship** for Ashley's grandmother and her family, the **incident** also inspired Ashley and three of her friends. The four eighth graders invented the Auto-MAT-ic, a **device** that protects elderly people from injury when they get out of bed at night.

3   The students entered the Auto-MAT-ic in the Christopher Columbus Awards, an annual science competition for middle school students. The competition encourages students to use science and **engineering know-how** to solve problems in their communities.

Safety Switches

4   The Auto-MAT-ic is a floor mat that **activates** a light connected to it. The mat contains a pressure-sensitive switch that when stepped on completes an *electrical circuit*. A circuit is a path of wires and switches through which an **electric current** flows. When the circuit in the mat is complete, the light goes on.

---

hardship difficulty
engineering building or constructing
know-how ability, knowledge
activates turns on, triggers
electric current flow of electrical power

Reading Strategy

Analyze Text Structure
What problem did Ashley and her friends find a solution for?

✓ Reading Check

1. **Recall facts** What grade was Ashley's group in when they invented the Auto-MAT-ic?

2. **Explain** How does the Auto-MAT-ic help the user?

3. **Speculate** Besides the elderly, who else might use the Auto-MAT-ic?

5

Ashley's team won one of the Columbus competition's top prizes, a $25,000 **grant** given to help turn a project into a **marketable** product. (Each team is allowed to spend only $100 on its entry.) With the money, the girls formed a company and partnered with an electronics **manufacturer.**

6

Reading Strategy

Analyze Text Structure
What possible problem does the microchip solve?

The partnership has enabled the girls to shrink the **circuitry** in the Auto-MAT-ic and put it on a small *integrated circuit*, or **microchip,** that will be part of the mat. The team hopes the Auto-MAT-ic will be manufactured for sale within a year.

7

Marilyn Hamot Ryan, one of Ashley's teachers at Saddle Brook Middle School in Saddle Brook, N.J., and the coach for the project, says that a Columbus Award does more than teach science and engineering. "I love to **motivate** the kids with the **prospect** of making a difference in their communities," she says. "It really comes down to, What can you do to make this a better place to live?"

Columbus Foundation Community Grant winners, the Auto-MAT-ic team

---

grant money given for a specific purpose
marketable sellable
manufacturer maker
circuitry arrangement of electrical wiring
microchip tiny piece of material that can hold a series of electrical pathways
prospect possibility

Silent Signals

8   The desire to make a difference in a community has **launched** Ryan's students to success at the Columbus Awards before. Several years ago, a Saddle Brook team submitted the IllumaCoach, a **device** that sends coaching signals to deaf soccer players. The team didn't win a big grant, but it did receive scholarship money ($3,000 per student) and has since **patented** the invention.

9   Kara Naegely, one of the three seventh graders who made up the team that year, says she had to learn how to work with electronics and radio **signals** to build the **device.** "It works almost like a **walkie-talkie**," she says.

10   The IllumaCoach has two parts. One is a handheld push-button controller. A coach pushes the buttons on the controller, sending radio waves to the second part, a small box that a deaf player wears on his or her wrist. The signal makes the wrist unit vibrate and display a pattern of colored lights. The pattern is a code that the coach and the player have worked out beforehand.

Reading Strategy

Analyze Text Structure
What problem did the IllumaCoach team invent a solution for? What was their solution?

Reading Check

1. **Recall details** What prize did the IllumaCoach team win?

2. **Analyze** The Latin root *lum* means "light" or "shine." Why is "IllumaCoach" an appropriate name for this invention?

---

patented registered an invention so that others can't produce it without permission
signals impulses or waves that carry sound
walkie-talkie radio **device** able to send and receive voice signals at short distances

Reading Strategy

Analyze Text Structure
What problem did the IllumaCoach team run into? What solution did they find?

11   Kara says the team had to **fine-tune** the *frequency* of the radio waves. Frequency is a measure of how many radio waves pass a point in a given amount of time. Radio signals that are broadcast to **devices** such as TVs, radios, and cell phones move on different frequencies. Kara says her team put the IllumaCoach on a **unique** frequency to prevent *interference,* the **garbled** messages that result when a receiver picks up multiple radio signals.

12   "We made sure the frequency was different than cell phones because we didn't want them to interfere," Kara says.

Straw Structures

13   The Saddle Brook team took the IllumaCoach to the Columbus Award finals in Florida in 2001. The same year, four girls from the Crow Indian Reservation in Crow Agency, Mont., won $25,000 for their entry, the Rez Protectors, a building made of straw.

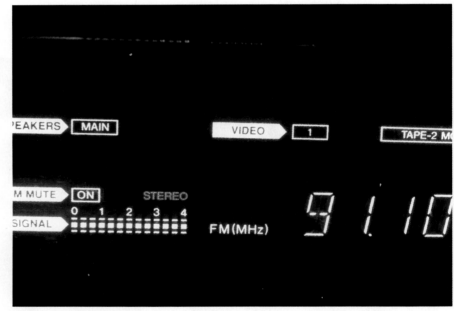

A radio frequency

---

unique one of a kind

14   Jack Joyce, the Crow team's science teacher and coach, says the girls were trying to answer a need for warm, inexpensive buildings on the reservation. Some community members worried that buildings made of straw would be **flimsy** or *flammable*—prone to **combustion**. "I call it the '**Three Little Pigs syndrome**,'" Joyce says. To **dispel** any doubts, the students ran experiments that showed that straw **bales** covered in plaster are safe, sturdy building blocks.

> ## Reading Strategy
> **Analyze Text Structure**
> What problem was the Crow team trying to solve?

15   When straw is packed together, it has a high **thermal resistivity**—heat does not flow easily through it. That **property** helps straw-bale buildings hold in warmth during the winter and keep it out during the summer. The girls demonstrated thermal resistivity by heating the air with a **blowtorch** on one side of a straw-bale wall and recording the temperatures on the other side.

16   The girls' project also excited Oprah Winfrey, and the talk-show host donated even more money. The girls have partnered with a construction company and built a straw-bale study hall on the reservation. "[The project] took science out of the textbook and out of the classroom," says Joyce, "and put it in real life."

> ## Build Your Knowledge
> Use context clues in the words, sentences, and paragraphs to find the meanings of the boldfaced words before reading their definitions below.

---

flimsy thin and weak
combustion catching on fire
Three Little Pigs syndrome fear that a house will fall down easily
dispel cause to go away
bales large, dense cubes of loose material, such as straw, tied together
thermal resistivity resistance to highs and lows in temperature
property quality
blowtorch hand-held tool that gives off a flame of very high temperature

> ## Reading Check
> 1. **Recall facts** What were the Crow team's buildings made of?
> 2. **Identify** Who helped the Crow team build their study hall?
> 3. **Make a judgment** Do you think the Rez Protectors are a worthwhile invention? Why or why not?

● **Apply the Reading Strategy**

Analyze Text Structure

Now complete the Reading Strategy graphic organizer.

1. Review the **Reading Strategy** on page 321.
2. Create a flow chart like the one below.
3. Look back at the reading. Note the three different problems presented in the article.
4. Identify the first problem in the box on the left. Then identify the solution, how it works, and whom it helps on the right.
5. Create a separate flow chart for each of the three problems and solutions in the article.

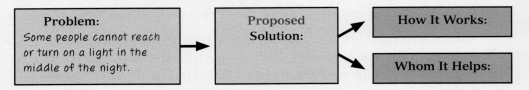

Problem:
Some people cannot reach or turn on a light in the middle of the night. → **Proposed Solution:** → **How It Works:** / **Whom It Helps:**

● **Academic Vocabulary**

Vocabulary for the Reading Comprehension Questions

Word	Explanation	Sample Sentence	Visual Cue
promote *verb*	to support; to contribute to the progress or growth of	Doctors **promote** a healthy diet that includes fruits and vegetables.	
outcome *noun*	end result or effect	The **outcome** of my studying all week was a good grade on the test.	

Draw a picture and write a sentence for each word.

✓ Checkpoint

1. If you had to **promote** a cause, what would you choose?
2. How is graduation day an example of an **outcome**?

Vocabulary Log

● Reading Comprehension Questions

Think and Discuss

1. **Recall details** Which two community service solutions won the Columbus competition's top prize?

2. **Evaluate** Imagine you were going to promote one of these inventions. Which would you choose? Why?

3. **Analyze the genre** Did the author present a clear, or coherent, **outcome** to the problem each team addressed? Explain your response.

4. **Analyze text features** Look back at the definition of unity on page 322. Do you think this selection has unity? Why or why not?

5. **Judge** What do you think of each of the inventions in this article? Did you like some more than others? Explain your answer and use Key Vocabulary words in your response.

6. **Revisit the Reading Focus Questions** Go back to page 322 and discuss the questions.

Workbook
page 212

Independent Practice
CD-ROM/Online

● Text Element

Definitions

Many magazine articles offer new information to readers. To help readers understand this material, articles often include **definitions** or explanations of words and phrases. In this way, an article can teach vocabulary that is specific to the article's topic.

"Community Service" describes award-winning science projects. To best describe the projects, author Chris Jozefowicz included a number of definitions.

Each word below is defined or explained in "Community Service." Find the word in the selection, and write down the definition the article provides.

1. electrical circuit (page 323)

2. integrated circuit (page 324)

3. frequency (page 326)

4. interference (page 326)

5. flammable (page 327)

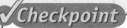

✓Checkpoint

1. How can an article teach vocabulary that is specific to the article's topic?

2. The five words from "Community Service" are related to what topic?

Workbook
page 213

Independent Practice
CD-ROM/Online

INAUGURAL ADDRESS

● About the Reading

An inaugural address is a formal speech given by someone who is about to begin his or her work in public office. In his inaugural address, President John F. Kennedy urged his listeners to build a peaceful, caring world.

● Build Background

America in 1961

John F. Kennedy took office as president of the United States in 1961. At that time, the nation was in a political struggle with the Soviet Union, which consisted of what is now Russia and several other countries in Eastern Europe. There was the possibility of a war. At the same time, the civil rights movement was demanding equality for African Americans. It was a difficult time to become the president of the United States.

Key Vocabulary

- abolish
- generosity
- mortal
- sacrifice
- summon

● Vocabulary From the Reading

Use Synonyms and Antonyms to Find Meaning

Synonyms are words that share the same, or nearly the same, meaning. Antonyms are words that are opposite in meaning. Use the synonyms and antonyms below to understand the meaning of the Key Vocabulary words. Discuss the meanings in a small group.

Key Vocabulary	Synonyms	Antonyms
abolish	erase	support, promote
generosity	spirit of giving, big-heartedness	cold-heartedness, unkindness
mortal	earthly, human	immortal, god-like
sacrifice	giving in, releasing	a win, gain, reward
summon	call up, assemble, invite	send away, drive off

✓ Checkpoint

1. Name a person whose **generosity** you admire. How does this person show his or her **generosity**?
2. Give an example of a small **sacrifice**. Give an example of a big one.

Vocabulary Log

Workbook page 214

Independent Practice CD-ROM/Online

● Reading Strategy

Recognize Author's Style

Recognizing an author's writing style is like thinking about someone's personality. To recognize the characteristics of an author's style, ask yourself these questions as you read "Inaugural Address."

1. Does the author use formal or informal language?
2. Does the author write in long sentences or short sentences? Does he repeat ideas?
3. Are the author's ideas simple, or are they complicated?
4. Does the author directly address the audience?

● Text Genre

Speech

A **speech,** or address, is a formal or informal presentation made by one person before an audience. Most formal speeches share the features below.

Speech	
audience	the listeners to a speech; a speech often addresses the audience directly
vivid language	strong, descriptive, active words or imagery
repetition	using a word or phrase two or more times to make a point or create a sense of rhythm

● Meet the Author

John Fitzgerald Kennedy was born in Brookline, Massachusetts, in 1917. He became a senator, and at the age of 43, the president. Kennedy was assassinated in 1963, barely a thousand days into his presidential term of office.

● Reading Focus Questions

As you read, think about these questions.

1. How does this selection relate to the theme of "making a difference"?
2. What is the purpose of an inaugural address?
3. What was Kennedy's specific purpose? What did he ask his audience to do?

Workbook
pages 215–216

Independent Practice
CD-ROM/Online

✓Checkpoint

1. In your own words, explain how an author's style can show his or her personality.

2. Identify one feature of a speech.

INAUGURAL ADDRESS

by John F. Kennedy

Reading Strategy

Recognize Author's Style Does the author directly involve the audience? How can you tell?

1   Vice President Johnson, Mr. Speaker, Mr. Chief Justice, President Eisenhower, Vice President Nixon, President Truman, Reverend Clergy, fellow citizens:

2   We **observe** today not a victory of **party,** but a celebration of freedom—symbolizing an end, as well as a beginning—**signifying renewal,** as well as change. For I have sworn before you and Almighty God the same **solemn** oath our **forebears prescribed** nearly a century and three-quarters ago.

3   The world is very different now. For **man** holds in his **mortal** hands the power to **abolish** all forms of human poverty and all forms of human life. And yet the same **revolutionary** beliefs for which our forebears fought are still at issue around the globe—the belief that the rights of man come not from the **generosity** of **the state,** but from the hand of God.

---

observe honor, celebrate
party a political organization (here, the Democratic Party)
signifying representing
renewal a new start
solemn serious
forebears ancestors (here, the nation's founders)
prescribed created
man all people
revolutionary drastically different
the state the nation

4   We dare not forget today that we are the **heirs** of that first revolution. Let the word go **forth** from this time and place, to friend and **foe** alike, that the **torch has been passed** to a new generation of Americans—born in this century, **tempered** by war, disciplined by a hard and bitter peace, proud of our ancient heritage, and unwilling to witness or permit the slow undoing of those human rights to which this nation has always been committed, and to which we are committed today at home and around the world.

5   Let every nation know, whether it wishes us well or ill, that we **shall** pay any price, bear any burden, meet any hardship, support any friend, oppose any foe, to assure the survival and the success of liberty....

6   In your hands, my fellow citizens, more than mine, will rest the final success or failure of our **course**. Since this country was founded, each generation of Americans has been **summoned** to give **testimony to** its national loyalty. The graves of young Americans who answered the call to service surround the globe.

> **Reading Strategy**
>
> **Recognize Author's Style** Does the author use formal or informal language?

✓ **Reading Check**

1. **Recall facts** According to paragraph 4, what has the nation always been committed to?

2. **Make inferences** What "young Americans" is Kennedy referring to in the last sentence of paragraph 6?

3. **Speculate** Why do you think Kennedy tells the audience in paragraph 6 that the success or failure of the nation rests in the hands of the audience?

---

heirs persons who inherit, who receive something from someone who has died
forth forward
foe enemy
torch has been passed responsibility has been given
tempered made stronger
shall will
course path to the future
testimony to proof of

7   Now the **trumpet summons** us again—not as a call to **bear arms,** though arms we need—not as a call to battle, though **embattled** we are—but a call to bear the **burden** of … a struggle against the common enemies of man: **tyranny,** poverty, disease, and war itself.

8   And so, my fellow Americans, ask not what your country can do for you; ask what you can do for your country.

9   My fellow citizens of the world, ask not what America will do for you, but what together we can do for the freedom of man.

10   Finally, whether you are citizens of America or citizens of the world, ask of us here the same high standards of strength and **sacrifice** which we ask of you. With a good conscience our only **sure** reward, with history the final judge of our **deeds,** let us go forth to lead the land we love, asking His blessing and His help, but knowing that here on earth God's work must truly be our own.

Reading Strategy

Recognize Author's Style What words and phrases does the author repeat in paragraphs 8 and 9?

---

trumpet the alarm that alerts us of our responsibility to our nation (figurative)
bear arms carry weapons of war
embattled troubled; in the midst of a struggle
burden heavy responsibility
tyranny a government in which one person rules with oppressive power
sure guaranteed
deeds actions

After Reading 2

Reading Comprehension Questions

Think and Discuss

1. **Recall facts** According to the end of "Inaugural Address," what is the only guaranteed reward for a life full of good deeds?

2. **Understand theme** What do you think is the theme of this speech? Point to examples that support your idea.

3. **Apply** Use the Key Vocabulary words **abolish** and **generosity** in sentences that describe Kennedy's inaugural address.

4. **Paraphrase** Explain paragraph 10 in your own words.

5. **Make a judgment** Do you think the nation still needs its citizens to make **sacrifices** for the nation? Do you think Kennedy would say the same thing in an inaugural address today? Explain your answer.

6. **Revisit the Reading Focus Questions** Go back to page 331 and discuss the questions.

Workbook page 217   Independent Practice CD-ROM/Online

Spelling

Commonly Misspelled Words

Workbook page 218   Independent Practice CD-ROM/Online

Writing Conventions

Punctuation: Using Ellipses and Brackets

Workbook page 219   Independent Practice CD-ROM/Online

Connect Readings 1 and 2

You have read two readings on the theme of making a difference: "Community Service" and "Inaugural Address." Use these activities to make connections between the readings.

1. With a partner, use this chart to compare the two readings.

Reading title	What is the genre of each selection?	Which selection is formal? Which is informal?	Which selection was more inspiring to you? Why?
COMMUNITY SERVICE			
INAUGURAL ADDRESS			

2. With a partner, ask and answer these questions.

   a. In what way have the students in "Community Service" done exactly what Kennedy urged his audience to do in "Inaugural Address"?

   b. How would you describe the style of each author? How does each author's style relate to the purpose of the selection he has written?

   c. Which author's style do you prefer? Why?

3. Revisit the Chapter Focus Question When you do something good for another person, are you also doing something good for yourself? Use examples from "Community Service" and "Inaugural Address" to answer this question.

● **Listening and Speaking**

Give a Persuasive Speech

Phrases for Conversation

Presenting a Problem

I'd like to tell you about a problem that we have . . . (in this school / city / classroom)

An example of this problem is . . .

Persuading

There are several solutions to this problem. First / Second / Third . . .

I believe we can solve this problem by . . .

We can solve this problem if we work together to . . .

If we don't solve this problem soon, . . .

When you give a persuasive speech, you try to convince your audience to take action or to change the way they think about something. For your persuasive speech, identify a problem in your school or community, and describe a course of action that you want your classmates to take to solve the problem.

1. Brainstorm a few issues in your community or your school. Think about problems that you and your classmates could help solve.

   a. Once you choose a topic, make a list that outlines the reasons it is important to solve this problem.

   b. Make another list of possible solutions—or focus on one very important solution.

   c. Finally, identify what will happen if this problem is never solved.

2. Organize your speech.

   a. First, state the problem. Describe it clearly, and provide examples of the issue.

   b. Next, present the solution. Focus on what your classmates can do to solve the problem.

   c. Finally, tell what will happen if the problem is not solved, and restate your solution.

3. Share your speech with your classmates. Keep a formal tone when speaking.

4. Be an active listener during your classmates' speeches by doing the following.

   a. Pay attention as you listen.

   b. Summarize the speaker's issue and solution to make sure you understand his or her point of view.

   c. Ask questions about the topic.

   d. Ask yourself whether you were persuaded by the speech. Do you agree with the solution the speaker **proposed**? Share your thoughts with your classmates.

Reading Fluency

CD-Assisted Reading Practice

Listening to a reading selection on an audio CD as you read can help you become a more fluent reader. Use the audio CD of "Inaugural Address" to practice this fluency activity.

1. Listen to the audio CD recording of this speech. Follow the speech in your book as you listen.

2. Listen closely to the speaker's voice as he speaks.

   a. Does his voice get higher or lower at the end of sentences?

   b. Does the speaker stress certain words? Which words?

3. Listen to the speech a second time, and read aloud with the CD recording.

4. Next, read aloud without the audio recording.

5. Finally, read the selection silently. Did following these five steps help you to read faster?

Vocabulary Development

Word Order

Often in formal speech or writing, the speaker or writer changes the **order of the words** in a sentence to emphasize the meaning of certain words or phrases, or to make a word or idea more powerful. See the following example from "Inaugural Address." The original word order brings attention to the most important part of the sentence.

Original sentence: "We observe today not a victory of party, but a celebration of freedom—"

Normal word order: "Today we are observing a celebration of freedom, not a party's victory."

Read the following sentences from "Inaugural Address." With a partner, decide how the original word order emphasizes certain words in the sentence.

1. "In your hands, my fellow citizens, more than mine, will rest the final success or failure of our course."

2. "Now the trumpet **summons** us again—not as a call to bear arms, though arms we need—not as a call to battle, though embattled we are—but a call to bear the burden of . . . "

3. "And so, my fellow Americans, ask not what your country can do for you . . . "

How can an idea or phrase be emphasized or made more powerful?

Vocabulary Log

Workbook page 220

Independent Practice CD-ROM/Online

● **Grammar**

Verbals: Infinitives, Gerunds, and Participles

A **verbal** is a word that expresses action or a state of being. Verbals are verbs that function as some other part of speech. Verbals can be infinitives, gerunds, or participles.

Infinitives

An **infinitive** is a verbal that functions as a noun or adverb. Form an infinitive by using the word **to** before a verb.

to dance   **to** play   **to** work   **to** learn

Infinitives		
example	part of speech	function
To dance onstage is exciting.	noun	subject of the sentence
She wanted **to play**.	noun	object of the verb *wanted*
The students study **to learn**.	adverb	shows purpose

Gerunds

A **gerund** is a verbal that functions as a noun. Form a gerund by adding **-ing** to a verb.

danc**ing**   play**ing**   driv**ing**

Gerunds		
example	part of speech	function
Dancing onstage is exciting.	noun	subject of the sentence
She wanted **acting** to be her career.	noun	object of the verb *wanted*
He will get in trouble for **driving** without a license.	noun	object of the preposition *for*

Participles

A **participle** is a verbal that is used as an adjective. It often ends in **-ing** or **-ed**. There are two kinds of participles: **present participles** and **past participles**.

Form a present participle by adding **-ing** to a verb.

chirp**ing**   eat**ing**   call**ing**   wal**king**

Form a past participle by adding **-ed** to a verb.

correct**ed**   publish**ed**   pack**ed**   prepar**ed**

Present Participles		
example	**part of speech**	**function**
The **chirping** birds woke me up.	adjective	modifies *birds*
The girl **playing** in the sand is my sister.	adjective	modifies *girl*
Past Participles		
example	**part of speech**	**function**
The book **published** ten years ago is still popular.	adjective	modifies *book*

Practice the Grammar Underline the verbal in each of the following sentences. Then identify each verbal as an infinitive, a gerund, a present participle, or a past participle.

1. Winning the Columbus prize was a great honor for the team.
2. They were excited to win the award.
3. The team worked to prevent injuries.
4. Their invention is interesting.

Use the Grammar Independently Write sentences using the different types of verbals. Follow the instructions below.

1. Use the infinitive *to wait* as the object of the verb *wanted*.
2. Use the gerund *studying* as the subject of a sentence.
3. Use the present participle *damaging* to modify the noun *winds*.
4. Use the past participle *opened* to modify the noun *window*.

Grammar Expansion

Verbs Followed by an Infinitive, a Gerund, or Either

Workbook
pages 223–224

Independent Practice
CD-ROM/Online

✓**Checkpoint**

1. Which **verbals** can be used as nouns?
2. How do you form a **present participle**?

Workbook
pages 221–222

Independent Practice
CD-ROM/Online

● **Writing Assignment**

Write a Response to Literature

> **Writing Prompt**
>
>   Write a response to literature essay that analyzes the writing style of John F. Kennedy. Then compare his writing style to your own. Include sentences or phrases from his speech. Make sure that the writing in your essay reflects the description of your own style. Use infinitives, gerunds, and participles in your essay.

Write Your Response to Literature Essay

1. **Read the student model.** In this example, a student compares her writing style to Edwidge Danticat's writing style.

Student Model

Every writer has a unique style. It reflects his or her personality, so if you are a quiet person, your writing might be very thoughtful and complex. Writing has to come from the heart, just like your personality. Edwidge Danticat and I are probably very different people because our writing styles are almost completely opposite.

Edwidge Danticat is the author of *Behind the Mountains*. It is a novel about a young girl named Celiane. Danticat's style is easy to follow. She writes in short sentences and uses description to help readers visualize the story. She doesn't repeat words, but her short sentences have a rhythm or beat to them. She uses quiet, simple words when she describes emotions, like "I wanted so badly to go," and "I tried to keep my back to the other students."

I like to describe my style as fast. I write choppy, short, speeding sentences. My writing is loud and exciting, like my personality. I like colorful words, and words that make noises, like "bang!" and "zip!" My writing sounds like conversations I have with friends.

Workbook
page 225

2. **Prewrite.**

    a. Begin by making a list of words and phrases that describe John F. Kennedy's writing style. Consider the words, phrases, and ideas in his "Inaugural Address." Read the speech again carefully and make sure you understand it.

    b. Find one example from his writing that supports each point you make about Kennedy's writing style.

    c. Then make a list of the characteristics of your writing style.

3. **Organize.** Use your lists to begin thinking about ideas for your essay. Put your ideas in a logical order.

4. **Write your essay.**

    a. Begin with an introduction that summarizes your topic. Include a thesis statement at the end of your introduction.

    b. Write two body paragraphs—one describing Kennedy's style, and one describing yours. Then write a conclusion that restates your thesis statement.

5. **Revise.** Read your essay. Then revise any sentences or points that seem unclear or misplaced.

    Use the **editing and proofreading symbols** on page 455 to mark any changes you want to make.

6. **Edit.** Use the **Writing Checklist** to help you find problems and errors.

7. **Share your composition with the class.**

> ## Writing Checklist
>
> **1.** I included an introduction, a body, and a conclusion.
>
> **2.** I described both Kennedy's style and my own.
>
> **3.** I included examples from Kennedy's address.
>
> **4.** I wrote in the style that I described as my own.
>
> **5.** I included gerunds, infinitives, and participles.

 **Writing Support**

Mechanics

Parallelism

Parallelism is the repetition of different ideas using the same grammatical **structure**. Parallelism can involve words, phrases, or whole sentences. Writers use parallelism to stress ideas or to create rhythm in their writing.

- . . . the **truth**, the whole **truth**, and nothing but the **truth**. (repeating words)
- "**Give me** liberty, or **give me** death!" (repeating phrases)
- "**Let freedom ring from** the mighty mountains of New York.

  Let freedom ring from the heightening Alleghenies of Pennsylvania.

  Let freedom ring from the snowcapped Rockies of Colorado." (repeating phrases)

Apply Check your composition for any parallelism. Do all the parallel words and phrases have the same grammatical **structure**?

Progress Check

How well did you understand this chapter? Try to answer the
questions. If necessary, go back to the pages listed for a review.

Skills	Skills Assessment Questions	Pages to Review
Vocabulary From the Readings	What do these words mean? • **device, fine-tune, garbled, incident, launch, motivate** • **abolish, generosity, mortal, sacrifice, summon**	320 330
Academic Vocabulary	What do these academic vocabulary words mean? • **structure, propose, logical** • **promote, outcome**	321 328
Reading Strategies	What is text **structure**? What is an author's style?	321 331
Text Genres	What is the text genre of "Community Service"? What is the text genre of "Inaugural Address"?	322 331
Reading Comprehension	What is "Community Service" about? What is "Inaugural Address" about?	329 335
Text Element	Why do magazine articles often define words for readers?	329
Spelling	Spell the following words correctly: *consceince, rist, truley.*	335
Writing Conventions	When are brackets used?	335
Listening and Speaking	**Phrases for Conversation** Give one phrase that you can use in a persuasive speech.	336
Vocabulary Development	Why might a writer want to change the order of the words in a sentence?	337
Grammar	Identify three kinds of **verbals.**	338–339
Writing Support: Mechanics	How does grammatical **structure** play a part in **parallelism**?	341

Assessment Practice

Read this passage. Then answer Questions 1 through 4.

The Peace Corps

1   In his inaugural address, President John F. Kennedy wanted to motivate listeners in the United States and all over the world. He described his vision of Americans working together with citizens from other countries to accomplish more. In March 1961, Kennedy launched the Peace Corps to try to make this happen.

2   In August 1961, the first Peace Corps volunteers went to Ghana and Tanzania, two African countries. Their mission included three goals: 1) to provide the people of other countries with trained workers, 2) to help people around the world better understand Americans, and 3) to help Americans better understand people around the world.

3   Today, the Peace Corps still works to meet those goals. More than 187,000 people have gone to 139 countries to heal, teach, build, and sacrifice themselves for the good of others.

---

1 Read this sentence from paragraph 1.

> **In March 1961, Kennedy <u>launched</u> the Peace Corps to try to make this happen.**

What does the word <u>launched</u> mean?
A   ended
B   blasted
C   started
D   landed

2 What is the text structure of this passage?
A   Problem / Solution
B   Cause / Effect
C   Compare / Contrast
D   Point / Counterpoint

3 Which of the following is not a goal of the Peace Corps?
A   to send skilled workers to other countries where they are needed
B   to earn money
C   to allow other countries to meet and get to know Americans
D   to provide Americans with a chance to learn about other countries and cultures

4 What is the genre of this text?
A   folktale
B   poem
C   historical nonfiction
D   magazine article

Writing on Demand: Response to Literature Essay

Write a response to literature essay that analyzes the writing style of Joseph Bruchac, the author of *Code Talker*. Then compare his writing style to your own. Include sentences or phrases from the text. Make sure that the writing in your essay reflects the description of your own style. **(20 minutes)**

> **Writing Tip**
> Try to use verbals such as infinitives, gerunds, and participles in your essay.

Apply & Extend

OBJECTIVES

Listening and Speaking

Present an autobiographical narrative

Media

Create a script for a radio advertisement

Writing

Write a research report

Projects

Independent Reading

● Listening and Speaking Workshop

Present an Autobiographical Narrative

> **Topic**
>
> An autobiographical narrative is a story you tell from your own life. You will present an oral autobiographical narrative about a time when you helped someone, or when someone helped you.

1. **Choose the Topic for Your Narrative**

   Think about times when you helped someone, or someone helped you. Choose one to tell about.

2. **Brainstorm**

   You will be speaking from the first-person point of view. Answer the following questions to help you brainstorm ideas for your narrative.

   a. What happened?

   b. When did it happen?

   c. Why did it happen?

   d. Where did it happen?

   e. Who was there?

3. **Plan**

   Use your answers to the questions in step 2 to plan your presentation. Try to remember as much detail as you can. Try to include sensory details and narrative devices such as describing the setting, comparing and contrasting characters, and creating suspense if appropriate to the story. Were there any sights, sounds, or smells that you remember from this event? What mood do you want to convey?

4. **Organize Your Presentation**

   a. Write each event from the story on a note card. Make sure the events are in the order in which they happened. For each event, write down what happened and as many details about it as you can remember. You will use your note cards when you give your presentation.

   b. Try to think of an interesting opening line to capture your audience's attention.

5. **Practice, Present, and Evaluate**

   Practice your presentation. As you practice, change your voice to show the emotions in the story. Then present your narrative to the class. Use gestures and eye contact during your presentation. Use the **Speaking Self-Evaluation** to evaluate your presentation. Use the **Active Listening Evaluation** to evaluate and discuss your classmates' presentations.

Active Listening Evaluation

1. The presentation told about an event from the presenter's life.

2. My favorite part of the presentation was _____ because _____ .

3. I would like to have heard more about _____ .

4. The speaker changed the tone of his or her voice to show the mood of the story.

5. The main emotion in the story was _____ .

Speaking Self-Evaluation

1. My presentation had an opening line that got the audience's attention.

2. My presentation answered the questions "who," "what," "when," "where," and "why."

3. I told about the events in the order in which they happened.

4. I included details to help my audience understand the story.

5. I spoke clearly and made eye contact with the audience.

● Media Workshop

Create a Script for a Radio Advertisement

In this activity, you will write a script for a radio advertisement. The advertisement will be for a local charity, an organization whose goal is to help the needy. It will be designed to get students your age to volunteer for the charity.

1. Find out about charities in your community. Use resources such as phone books, newspapers, and the Internet to find local charities.

2. Choose a charity that interests you, or one that you think you might like to volunteer for. Then find out more about the charity. Call and ask for information about the service the charity offers. Whom does the charity help? What do the charity's volunteers do?

3. Write your radio script based on what you have learned about your charity. Keep the following in mind when you write your script.

   a. Remember your audience. You are trying to get people your own age interested in volunteering. What could you include in your script to accomplish this?

   b. Think about your tone of voice. How can you use your voice to get your message across?

   c. Think about persuasive language. What words and phrases can you use to persuade people to volunteer for your charity?

4. Present your script to the class. Ask for feedback. Would other students be persuaded to volunteer for your charity? Why or why not?

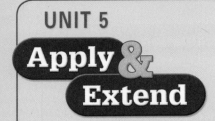

Apply &
Extend

● Writing Workshop
Write a Research Report

When you write a research report, you look for information about a topic from different sources, such as books, print and online encyclopedias, Web sites, and magazines. You then show that you understand the information by writing about it in your own words in a report, giving credit to the sources you used.

> **Writing Prompt**
>
> Choose a historical figure who has made a difference in the world. Research the person's life and work. Write a research report telling about the person's life and how he or she made a difference in the world.

PREWRITE

1. Read the student model on the next page. It will help you understand how to write a research report.

2. First, choose a person to write about. Then ask questions like those listed below. Research to find the answers. Use books from your school library, the Internet, and other resources. Take notes on the information you find.

   a. Why is this person important?

   b. How has this person made the world a better place?

   c. What are the most important events in this person's life?

3. After you have researched the person's life, use a timeline to organize the information you found. Write each event from the person's life and the date it occurred on your timeline.

4. As you conduct your research, be sure to take notes on where you find your information. You will need to list these sources at the end of your report.

WRITE A DRAFT

1. Write your introduction. The introduction should explain the main idea of your report.

2. Write the body of your report. The body should consist of three or more paragraphs telling about important events in the life of your subject.

3. Write your conclusion. Your conclusion should restate the main idea of your report.

Jackie Smith

The Life of Rosa Parks

One person who made the world a better place was Rosa Parks. She was an important leader of the civil rights movement in the United States.

Rosa Parks was born Rosa Louise McCauley in Tuskegee, Alabama, on February 4, 1913. She went to the Alabama State Teacher's College High School. She married Raymond Parks in 1932.

Rosa and her husband were both members of the National Association for the Advancement of Colored People (NAACP). Rosa's involvement in the Montgomery Bus Boycott made her famous. The boycott started in 1955 after Rosa was arrested for refusing to give up her seat on a city bus to a white man. When she was arrested, African Americans in Montgomery organized a boycott of the bus system. This meant that they refused to ride the buses again until they were treated fairly. The boycott lasted for 381 days, until the United States Supreme Court declared that segregation on buses was not allowed by the U.S. Constitution.

Rosa Parks moved to Detroit, Michigan, in 1957. She worked for U.S. Representative John Conyers from 1965 to 1988. In 1987, she helped found the Rosa and Raymond Parks Institute for Self Development. Rosa Parks died on October 24, 2005, at the age of 92.

Rosa Parks made a difference by participating in the civil rights movement. In this way, she made the world a better place.

Sources:

Parks, Rosa and Jim Haskins. Rosa Parks: My Story, New York: Dial Books, 1992.

The Rosa and Raymond Parks Institute for Self Development, www.rosaparks.org.

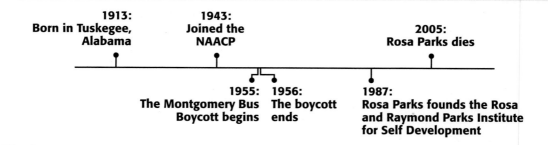

1913:
Born in Tuskegee, Alabama

1943:
Joined the NAACP

2005:
Rosa Parks dies

1955:
The Montgomery Bus Boycott begins

1956:
The boycott ends

1987:
Rosa Parks founds the Rosa and Raymond Parks Institute for Self Development

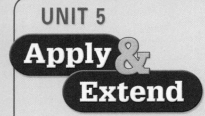
REVISE

1. Review your report. Is it clear and easy to read? Look for any places where the ideas do not flow in a logical order.

2. Exchange your report with a partner. Ask your partner to use the **Peer Review Checklist** to review your report.

3. Revise your draft using the **Revising and Editing Checklist**. Make any changes necessary to make your research report clearer and better organized.

4. Use the **editing and proofreading symbols** on page 455 to help you mark the changes you need to make.

EDIT

1. Use the **Revising and Editing Checklist** to evaluate your report again.

2. Fix any errors in grammar, spelling, and punctuation.

Revising and Editing Checklist

1. My report tells about a person who has made a difference in the world.

2. My report tells about the most important events in the person's life.

3. I included dates of important events.

4. I included a timeline.

5. I listed my sources at the end of my report.

6. I used perfect tenses and verbals.

Peer Review Checklist

1. The report gives information about a person's life.

2. The events of the person's life are given in the order they happened.

3. One new thing I learned from the report is _____ .

4. I would have liked to learn more about _____ .

PUBLISH

1. Write your report in your best handwriting so that it is clear and easy to read. Or, use a computer to write your report. Be sure to use appropriate margins and spacing.

2. Draw the final version of the timeline for your report. You may want to illustrate the events on your timeline.

● Projects

Choose one or more of the following projects to explore the theme of making a difference further.

PROJECT 1

Volunteer at a Local Organization.

1. Choose an organization that helps people in your community. Find out what the organization does and how it helps people.
2. Fill out an application to volunteer at this organization. Be ready to supply your name, address, and phone number, and possibly the name and phone number of a parent or caregiver. Also be ready to say why you want to volunteer at that organization and what you want to do there. Remember to complete all of the steps of the application.
3. Spend a day volunteering at the organization.
4. After you volunteer, create a presentation summarizing your experience. Present it to the class. If possible, create a PowerPoint presentation about your experience.

PROJECT 2

Analyze a Speech That Made a Difference.

Sometimes a speech can change the way people think. One of the most important speeches in American history was Martin Luther King Jr.'s "I Have a Dream" speech.

1. Find a recording of the "I Have a Dream" speech online.
2. Listen to the recording. As you listen, think about what made the speech so effective.
3. Make a list of devices that King used to make his speech effective. Discuss your list with a partner.

PROJECT 3

Dramatize a Situation in Which Someone Makes a Difference.

1. With a group, brainstorm some situations in which one person helps another.
2. Choose one situation and write a script about it. Include dialogue that shows what the people in the scene are thinking and feeling. Also include stage directions that tell the actors what to do and how to say their lines.
3. Perform your scene for the class. After each performance, discuss how words and actions showed what the people in the scene were thinking. How did things like word choice, pitch, and tone of voice work with the postures and gestures the actors used?

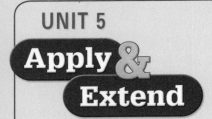

UNIT 5

Apply & Extend

● Independent Reading

Explore the theme of making a difference further by reading one or more of these books.

Code Talker by Joseph Bruchac, Dial Books, 2005.

Throughout World War II, Navajo code talkers helped the United States by sending messages in a code based on the Navajo language. They played an important part in helping win the war. This novel tells the story of Ned Begay, a 16-year-old boy who becomes a code talker. The experience changes Ned's life.

Through My Eyes by Ruby Bridges, Scholastic, 1999.

In this autobiography, Ruby Bridges tells the true story of how she helped to integrate a school in 1960. Ruby was the first African-American student at the all-white William Frantz Public School in New Orleans, Louisiana. She had to face angry mobs of protesters and learn all by herself in her own classroom. Her courage created new opportunities for other African-American students.

Snow Goose by Paul Gallico, Knopf, 1971.

A lonely artist and a young girl work together to take care of an injured snow goose during World War II. Their actions cause them to become involved in the rescue of stranded British soldiers at Dunkirk.

Promises to the Dead by Mary Downing Hahn, Clarion Books, 2000.

During the Civil War, a dying woman asks Jesse Sherman for help. The woman asks Jesse to help her seven-year-old son escape slavery. Jesse becomes trapped between the two sides in the war in an attempt to keep his promise.

Journey for Peace: The Story of Rigoberta Menchu by Marlene Brill, Dutton Books, 1996.

Rigoberta Menchu led a struggle for the rights of Mayan Indians in Guatemala. Her efforts to make a difference in the lives of poor Guatemalans led to her receiving the Nobel Peace Prize. This book tells the story of her quest to end violence in Guatemala.

Milestones to Achievement

● Writing: Revise and Edit

Read this rough draft of a student's business letter, which may contain errors. Then answer Questions 1 through 4.

(1) 1256 Sunshine Lane
(2) San Francisco, CA 92501
(3) September 6, 2009

(4) Super Foods Supermarket Headquarters
(5) 18 Second St.
(6) Sacramento, CA 94203

(7) To Whom it May Concern:

(8) My name is Javier Fuentes. (9) I volunteer with other students at an organization that takes donations of food and clothing. (10) <u>I am writing request</u> your help to meet our goal of providing full Thanksgiving dinners for 50 families this year. (11) I thinked you might be able to help us.

(12) I would like to give you more information about the group I volunteer for. (13) The name of our group is Give Back, and this is the third year that <u>we had helped</u> in the community. (14) Thanksgiving is our most important time, and we will be working very hard to reach our goal.

(15) We would like to know if Super Foods Supermarket would like to help Give Back. (16) Your generousity would be appreciated by us.

(17) Sincerely,

(18) *Javier Fuentes*
(19) Javier Fuentes

---

1 What is the correct way to write the underlined part of sentence 10?

- A   I am writing requested
- B   I am writing am requesting
- C   I am writing to request
- D   I am writing requests

2 What is the correct way to write the underlined part of sentence 13?

- A   we will have helping
- B   we will have helped
- C   we have helping
- D   we have helped

3 How can you correct the word "thinked" in sentence 11?

- A   Change to *thought.*
- B   Change to *thinking.*
- C   Change to *will have thought.*
- D   Change to *have thought.*

4 Which word is misspelled?

- A   volunteer
- B   generousity
- C   consists
- D   donation

⏱ Writing on Demand: Business Letter

Write to an organization that you admire. Ask for their help with a cause that you are involved in. Explain how you are involved with the cause and how this organization can help. **(20 minutes)**

Read this speech. Then answer Questions 1 through 8.

A Day to Volunteer

1   Principal Lee, Vice Principal Hernández, teachers, community leaders, and my fellow students:

2   Welcome to East Side School's first annual Volunteer Day. As the student body president, I would like to recognize many people for their work in making this day happen. I would like to say thank you to my English teacher, Mrs. Chung, who had helped me even before we decided to make this day a reality. Also, thank you to all the community leaders for their generosity; they have given us the school buses and the supplies we needed. Finally, I want to thank all of you, my hardworking fellow students, for sacrificing your time and energy to make today possible.

3   Before we begin the first annual Volunteer Day, I want to talk about the day's goals and what you will be seeing and doing. You will learn about the homeless and their need for shelter, food, and clothes. You will go to a day care center that needs repairs, and you will visit a retirement home. Let today motivate you to become a lifelong volunteer. You may only give twenty people sandwiches today, but think how many it would be if you did it once a month for the rest of your life. You may only paint one room in a day care center, but think how much help you could offer in a year. You may only spend several hours with an elderly person, but it could be the beginning of a friendship that could last many years. Finally, before the day is over, you will have given your time and energy, but you also will have received something in return: a thank you, a smile, or a hug.

4   Now let's get out there and give it all we've got! Let's show the world what East Side School can do to make the world a better place.

1 What does the word <u>generosity</u> mean in the following sentence from paragraph 2?

> Also, thank you to all the community leaders for their <u>generosity</u>; they have given us the school buses and the supplies we needed.

A giving

B learning

C accomplishing

D teaching

2 What does the word <u>sacrificing</u> mean in the following sentence from paragraph 2?

> Finally, I want to thank all of you, my hardworking fellow students, for <u>sacrificing</u> your time and energy to make today possible.

A purchasing

B getting rid of

C giving up something to achieve a goal

D storing

3 Who is making this speech?

A the principal of East Side School

B a teacher from East Side School

C a community leader

D the student body president of East Side School

4 What does the speaker hope will happen during Volunteer Day?

A Students will learn what it feels like to be homeless.

B Students will learn what it feels like to be elderly.

C Students will help others and learn from them.

D Students will start their own homeless shelters, day cares, and nursing homes.

5 Which sentence contains an example of the past perfect?

A Now let's get out there and give it all we've got!

B I would like to say thank you to my English teacher, Mrs. Chung, who had helped me even before we decided to make this day a reality.

C Also, thank you to all the community leaders for their generosity; they have given us the school buses and the supplies we needed.

D You will go to a day care center that needs repairs, and you will visit a retirement home.

6 Which of these contains an idiom?

A You may only spend several hours with an elderly person, but it could be the beginning of a friendship that could last many years.

B Also, thank you to all the community leaders for their generosity; they have given us the school buses and the supplies we needed.

C Let today motivate you to become a lifelong volunteer.

D Now let's get out there and give it all we've got!

7 Which sentence includes a verbal?

A I want to talk about the day's goals.

B You will learn about the homeless and their need for shelter, food, and clothes.

C You will go to a day care center that needs repairs, and you will visit a retirement home.

D Welcome to East Side School's first annual Volunteer Day.

8 Which phrase begins a section of parallelism?

A Before we begin

B Welcome to

C You may only

D Let today

Leadership

Explore the Theme

1. What does it mean to be a **leader**?
2. Think about the picture of the coach. A coach directs a team so all the players know what to do. What would happen if the team members did not follow the coach?
3. Do you think you would make a good **leader**? Why or why not?

Theme Activity

There have been many famous leaders throughout history. However, you may also know leaders in your own community or school. Make a list of all the leaders you can think of. Then write an explanation of what made or makes this person a leader.

Leader	What This Person Did/Does

CHAPTER 1

Objectives

Reading Strategies
Analyze character;
Identify the main idea

Listening and Speaking
Give a research presentation

Grammar
Learn conditional clauses

Writing
Write a persuasive essay

Academic Vocabulary

dialogue	affect
justify	judge

Academic Content

Biography of freedom fighter Iqbal Masih

Labor leaders Dolores Huerta and César Chávez

● Chapter Focus Question
What qualities must a good leader have?

Reading 1 — **Literature**
Novel (excerpt)
Iqbal
by Francesco D'Adamo

Reading 2 — **Content: Social Studies**
Textbook
The Equal Rights Struggle Expands

Iqbal

● About the Reading
Sometimes, a person who at first does not seem very powerful discovers the strength and ability to be a great leader. In *Iqbal* you will read about such a person.

Build Background

Iqbal Masih

Iqbal is a story based on the real-life experiences of a young boy from Pakistan named Iqbal Masih. When he was 4 years old, Iqbal's family sold him to a moneylender. Iqbal was to work until his family's loan was paid. But like so many children in this situation in Pakistan, Iqbal's release never occurred. He worked for years at a carpet factory, in chains, for 14 or more hours each day and with little to eat or drink. When he was 10, Iqbal escaped. He joined an organization that fought to save child workers. With their help, Iqbal rescued thousands of children from a life of slavery. He also brought international attention to the issue of child labor. In 1994, when he was barely 12 years old, Iqbal won the Reebok Human Rights Award for his work. In 1995, Iqbal was killed, possibly by someone within the carpet industry who made money from the child labor that Iqbal tried to end.

As this excerpt begins, Iqbal has been freed from the factory where he worked. He is still living with the group who freed him— the Liberation Front, run by a man named Eshan Khan—at their headquarters, along with a few other children like him.

Use Prior Knowledge

Brainstorm About Fighting for a Cause

A cause is an effort that focuses on a goal—usually a serious and challenging goal. People often work on causes that help others. Iqbal's cause, for example, was ending child labor. His goal was to free the children who were sold into slavery.

Brainstorm with a partner to make a list of important causes. For each of these causes, choose a well-known person who would be a good leader or representative for that cause.

Cause	Leader

Key Vocabulary

- companion
- courageous
- distribute
- immense
- timid
- tireless

● Vocabulary From the Reading
Learn, Practice, and Use Independently

Learn Vocabulary Use the context (the other words and phrases in the sentence) to determine the meaning of the **highlighted** word.

1. My **companions** and I spent the afternoon washing dogs at the shelter. We all like to help animals.

2. My friend and her dog help to rescue hikers who are lost in the mountains. They are a **courageous** team, searching even in terrible weather conditions.

3. Suzanne **distributes** food to needy families all over her town. Sometimes it takes her hours to deliver food to so many houses.

4. Toby is an **immense** dog; he weighs nearly 140 pounds, and his back is as high as my waist.

5. Many of the dogs at the shelter are **timid**. They won't come up to you, even if you offer them a treat.

6. Suzanne's **tireless** work is impressive. Although she could use a break, she keeps working until every dog is clean and happy.

Practice Vocabulary Use all of the Key Vocabulary words to describe the pictures below. Each picture can be described by more than one vocabulary word.

✓Checkpoint

1. Identify three jobs that require the worker to be **courageous**.

2. Identify one kind of animal that is usually **timid**.

Use Vocabulary Independently For each Key Vocabulary word, write a sentence that describes one of the pictures above.

Vocabulary Log

Workbook page 229

Independent Practice CD-ROM/Online

● Academic Vocabulary

Vocabulary for the Reading Strategy

Word	Explanation	Sample Sentence	Visual Cue
dialogue *noun*	a conversation between two or more people or characters	Marco and Luisa are practicing their **dialogue** for the school play.	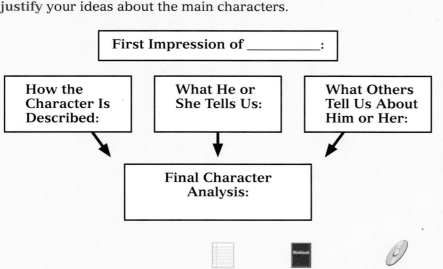
justify *verb*	to give a reason for an action	Josh uses information from several textbooks to **justify** his answer.	

Draw a picture and write a sentence for each word.

● Reading Strategy

Analyze Character

To analyze character, look for details that reveal the personality of a person in a story. Think about what the person says and does. Think about what is revealed in **dialogues** between him or her and other characters. This information will give you insight into the character.

As you read, note these details about the main characters. When you finish *Iqbal*, you will fill in the flow chart below to analyze and **justify** your ideas about the main characters.

First Impression of _____:

How the Character Is Described:

What He or She Tells Us:

What Others Tell Us About Him or Her:

Final Character Analysis:

> **√Checkpoint**
> 1. What is a **dialogue**?
> 2. What does it mean to **justify** your ideas?

Vocabulary Log

Workbook page 230

Independent Practice CD-ROM/Online

Build Your Knowledge

Who is the narrator of this novel? Look for clues in the reading that tell you it is a girl named Fatima. She is another child who Eshan Khan freed from a moneylender. The story about Iqbal is told from her first-person point of view.

● Text Genre

Novel

A **novel** is a long work of fiction. *Iqbal* is a special kind of fiction called a **fictional account.** In a fictional account, the characters and events are based on real people, but the author adds his or her own creative details. Most novels share the features below.

Novel	
characters	people in a novel or story
mood	feeling the author wants the reader to experience while reading scenes or moments in the novel
setting	where and when a story takes place
conflict	a problem or struggle at the center of a story

● Meet the Author

Francesco D'Adamo has written books for readers of all ages. He has won notable awards for his children's books, many of which were first published in Italy. *Iqbal* is the first of D'Adamo's books to be published in the United States, and it has been translated into 10 languages. D'Adamo lives in Milan, Italy.

● Reading Focus Questions

As you read, think about these questions.

1. How does *Iqbal* relate to the theme of "leadership"?
2. What do you think was the author's purpose for writing *Iqbal*?
3. Do you think it is possible for a child to be a leader? Why or why not?

✓Checkpoint

1. What is a **fictional account**?
2. What is a **conflict**?

Workbook
page 231

Independent Practice
CD-ROM/Online

Iqbal

by Francesco D'Adamo

1   That same evening, after dinner, Iqbal made a **solemn declaration** to the men and women who were meeting in the big downstairs room: "I want to stay and help you free all the children who are slaves in Pakistan."

2   Eshan Khan looked at him and smiled.

3   "That's not possible, Iqbal. You were very **courageous** when you **rebelled** and helped us rescue your **companions**, but you can't stay here with us. You belong to your family. What would your father and mother say if we didn't take you home to them?"

Reading Strategy

Analyze Character
Which of Eshan Khan's words reveal something about Iqbal's character?

4   "What good will it do me to go home, if after a year or even sooner I'm a slave again? Or Maria, or Fatima? Or the others? How many children are out there working the way we were?"

5   "We don't know for sure. There are hundreds of **clandestine** carpet factories just in Lahore, and in the countryside there are the brick-making **kilns.** Up toward the mountains there are the mines. And then there are the farm slaves . . . tens of thousands of children, hundreds of thousands, maybe . . ."

6   "You want to free them," said Iqbal. "And, so do I."

7   Maria and I watched, our mouths wide open, we were so impressed. Iqbal was talking like an adult.

Loom for making carpets

Reading Check

1. **Recall details**
   According to Eshan Khan, who does Iqbal belong to?

2. **Recall details**
   Does Eshan Khan know how many children are working as slaves? Why not?

3. **Analyze character**
   Why are Maria and the narrator impressed with Iqbal?

---

solemn serious, not to be taken lightly
declaration statement
rebelled resisted, fought against
clandestine hidden, secret
kilns ovens in which clay is baked into bricks

8   "Think it over, Eshan," one of the men said. "The boy is clever and could be useful. You know how hard it is to get the **magistrates** to **intervene**. Iqbal could sneak in and talk to the children, who would trust him. He can find the proof we need. If it hadn't been for him, we would never have been able to stop Hussain Khan."

9   Eshan Khan continued to shake his head.

10   "No. He'd have to learn so many things. . . ."

Reading Strategy

Analyze Character
What does Iqbal's dialogue with Eshan Khan reveal about Iqbal?

11   "I'll learn," Iqbal promised. "I've already learned to read and write. Well . . . a little, anyway."

12   "It's too dangerous. The carpet merchants and the kiln owners are very powerful. The moneylenders are **influential.** The police tend to protect them—you've already seen that. And the magistrates just look the other way. All of us here have been threatened and **persecuted.** No, we can't allow it."

13   Iqbal stood up and drew himself to his tallest, which actually wasn't very tall. He looked **immensely** tall to us, though, as if he could touch the ceiling.

14   "I'm not afraid," he said. "I'm not afraid of anybody."

15   They believed him.

---

magistrates civil officers with limited power to administer and enforce the law
intervene step in to stop something; here, defend the children against the factory owners and moneylenders
influential powerful
persecuted treated unfairly or harshly

16   Iqbal went home to visit his family. Ten days later Eshan Khan brought him back, and he spent the rest of the day closed up in his room. Toward evening he came out and said, "My mother cried and my father was frightened for me, but now they understand my choice, and they approve. I've promised that I'll go back as often as I can, especially for our holidays, but I want to stay here, Fatima. I want to study. I want to learn everything I can. I want to be a famous lawyer and free all the children in Pakistan."

17   "Good for you, Iqbal!" exclaimed Maria.

18   I said the same, but my voice **trembled.**

19   Iqbal did study. We all did. He also took part in the meetings of the Liberation Front, listening so carefully that his forehead would become wrinkled with the effort to understand.

20   Less than a month after we had been rescued, Iqbal managed to sneak into a carpet factory that was hidden in a damp cellar in the northern outskirts of Lahore. He found thirty-two children covered with **scabies** and wounds, so thin their ribs almost cut through their skin. He spoke to them. He showed them the scars on his hands to win their trust, and he took photos of the chains, the **looms,** the water seeping in. The place was raided three days later by some men from the Liberation Front, accompanied by a magistrate and policemen, who arrested the **proprietor** and freed the children.

> **Reading Strategy**
>
> **Analyze Character**
> What do Iqbal's actions with the children reveal about his character?

✓
Reading Check

1. **Recall facts** What does Iqbal want to become?

2. **Recall facts** What does Iqbal do to win the trust of the children in the carpet factory?

3. **Draw conclusions** Do you think Iqbal had to win the children's trust?

---

trembled shook or wavered
scabies an itchy rash that is caused by the bites of very small insects
looms carpet-weaving machines
proprietor owner and operator

21   All that night and throughout the next day Maria and I worked alongside Eshan Khan's wife and the other women, carrying pots of hot water back and forth for baths and making beds for the new arrivals.

22   Were they ever dirty! It was hard to believe that we were like that when we arrived.

23   Iqbal continued to take his declaration seriously. Over the next few months, he helped close eleven more factories. Almost two hundred children were liberated. They all passed through **Headquarters,** which at times looked like an **orphanage**! They were cared for and then sent back to their families. All the children told the same story, "our" story. They came from isolated villages in the middle of the countryside; there was a bad harvest or an illness, and the families had to ask for loans from the moneylenders. Then the families had to **bond** their children to pay back the debt.

Reading Strategy

Analyze Character
What does Iqbal's hard work indicate about his character?

24   Iqbal wanted to do more.

25   "We have to hit the moneylenders," Iqbal said. "They're to blame for everything."

26   By now he had taken his place in the meetings of the adults, speaking up with **authority**. He was **tireless**. The minute he finished one mission, he began another.

27   "We have to send them all to prison, every single one!" he would say.

28   Maria and I were uncomfortable when he was out **scoping** illegal factories. We worried and waited anxiously for his return.

Headquarters the office and home site of the Liberation Front organization
orphanage temporary home for children without families to live with
bond give for labor as a way of repaying a loan
authority knowledge and expertise
scoping spying on, studying in secret

29   One night he didn't come home and we were afraid something had happened to him. He returned the next morning with a black eye and a cut on his cheek.

30   "I found another workshop," he said, "but they caught me. They smashed the camera, too. Let's just wait a few days, then I'll go back."

31   Eshan Khan was proud of him and treated him like a son. And Maria and I were treated like daughters. We had everything we needed, but still I **fretted** sometimes. Iqbal's and my **paths** were going in different directions, and I felt that soon we would have to separate. I was also occupied by thoughts of my family. Sooner or later my relatives would be found. What would I do then?

32   But there were problems much more important than mine. Eshan Khan was worried. "We have to be careful," he said, "Because *they*, the moneylenders and the people who get rich by **exploiting** children, won't give in so easily. The more children we liberate, the more exploiters we accuse, the more they will try to silence us. That's what they're afraid of . . . our voice. They get rich and fatten where there's silence and ignorance."

Reading Strategy

Analyze Character
What does Iqbal's desire to go back reveal about his character?

Reading Check

1. **Recall details** How do Eshan Khan and the Liberation Front treat the children who are staying with them?

2. **Identify text evidence** Identify two pieces of evidence that indicate how dangerous the Liberation Front's work can be.

3. **Make an inference** What do you think Eshan Khan means when he says the moneylenders "will try to silence us"?

---

fretted worried
paths directions in life
exploiting taking terrible advantage of

A vegetable market in Lahore, Pakistan

Reading Strategy

Analyze Character
What does Eshan Khan's **statement** reflect about his character? Explain your answer.

33 One evening I overheard Eshan Khan talking softly to his wife.

34 "It's Iqbal who worries me. By now they know him. They know that it's thanks to him that we can find them. He's so enthusiastic, but he's **rash.** We'll have to be more cautious."

35 Soon there were two men on guard in the big downstairs room.

36 One night something woke us. We heard strange noises, then gunshots. Then there were shouts and the sound of running feet.

37 "What's happening?" we asked.

38 No one answered.

39 Out in the street some people shook their fists at us, and there were tough-looking men on the sidewalk in front of Headquarters. They would stand there for hours, watching us go in and out.

40 When I thought about Eshan Khan's *they*, I thought of Hussain Khan, but I also realized *they* had to be something even bigger and much worse.

41 Then came the **episode** in the market to **reinforce** my fears.

42 Even in a city as big and modern as Lahore, the outdoor market is the true center of life and activity. Sooner or later during the day everybody passes through, perhaps to shop and meet friends, perhaps simply to look at people. **Periodically** the activists of the Liberation Front would go to the market, where they would build a little platform to speak from. Over the platform they hung a banner that said NO MORE CHILD LABOR, and there were signs with slogans against bonded labor and slavery.

---

rash quick and foolish
episode event
reinforce support, make stronger
periodically from time to time

43 The volunteers **distributed handouts** exactly like the one Iqbal had brought back to us at Hussain Khan's. The men gave short speeches, using a big trumpet-thing they called a **megaphone.**

44 A little crowd always gathered. The merchants, especially the richest ones, ridiculed and insulted the speakers. They even threw things at them. The majority of the audience listened **passively.** Only a few had enough nerve to show **timid** approval. These were usually farmers or laborers, usually people who understood what it meant to lose a child in that way. At least, that's what Iqbal told us, for Maria and I weren't allowed to go. They said it was too dangerous.

45 That day Iqbal spoke, too. He stood balanced **precariously** on a fruit crate, holding the heavy megaphone. Despite his shyness and embarrassment, despite the shouting, the whistling, and the racket of the onlookers, he managed to talk about his experience. He spoke about Hussain Khan and the carpet factory, about children chained to their looms. Then he named names. He shouted all the names he had heard during the meetings at Headquarters, the names of the great moneylenders, the names of rich, important, mysterious men who lived in luxury in the center of town, who traveled, who had business all over the world: Eshan Khan's *they.*

46 He called them **flesh merchants,** exploiters, **vultures.**

> **Reading Strategy**
>
> **Analyze Character** How does Iqbal look, feel, and act at the market? What does this reveal about his characer?

A megaphone like the one used by the Liberation Front in the market

✓ **Reading Check**

1. **Recall facts** How do the merchants show their disapproval of the men's speeches?

2. **Draw conclusions** According to paragraph 44, only a few people in the crowd were brave enough to show any approval of Iqbal's words. Who or what was the crowd afraid of?

---

handouts papers with information on them
megaphone a hollow tube placed against the mouth used to make the voice louder
passively without action or expression
precariously without stability or firmness
flesh merchants people who sell or trade other people
vultures birds that feed on the dead animals they find; here, dangerous, greedy people

47   A **riot** broke out in the square. A small group tried to attack the platform, pushing, slapping. The police had to intervene, not very **willingly**.

48   *They* weren't in the square, of course. They don't go to the open-air market, but evidently they have lots of supporters.

49   The next morning, Eshan Khan came in with a pile of newspapers under his arm. There were articles in all of Lahore's papers, and also in a Karachi paper. Two of them even had printed photos of Iqbal, standing on the platform with that funny trumpet-thing in front of his mouth.

50   One of the papers called him "the **courageous** child who had **denounced** his **oppressors**," and another talked about the "shameful exploitation of a child's innocence."

Reading Strategy

Analyze Character
What does this dialogue indicate about Iqbal?

51   "This is a good thing, isn't it, Father?" he asked Eshan Khan. "You said that *they* keep getting stronger thanks to ignorance and silence. Well, this isn't silence."

52   "Yes, Iqbal," Eshan Khan said, "this is good for our cause."

53   But he didn't seem convinced. He looked worried.

---

riot public disturbance
willingly eagerly, happily
denounced publicly blamed
oppressors those who would crush or overpower others

54   I remember that period so well. Iqbal was happy, enthusiastic about everything, hungry and thirsty for anything new.

55   We were beginning to get used to our new life, to freedom. We could go out whenever we wanted . . . well, almost. Eshan Khan's wife kept a close eye on us. Once she gave us some money and we went to the movies. It was just like Karim said. We saw an Indian film that lasted four hours and I cried the whole time. Iqbal was nasty and wouldn't go see it a second time. We discovered television. We listened to strange music that came from far away— from America, they said.

56   Iqbal was full of plans for the future. He talked about them to Maria and me. He wasn't afraid of all the new things. I was, at least a little. Everything was happening so fast, or maybe I was afraid the happy dream would end, too fast.

57   One day a foreign person in strange clothes came to Headquarters. He said he was an American reporter. He interviewed Iqbal and Eshan Khan for two hours. A few days later an **international correspondent** came.

58   "When people abroad know about our cause, they'll help us and we'll be safer," said Eshan Khan.

59   One night we were awakened by a loud explosion. We could hear screams and see flames rising up to the windows on the second floor. We tried to go downstairs but Eshan Khan stopped us.

60   "You stay here!" he roared.

61   Someone had thrown two **incendiary** bombs against Headquarters. A man was injured and had to go to the hospital. *They* had sent a warning.

Reading Strategy

Analyze Character
What does this paragraph suggest about the differences between Iqbal and the narrator?

Reading Check

1. **Recall facts** Who interviews Iqbal and Eshan Khan at Headquarters?

2. **Make inferences** Why do you think Iqbal—a child—is included in the interview?

3. **Predict** Do you think the Liberation Front will be successful against the moneylenders and merchants who exploit children? Why or why not?

---

international correspondent journalist who covers news from all over the world
incendiary fire-causing

● Apply the Reading Strategy

Analyze Character

Now complete the Reading Strategy flow chart.

1. Review the **Reading Strategy** on page 359 and copy the flow chart.

2. Look back at the reading. Analyze the character of Iqbal. Fill in the chart as you find information that fits into each space.

3. Use the last space in the chart to **justify** your impression of Iqbal. Then repeat the chart for the remaining major characters.

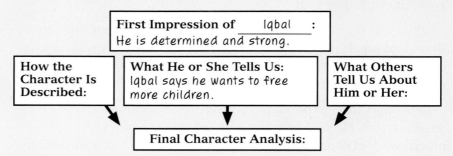

First Impression of _____Iqbal_____ :
He is determined and strong.

| How the Character Is Described: | What He or She Tells Us:
Iqbal says he wants to free more children. | What Others Tell Us About Him or Her: |

Final Character Analysis:

● Academic Vocabulary

Vocabulary for the Reading Comprehension Questions

Word	Explanation	Sample Sentence	Visual Cue
affect *verb*	to influence or have an impact on someone or something	The trainer **affects** the behavior of the horse.	
judge *verb*	to consider something and then give an official decision	The umpire **judges** each pitch and decides if it is a strike.	

Draw a picture and write a sentence for each word.

✓Checkpoint

1. In what way can the weather **affect** someone's mood?

2. What kinds of things can be **judged**?

Vocabulary
Log

Reading Comprehension Questions

Think and Discuss

1. **Recall facts** Where did Iqbal work as a bonded slave?

2. **Describe** Using the Key Vocabulary words, describe the characters in *Iqbal*. Look for clues in the text to help you write each description.

3. **Identify mood** What is the mood of this selection?

4. **Connect ideas** How does Iqbal's conflict with the moneylenders **affect** the mood of the work? How does the setting **affect** the mood? How does the setting **affect** the conflict in the story?

5. **Judge** Think about the information in the **Build Background** on page 357. Does Iqbal's character in the novel seem like the same person you read about? Do you think the events in this story could have really happened?

6. **Revisit the Reading Focus Questions** Go back to page 360 and discuss the questions.

Workbook
page 232

Independent Practice
CD-ROM/Online

Literary Element

Simile

A **simile** is a comparison of two different or unlikely things. Similes use the words *like* or *as* to make these comparisons. Even though a simile compares two things that seem very different, a simile highlights the shared characteristics of these two things.

In *Iqbal*, for example, the narrator tells readers that the headquarters of the Liberation Front looked "like an orphanage." The headquarters is not an actual orphanage—the children who stay there have family in Pakistan. However, when the children are rescued, many will stay at Headquarters at the same time. The narrator suggests that so many children living in one place is typical of orphanages.

Read each simile below. Then explain the similarity that the simile points out.

1. Iqbal is **as small as a mouse**, but his strength of character is **immense**.

2. The incendiary device was **as loud as thunder** when it exploded.

3. The outdoor market is **like a carnival.**

4. The merchants are **as stubborn as mountains.**

5. Iqbal is **like an angel** to the children in the factory.

1. Create a **simile** that describes Eshan Khan.

2. Create a simile that describes the market.

Workbook
page 233

Independent Practice
CD-ROM/Online

The Equal Rights Struggle Expands

● About the Reading

In *Iqbal*, you read about how a young boy became a leader in the struggle to free children from terrible working conditions in Pakistan. In "The Equal Rights Struggle Expands," you will read about leaders who fought for fair working conditions for farm workers in the United States.

Dolores Huerta and César Chávez formed the National Farm Workers Association in 1962.

● Build Background

The United Farm Workers Union

In the 1950s, Mexican-American farmers began a long fight for fair working conditions in the agricultural, or farming, industry in the United States. Farming was one of the country's largest businesses. Its success was due, in large part, to farm workers. However, the workers were given poor housing and paid low wages. It was clear that the farm workers needed a labor union, an organization that would protect and defend them. Dolores Huerta and César Chávez worked together to create a union that would later be called the United Farm Workers.

● Vocabulary From the Reading

Use Context Clues to Determine Meaning

Read each sentence below. Use the context to figure out the meaning of each **highlighted** word. Discuss the meanings with a small group.

1. Joey wanted to help end poverty. He became an **activist** for that cause, raising money and volunteering his time to help the poor.
2. Our teacher knows we want to succeed, which is why he **advocates** studying, doing homework, and participating in class.
3. When the grape growers treated their farmers badly, buyers stopped buying grapes. This **boycott** continued until the grape growers improved conditions for their workers.
4. I gave a small **contribution** during the fundraiser. The charity raised nearly one million dollars that night.
5. The union spoke to the farm owners and **negotiated** a new contract for the employees, one that gave them better pay.
6. The workers called for **reform** because they didn't like how they were treated. They made a list of the changes they wanted and then they talked to their employer about the list.

Key Vocabulary

activist

advocate

boycott

contribution

negotiate

reform

✓ Checkpoint

1. What kinds of **contributions** can be made to a charity?
2. What kind of behavior do doctors **advocate**?

Vocabulary Log

Workbook page 234

Independent Practice CD-ROM/Online

● Reading Strategy

Identify the Main Idea

The **main idea** of a piece of writing is the most important, or central, message. In informational texts, the main idea is surrounded by facts and details. As a reader, you must identify the main idea in order to understand how the details relate to it.

1. As you read, note the main idea of each paragraph and section.

2. Note the details and facts that relate to the main idea.

3. Make sure you understand the main idea before moving on to the next paragraph or section.

● Text Genre

Informational Text: Social Studies Textbook

"The Equal Rights Struggle Expands" is a selection from a social studies textbook. Textbooks are used by students who are learning about a particular content area. Many social studies textbooks contain the features below.

Social Studies Textbook	
primary sources	documents created at the time of an event or quotations from a person who lived at that time
summaries	brief statements that cover the most important features of a reading selection
boxed items	comments or activities that relate to, but are separate from, the main text; they often appear to the side of the main reading

● Reading Focus Questions

As you read, think about these questions.

1. How does this reading connect to the theme of "leadership"?

2. What do you think is the purpose of reading about Huerta and Chávez now?

3. Who might be inspired by their story?

✓**Checkpoint**

1. How are **main ideas** supported in an informational text?

2. Would the John F. Kennedy speech in Unit 5 be considered a primary source? Explain your answer.

Workbook
pages 235–236

Independent Practice
CD-ROM/Online

The Equal Rights Struggle Expands

Activist Dolores Huerta

Reading Strategy

Identify the Main Idea
What is the main idea of the section titled "One American's Story"?

One American's Story

1   During the first half of the twentieth century, efforts by farm workers to organize labor unions had been **suppressed** by farm owners. In the 1950s and 1960s, Mexican-American **activists** continued to organize, inspired by African Americans in the civil rights movement. Dolores Huerta was teaching the children of farm workers in California when she realized what her **contribution** would be.

2   PRIMARY SOURCE

"I couldn't stand seeing kids come to class hungry and needing shoes. I thought I could do more by organizing farm workers than by trying to teach their hungry children."
        —Dolores Huerta, *Biography of Dolores Huerta*

3   Huerta went on to help **found** the first farm workers' union in 1962. She became the union's chief negotiator for contracts, guaranteeing farm workers fair wages, **benefits**, and **humane** working conditions.

Other Minorities Organize

4   **KEY QUESTION**

How did other minorities fight for civil rights?

5   The civil rights movement sent **shock waves** through American society. Many people **reconsidered** issues of equality and **discrimination** and became politically involved in their communities. The civil rights movement encouraged other minorities in their fight for equal rights.

---

suppressed held back, kept down
found establish, create
benefits a service (like health insurance) or a right (as to take vacation time) provided by an employer in addition to wages or salary
humane compassionate or sympathetic
shock waves feelings of great surprise or disruption
reconsidered thought again about
discrimination unfair treatment due to things such as race, gender, age, and religion

6   **Mexican Americans Unite**   **Latinos** trace their roots to Spanish-speaking Latin American countries. The Latino population in the United States is extremely diverse. It includes people from many places, including Mexico, Puerto Rico, Cuba, and Central and South America. Each group has its own social and political concerns. For example, Mexican Americans are concerned about immigration and citizenship. Puerto Ricans are already U.S. citizens; therefore immigration issues aren't their primary concern.

7   Like African Americans, Mexican Americans united to fight for equality. In the 1950s, César Chávez, a Mexican-American farm worker and labor organizer, began working with Dolores Huerta to create a labor union. Chávez had been inspired by the nonviolent **tactics** of Gandhi and Martin Luther King Jr. In 1962, Chávez and Huerta founded what would become the United Farm Workers Organizing Committee (UFWOC). In 1965, when California's grape growers refused to recognize the union, Chávez launched a nationwide grape **boycott**. The **boycott** succeeded, and in 1970 Huerta **negotiated** a favorable contract between grape growers and the UFWOC.

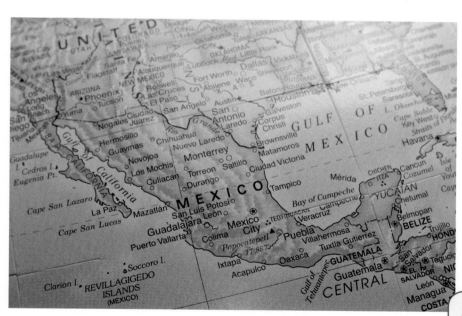

> **Reading Strategy**
>
> **Identify the Main Idea** What is the main idea of the text on this page?

> ✔
> **Reading Check**
> 1. **Recall facts** The Latino population in the United States includes people from what places?
> 2. **Draw conclusions** Why do you think the boycott succeeded?

---

tactics methods

Reading Strategy

Identify the Main Idea
Write one sentence that summarizes the main idea of paragraph 8.

8   The farm workers' struggle inspired Mexican Americans in cities to organize. In 1968, students in Los Angeles walked out of classes to **press** their demands for **reform** in the school system. They wanted better facilities, more courses on Mexican-American topics, and more Mexican-American teachers. At first, school authorities had protesters arrested. Later, they admitted to the poor conditions, and many **reforms** were eventually made. In 1970, Mexican Americans formed *La Raza Unida* (lah RAH•sah oo•NEE•dah), meaning the united people, to elect Mexican Americans to public office and to **advocate** for better jobs, pay, housing, and education.

History Makers

César Chávez   1927–1993

9   César Chávez helped to improve the working conditions of farm workers. In 1962 he started an organization that became the United Farm Workers union. Through nonviolent protests, **boycotts**, and voter registration drives, this group brought national attention to the workers' struggle for equal and fair treatment.

Dolores Huerta   b. 1930

10   Huerta was a founding member of the National Farm Workers Association (NFWA) with César Chávez. Huerta's work helped bring about important legislation. The California Agricultural Labor Relations Act of 1975 allows farm workers to collectively organize and **bargain**. The Immigration Act of 1985 resulted in over a million farm workers receiving **amnesty**. Today, Huerta continues to help improve the lives of immigrants, women, and young people.

---

press push
bargain negotiate contracts
amnesty forgiveness, without paying a price, for any wrongs committed

Reading Primary Sources

An Open Letter

[11] **SETTING THE STAGE** In a 1969 letter, César Chávez denied accusations that he had used violence to win decent wages and better benefits for farm workers.

[12]   Today … we remember the life and sacrifice of Martin Luther King Jr., who gave himself totally to the nonviolent struggle for peace and justice. In his letter from Birmingham Jail, Dr. King describes better than I could our hopes for the **strike** and **boycott**: "Injustice must be exposed, with all the **tension** its exposure creates, to the light of human conscience and the air of national opinion before it can be cured." For our part, I admit that we have **seized** upon every tactic and strategy **consistent** with the **morality** of our cause to expose that injustice and **thus** to **heighten** the **sensitivity** of the American conscience so that farm workers will have without bloodshed their own union and the dignity of bargaining with their **agribusiness** employers….

Our Cause

[13]   Farm workers were excluded from the National Labor Relations Act of 1935—the law that gives most Americans the right to organize a union. Chávez wanted lawmakers to allow farm workers to organize unions.

1. Why do you think farm workers wanted to organize a union?

Reading Strategy

Identify the Main Idea Which sentence in the boxed item is the main idea of Chávez's letter?

Reading Check

1. **Recall details** In what year did Chávez write his letter?

2. **Identify** What primary source does Chávez cite in his letter?

3. **Speculate** Why do you think it was important to Chávez to use only nonviolent tactics to draw attention to his cause?

---

strike refusal to work
tension discomfort
seized taken
consistent in keeping with
morality sense of right and wrong
thus by doing so
heighten increase
sensitivity compassion
agribusiness farming business

Reading Strategy

Identify the Main Idea
What is the main idea of paragraph 14?

14   Our strikers here in Delano and those who represent us throughout the world are well trained for this struggle. … they have been taught not to **lie down and die** or to flee in shame, but to resist with every ounce of human **endurance** and spirit. To resist not with **retaliation** in kind but to overcome with love and compassion, with **ingenuity** and creativity, with hard work and longer hours, with **stamina** and patient **tenacity**, with truth and public **appeal**, with friends and allies, with mobility and discipline, with politics and law, and with prayer and **fasting**. They were not trained in a month or even a year; after all, this new harvest season will mark our fourth full year of strike and even now we continue to plan and prepare for the years to come… .

15   We shall overcome and change it not by retaliation or bloodshed but by a determined nonviolent struggle carried on by those masses of farm workers who intend to be free and human.

—*César E. Chávez*

Our Cause

16   During the civil rights era, protesters often received extensive training before participating in marches, demonstrations, and **sit-ins**. Chávez explains that farm workers were also trained for the struggle.

2. Why might training for nonviolent protest be necessary?

---

lie down and die accept failure
endurance ability to withstand hardship
retaliation fighting back
ingenuity cleverness
stamina ability to keep going
tenacity persistence in seeking something valued or desired
appeal plea, begging for sympathy
fasting refusal to eat
sit-ins acts of protest where people sit in seats or on a floor and refuse to leave

Reading Comprehension Questions

Think and Discuss

1. **Recall facts** When did Dolores Huerta help found the first farm workers union?

2. **Identify** Identify each of the primary sources cited in "The Equal Rights Struggle Expands." How did each source relate to the selection?

3. **Summarize** Write a brief paragraph that summarizes the reading. Use the Key Vocabulary words in your summary.

4. **Explain** What is the purpose of the boxed items in this selection?

5. **Ask questions** If you could interview Chávez or Huerta today, what two questions would you ask them?

6. **Revisit the Reading Focus Questions** Go back to page 373 and discuss the questions.

Workbook
page 237

Independent Practice
CD-ROM/Online

Spelling

The Suffixes -er and -or

Workbook
page 238

Independent Practice
CD-ROM/Online

Writing Conventions

Spelling: Contractions

Workbook
page 239

Independent Practice
CD-ROM/Online

Connect Readings 1 and 2

You have read two readings on the theme of leadership: *Iqbal* and "The Equal Rights Struggle Expands." Use these activities to make connections between the readings.

1. With a partner, use this chart to compare the structure of the two readings.

Reading title	What is the text genre?	Which reading used primary sources?	Which reading did you find most interesting? Why?
Iqbal			
The Equal Rights Struggle Expands			

2. With a partner, ask and answer these questions.
   a. How did both authors use real events and people in the selections?
   b. What challenges did Iqbal share with Huerta and Chávez?
   c. Which reading is meant to both entertain and inform readers?

3. **Revisit the Chapter Focus Question** What qualities must a good leader have? Use examples from *Iqbal* and "The Equal Rights Struggle Expands" to answer this question.

Phrases for Conversation

Giving Compliments

That was great!
Good job!
Terrific!
Well done!

● Listening and Speaking

Give a Research Presentation

Research a leader who inspires you in some way. Present a brief speech that describes the person and his or her accomplishments. Include visual aids to add interest to your speech.

1. Brainstorm a brief list of people you find inspiring, and think about why he or she is inspiring to you.

2. Choose one person from your list.

   a. Go to your library and research this person. Use the Internet as well as books and print or online encyclopedias.

   b. Create a timeline, or chronology, of the person's life and accomplishments.

   c. Include a photograph of the person and, if possible, an example of his or her work.

3. Organize your speech.

   a. Your speech should follow the order of events in the timeline you created.

   b. Be sure to include the reason why you chose this person as the subject of your presentation.

   c. Edit your speech, adding active verbs, vivid descriptions, and colorful details to make your speech interesting.

4. Rehearse your presentation. Be sure to practice how you will share your visual aids with the class.

5. Give your speech to your classmates.

6. After listening to your classmates' speeches, compliment them on their presentations.

Martin Luther King Jr. and Amelia Earhart were two inspirational American leaders.

● Reading Fluency

Reading Silently

Reading silently helps you to read faster and become a more fluent reader.

1. Listen to the audio recording of page 361 of *Iqbal*. Read along as you listen.

2. Then silently reread paragraphs 1–7 two times. Read the paragraphs within 1.5 minutes. You will be reading 200 words per minute. Your partner will time your readings.

3. Reread the page two more times. Each time you reread the passage, try to increase your reading rate.

● Vocabulary Development

Suffix: -ion

A **suffix** is a word part that is added to the end of a word. A suffix can change the meaning of a word, and it often changes a word's part of speech. The suffixes **-tion** and **-sion** change a word into a noun. For example, the verb *impress* changes to a noun when it becomes *impression*. *Isolate* becomes the noun *isolation*. Note that spelling changes are sometimes necessary.

Add a **-tion** ending to each of the following words.

1. **negotiate**
2. populate
3. direct
4. immigrate

Add a **-sion** ending to each of these words.

5. suppress
6. success
7. express
8. confuse

Vocabulary
Log

Workbook
page 240

Independent Practice
CD-ROM/Online

● Grammar

Conditional Clauses

Use conditional clauses beginning with **if, unless,** and **even if** to express:

- a real or possible situation that occurs in the present. Both the conditional clause and the main clause are in the present tense.

  If you heat ice, it melts.

  I am always cold **even if I wear a sweater.**

- a real or possible situation in the future. The conditional clause is in the present tense, and the main clause is in the future tense.

  Your feet will get wet **if you walk through the puddle.**

  Unless you do your homework, you will not get a good grade on the test.

Note

When the conditional clause is at the beginning of the sentence, use a comma after the clause. Do not use a comma if the clause follows the main clause.

Practice the Grammar Using the two sentences in each item below, create one sentence by making one of them a conditional clause with *if, even if,* or *unless.* Underline the conditional clause.

nothing will change / the Liberation Front is silent.

Nothing will change if the Liberation Front is silent.

1. you demand better working conditions / the employers might not listen
2. the Liberation Front will accomplish more / Iqbal helps them
3. the world knows about the Liberation Front / more children will be helped
4. the world will know about Iqbal / newspapers print stories about him
5. the child labor laws change / more children will be in danger

---

Use the Grammar Independently Write three sentences with conditional clauses. Use *if, even if,* and *unless* in your sentences.

Conditional clauses can also be used to express unreal or imaginary situations. Use these clauses to express:

- an unreal situation in the present used to express what would happen in an imaginary situation.

  If I had more time, I would read more.

  We would go to the party **if Dad gave us permission.**

  To create these sentences, use one of the following structures:

  Conditional clause **(If + past tense),** + main clause **(would + verb).**

  Main clause **(would + verb)** + conditional clause **(if + past tense).**

Note

When using the verb *to be* in the conditional clause, use *were* instead of *was* for subjects I / he / she / it.

  If I were older, I would have a driver's license.

- an unreal situation in the past used to express how something could have happened differently.

  If I had gone to the game, I would have caught that fly ball.

  He would have gone to the party **if he had been invited.**

  To create these sentences, use one of the following structures:

  Conditional clause **(If + past perfect tense),** + main clause **(would have + verb).**

  Main clause **(would have + verb)** + conditional clause **(if + past perfect tense).**

Grammar Expansion

Conditional Expressions with Modals *should*, *could*, and *might*

Workbook
page 244

Independent Practice
CD-ROM/Online

Practice the Grammar Match each sentence beginning with the correct ending.

1. The students would learn more about their culture

2. The growers would suffer

3. If Huerta and Chávez had not worked together,

4. If the employers didn't listen to their workers,

a. they would not have formed the National Farm Workers Association.

b. if the schools gave classes on Mexican-American topics.

c. if the workers held a boycott.

d. reforms would not be made.

✓*Checkpoint*

1. Write a sentence using a conditional clause to express an unreal situation in the present.

2. When do you use a comma with a conditional clause?

Use the Grammar Independently Complete the following sentences with an appropriate main or conditional clause.

1. Mark would have bought the bicycle . . .

2. If Larissa were good at sports, . . .

Workbook
pages 241–243

Independent Practice
CD-ROM/Online

● Writing Assignment

Write a Persuasive Essay

> ### Writing Prompt
>
> Write an essay that persuades your readers of one way they can lead others and why it is important. Be sure to include conditional clauses.

Write Your Persuasive Essay

1. **Read the student model.** In this model, a student tells why it is important for people to act as role models for children. Look for ways the writer tries to persuade the reader.

Student Model

Children follow by example. Therefore, it is very important for all adults and teenagers to act as role models for children.

Children admire the older people around them. Because of this, they often imitate what they see others doing. If you do the wrong thing, they might do it, too. So we must think about every action we take and whether we would want a child to do it, too.

If you think of yourself as a role model, it will help you to remember to do what is good for you and others. This can include following the rules in school, listening to your teacher, and doing what you are told.

When you act as a good role model, you are also telling the people around you that they can trust you. By acting mature and being a good role model, people know that they can count on you.

Think of yourself as a role model. Remember that children look up to us to know right from wrong. There will often be a child watching what you do and how you do it. Don't you want to show the child what is right?

2. Prewrite.

a. Begin by brainstorming ideas. Think about the little ways that someone can show leadership.

b. Choose one way that seems easy to accomplish, yet is important.

c. Think of ways to persuade your reader. For example, you can use the example of a famous person who demonstrates leadership behavior. You can also appeal to your reader's emotions by suggesting how showing leadership can change his or her life as well as the lives of others.

3. Write your essay. Include an introduction that ends in a thesis statement. Put your persuasive technique in the body. End your essay with a summary of your main points.

4. Revise. Read your essay aloud. Revise any sentences or paragraphs that seem unclear or misplaced. Make sure your ideas are well-organized and consistent.

Use the **editing and proofreading symbols** on page 455 to mark any changes you want to make.

5. Edit. Use the **Writing Checklist** to help you find any errors.

6. Read your essay to the class.

> ### Writing Checklist
>
> **1.** I wrote an introduction, a body, and a conclusion.
>
> **2.** I clearly stated the thesis of my essay.
>
> **3.** I used conditional clauses.
>
> **4.** I proofread my work.

Writing Support

Spelling

Spelling Rules and Frequently Misspelled Words

English has many spelling rules. Here are a few of those rules.

- *i* before *e*, except after *c* or when it sounds like an *a*
  Examples: piece, ceiling, neighbor

- Change *y* to *i* before adding *-es*
  Examples: candy ➞ candies, sky ➞ skies, penny ➞ pennies

- Double the final consonant in many words before adding *-ing* or *-er*
  Examples: pin / pinning; bat / batting; hot / hotter

These words are commonly misspelled:

    argument conscience grateful misspell noticeable

    possession privilege separate vacuum Wednesday

Apply Check for commonly misspelled words. Have you spelled them correctly?

Workbook
pages 246–248

Independent Practice
CD-ROM/Online

Progress Check

How well did you understand this chapter? Try to answer the questions. If necessary, go back to the pages listed for a review.

Skills	Skills Assessment Questions	Pages to Review
Vocabulary From the Readings	What do these words mean? • **companion, courageous, distribute, immense, timid, tireless**	358
	• **activist, advocate, boycott, contribution, negotiate, reform**	372
Academic Vocabulary	What do these academic vocabulary words mean? • **dialogue, justify**	359
	• **affect, judge**	370
Reading Strategies	What does it mean to analyze character?	359
	In a textbook, what kind of material often surrounds the **main idea**?	373
Text Genres	What is the text genre of *Iqbal*?	360
	What is the text genre of "The Equal Rights Struggle Expands"?	373
Reading Comprehension	What is *Iqbal* about?	371
	What is "The Equal Rights Struggle Expands" about?	379
Literary Element	What is a **simile**?	371
Spelling	What part of speech is formed when the suffix *–er* or *–or* is added to a verb?	379
Writing Conventions	Give the contraction form of "will not."	379
Listening and Speaking	**Phrases for Conversation** Identify one way to compliment someone's performance.	380
Vocabulary Development	What noun do you create when you add the suffix *-ion* to the word *create*?	381
Grammar	Give an example of a sentence with a conditional clause.	382–383
Writing Support: Spelling	What happens to the final *–y* in words when they become plural?	385

Assessment Practice

Read this passage. Then answer Questions 1 through 4.

Jackie Robinson

1   Jackie Robinson was an admirable man and a leader in many ways. He was a baseball player, a writer, and a civil rights activist. In 1947, he became the first African American in the 20th century to play professional baseball. Even though players and fans were sometimes cruel to him, Jackie was courageous. In 1947, he was named Rookie of the Year. He went on to win many other awards during his baseball career.

2   Jackie Robinson was like a champion both on the field and off the field. During the 1960s, he was involved in politics and wrote for a newspaper. He supported civil rights leaders like Martin Luther King Jr. and Malcolm X, and worked for the rights of all people.

3   In 2007, ballparks around the country held Jackie Robinson Day to honor Robinson for his contributions to baseball and to the country. If Jackie Robinson had not broken baseball's color barrier, America would have missed the chance to know a remarkable player and a courageous man.

1 **What does the word <u>courageous</u> mean in the following sentence?**

> Even though players and fans were sometimes cruel to him, Jackie was <u>courageous</u>.

  A kind   **B** angry

  C brave   **D** upset

2 **What is the main idea of this passage?**

  A Robinson was a civil rights activist.

  B Robinson was Rookie of the Year.

  C Robinson was a remarkable player and a courageous man.

  D Robinson won many awards.

3 **What is a simile in the passage?**

  A Jackie Robinson was like a champion both on the field and off the field.

  B He went on to win many other awards during his baseball career.

  C He was a baseball player, a writer, and a civil rights activist.

  D Jackie Robinson was an admirable man and a leader in many ways.

4 **What is the text genre for this passage?**

  A poem

  B persuasive essay

  C textbook excerpt

  D autobiographical short story

Writing on Demand: Persuasive Essay

Write a persuasive essay about an important leader. Use examples from his or her life to persuade your audience that the person was or is a strong leader. **(20 minutes)**

> **Writing Tip**
> Include a thesis statement in your essay and support it with details from the person's life.

CHAPTER 2

Objectives

Reading Strategies
Distinguish fact from opinion; Recognize imagery

Listening and Speaking
Role-play an interview

Grammar
Learn to avoid shifts in writing; Learn the active and passive voices

Writing
Write a research essay

Academic Vocabulary

distinguish	factor
locate	resource

Academic Content

A nationwide science contest

Slavery and the Underground Railroad

● Chapter Focus Question
What can a really good leader teach you?

Reading 1 **Content:** Science
Brochure and newspaper article
Science Olympiad
He's Teacher, Student, and Cheerleader
by Eric Carpenter

Reading 2 **Literature**
Historical novel (excerpt)
Harriet Tubman: Conductor on the Underground Railroad
by Ann Petry

Science Olympiad

● About the Reading

Have you ever attended a science fair? Imagine a science competition that involves students from schools across the country. You are going to read about such an event that tests talented high-school students on all different areas of science, with the best and brightest taking home the first place prize.

Build Background

The Original Olympiad

Science Olympiad is a science competition that takes its name from the ancient Olympic Games in Greece. The original games were held in the city of Olympia in 776 BCE. They were meant to present the athletic talents of the competitors. In the modern Olympic Games, athletes compete in specialized events, like swimming and gymnastics. In the Olympiad that you will read about, science is the main event.

Use Prior Knowledge

Imagine an Academic Olympiad

At the Science Olympiad, students compete in different areas of science.

There are many different areas of science. How do you know? Copy the graphic organizer. Then work with a partner to fill in the graphic organizer with as many different areas of science as you can. Add more circles as needed. Finally, discuss what you know about one or more of these areas of science.

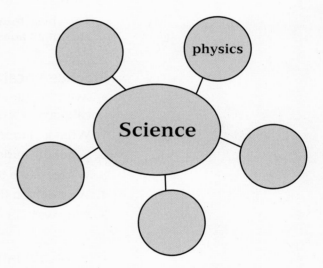

Key Vocabulary

assembly

achievement

curriculum

prestige

tournament

● Vocabulary From the Reading
Learn, Practice, and Use Independently

Learn Vocabulary Use the context clues to determine the meaning of the **highlighted** word in each sentence.

1. All the students in the school met for an **assembly** in the cafeteria. They listened to a presentation about the rules for running for class president.

2. Leah worked hard all year long, and she got straight A's. At graduation she was awarded for her **achievement**.

3. An English **curriculum** includes writing, grammar, and literature.

4. Tom's job at the university brings him a lot of **prestige**. He is very well-respected and is often asked to travel to other universities to give speeches.

5. The chess **tournament** lasted two weeks. There were events for kids of all ages to compete in.

Practice Vocabulary Read each of the following questions. Then answer the question with a sentence that includes one of the Key Vocabulary words.

1. What is happening in the school auditorium right now?
2. What do students learn at school?
3. Where can a tennis player compete in a series of events?
4. Why do you think the businessman wants to become governor?
5. Why was Lucy given an award in English class?

Use Vocabulary Independently Write a short paragraph that uses all of the Key Vocabulary words.

✓Checkpoint

1. What might be included in an art **curriculum**?

2. How can someone's **achievement** be recognized?

Vocabulary Log

Workbook page 249

Independent Practice CD-ROM/Online

● Academic Vocabulary

Vocabulary for the Reading Strategy

Word	Explanation	Sample Sentence	Visual Cue
distinguish *verb*	to see or understand differences	I cannot **distinguish** between the identical twins. I never know which one I'm talking to.	
locate *verb*	to find	Angela **locates** the train station on the city map by looking for the street name.	

Draw a picture and write a sentence for each word.

● Reading Strategy

Distinguish **Fact from Opinion**

A fact is information that is true and that can be proven.

Sandy watched a movie last night.

An opinion is a person's feelings or beliefs about something. Opinions cannot be proven. Words like *think, feel, best, worst,* and *believe* often express an opinion.

Sandy thought that the movie was very good.

To **distinguish** a fact from an opinion, look for factual proof or clue words that indicate opinions.

As you read, **locate** statements of fact and opinion. When you finish reading, you will complete the chart below to help you **distinguish** facts from opinions.

Facts	Proof	Opinions	Clues

✓Checkpoint

1. What does the word **distinguish** mean?
2. How can you **distinguish** between facts and opinions?

Vocabulary Log

Workbook page 250

Independent Practice CD-ROM/Online

● Text Genre

Informational Texts: Brochure and Newspaper Article

In Unit 5, Chapter 1, you learned that **brochures** are short documents that communicate specific information, and that they often include features like headings and testimonials. The first reading in this chapter includes a brochure and another type of informational text, a **newspaper article.** Newspaper articles report on current events in a community or in the world. Below are some common features of newspaper articles.

Newspaper Articles	
facts and opinions	facts, such as dates, events, names, and services, can be proven; opinions cannot be proven
current events	actual activities happening at the present time
interviews	meetings where information is gathered from someone

● Meet the Author

Eric Carpenter was born and raised in California. Carpenter developed a love of writing at an early age and has pursued that passion as an adult. He has been a reporter and writer for the Orange County Register since 1995.

● Reading Focus Questions

As you read, think about these questions.

1. How can students learn to become leaders?
2. What do you think is the purpose of each of the readings in this section?
3. Do you think the Science Olympiad is a worthwhile competition? Why or why not?

✓ Checkpoint

1. What is an example of a **current event**?
2. Give an example of a **fact**. Give an example of an **opinion**.

Workbook
page 251

Independent Practice
CD-ROM/Online

Science Olympiad

We have a mission.

1   Science Olympiad is a national **non-profit** organization dedicated to improving the quality of **K–12** science education, increasing male, female, and minority interest in science and providing recognition for outstanding **achievement** by both students and teachers. These goals are achieved by participating in Science Olympiad **tournaments**, **incorporating** Science Olympiad into classroom **curriculum**, and attending teacher-training **institutes**.

America's Most Exciting Science Competition

2   Imagine 5,000 people cheering for a high school junior who designed a robot that could play **billiards**. Imagine an academic **pep rally**, with the mayor of your town sending off a bus load of 13-year-old chemists, **geologists**, and **astrophysicists** in a **confetti-filled** parade. Imagine a girl getting a chance to meet with the head of the Centers for Disease Control and Prevention, an astronaut, a famous **pediatric neurosurgeon**, or a U.S. president. Imagine Science Olympiad.

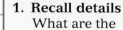

SCIENCE OLYMPIAD
™
Exploring the World of Science

Reading Strategy

Distinguish **Fact From Opinion** Would you label this heading a fact or an opinion? How do you know?

✔ *Reading Check*

1. **Recall details** What are the three goals of the Science Olympiad?

2. **Speculate** If you could meet any of the people mentioned in the reading, who would you want to meet, and why?

---

non-profit dedicated to serving others without earning money for its owners
K–12 kindergarten through grade 12
incorporating including
institutes sessions, programs
billiards variation on the game of pool
pep rally assembly to build enthusiasm among students
geologists scientists who study the Earth's development
astrophysicists scientists who study stars, planets, and their behavior
confetti-filled covered with tiny pieces of colored paper
pediatric neurosurgeon doctor who performs brain surgery on children and babies

An Alternative to Science Fairs

Reading Strategy

Distinguish Fact From Opinion Locate a fact in this paragraph. How do you know it is a fact?

3   Fulfilling a desire to bring excitement to science competitions, Science Olympiad was founded in 1983 by educators Dr. Gerard J. Putz and John C. Cairns. After successful **tournaments** were held in Michigan and Delaware, the program began to attract interest from school districts all around the country. What began as a **grassroots assembly** of science educators has now become one of the **premier** science competitions in the nation. Currently, Science Olympiad has members in all 50 states and Canada, totaling more than 14,500 actively participating K–12 schools.

4   At the competitive level, elementary, middle, and high school students with a **knack** for science have a chance to excel outside of the classroom. Secondary teams advancing to state and national **tournaments** are celebrated at pep rallies, travel to major universities, make new friends, and experience what it's like to be a star in the community, all without throwing, catching, or hitting a ball. One of Science Olympiad's most important goals is to bring academic competition to the same level of recognition and praise normally **reserved** for athletic competitions in this country.

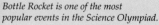
Bottle Rocket is one of the most popular events in the Science Olympiad.

---

grassroots local
premier highest-quality
knack special talent or ability
reserved set aside, kept for a special purpose

The Nuts and Bolts of Competition

5   Much like a football or soccer team, Science Olympiad teams prepare throughout the year for **tournaments**. Some have paid coaches, some have volunteers; most practice every week, some practice every day. Each team is allowed to bring 15 students who may participate in one or all of the events within a **division**.

6   Science Olympiad competitions are like academic **track meets**, consisting of a series of 23 individual and team events. Each year, events are updated to reflect the ever-changing nature of the latest advances in biology, earth science, chemistry, physics, computers, astronomy, engineering, and technology. By combining events from all **disciplines,** Science Olympiad encourages a wide **cross-section** of students to participate. Emphasis is placed on active, hands-on, group participation. Through the Olympiad, students, teachers, coaches, principals, business leaders, and parents bond together and work toward a shared goal.

7   Teamwork is a required skill in most scientific careers today, and Science Olympiad encourages group learning by designing events that **forge** alliances. In "Bridge Building," an engineering **whiz** and a kid from wood shop can become gold medalists. Similarly, a talented builder and a student with a good scientific vocabulary can excel in "Write It, Do It." Science Olympiad seeks to shatter the **isolated** scientist stereotype.

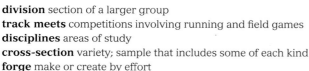

division section of a larger group
track meets competitions involving running and field games
disciplines areas of study
cross-section variety; sample that includes some of each kind
forge make or create by effort
whiz person with talent
isolated alone, separated from others

> ## Reading Strategy
>
> **Distinguish Fact From Opinion** Is each sentence in this paragraph a fact or an opinion? How do you know?

> ## ✓ Reading Check
>
> 1. **Recall details** How many individual and team events are held at each Science Olympiad?
>
> 2. **Draw conclusions** Why does Science Olympiad keep its events up-to-date?

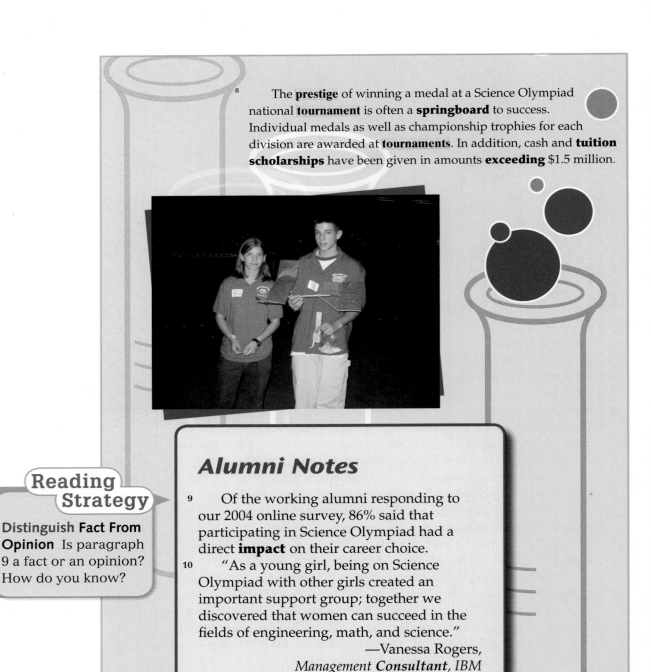

8 The **prestige** of winning a medal at a Science Olympiad national **tournament** is often a **springboard** to success. Individual medals as well as championship trophies for each division are awarded at **tournaments**. In addition, cash and **tuition scholarships** have been given in amounts **exceeding** $1.5 million.

Reading Strategy

Distinguish Fact From Opinion Is paragraph 9 a fact or an opinion? How do you know?

Alumni Notes

9 Of the working alumni responding to our 2004 online survey, 86% said that participating in Science Olympiad had a direct **impact** on their career choice.

10 "As a young girl, being on Science Olympiad with other girls created an important support group; together we discovered that women can succeed in the fields of engineering, math, and science."

—Vanessa Rogers,
*Management **Consultant**, IBM*

---

springboard something that leads to another action
tuition scholarships gifts of money to be used to pay for college courses
exceeding greater than
impact effect
consultant person paid to advise or guide others

He's Teacher, Student, and Cheerleader

"Mr. J," Troy Olympiad adviser, can't get enough of passing on knowledge.

by Eric Carpenter

Troy High School science teacher Dan Jundanian

1   FULLERTON Dan Jundanian's heart raced. He nearly fell off the edge of his seat.

2   And when the announcement came Saturday night that the students on his Troy High School Science Olympiad team had **captured** the national title, he leapt from his chair to offer congratulations.

3   Seeing his students succeed never gets old for Jundanian.

4   The silver-bearded biology teacher simply known as "Mr. J" has led a team from Troy to the National Science Olympiad for nine straight years. They've won five times—more than any other school in the 20-year history of the competition testing students' biology, chemistry, and **engineering** skills.

5   "Every year, I get attached. I see the hundreds of hours the kids spend preparing, and I want them to experience the thrill of a national championship," he said. "Knowing that I played some part in helping them get to that . . .. How can that ever be **old hat**?"

6   Jundanian, 59, **scouts** his classes for team members. Throughout the school year, he stays late for after-school study sessions. At the **tournament**, he's part technical adviser, part cheerleader.

7   His enthusiasm for science is **contagious**. He's been teaching biology at Troy since 1969.

This newspaper article tells about a teacher who coaches his students in the Science Olympiad that you just read about.

Reading Strategy

Distinguish **Fact From Opinion** Find an opinion on this page. How do you know it is an opinion?

Reading Check

1. **Recall details** What made Dan Jundanian leap off of his chair?

2. **Explain** How is Jundanian "part technical adviser, part cheerleader"?

---

captured caught, took hold of
engineering science of building structures
old hat boring
scouts searches
contagious able to spread from one person to the next

8 He still enjoys teaching because, he said, he's still learning.

9 "I'm always reading, discovering new things, and I can't wait to pass it along to my students."

10 Jundanian's classroom is packed with reminders of his discoveries. The walls are lined with butterflies and bugs he's collected over the years. … A live African bullfrog and a California king snake rest in cages next to students.

11 "If they're not looking at me, I at least want them to be looking at some kind of biology all the time," he said. "I want to spark their interest."

12 Jundanian's passion for science was sparked as a kid in Ohio. He spent hours **scouring** fields and river banks for insects, lizards, fish, and snakes. As long as he kept his **creepy crawlers** in the garage, his mother didn't mind. …

13 From those early experiences, his excitement for science continued into high school, when his family moved to California.

14 He chose to **major** in biology at California State University, Fullerton, with the hope of someday becoming a national park **ranger**. But soon his ambition changed to teaching. He came from a family of teachers. His dad was a math instructor.

Reading Strategy

Distinguish Fact From Opinion Is the information in this paragraph fact or opinion? Explain your response.

---

scouring searching a place thoroughly
creepy crawlers (slang) bugs or rodents that crawl or slither
major to study as one's main field in college
ranger official who watches over and cares for a park

15   Jundanian enjoys sharing his passion for learning. ...

16   He found a job at Troy High, across the street from the university. When the school's attendance **boundary** started to shrink in the early 1980s, administrators made Troy a "science **magnet**," focusing the **curriculum** on math, science, and computer technology. Before long, Troy was attracting students from four counties.

17   "The students are learning at a higher level each year," Jundanian said. "They are constantly challenging us to stay current."

18   He has **re-enrolled** in several university classes and is always reading textbooks and new studies to keep up-to-date.

19   Jundanian and fellow teacher Kurt Wahl started the Science Olympiad team in 1987 to challenge the brightest science students. By 1994, they had won the state **tournament**. In 1996, they captured their first national title.

20   At this year's **tournament**, Jundanian ran into a former student, Mark Rudner, who is finishing an engineering degree at Caltech.

21   "He was telling me about the projects he was working on and, I'll say it, I had no idea what he was talking about," Jundanian said, laughing.

22   "Some of these kids move way past me. I'm just happy knowing I helped them get there."

> ## Reading Strategy
>
> **Distinguish Fact From Opinion** Locate one fact in this paragraph.

> ## ✔ Reading Check
>
> 1. **Recall details**
>   Who is Mark Rudner?
>
> 2. **Draw conclusions**
>   Do you think Jundanian is proud of his students? How do you know?

---

boundary limit
magnet school with a specialized curriculum
re-enrolled entered again

Apply the Reading Strategy

Distinguish Fact from Opinion

Now that you have read "Science Olympiad" and "He's Teacher, Student, and Cheerleader," you are ready to complete the Reading Strategy chart.

1. Review the **Reading Strategy** on page 391 and copy the chart.
2. Look back at the reading. **Locate** statements of fact and opinion. Then complete the chart below to help you to **distinguish** facts from opinions.

Facts	Proof	Opinions	Clues
Science Olympiad is a national non-profit organization	You can look the organization up on the Internet.	It is America's most exciting science competition.	"Most exciting" cannot be proven, and is something people might disagree about.

Academic Vocabulary

Vocabulary for the Reading Comprehension Questions

Word	Explanation	Sample Sentence	Visual Cue
factor *noun*	someone or something that actively contributes to a result	Anna's speed was the biggest **factor** in our win at last week's soccer game.	
resource *noun*	a supply of support, money, knowledge, or anything needed	The donated money gives the university the **resources** it needs to build a new library.	

Draw a picture and write a sentence for each word.

✓Checkpoint

1. Identify one person who is a **factor** in your success at school.
2. Name a **resource** at your library that is helpful to students.

Vocabulary Log

Reading Comprehension Questions

Think and Discuss

1. **Recall details** Students in what grade levels compete in the Science Olympiad?

2. **Recall details** What **resources** does Jundanian use to keep his science knowledge up-to-date?

3. **Summarize** Summarize the two readings using the Key Vocabulary words on page 390.

4. **Draw conclusions** Do you think teachers are an important **factor** in the teams' successes? Explain your answer.

5. **Make a judgment** Do you think Troy High School's success should be featured in the Science Olympiad brochure? Why or why not?

6. **Revisit the Reading Focus Questions** Go back to page 392 and discuss the questions.

Workbook
page 252

Independent Practice
CD-ROM/Online

Text Elements

Purpose and Audience

Every piece of writing has a **purpose** and an **audience** for whom it is written. The purpose is the goal the author has for writing. Some purposes, or goals, are to entertain, to inform, or to persuade. The audience is the group of readers the author is writing for. Authors know whether their readers are young or old, new to the book's subject matter or experts on the topic. Knowing the purpose and audience helps writers determine what they write about—or the focus—and how they write it.

Reading 1 includes a brochure and a newspaper article that both focus on the Science Olympiad competition. Each of these has its own purpose and audience. For each of the reading selections below, name the purpose and the audience.

Title	Purpose	Audience
Science Olympiad		
He's Teacher, Student, and Cheerleader		

✓Checkpoint

1. Name the different **purposes** a piece of writing can have.

2. How do the purpose and the **audience** relate to the focus of a selection?

Workbook
page 253

Independent Practice
CD-ROM/Online

Harriet Tubman: Conductor on the Underground Railroad

● About the Reading

In "He's Teacher, Student, and Cheerleader," you read about a man who led his students to academic success. In this selection, you will read about a woman who led people from slavery to freedom.

Portrait of Harriet Tubman

● Build Background

The Underground Railroad

Harriet Tubman was born into slavery in the early 1820s, and she escaped from her plantation master in 1849. Some accounts say that she led approximately 300 slaves along the Underground Railroad. The Underground Railroad was a pathway of safe houses that stretched from the southern United States to Canada. In these places, a runaway slave could rest, eat, and hide from bounty hunters, people paid to return escaped slaves to their masters in the South. With Tubman's help, escaped slaves passed through cities such as Camden, Delaware; Philadelphia, Pennsylvania; and Rochester, New York.

● Vocabulary From the Reading

Use Context Clues to Determine Meaning

Use the information in each sentence to determine the meaning of the **highlighted** word.

1. After the team lost, they felt **discouraged**. They didn't think they would be able to win any more games.
2. After a long day of working on the farm, Joey came home **disheveled**. His shirt was torn, his pants were dirty, and his hair was a mess.
3. Maura saw her friends cheering her on, and even though she was tired, it was the **incentive** she needed to finish the marathon.
4. The mother hen **pursues** her chicks as they run into the field. She will not let any of them run too far from her.
5. When my sister and I arrived home, we realized we had lost our keys. It was raining, so we looked for **shelter** until our mother came home.

Key Vocabulary

discouraged
disheveled
incentive
pursue
shelter

✓Checkpoint

1. Describe a **disheveled** room.
2. What **incentive** do you need to get up early on a Saturday morning?

 Vocabulary Log   Workbook page 254   Independent Practice CD-ROM/Online

Reading Strategy

Recognize Imagery

Writers choose specific words that help readers form mental pictures. This is called **imagery.** Imagery helps you to imagine the sights, sounds, feel, smell, and taste of things in the reading. Through the use of imagery, writers create emotion and mood.

As you read, note words and phrases that relate to the senses and help you see, hear, feel, smell, and taste.

Sight: clear night when the North Star was visible

Text Genre

Historical Novel

Historical novels tell the stories of specific people and events in history. They contain details that reflect that time period, for example, the way people dressed, spoke, traveled, and ate. Historical novels have the following features:

Historical Novel	
plot	the action of the story
historical setting	where and when a story takes place
historical details	every aspect of life in another time period, such as the way people lived, how they behaved, and what they wore

Meet the Author

Ann Petry was born in 1908. At a time when few African-American women were professional writers, Petry published a number of books. Petry lectured and wrote until her death in 1997.

Reading Focus Questions

As you read, think about these questions.

1. How does *Harriet Tubman: Conductor on the Underground Railroad* relate to the theme of leadership?
2. Why do you think Petry chose Tubman as her subject?
3. In what ways was Tubman an unlikely leader in her day?

✓**Checkpoint**

1. What is **imagery**?
2. Write four words that could help the reader imagine a hot day.

Workbook
pages 255–256

Independent Practice
CD-ROM/Online

Harriet Tubman: Conductor on the Underground Railroad

by Ann Petry

1   Along the Eastern Shore of Maryland, in Dorchester County, in Caroline County, the masters kept hearing whispers about the man named Moses, who was running off slaves. At first they did not believe in his existence. The stories about him were fantastic, unbelievable. Yet they watched for him. They offered rewards for his capture.

The North Star

2   They never saw him. Now and then they heard whispered rumors to the effect that he was in the neighborhood. The woods were searched. The roads were watched. There was never anything to indicate his **whereabouts.** But a few days afterward, a **goodly** number of slaves would be gone from the **plantation.** Neither the master nor the **overseer** had heard or seen anything unusual in the **quarter.** Sometimes one or the other would **vaguely** remember having heard a **whippoorwill** call somewhere in the woods, close by, late at night. Though it was the wrong season for whippoorwills . . .

3   Harriet Tubman could have told them that there was far more involved in this matter of running off slaves than signaling the would-be runaways by imitating the call of a whippoorwill, or a hoot owl, far more involved than a matter of waiting for a clear night when the North Star was visible.

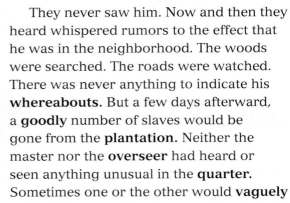

Reading Strategy

Recognize Imagery
Which sense does this image appeal to?

4   In December, 1851, when she started out with the band of fugitives that she planned to take to Canada, she had been in the vicinity of the plantation for days, planning the trip, carefully selecting the slaves that she would take with her . . .

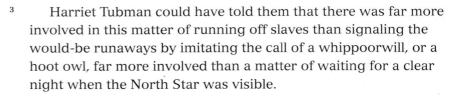

whereabouts location
goodly significant
plantation large estate in the South that used slaves for labor
overseer supervisor
quarter area of plantation where slaves lived
vaguely without clarity
whippoorwill small, nighttime bird

5   But there were so many of them this time. She knew moments of doubt when she was half-afraid, and kept looking back over her shoulder, imagining that she heard the sound of pursuit. They would certainly be **pursued.** Eleven of them. Eleven thousand dollars' worth of flesh and bone and muscle that belonged to Maryland planters. If they were caught, the eleven runaways would be whipped and sold South, but she—she would probably be hanged.

6   They tried to sleep during the day but they never could wholly relax into sleep. She could tell by the positions they assumed, by their restless movements. And they walked at night. Their progress was slow. It took them three nights of walking to reach the first stop. She had told them about the place where they would stay, promising warmth and good food, holding these things out to them as an **incentive** to keep going.

7   When she knocked on the door of a farmhouse, a place where she and her **parties** of runaways had always been welcome, always been given **shelter** and plenty to eat, there was no answer. She knocked again, softly. A voice from within said, "Who is it?" There was fear in the voice.

8   She knew instantly from the sound of the voice that there was something wrong. She said, "A friend with friends," the password on the Underground Railroad.

Reading Strategy

Recognize Imagery
Which sense does this image relate to?

Harriet Tubman's home in Auburn, New York

✓ **Reading Check**

1. **Recall facts** How many slaves does Tubman have with her?

2. **Speculate** Why do you think Tubman's punishment would be worse than the others' if they got caught?

---

parties groups

9   The door opened, slowly. The man who stood in the doorway looked at her coldly, looked with **unconcealed astonishment** and fear at the eleven **disheveled** runaways who were standing near her. Then he shouted, "Too many, too many. It's not safe. My place was searched last week. It's not safe!" and slammed the door in her face.

10   She turned away from the house, frowning. She had promised her passengers food and rest and warmth, and instead of that, there would be hunger and cold and more walking over the frozen ground. Somehow she would have to **instill** courage into these eleven people, most of them strangers, would have to feed them on hope and bright dreams of freedom instead of the fried pork and corn bread and milk she had promised them.

11   They stumbled along behind her, half-dead for sleep, and she urged them on, though she was as tired and as **discouraged** as they were. She had never been in Canada but she kept painting **wondrous** word pictures of what it would be like. She managed to **dispel** their fear of pursuit, so that they would not become hysterical, panic-stricken. Then she had to bring some of the fear back, so that they would stay awake and keep walking though they drooped with sleep . . .

Reading Strategy

Recognize Imagery
What descriptive words in paragraph 11 help you form an image of the condition of the runaways?

---

unconcealed visible, open to view
astonishment surprise
instill to give by example or by teaching
wondrous fantastic, impressive
dispel scatter

12   That night they reached the next stop—a farm that belonged to a German. She made the runaways take **shelter** behind trees at the edge of the fields before she knocked at the door. She hesitated before she approached the door, thinking, suppose that he, too, should refuse **shelter,** suppose— Then she thought, Lord, I'm going to hold steady on to You and You've got to see me through—and knocked softly.

13   She heard the familiar **guttural** voice say, "Who's there?"

14   She answered quickly, "A friend with friends."

15   He opened the door and greeted her warmly. "How many this time?" he asked.

16   "Eleven," she said and waited, doubting, wondering.

17   He said, "Good. Bring them in."

18   He and his wife fed them in the lamplit kitchen, their faces glowing, as they offered food and more food, urging them to eat, saying there was plenty for everybody, have more milk, have more bread, have more meat . . .

19   Two nights later she was aware that the feet behind her were moving slower and slower. She heard the **irritability** in their voices, knew that soon someone would refuse to go on . . .

Reading Strategy

Recognize Imagery
Which senses do these images relate to?

✓ **Reading Check**

1. **Recall facts** Where does Tubman hide the runaways before knocking on the farmhouse door?

2. **Make inferences** The farmer says, "How many this time?" What do his words suggest about his work with Tubman and the Underground Railroad?

3. **Speculate** Why do you think the man and his wife help the slaves?

---

guttural spoken deep in the throat
irritability annoyance

20   She tried to explain to them why none of them could go back to the plantation. If a runaway returned, he would turn **traitor,** the master and the overseer would force him to turn traitor. The returned slave would **disclose** the stopping places, the hiding places, the cornstacks they had used with the full knowledge of the owner of the farm, the name of the German farmer who had fed them and sheltered them. These people who had risked their own security to help runaways would be ruined, fined, imprisoned.

21   She said, "We got to go free or die. And freedom's not bought with dust" . . .

Reading Strategy

Recognize Imagery
What descriptive words in paragraph 22 help you form a mental picture of Harriet Tubman?

22   She gave the impression of being a short, muscular, **indomitable** woman who could never be defeated. Yet at any moment she was **liable** to be **seized** by one of those curious fits of sleep, which might last for a few minutes or for hours.

23   Even on this trip, she suddenly fell asleep in the woods. The runaways, **ragged**, dirty, hungry, cold, did not steal the gun as they might have, and set off by themselves, or turn back. They sat on the ground near her and waited patiently until she awakened. They had come to trust her **implicitly,** totally. They, too, had come to believe her repeated statement, "We got to go free or die." She was leading them into freedom, and so they waited until she was ready to go on.

---

traitor person who betrays someone else
disclose tell or show something that was secret
indomitable unstoppable
liable likely
seized grasped
ragged having a worn edge, shabby
implicitly without reservation

Reading Comprehension Questions

Think and Discuss

1. **Recall details** In what state does this story take place?

2. **Analyze character** What four adjectives would you use to describe Harriet Tubman's character?

3. **Summarize** Summarize this reading using as many Key Vocabulary words as you can.

4. **Speculate** How has the author created a character who is similar to the real Harriet Tubman? Use what you learned about Tubman on page 402 to answer.

5. **Analyze and apply** What positive message does Tubman's story offer to readers today?

6. **Revisit the Reading Focus Questions** Go back to page 403 and discuss the questions.

Workbook
page 257

Independent Practice
CD-ROM/Online

Connect Readings 1 and 2

You have read two readings on the theme of leadership: "Science Olympiad" / "He's Teacher, Student, and Cheerleader" and *Harriet Tubman: Conductor on the Underground Railroad*. Use these activities to make connections between the readings.

1. With a partner, use this chart to compare the two readings.

Reading title	What is the genre of each reading?	Which character represents leadership?	Which reading did you enjoy more? Why?
Science Olympiad **He's Teacher, Student, and Cheerleader**			
Harriet Tubman: Conductor on the Underground Railroad			

2. With a partner, ask and answer these questions.

   a. What leadership qualities do Dan Jundanian and Harriet Tubman share?

   b. What is one message that both selections offer readers?

3. Revisit the Chapter Focus Question What can a really good leader teach you? Use examples from the readings.

Spelling

Compound Words

Workbook
page 258

Independent Practice
CD-ROM/Online

Writing Conventions

Punctuation: Titles of Works

Workbook
page 259

Independent Practice
CD-ROM/Online

Listening and Speaking

Role-play an Interview

With a partner, role-play an interview between a modern-day journalist and one of the runaway slaves. When you finish, switch positions.

Phrases for Conversation

Asking for Clarification

I'm not sure I understand what you mean.

Could you please clarify what you mean?

Could you please repeat that?

1. Decide on your roles. One of you will be the interviewer, and the other will be the one being interviewed.

2. JOURNALIST: Create a list of questions to ask your partner. Your interview topics should include:

   a. the slave's decision to run away.

   b. who helped him or her along the way.

   c. the slave's advice to someone facing the decision to stay a slave or to go free.

3. RUNAWAY SLAVE: Listen carefully to each question. Ask the interviewer to explain or clarify any unclear questions. Ask questions in return if necessary.

4. RUNAWAY SLAVE: Answer each question as though you were that person, using "I" and "we" and adding logical details from that person's experiences. Tell the story of your experiences.

5. Switch roles and do the role play again.

6. When you finish, discuss your interviews with the class.

Harriet Tubman (left, holding pan) with slaves she helped, about 1900

● Reading Fluency

Rapid Word Recognition

Rapidly recognizing words helps you increase your reading rate. It is an important characteristic of a fluent and accurate reader.

1. With a partner, review the words below.

2. Read the words from left to right aloud for one minute. Use appropriate pacing. Do not read so fast that you cannot pronounce the words correctly. Your partner can time you as you read.

3. How many words did you read in one minute? Count the words and record your results.

4. Compare your results to the results you had on page 311. Did you recognize more words in less time?

announcement	technical	interest	pictures	managed
security	managed	pictures	announcement	interest
security	technical	announcement	managed	security
interest	managed	security	interest	pictures
security	pictures	announcement	technical	managed

● Vocabulary Development

Spelling of Derivatives

Many English words are **derived,** or come, from other words—sometimes from words in other languages. These words are called **derivatives.** For example, the derivative *position* comes from the Latin root *pos,* which means "to place or put." When you add prefixes or suffixes to derivatives, like **re**position, you create a new derivative.

It is important to spell the new word correctly. Many times you will need to delete one or more letters from the original word to make the derivative.

Add the prefix or suffix indicated to each of the words below to form a new derivative. When you finish, check your work with a dictionary.

recognize + -tion (the act of taking notice) = recognition

1. capture + -tive (one who has been taken by force)

2. compute + -er (an electronic device that processes data)

3. un- + necessary (not necessary, needless)

4. celebrate + -tion (a ceremony that honors someone or something)

✓*Checkpoint*

1. What is a **derivative**?

2. What word do you form when you add the prefix *un-* to the word *equal*?

Vocabulary Log

Workbook page 260

Independent Practice CD-ROM/Online

● Grammar

Avoiding Subject and Verb Shifts in Writing

Use a consistent subject and verb tense within a single sentence to avoid a shift in your writing. If the subject or tense changes, the meaning of the sentence will change.

- Avoid **shifts in subject** by using one subject throughout a sentence. Check pronouns against the subject introduced earlier in the sentence.

  incorrect: The **passengers** should sit so **you** do not fall while the bus is in motion.

  correct: The **passengers** should sit so **they** do not fall while the bus is in motion.

- Avoid **shifts in verb tense** by being consistent with the tense you are writing in.

  incorrect: The girls **laughed** out loud, and then they **walk** away.

  correct: The girls **laughed** out loud, and then they **walked** away.

Build Your Knowledge

Be sure that you have subject-verb agreement when the subject is compound. For example, The **boy and girl** *walk* to school together everyday.

Practice the Grammar Tell why the underlined words in the following sentences show shifts in writing. Then change the wrong word or phrase to correct the error.

1. She and the runaway slaves used the Underground Railroad, which led <u>you</u> to the free states and Canada.
2. A runaway herself, she left on the road to freedom with her brothers, who later <u>turn</u> back and <u>leave</u> Tubman on her own.
3. Tubman traveled from farmhouse to farmhouse at night when most people <u>are</u> sleeping.
4. The slaves traveled to the safe houses, where <u>she</u> ate and slept.
5. She believed in equality for everyone, which is why <u>you</u> joined the Union Army during the Civil War.

Grammar Expansion

Reported Speech (Direct and Indirect Quotes)

Workbook
page 262

Independent Practice
CD-ROM/Online

Use the Grammar Independently Write a paragraph about the Science Olympiad. For each sentence, identify the subject and the verb tense. Make sure that there are no shifts in writing in the sentences.

✓**Checkpoint**

1. In your own words, explain what a **shift in writing** is.
2. How does a shift in verb tense affect the meaning of a sentence?

Workbook
page 261

Independent Practice
CD-ROM/Online

● Grammar

Active Voice and Passive Voice

In the **active voice,** a sentence shows an action performed by the subject.

The **wind** *pushed* the little boat.

The **dog** *chased* the squirrel away.

In the **passive voice,** the subject receives the action of the verb. The passive voice uses a form of the helping verb *be* (*is, am, are, was, were*), and what is performing the action is moved toward the end of the sentence. Use the passive voice when the action is more important than who or what is doing the action.

The little **boat** was *pushed* by the wind.

The **squirrel** was *chased* by the dog.

To change a sentence from the passive voice to the active voice, look for what is performing the action. This often follows the word *by.*

The theater was closed **by** the manager. ⟶ The manager closed the theater.

In many forms of writing, active voice is preferable to passive voice. The passive voice is less forceful and can make the meaning of the sentence unclear.

Practice the Grammar Change each sentence below from the passive voice to the active. Do not change the meaning of the sentence.

1. The robot was built by the Science Olympiad students.
2. The award was won by the robot team.
3. The winners were chosen by the judges.
4. During the competition, the students were helped by the teachers and volunteers.
5. A celebration was held by all the students who competed.

Use the Grammar Independently Write a brief paragraph about Harriet Tubman and the Underground Railroad. Use at least two sentences in the passive voice, and two in the active voice.

Grammar Expansion

Passive Voice in Different Verb Tenses

Workbook page 264

Independent Practice CD-ROM/Online

✓**Checkpoint**

1. In the **passive voice,** where in the sentence is the person or thing doing the action usually found?

2. Create a passive voice sentence. Then change it to an **active voice** sentence.

Workbook page 263

Independent Practice CD-ROM/Online

● Writing Assignment

Write a Research Essay About a Historical Period

> **Writing Prompt**
>
> Write a research essay about a historical period. Identify the era, or time period, and describe the clothing, transportation, and other details of daily life. Write an introduction, body, and conclusion. Include one quotation from a source in your essay. Use the active voice whenever possible and logical.

About Research Essays

A research essay uses a variety of sources, such as biographies, informational texts, and Web sites. Sentences taken directly from those sources are called **quotations**. These add value and credibility to your essay. Always be sure to cite your sources at the end.

Write Your Research Essay

1. **Read the student model.**

Student Model

Ancient Egypt is a very interesting historical period. Between 3050 and 30 BCE, powerful kings called pharaohs ruled Egypt. The people accomplished many things, such as building the pyramids. Daily life, including work and keeping healthy, was very different from today.

There were different classes of people. The peasant men worked as farmers and shepherds, the middle class were artisans and merchants, and the upper class included priests and the pharaoh. In What Life Was Like on the Banks of the Nile, we learn that women participated in the society, and that they "possessed rights, responsibilities, and privileges not seen anywhere else in that era."

Keeping oneself attractive and in good health was important. As stated in What Life Was Like on the Banks of the Nile, "In the Nile Valley, beauty and personal adornment were important to rich and poor alike, and not just for vanity's sake." They used oils that protected their skin. But many people did not live past the age of 35.

Workbook
page 265

2. Prewrite.

   a. Choose a time period that interests you. Think of questions about that time period that you want to answer in your essay.

   b. In your school library, locate one or two books on this era. Make sure the books describe what daily life was like.

   c. As you read, locate a few quotations to include in your essay. Write the sentences down exactly as they are in the source.

3. Write your essay.

   a. Begin with an introduction in which you identify the era. Tell your readers which areas of daily life you plan to explore in the body of your paper.

   b. In the body, write specific information about the era. Include one of the sentences from your sources, and write the author's name and the title of the book. If the source does not have an author, simply include the title.

   c. End your essay with a conclusion that summarizes how life was different in this era.

4. Revise. Read your essay. Revise any sentences or paragraphs that seem unclear or misplaced. Use the **editing and proofreading symbols** on page 455 to mark any changes you want to make.

5. Edit. Use the **Writing Checklist** to help you find any problems and errors.

6. Read your composition to the class.

Writing Checklist
1. I described details of daily life.
2. I included an introduction, body, and conclusion.
3. I used at least one direct quotation from a source.
4. I included the title and author of my source.
5. I corrected any shifts in writing.
6. I used the active voice.

 Writing Support

Mechanics

Quotation Marks

Use **quotation marks** around the exact words, phrases, or sentences you take from a published source. Always identify where the quotation is from; never copy without identifying the source.

- Place periods and commas within the quotation marks at the end of the quotation.

  As noted in *What Life Was Like on the Banks of the Nile*, "Each summer, when the Nile overflowed its banks and replenished the parched earth, the people of ancient Egypt witnessed anew the miracle of creation."

  Note that a quotation begins with a capital letter when it is a full sentence.

- Phrases can be quoted from sources. Use quotation marks to set them off from your own writing, and use a lowercase letter to begin the quotation.

  The book *What Life Was Like on the Banks of the Nile* states that "the tombs of the pharaohs took on great importance."

Apply Check to be sure you used quotation marks correctly in your essay.

Workbook
pages 266–268

Independent Practice
CD-ROM/Online

Progress Check

How well did you understand this chapter? Try to answer the questions. If necessary, go back to the pages listed for a review.

Skills	Skills Assessment Questions	Pages to Review
Vocabulary From the Readings	**What do these words mean?**	
	• achievement, assembly, curriculum, prestige, tournament	390
	• discouraged, disheveled, incentive, pursue, shelter	402
Academic Vocabulary	What do these academic vocabulary words mean?	
	• distinguish, locate	391
	• factor, resource	400
Reading Strategies	What is the difference between a fact and an opinion?	391
	What does imagery do for a reader?	403
Text Genres	What are the text genres of "Science Olympiad" and "He's Teacher, Student, and Cheerleader"?	392
	What is the text genre of *Harriet Tubman: Conductor on the Underground Railroad*?	403
Reading Comprehension	What are "Science Olympiad" and "He's Teacher, Student, and Cheerleader" about?	401
	What is *Harriet Tubman: Conductor on the Underground Railroad* about?	409
Text Element	Explain what **purpose** and **audience** are.	401
Spelling	Give three examples of compound words.	409
Writing Conventions	What titles are italicized?	409
Listening and Speaking	**Phrases for Conversation**	
	How can you ask for clarification?	410
Vocabulary Development	What is a **derivative**?	411
Grammar	What is a shift in writing?	412
	Give an example of an **active voice** sentence.	413
Writing Support: Mechanics	Where are quotation marks used?	415

Assessment Practice

Read this passage. Then answer Questions 1 through 4.

Local Teen Helps Classmates During School Fire

1   NEWTOWN—Francesca Gómez is glad that she paid attention during all those fire drills at school. Her classmates are glad, too.

2   During the fire that destroyed part of Newtown Middle School last Monday, Gómez, an eighth-grade student, led four classmates safely out of the school.

3   "I saw an assembly of students in the band room right before the fire alarm sounded," Gómez recalls. "They had music playing on the stereo that was very loud. A few minutes later, the alarm went off. I was about to go outside, but then I remembered those students. I wondered if they could hear the alarm."

4   Gómez ran back to the room. The students saw her shouting at them but couldn't hear what she was saying. They turned down the music and heard her say, "Fire!" That was all the information they needed, and the students were led by Francesca out a nearby door.

---

1   **What does the word <u>assembly</u> mean in the following sentence?**

> I saw an <u>assembly</u> of students in the band room right before the fire alarm sounded.

A   shelter   B   team

C   classroom   D   group

2   **Which statement is an opinion?**

A   I wondered if they could hear the alarm.

B   A few minutes later, the alarm went off.

C   They had music playing on the stereo that was very loud.

D   Gómez ran back to the room.

3   **What characteristic does the following sentence have?**

> The students were led by Francesca out a nearby door.

A   an incorrect shift in subject

B   the passive voice

C   an incorrect shift in verb tense

D   the active voice

4   **What is the text genre for this passage?**

A   brochure

B   short story

C   persuasive essay

D   newspaper article

Writing on Demand: Essay

    Write an essay about a historical period that a relative or another adult you know lived through. Mention at least one historical event that took place during that time period. Include information on the trends in clothes, music, and entertainment. **(20 minutes)**

> **Writing Tip**
> Write an introduction, body, and conclusion for your essay. Use the active voice.

Apply & Extend

OBJECTIVES

Listening and Speaking
Give a persuasive speech

Media
Understand workplace documents

Writing
Write a response to literature essay

Projects

Independent Reading

● Listening and Speaking Workshop
Give a Persuasive Speech

> **Topic**
>
> Imagine you are running for president of your school's student government. Write a speech telling why you believe you are the best candidate.

1. **Brainstorm**

   a. In this unit, you read about people who are leaders. Think about how each of these people showed the qualities of leadership. What qualities do you think are important for a leader to have?

   b. Decide on a focus for your speech. Think of reasons why you would make a good student government president. Take notes on your reasons.

   - What are some qualities you have that would make you a good leader? On what occasions have you demonstrated these qualities?

   - What are some improvements you would make to your school if you were elected?

2. **Plan**

   Think of evidence you can use to support your position. Keep in mind the point of view of your listeners. What evidence are they likely to find persuasive?

3. **Organize Your Speech**

   Write down reasons why you should be elected on note cards. Write one reason on each card. Then write evidence and details to support each reason. Be sure your speech is organized in a way that will make it easy for your listeners to understand.

4. **Practice, Present, and Evaluate**

   Practice your speech. As you practice, emphasize key points by changing your tone of voice and using gestures. Raise your voice and increase your pace when you want to say something you feel is important. Then give your speech. Ask for feedback from your listeners. Use the **Speaking Self-Evaluation** to evaluate your speech. Use the **Active Listening Evaluation** to evaluate and discuss your classmates' speeches.

Media Workshop

Understand Workplace Documents

Workplace documents can include memos, employee handbooks, and other kinds of instructions. The excerpt below is from a set of instructions for what to do in case of a fire.

> **In Case of Fire . . . Remember These Tips!**
> - Follow instructions from your manager.
> - Do not try to carry equipment or other items with you.
> - Leave the office quickly and quietly.
> - Use the stairs. Do not use the elevators.
> - Meet behind the fence in the parking lot. Do not try to re-enter the building.

1. Read the excerpt. Answer the following questions.
   a. What kind of information does the excerpt give?
   b. Who is the excerpt written for?
   c. Why are the directions in the excerpt important?

2. Work with a group. Think of how you would use the excerpt to identify and communicate information.
   a. Each student should write one question that the excerpt can answer, such as "Where should I go after I leave the building?"
   b. Work as a group to answer each student's question. Point out the parts of the excerpt you used to explain your answer.

3. Sometimes directions like those in the excerpt are spoken instead of written down. With your group, practice following spoken directions.
   a. One person should read a line of the directions aloud.
   b. The group should work together to follow the spoken directions.

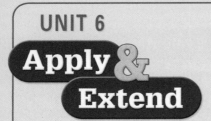
● **Writing Workshop**
Write a Response to Literature

  When you write a response to literature, you tell what you think about something you have read. A response to literature includes a main idea about the reading as well as details and examples to support the main idea.

> **Writing Prompt**
>   Choose one of the readings from Unit 6. Write an essay telling how the people in the reading showed qualities of leadership.

PREWRITE

1. Read the student model on the next page. It is a response to literature essay about the article "Searching for Sacagawea" by Margaret Talbot. In it, the writer tells how Sacagawea showed leadership.
2. Choose the reading that you will respond to.
3. Think about these questions. Take notes on your ideas.
   a. Who were the people in the reading?
   b. What qualities did the people have that made them good leaders?
   c. How did they show these qualities?
4. Use an outline to help organize your writing.

WRITE A DRAFT

1. First, write your introduction. It should tell which reading you will write about and briefly state the main idea of your essay.
2. Write the body of your essay. The body should have at least three paragraphs. Each paragraph should include supporting statements that link back to your main idea. Use information from the reading to support your ideas.
3. Write the conclusion. The conclusion should return to the central idea of your essay. Your conclusion may also compare your subject to other people you have read about, such as Iqbal Masih and Harriet Tubman.

Writing Suggestion

  Use a thesaurus to make your writing more interesting. Look up words to find synonyms. This will help you vary your choice of words as you write.

Student Model

Liz Garcia

Sacagawea: A Brave Leader

The introduction should tell which work of literature you are writing about.

In the article "Searching for Sacagawea," Margaret Talbot shows that Sacagawea had many qualities of a good leader. She was strong and determined, and she was able to stay calm in difficult situations. These qualities allowed her to play an important part in American history.

Sacagawea was originally from the Shoshone group of Native Americans. When she was about 13, she was taken captive by a group called the Hidatsa. She must have been a strong person in order to survive. Being a strong person is one quality that helped make her a good leader.

Sacagawea had knowledge about many things. Sacagawea was only 17 when she and her husband joined Lewis and Clark on their expedition. Sacagawea helped Lewis and Clark on their journey in several ways. First, she showed them wild plants that they could eat on their journey. She also served as a translator. When the expedition reached the area where the Shoshone lived, Sacagawea was able to tell Lewis and Clark where they were.

When responding to literature, you should give examples from the work.

Sacagawea's actions show that she was curious about the world around her. One example of this occurred when Clark told the group that he would take some of them out to the ocean to see a beached whale. Sacagawea told Clark that she had never seen the ocean, and she really wanted to go. He agreed, and the next day the group traveled to the ocean. Curiosity is another quality that helped make her a leader.

The best example of Sacagawea showing qualities of leadership is an event that took place as the group traveled on the Missouri River. The boat that Sacagawea and her husband were in was hit by high winds, causing it to nearly tip over. Sacagawea reached into the water and saved the group's supplies. This act, which showed that she knew how to stay calm during a stressful situation, is another important ability for a leader to have.

Your response should have one central idea that is stated in the introduction and conclusion.

Sacagawea's strength, knowledge, curiosity, and calmness were some qualities of leadership that she showed during the Lewis and Clark expedition. She is remembered for her contributions to one of American history's greatest journeys.

REVISE

1. Review your essay. Are your ideas well organized? Use the **Revising and Editing Checklist** to help you evaluate and edit your draft.

2. Exchange your essay with a partner. Ask your partner to use the **Peer Review Checklist** to review your essay.

3. Revise your draft. You may want to rearrange sentences or paragraphs to make your essay clearer.

4. Use the **editing and proofreading symbols** on page 455 to help you mark the changes you need to make.

EDIT

1. Reevaluate your essay using the **Revising and Editing Checklist.**

2. Fix any errors in grammar, spelling, and punctuation.

Peer Review Checklist

1. The essay includes a clear main idea.

2. The essay has an introduction, body, and conclusion.

3. This essay helped me understand more about the character.

4. My favorite part of the essay is _____ .

5. The essay would be better if _____ .

Revising and Editing Checklist

1. My introduction tells which reading I am writing about.

2. My introduction includes a clear main idea.

3. The body of my essay includes ideas and statements that relate to my main idea.

4. I used examples from the text to support my ideas.

5. My conclusion returns to the main idea stated in my introduction.

6. I used conditional clauses correctly.

7. I used a consistent subject and verb tense in my writing.

PUBLISH

1. Write your essay in your best handwriting. Or use a computer and word processing program to write your essay. Be sure to use appropriate margins and spacing. If you use a computer, use a spell check.

2. Read your essay to the class. Read slowly and clearly, changing your tone of voice to reflect the different ideas in your essay.

● Projects

Choose one or more of the following projects to explore the theme of leadership further.

PROJECT 1

Make a Poster for a Political Candidate.

1. Make a poster to go with the speech you wrote in the Listening and Speaking Workshop on page 418.

2. Your poster should illustrate the reasons that you would be a good president of your student government.

3. Use a computer to find illustrations for your poster. Print photographs or graphics from the Internet, or make a chart or other graphic organizer using a word processing program.

PROJECT 2

Use a Bibliography to Learn More About a Leader.

1. Look in your classroom or school library for a book about a leader.

2. Find the book's bibliography. The bibliography is found at the end of the book. Choose one of the sources you find listed.

3. Find the source and read it. Decide what kind of writing would be best to present the information you learned, for example, an essay, a poem, or a play.

PROJECT 3

Make a Documentary About Leadership.

1. Find a documentary in your school library. View the documentary. Analyze how elements like graphics, motion, color, and narration help communicate the film's point.

2. Work with a group. Make a documentary about some important leaders. Using information from the documentaries you viewed, include facts and details about their leadership. How did they show qualities of leadership?

3. Present your group's documentary to the class.

PROJECT 4

Research Publishing Laws.

1. Go to your school or local library to investigate terms that describe different publishing laws.

2. Use a dictionary and online resources to find the terms **slander, libel, copyright,** and **plagiarism.**

3. Then look for news articles where these terms can be found. Choose an article, read it, and present to the class a summary of the article.

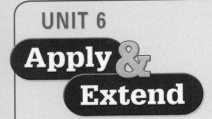

● Independent Reading

Explore the theme of leadership further by reading one or more of these books.

Iqbal by Francesco D'Adamo, Simon and Schuster, 2005.

Fatima is a young girl in Pakistan whose family has sold her into servitude to pay her father's debt. She and other children work long hours in a cramped, hot carpet factory. One day, a boy named Iqbal comes to rescue the children. Iqbal bravely fights for the rights of children.

Harriet Tubman: Conductor on the Underground Railroad by Ann Petry, Amistad, 2007.

This biography offers a detailed portrait of Harriet Tubman, the woman nicknamed "Moses" for her work leading slaves to freedom. Learn about how her bravery, strength, and determination made an impact on our country's history.

Indian Chiefs by Russell Freedman, Holiday House, 1988.

This book examines the lives of six of the greatest American Indian leaders of the 1800s. It includes information on Red Cloud of the Oglala Sioux, Santanta of the Kiowas, Quanah Parker of the Comanches, Washakie of the Shoshones, Joseph of the Nez Perces, and Sitting Bull of the Hunkpapa Sioux.

The King's Swift Rider: A Novel on Robert the Bruce by Mollie Hunter, HarperCollins, 1998.

A sixteen-year-old boy named Martin Crawford is hunting on a Scottish moor when he rescues a man who is being chased by several soldiers. The man turns out to be Robert the Bruce, the leader of the Scottish rebels who are fighting the English king. Martin joins Scotland's rebel army as a messenger spy. This novel is based on the life of Robert the Bruce, the leader in Scotland's War for Independence.

Saladin: Noble Prince of Islam by Diane Stanley, HarperCollins, 2002.

This illustrated biography tells the story of the 12th-century ruler Saladin. A skilled leader who showed compassion for those he conquered, Saladin was praised even by his enemies. The book includes background information on the Crusades, during which Saladin became famous.

Heinle Reading Library

Martin Luther King, Jr. by Herb Boyd

Read to find out why Martin Luther King, Jr. is remembered as a great American leader. The book begins with his childhood in the segregated South and tells about his days as a minister. It also focuses on King's role in the civil rights movement and how he won the Nobel Peace Prize in 1964, four years before his death.

Writing: Revise and Edit

MILESTONESTRACKER

Read this rough draft of a student's persuasive essay, which may contain errors. Then answer Questions 1 through 4.

An Everyday Leader

(1) Anyone can be a leader. (2) A good leader does not have to be talkative or social. (3) Shy people can be excellent leaders, too. (4) Leaders are followed by people for many reasons. (5) Whether you are timid or bold, you should think about how you can be a good leader every day.

(6) What is a good leader? (7) If you are honest even when no one is watching, you are a good leader. (8) If you help others even when you are busy or tired, you are a good leader. (9) If you are kind and friendly to those whom others tease, you are a good leader. (10) Good leadership does not depend on your achievements. (11) The one trait that all great leaders have in common is that they tirelessly give more than they recieve.

(12) You can be a quiet, shy leader or a talkative, social one. (13) Things may not always go your way, but a good leader does not get disheveled easily. (14) If we were all true leaders, the world is a happier place.

1 How should the misspelled word in sentence 11 be corrected?

A comon

B triat

C receive

D tirelesslie

2 Which word is a better choice than disheveled in sentence 13?

A courageous

B immense

C reformed

D discouraged

3 How can you correct sentence 14?

A Change *is* to *are*.

B Change *is* to *being*.

C Change *is* to *have been*.

D Change *is* to *would be*.

4 Which sentence in the passage uses the passive voice?

A sentence 3

B sentence 4

C sentence 10

D sentence 12

Writing on Demand: Formal Letter

Write a formal letter to your teacher that describes the strong leadership qualities of someone you know. Include information about the person's role and what makes him or her a good leader. **(20 minutes)**

Writing Tip

Check for shifts in writing. Make sure all the verbs and nouns in your sentences agree.

Read this historical fiction. Then answer Questions 1 through 8.

Harriet Beecher Stowe in Washington

1   Harriet sat in the comfortable wooden chair, her hands folded in her lap. She couldn't help feeling a little nervous, not because of whom she was about to meet, but because of what she had to say to him.

2   As she waited, Harriet reflected on how much her life had changed recently. In ten years, she had gone from being a schoolteacher to an activist for the rights of millions of people she didn't know. It was all because she wrote a book. After *Uncle Tom's Cabin* was distributed, the reactions were strong. People in the North saw the story as an incentive to end slavery. People in the South saw it as another reason to pursue secession. Harriet knew that if she had not written the book, the country would not be so divided. All she wanted was to use her pen like a key to unlock the chains of slavery.

3   The door opened at last, and the tall man in the dark suit walked in. Harriet stood. She was surprised by how tired and disheveled he looked, but he still smiled kindly at her. Harriet felt a new appreciation for his courageous leadership in these difficult times.

4   "Hello, Ms. Stowe," he said. "So you're the little woman who wrote the book that started this great war!"

5   "There is nothing great about war, Mr. President," Harriet replied.

6   "No, indeed there is not," Lincoln answered, as the smile left his face. "But your contribution to our current situation has been great. If you had decided to keep teaching, the world would not know the misery of the slave."

7   "Knowing is half the battle, Mr. President," Harriet said. "Now is the time to act. The war goes on, but you must do more. You must end slavery."

1 What does the word <u>incentive</u> mean in the following sentence from paragraph 2?

> People in the North saw the story as an <u>incentive</u> to end slavery.

A motivation

B decision

C belief

D obstacle

2 What does the word <u>disheveled</u> mean in the following sentence from paragraph 3?

> She was surprised by how tired and <u>disheveled</u> he looked, but he still smiled kindly at her.

A confused

B courageous

C disordered

D disappointed

3 Whom is Harriet waiting to meet?

A a schoolteacher

B President Lincoln

C Uncle Tom

D a slave

4 What does Harriet want?

A to start a war

B to divide the country

C to write a book

D to end slavery

5 Which is an example of a simile from the passage?

A "Knowing is half the battle, Mr. President," Harriet said.

B People in the South saw it as another reason to pursue secession.

C All she wanted was to use her pen like a key to unlock the chains of slavery.

D As she waited, Harriet reflected on how much her life had changed recently.

6 Which is an example of the passive voice?

A Harriet stood.

B As she waited, Harriet reflected on how much her life had changed recently.

C Harriet felt a new appreciation for his courageous leadership in these difficult times.

D After *Uncle Tom's Cabin* was distributed, the reactions were strong.

7 Which is an example of a conditional clause?

A knowing is half the battle

B you must end slavery

C If you had decided to keep teaching

D she had gone from being a schoolteacher to an activist

8 Which noun is NOT formed by adding the suffix *-ion* to a verb?

A appreciation

B million

C reaction

D contribution

MILESTONES HANDBOOK

◯ Nouns

- **Nouns** name a person, place, or thing.
- **Singular nouns** are nouns that name one person, place, or thing.
- **Plural nouns** are nouns that name more than one person, place, or thing.

Regular Plural Nouns

Singular	Plural	Spelling Rule
book	book**s**	most nouns: add **-s**
bus lunch	bus**es** lunch**es**	nouns that end in **s, x, z, ch, sh:** add **-es**
baby family	bab**ies** famil**ies**	nouns that end in a **consonant + y:** change the **y** to **i** and add **-es**
loaf knife	loa**ves** kni**ves**	nouns that end in **f** or **fe:** change the **f** or **fe** to **-ves**

Irregular Plural Nouns

Some nouns are irregular in the plural form.

Singular	Plural	Singular	Plural
man	**men**	child	**children**
woman	**women**	mouse	**mice**

Possessive Nouns

- To show possession with **names** and **singular nouns,** use an apostrophe + **s** (**'s**).
- To show possession with **plural nouns ending in s,** use only an apostrophe (**'**).
- To show possession with **irregular plurals,** use an apostrophe + **s** (**'s**).

Statement	Sentence with Possessive Noun
Sara has a nice apartment.	Sara**'s** apartment is nice.
The boy has a TV in his room.	The boy**'s** TV is in his room.
The girls have a big bedroom.	The girls**'** bedroom is big.
The men have blue hats.	The men**'s** hats are blue.

Count and Noncount Nouns

- **Count nouns** are nouns you can count. They are singular or plural.
- You use **a, an, the,** or a **number** with count nouns.

    I have **one egg.** I have **12 carrots.**

    I made **a salad.** I made it with **a tomato** and **an onion. The salad** was delicious.

- **Noncount nouns** can't be counted. They are singular. Don't use **a, an,** or **numbers.**

    I like **juice.** I eat **cheese.** I always drink **milk.**

Compound Nouns

A **compound noun** is a noun that is made up of two or more words. Most compound nouns are formed by nouns modified by other nouns or by adjectives.

    tooth + brush = toothbrush
    soft + ball = softball
    hand + shake = handshake

Articles

There are three articles: **a, an,** and **the.** Articles are used with nouns.

Indefinite Articles: a, an

- Use **a** and **an** with singular and plural count nouns when the noun is not specific.
- Use **a** before a word beginning with a consonant sound.

    I have **a** cousin in Chicago.

- Use **an** before a word beginning with a vowel sound.

    I have **an** uncle in Tampa.

Definite Article: the

- Use **the** before a specific noun.

    I do not usually like rice, but **the** rice your mother makes is great.

- Use **the** before names of:

regions of countries that are directions	I live in **the** South.
mountains, lakes, and islands	We go camping in **the** Rockies.
that are plural	**The** Caribbean Islands are beautiful.
large bodies of water and deserts	**The** Pacific is the largest ocean.

- Do not use **the** before names of:

continents, countries, states, cities	South America is very large.
	Miami is in Florida.
exception: the United States	I live in **the** United States.
mountains, lakes, and islands	Mount McKinley is in Alaska.
that are singular	My aunt is from Puerto Rico.

○ Pronouns

A **pronoun** takes the place of a noun or refers to a noun.

> My brother is sick today. **He** has a cold.

Subject Pronouns

- **Subject pronouns** take the place of subject nouns.

Subject Pronoun	Sentence	Subject Pronoun	Sentence
singular		**plural**	
I	**I** am Mario.	we	**We** are in class.
you	**You** are a student.	you	**You** are students.
he	**He** is a teacher.		
she	**She** is a lawyer.	they	**They** are in the office.
it	**It** is my pen.		

Object Pronouns

- **Object pronouns** take the place of object nouns.
- They show to whom something happened or who received something.
- They come after a verb or preposition.

Object Pronoun	Sentence	Object Pronoun	Sentence
singular		**plural**	
me	Min likes **me.**	us	They live next door to **us.**
you	Fatima works with **you.**	you	Ben helps **you** on Mondays.
him	Cosima knows **him.**		
her	Javier is walking with **her.**	them	The teacher helps **them** every day.
it	Victor bought **it.**		

Possessive Pronouns

Possessive pronouns tell who owns or has something.

Possessive Pronoun	Sentence	Possessive Pronoun	Sentence
singular		**plural**	
mine	This book is **mine.**	ours	That car is **ours.**
yours	**Yours** is on the table.	yours	Where did you park **yours**?
his	Matteo is reading **his.**		
hers	Irina doesn't have **hers.**	theirs	They brought **theirs** last week.
its	The cat has its food. The dog wants **its.**		

○ Adjectives

- **Adjectives** describe nouns.
- Adjectives can come before nouns: I have a **loud** voice.
- Adjectives can come after the verb **be:** My voice is **loud.**

Comparative Adjectives

Comparative adjectives compare two things.

Adjective	Comparative	Spelling Rule
tall	tall**er**	most one-syllable adjectives: add **-er**
dry happy	dr**ier** happ**ier**	one- and two-syllable adjectives that end in **y:** change the **y** to **i** and add **-er**
careful difficult	**more** careful **more** difficult	two or more syllable adjectives: put **more** in front of the adjective

Irregular comparatives

good / **better**
bad / **worse**

Superlative Adjectives

Superlative adjectives compare three or more things.

Adjective	Superlative	Spelling Rule
tall	**the** tall**est**	most one-syllable adjectives: add **-est**
dry happy	**the** dr**iest** **the** happ**iest**	one- and two-syllable adjectives that end in **y:** change the **y** to **i** and add **-est**
careful difficult	**the most** careful **the most** difficult	two or more syllable adjectives: put **most** in front of the adjective

Irregular superlatives

good / **the best**
bad / **the worst**

Possessive Adjectives

Possessive adjectives tell who something belongs to. They come before nouns.

Possessive Adjective	Sentence	Possessive Adjective	Sentence
singular		**plural**	
my	I am a student. **My** name is Matt.	**our**	We are in school. **Our** teacher is Mr. Dunn.
your	You are a teacher. **Your** class is in Room 21.	**your**	You are good students. **Your** grades are excellent.
his	Sam is a student. **His** teacher is Mrs. Martin.	**their**	Mrs. Ho and Mr. Dunn are teachers. **Their** students are in class.
her	Meg is in class. **Her** books are here.		
its	The computer is in the office. **Its** screen is on.		

○ Prepositions

- **Prepositions** and the words that follow them can tell *where, when,* and *how* something happens.

  > She is playing **in** the park. (where)
  > They go to school **at** 7:00. (when)
  > Mary walks **with** energy. (how)

- A **prepositional phrase** is a preposition and the words that follow it.

  > She put the plate **on the table.**

Common Prepositions		
about	below	of
above	between	on
against	by	over
around	for	through
at	from	to
before	in	under

○ Conjunctions

- **Conjunctions** can join words, phrases, or clauses (parts of a sentence with a subject and a verb).
- Conjunctions can join two independent clauses (clauses that can stand alone). Use these conjunctions: **and, or, but, so.**

  > Maria did her homework, **and** I helped her.
  > We can eat at home, **or** we can go to a restaurant.
  > I want a glass of milk, **but** we don't have any.
  > It's raining, **so** you need your umbrella.

- Conjunctions can join an independent clause (a clause that can stand alone) with a dependent clause (a clause that cannot stand alone). Use these conjunctions: **before, when, after, because, although.** The dependent clause can come first or second.

  > **Before** I came here, I lived in Haiti.
  > I learned English **when** I came to the United States.
  > **After** I learned English, I made lots of friends.
  > He took the job **because** he wanted the experience.
  > I walked to the mall **although** it is a mile away.

*For more about clauses, see page 446.

○ Adverbs

- **Adverbs** describe verbs, adjectives, or other adverbs. They often answer the questions "how?" or "how frequently?"

  > It snows **often** in Boston.

- Many adverbs end with **-ly.**

  > The man spoke **softly.**

○ Interjections

- **Interjections** are words that express strong feelings.
- They are often followed by an exclamation point.

  > **Hooray!** It's snowing.

○ Verbs

A **verb** is an action word.

Simple Present Tense

Use the **simple present tense** to tell about an action that generally happens or is true now.

Simple Present Tense of *be*	
singular	**plural**
I **am** Mario.	We **are** in class.
You **are** a student.	You **are** students.
He **is** a teacher.	
She **is** a lawyer.	They **are** in the office.
It **is** my pen.	

Contractions

I am = I'm
you are = you're
he is = he's
she is = she's
it is = it's
we are = we're
they are = they're

Simple Present Tense of Regular Verbs				
affirmative		**negative**		
subject	**verb**	**subject**	**verb**	
I You We They	**read.**	I You We They	**do not**	**read.**
He She It	**read<u>s</u>.**	He She It	**does not**	**read.**

Contractions

do not = don't
does not = doesn't

Present Progressive Tense

- The **present progressive tense** of a verb tells about an action happening right now.
- The present progressive uses **am, is,** or **are** and the **-ing** form of a verb.

Present Progressive Tense					
affirmative			**negative**		
I	**am**		I	**am not**	
He She It	**is**	**walking.**	He She It	**is not**	**walking.**
We You They	**are**		We You They	**are not**	

Present Progressive: *-ing* Spelling Rules

Present Progressive: *-ing* Spelling Rules	
rule	**examples**
Add **-ing** to the end of most verbs.	ask → ask**ing** go → go**ing**
For verbs that end in **e**, drop the **e** and add **-ing.**	dance → danc**ing** invite → invit**ing**
For verbs with one syllable that end in a vowel + a consonant, double the consonant and add **-ing.**	stop → sto**pping** run → ru**nning**
Do not double the consonant **w, x,** or **y.**	draw → draw**ing** fix → fix**ing** play → play**ing**
Double the consonant for verbs with two syllables that end in a consonant + vowel + consonant, with the stress on the last syllable.	begin → begi**nning** admit → admi**tting**
Do not double the consonant for verbs with two syllables that end in a consonant + vowel + consonant if the stress is *not* on the last syllable.	listen → listen**ing** open → open**ing**

Present Perfect Tense

- Use the **present perfect tense** to say that something happened in the past, when the exact time is not important.
- It is also used to talk about something that started in the past and continues to the present.
- The present perfect tense uses **have/has** and the past participle of a verb.
- The past participle of regular verbs ends in **-ed** or **-d:** walk**ed,** danc**ed.**
- See page 437 for a list of irregular past participles.

Present Perfect Tense					
affirmative			**negative**		
I	**have**	already **walked.**	I	**have not**	already **walked.**
He She It	**has**		He She It	**has not**	
We You They	**have**		We You They	**have not**	

Contractions

have not = haven't
has not = hasn't

- Use the **present perfect tense** with *for* and *since* to talk about something that started in the past and continues to the present.

  John **has lived** in Florida for ten years.

  They **have been** sick since Monday.

Irregular Past Participles

Base	Past Participle	Base	Past Participle
be	been	leave	left
become	become	lie	lain
begin	begun	lose	lost
break	broken	make	made
bring	brought	mean	meant
build	built	meet	met
buy	bought	pay	paid
choose	chosen	put	put
come	come	read	read
cost	cost	ride	ridden
cut	cut	run	run
do	done	say	said
draw	drawn	see	seen
drink	drunk	sell	sold
drive	driven	send	sent
eat	eaten	sing	sung
fall	fallen	sit	sat
feel	felt	sleep	slept
find	found	speak	spoken
fly	flown	spend	spent
get	gotten	stand	stood
give	given	swim	swum
go	gone	take	taken
grow	grown	teach	taught
have	had	tell	told
hear	heard	think	thought
hold	held	understand	understood
keep	kept	wear	worn
know	known	win	won
lay	laid	write	written

Imperatives

- Use the **imperative** to give instructions, directions, or orders.
- The imperative is like the simple present without a subject. The implied subject is *you*.
- Strong orders end with an exclamation point (**!**).

Imperatives		
simple present	**imperative**	**negative imperative**
You turn left at the library.	**Turn** left at the library.	**Do not (Don't) turn** left at the library.
You take the bus.	**Take** the bus**!**	**Do not (Don't) take** the bus**!**

Simple Past Tense

Use the **simple past** tense of a verb to tell about an action that happened in the past.

Simple Past Tense of Regular Verbs

- Add **-ed** or **-d** to form the simple past tense of a regular verb.
- Contraction: **did not = didn't**

Verb	Simple Past	Affirmative Sentence	Negative Sentence
play	play**ed**	Sue **played** volleyball last week.	Sue **did not play** volleyball last week.
dance	danc**ed**	I **danced** yesterday.	I **did not dance** yesterday.

Simple Past Tense of Irregular Verbs

Irregular verbs have special forms.

Base	Simple Past	Base	Simple Past	Base	Simple Past	Base	Simple Past
be	was/were	eat	ate	leave	left	sing	sang
become	became	fall	fell	lie	lay	sit	sat
begin	began	feel	felt	lose	lost	sleep	slept
break	broke	find	found	make	made	speak	spoke
bring	brought	fly	flew	mean	meant	spend	spent
build	built	get	got	meet	met	stand	stood
buy	bought	give	gave	pay	paid	swim	swam
choose	chose	go	went	put	put	take	took
come	came	grow	grew	read	read	teach	taught
cost	cost	have	had	ride	rode	tell	told
cut	cut	hear	heard	run	ran	think	thought
do	did	hold	held	say	said	understand	understood
draw	drew	keep	kept	see	saw	wear	wore
drink	drank	know	knew	sell	sold	win	won
drive	drove	lay	laid	send	sent	write	wrote

Simple Past Tense of *be*

Simple Past Tense of *be*		
subject	**simple past of *be***	**statement**
I He She It	**was** **was not**	I **was** at school yesterday. She **was not** at school on Monday.
We You They	**were not** **were**	We **were not** thirsty. You **were** hungry.

Contractions

was not = wasn't
were not = weren't

Past Progressive Tense

- The **past progressive** form of a verb tells about an action that was happening at a particular time in the past or when something else happened.
- The past progressive uses the simple past tense of **be** and the **-ing** form of a verb.

Past Progressive Tense					
affirmative			**negative**		
I	**was**	eat**ing** dinner when a fire engine went by.	I	**was not**	eat**ing** dinner at 8:00 last night.
He She It	**was**		He She It	**was not**	
We You They	**were**		We You They	**were not**	

Past Perfect Tense

- Use the **past perfect tense** to talk about a past action or event that took place before another event took place in the past.
- The past perfect tense uses **had** and the past participle of a verb.
- See page 437 for a list of irregular past participles.

Past Perfect Tense					
affirmative			**negative**		
I	**had**	**studied** hard before the test yesterday.	I	**had not**	**studied** hard before the test yesterday.
He She It	**had**		He She It	**had not**	
We You They	**had**		We You They	**had not**	

Contractions

I had = I'd
you had = you'd
he had = he'd
she had = she'd
we had = we'd
they had = they'd

Future Tense

The **future tense** describes events in the future.

Future Tense with *will*

- One way to show the future tense is to use **will** before the main verb.
- Use **will** with all subject nouns and pronouns.

Future Tense with *will*	
affirmative	**negative**
I **will** go to the mall tonight.	I **will not** go to the mall tonight.
You **will** go at noon.	You **will not** go at noon.
He **will** buy a hat tomorrow.	He **will not** buy a hat tomorrow.
She **will** go next Tuesday.	She **will not** go next Tuesday.
It **will** be fun.	It **will not** be fun.
We **will** pay now.	We **will not** pay now.
They **will** use a credit card.	They **will not** use a credit card.

Affirmative Contractions

I will = I'll
you will = you'll
he will = he'll
she will = she'll
it will = it'll
we will = we'll
they will = they'll

Negative Contraction

will not = won't

Future with *going to* + verb

- You can also show the future time by using **be** + **going to** before the main verb.
- This is more informal than **will.**

Future Tense with *be* + *going to*	
affirmative	**negative**
I **am going to** go to the mall tonight.	I **am not going to** go to the mall tonight.
You **are going to** go at noon.	You **are not going to** go at noon.
He **is going to** buy a hat tomorrow.	He **is not going to** buy a hat tomorrow.
She **is going to** go next Tuesday.	She **is not going to** go next Tuesday.
It **is going to** be fun.	It **is not going to** be fun.
We **are going to** pay now.	We **are not going to** pay now.
They **are going to** use a credit card.	They **are not going to** use a credit card.

Future Perfect Tense

- Use the **future perfect tense** to say that something will be completed in the future or at the time of another action in the future.

Present Perfect Tense					
affirmative			**negative**		
I	**will have**	already **eaten** by 8:00 tonight.	I	**will not have**	already **eaten** by 8:00 tonight.
He/She/It	**will have**		He/She/It	**will not have**	
We/You/They	**will have**		We/You/They	**will not have**	

○ Question Types

- There are two types of questions: *yes/no* **questions** and **information questions**.
- The answer to a *yes/no* question is either *yes* or *no*.
- The answer to an information question is a piece of information.

Yes/No Questions with *be*

Simple Present

To ask *yes/no* questions with **be,** put **am, is,** or **are** before the subject.

Present Progressive

- To ask *yes/no* questions with **be,** put **am, is,** or **are** before the subject.
- Use the **-ing** form of the verb after the subject.

Simple Past

- To ask *yes/no* questions with **be,** put **was/were** before the subject.
- Use the base form of the verb after the subject.

Future

- To ask *yes/no* questions with **be,** put **will** before the subject.
- Use the base form of the verb after the subject.

	statement	*yes/no* question	short answer
Yes/No **Questions with *be***			
Simple Present	The kitchen **is** big.	**Is** the kitchen big?	Yes, **it is.** No, **it isn't.**
	The rooms **are** small.	**Are** the rooms small?	Yes, **they are.** No, **they aren't.**
Present Progressive	She **is being** serious.	**Is** she **being** serious?	Yes, **she is.** No, **she isn't.**
Simple Past	The window **was** open.	**Was** the window open?	Yes, **it was.** No, **it wasn't.**
	The doors **were** closed.	**Were** the doors closed?	Yes, **they were.** No, **they weren't.**
Future	You **will be** here tomorrow.	**Will** you **be** here tomorrow?	Yes, I **will.** No, I **won't.**
	My parents **will be** busy this weekend.	**Will** my parents **be** busy this weekend?	Yes, they **will.** No, they **won't.**

Yes/No Questions with Verbs Except *be*

Simple Present

- To ask *yes/no* questions with all verbs except **be,** put **do** or **does** before the subject.
- Use the base form of the verb after the subject.

Present Progressive

- To make *yes/no* questions with all verbs except **be,** put **am, is,** or **are** before the subject.
- Use the **-ing** form of the verb after the subject.

Simple Past

- To ask *yes/no* questions with all verbs except **be,** put **did** before the subject.
- Use the base form of the verb after the subject.

Future

- To make *yes/no* questions with all verbs except **be,** put **will** before the subject.
- Use the base form of the verb after the subject.

Yes/No Questions with Verbs Except *be*			
	statement	*yes/no* question	short answer
Simple Present	He **likes** the house.	**Does** he **like** the house?	Yes, he **does.** No, he **doesn't.**
	They **study** in the kitchen.	**Do** they **study** in the kitchen?	Yes, they **do.** No, they **don't.**
Present Progressive	You **are sitting** in the living room.	**Are** you **sitting** in the living room?	Yes, I **am.** No, **I'm not.**
	She **is learning** how to drive.	**Is** she **learning** how to drive?	Yes, she **is.** No, she **isn't.**
Simple Past	You **ate** in the kitchen.	**Did** you **eat** in the kitchen?	Yes, I **did.** No, I **didn't.**
	You **read** a book in the living room.	**Did** you **read** a book in the living room?	Yes, we **did.** No, we **didn't.**
Future	He **will graduate** in 2010.	**Will** he **graduate** in 2010?	Yes, he **will.** No, he **won't.**
	We **will have** a test on Friday.	**Will** we **have** a test on Friday?	Yes, we **will.** No, we **won't.**

Information Questions

- Information questions start with a question word.
- Another name for information questions is **wh-** questions because most question words begin with **wh-** (**who, what, when, where, why**).
- The answer to an information question is a specific piece of information.

	Question Word	Helping Verb	Subject	Main Verb	
Simple Present	Who	do	you	see	in the picture?
Simple Past	What	did	you	see	at the museum?
Present Progressive	Why	are	you	watching	the movie?
Future Tense	Where	will	you	see	your friends?

◯ Frequently Misused Verbs

Certain verbs are frequently misused.

Misused Verbs	Example
lie = to rest in a horizontal position	Present: I **lie** in my bed to take a nap. Past: The cat **lay** in the shade.
lay = to put something down	Present: **Lay** your keys on the table. Past: We **laid** a new rug on the floor.
sit = to take a sitting position	Present: I **sit** in the first row in class. Past: She **sat** quietly for 15 minutes.
set = to put or place something	Present: Please **set** the dish on the table. Past: I don't know where I **set** my keys.
rise = to go or get up	Present: My father usually **rises** at 6:00. Past: Yesterday, he **rose** at 7:00.
raise = to lift or bring something up	Present: **Raise** your hand if you have a question. Past: I **raised** my voice so the teacher could hear me.

◯ Complete Sentences

- A sentence is a group of words. The words express a complete thought.
- A complete sentence has a subject and a verb.
- The subject tells who or what the sentence is about. The subject can be a noun or a pronoun.
- The verb tells about the subject.
- A complete sentence begins with a capital letter.
- A complete sentence ends with a punctuation mark:
  a period (**.**), a question mark (**?**), or an exclamation point (**!**).

Complete Sentences	Incomplete Sentences
My brother is in your math class.	Julien your brother. (no verb)
She needs a pen.	Exercises every day. (no subject)

Subject-Verb Agreement

- The **subject** and **verb** in a sentence must **agree** in number.
- When a subject is singular, the verb must be a singular form.
- When the subject is plural, the verb must be a plural form.

Subject-Verb Agreement	
singular subject + singular verb	**plural subject + plural verb**
She is a doctor.	**They are** teachers.
The man cooks breakfast every day.	**The children cook** dinner on the weekend.

Agreement with Compound Subjects

- A **compound subject** has two or more parts.
- The subjects are combined with conjunctions, such as **and** and **or.**
- If the conjunction is **and,** the verb is usually plural.
      Alex and Bob **play** soccer.
- If the conjunction is **or,** the verb agrees with the subject closest to the verb.
      A pen or a pencil **is** required.
      A book or two notebooks **are** required.

Declarative Sentence

- A **declarative sentence** states (or "declares") an idea, fact, or information.
- A declarative sentence usually ends in a period (**.**).
    > My grandmother is a wise woman.
    > John and Johanna are twins.

Interrogative Sentence

- An **interrogative sentence** asks a question.
- An interrogative sentence usually ends in a question mark (**?**).
- An interrogative sentence can ask for a *yes/no* answer or for specific information.
    > Do you like tacos? (Answer: *yes* or *no*)
    > Where were you born? (Answer: a specific place)

Imperative Sentence

- An **imperative sentence** gives an order or command.
- An imperative sentence does not include a subject. It uses the base form of the verb.
- An imperative sentence ends in a period (**.**) or an exclamation point (**!**).
    > Please shut the door.
    > Be careful!

Exclamatory Sentence

- An **exclamatory sentence** shows strong feeling.
- An exclamatory sentence ends in an exclamation point (**!**).
    > I really like my English class!
    > Hurry up! We're late.

○ Sentence Types

Clauses

- Most sentences are made of **clauses.** Clauses have at least one **subject** and one <u>verb</u>.
  Raoul <u>did</u> his homework.
- An **independent clause** can stand alone as a sentence. It expresses a complete thought.
  Raoul did his homework.
- A **dependent clause** cannot stand alone as a sentence. It must be used with an independent clause.
  <u>Before he went to bed</u>, <u>Raoul did his homework.</u>
      [dependent clause]   [independent clause]

Sentence Types

There are different sentence types. Using different types of sentences can make your writing more interesting.

Simple Sentence	Feature	Example
	one independent clause (there is no dependent clause)	Raoul got up early.

Compound Sentence	Feature	Example
	two independent clauses joined by a conjunction such as **and, but, or, nor, so, yet** (there is no dependent clause) NOTE: A comma links the two independent clauses.	Raoul got up early, **and** then he left for school.

Complex Sentence	Feature	Example
	an independent clause and at least one dependent clause	Although he went to bed late, Raoul got up early.
	an independent clause and a dependent clause joined by relative pronouns such as **who, that, which, whose, where**	Raoul read the book **that** his English teacher assigned.

Compound-Complex Sentence	Feature	Example
	at least two independent clauses and at least one dependent clause	Because I am a good student, some people expect me to speak perfectly, and other people expect me to write perfectly.

How to Use a Dictionary and a Thesaurus

○ How to Use a Dictionary

A good dictionary is an important reference tool. A dictionary can help your writing because it helps you to understand and select appropriate words for your writing.

Dictionaries are available in printed book form, on CD-ROM, and online.

Features of a Dictionary

- Word entries are organized alphabetically from A to Z.
- An entry starts with a headword. The headword shows how the word is broken into syllables.
- After the headword, you will find the pronunciation and syllable stress. Dictionaries use symbols to represent sounds. These symbols are used to help you pronounce the word in a way that most people will understand. The pronunciation also shows which syllable is stressed.
- Next, you'll find grammatical information. For each word, there is an abbreviation that tells you the part of speech—noun, pronoun, adjective, verb, adverb, preposition, conjunction, or interjection—that the word represents.
- Next is the definition—what the word means. When there are multiple meanings, the meanings are numbered.
- Entries often include an example sentence to show how to use the word in context.
- Some dictionaries also include the origin of the word. English has been spoken for about 1,500 years, so knowing word origins helps you understand when a word came into the language and where it came from.
- Some dictionaries also include synonyms (words with similar meanings) and antonyms (words with opposite meanings).

> **mile•stone** /ˈmaɪlˌstoʊn/ *n.*
> **1** a marker, such as a stone — that indicates the distance in miles: *Many years ago, the main road between Boston and New York had milestones next to it.* **2** an important achievement, event: *Getting her college degree was a milestone in her life.*
> [from Old English]
> *synonym* accomplishment, achievement, event

pronunciation
part of speech
definition
example sentence
origin
synonym

○ How to Use a Thesaurus

A thesaurus is another important reference tool.
- A thesaurus includes words and their **synonyms**—words that have the same or similar meanings.
- Some thesauruses also include **antonyms**—words that have opposite meanings.
- It may also include related words or concepts.
- Thesauruses are available in printed book form, on CD-ROM, and online.
- Use a thesaurus to help you vary your word choices and make your writing more interesting.
- When you know the meaning of the synonym or the antonym of an unknown word, you can determine that word's meaning.

> **sympathy** *n.*
> **1** understanding, concern.
> *antonym* indifference **2** accord, support of someone/something.
> *antonym* hostility
> *Related words* humanity, kindness, pity

synonyms
antonym
related words

Spelling

Spelling Rules

i before *e* except after *c* or when pronounced *ay*

- **i** before **e:** fr**ie**nd, br**ie**f, n**ie**ce, f**ie**rce
- after **c:** rec**ei**ve, c**ei**ling
- pronounced *ay*: **ei**ght, n**ei**ghbor, w**ei**gh, th**ei**r

q and *u*

- Always put the letter **u** after the letter **q: qu**ick, **qu**estion, **qu**iz.

Noun Plurals

- Add **-s** to form the plural of most nouns.
    paper / paper**s**
- For nouns ending in **-s, -x, -z, -ch, -sh:** add **-es.**
    gas / gas**es**   box / box**es**   sandwich / sandwich**es**   dish / dish**es**
- For nouns ending in consonant + **y:** change the **y** to **i** and add **-es.**
    family / famil**ies**
- For nouns ending in **-f** or **-fe:** change the **-f** or **-fe** to **-ves.**
    loaf / loa**ves**   life / li**ves**
- For nouns ending in vowel + **o:** add **-s.**
    radio / radio**s**
- For nouns ending in consonant + **o:** add **-es.**
    tomato / tomato**es**

Suffixes

- When adding a suffix that begins with a vowel: drop a final silent **-e.**
    combine / combin**ation**   remove / remov**able**
- When adding a suffix that begins with a consonant: keep the final silent **-e.**
    achieve / achiev**ement**   care / care**ful**
- When adding a suffix to a one-syllable word that ends in vowel + consonant: double the consonant.
    hit / hi**tting**   stop / sto**pped**
- Change a final **y** to **i,** except when adding **-ing.**
    day / da**ily**   try / tr**ied**   play / play**ing**

Frequently Misspelled Words

address	broccoli	embarrass	government	jewelry	library	necessary	prejudice	scissors	through
arctic	calendar	exercise	height	judgment	mathematics	neighbor	raspberry	separate	truly
beginning	definite	fascinate	humorous	ketchup	miniature	occasion	receive	sincerely	until
believe	desperate	February	independent	knowledge	misspell	piece	rhythm	special	Wednesday
bicycle	disastrous	foreign	jealous	leisure	mysterious	precede	science	thorough	weird

◯ Homophones

- **Homophones** are words that have the same pronunciation but different spellings and meanings.

Homophone	Example
to = part of a verb infinitive; also a preposition	I want **to** read my book. I went **to** the store for my grandfather.
two = the number 2	My **two** shoes are beside the bed.
too = also	My books are at home. My notebook is, **too.**
it's = it is	I lost my backpack. **It's** not in my bedroom.
its = possessive adjective	I like that house and especially **its** porch.
their = possessive adjective	**Their** room is usually messy.
they're = they are	**They're** always quiet.
there = place	My house is over **there** by the shopping mall.
your = possessive adjective	When is **your** birthday?
you're = you are	**You're** the best teacher in the school.

Other homophones

buy (to purchase) / **by** (a preposition) /
    bye (short form of good-bye)
fir (tree) / **fur** (animal hair)
hair (on your head) / **hare** (animal)

pair (two) / **pear** (fruit)
peace (quiet; no war) / **piece** (part of something)
scene (part of a play) / **seen** (past participle of the verb *see*)
write (form letters or words) / **right** (correct; a direction)

◯ Homographs

- **Homographs** are words that are spelled the same but have different meanings.
- They may or may not have the same pronunciation.

Homograph	Example
dove = a small bird	A white **dove** flew by.
dove = past tense of the verb *dive* (different pronunciation)	I **dove** into the swimming pool.
just = fair and reasonable	My mother is a **just** person.
just = a short time ago (same pronunciation)	The baby **just** fell asleep.
tear = rip	He has a **tear** in his shirt.
tear = water from the eye (different pronunciation)	There are **tears** in her eyes.
well = in good health	Marco doesn't feel **well.**
well = a hole made in the ground to reach water, oil, etc. (same pronunciation)	There is no water left in the **well.**

Roots, Prefixes, Suffixes

◯ Common Greek and Latin Word Roots

Greek Root	Meaning	Example
astro	star	astronaut
auto	self	automatic
biblio	book	bibliography
bio	life	biology
meter	measure	speedometer
micro	small	microscope
sphere	ball	hemisphere
tele	from afar	telephone

Latin Root	Meaning	Example
centi	hundred	centipede
contra	against	contrary
dict	say, speak	dictate
fract	break	fraction
man	hand	manual
pop	people	population
struct	build	construct
vid/vis	see	video/visual

◯ Prefixes

- A **prefix** is a group of letters added to the beginning of a word.
- The word it is added to is called the **root word.**
- The prefix changes the meaning of the root word.

Prefix	Meaning	Example
anti-	against	antifreeze
bi-	two	bicycle
dis-	not, opposite	dislike
inter-	between	international
mid-	middle	midway
mis-	not, incorrectly	misunderstand
over-	over	overlook
pre-	before	preview
re-	back, again	rewrite
super-	above	superstar
un-	not	unhealthy

◯ Suffixes

- A **suffix** is a group of letters added to the end of a root word.
- A suffix changes the meaning of the root word.

Suffix	Meaning	Example
-able	can be done	removable
-en	made of	wooden
-er, -or	one who	worker, actor
-ful	full of	careful
-ist	one who	dentist
-less	without	fearless
-ment	action or process	enjoyment
-ness	condition of	kindness
-ous	possessing the qualities of	gaseous
-tion	act, process	attraction

Syllabication

- A **syllable** is a unit of pronunciation.
- A syllable contains only one vowel sound.
- A word can have one or more syllables.
- Dividing words into syllables helps you learn how to pronounce them.

Closed Syllables

- A closed syllable ends in a consonant.
- A closed syllable has one vowel.
- The vowel sound in a closed syllable is short.

    sat, run, nap/**kin**, **sub**/**ject**

Open Syllables

- An open syllable ends in a vowel.
- The vowel sound in an open syllable is usually long.

    me, no, she, mu/sic, **ta**/ble, **o**/pen

Final -e Syllables (VCe)

- A final **-e** syllable ends in a vowel (V), a consonant (C), and a final **-e.**
- The final **-e** is silent and makes the earlier vowel long.

    make, cute, hope a/**lone**, in/**side**

Vowel Digraphs (Vowel Teams)

- A vowel digraph (or vowel team) is created when two vowels together form one vowel sound in the same syllable.
- The vowel sound in a vowel digraph syllable is long.

    boat, meat, ex/**plain,** re/**peat, sea**/son

r-Controlled Vowels

- **r**-controlled vowels contain a vowel followed by an **r.**
- The vowel sound is affected by the **r.**
- When dividing a word into syllables, the vowel and the *r* usually stay in the same syllable.

    car, her, bird, but/**ter,** en/**ter, per**/son

Consonant + -le

- A common syllable spelling pattern is a consonant + **-le.**
- The **e** is silent.
- The syllable appears at the end of a word.

    ta/**ble,** cir/**cle,** ti/**tle**

Punctuation

Period (.)

Declarative Sentence	A statement is called a declarative sentence. Put a period at the end of a declarative sentence.	Today is the first day of school**.**
Abbreviations	An abbreviation is a short form of a word. Put a period at the end of an abbreviation.	Tuesday → Tues**.** inch → in**.**

Question Mark (?)

Questions	A question is also called an interrogative sentence. Put a question mark at the end of a question.	What is your name**?** Are you going to the party**?**

Exclamation Point (!)

Exclamations and Emphasis	An exclamation point at the end of a sentence shows strong feelings or surprise. Use exclamation points with exclamatory sentences and with imperative sentences for emphasis.	The burrito was delicious**!** Don't eat the lettuce**!** I didn't wash it yet**!**

Comma (,)

Items in a Series	Use a comma after each part of a series. A series has three or more parts.	I have a pen**,** a pencil**,** and a book.
In Dates	Use a comma after the day in a date.	September 13**,** 2009
In Addresses	Use a comma before an apartment number. Use a comma after a city.	126 First St.**,** Apt. 3A Santa Ana**,** CA 92701
In Letters	Use a comma after the greeting and the closing in a friendly letter.	Dear Aunt Mary**,** Your friend**,**
In Compound Sentences	Use a comma to link independent clauses in a compound sentence joined by conjunctions: **and, but, or, nor, for, so, yet.** The comma comes before the conjunction.	I like apples**,** but I prefer strawberries. You need to leave now**,** or you'll miss the bus.

Apostrophe (')

Contractions	An apostrophe takes the place of missing letters in contractions.	it is → it**'**s he will → he**'**ll
Possessives	An apostrophe + **s** indicates possession. If the word is singular and ends in **s,** add **'s.** If the word is plural and ends in **s,** just add an apostrophe.	the girl**'s** book Lois**'s** book the boys**'** house

Quotation Marks (" ")

Quotations	Quotation marks show the exact words people say. Put quotation marks where the speaker's words start and stop. Put a comma between the quote and the speaker of the quote.	"Let me clean the car," Ramón said. Ramón said, "Let me clean the car."
Titles	Use quotation marks for titles of articles in newspapers and magazines, poems, songs, and short stories.	Did you read the article "New Park Opens" in *The Daily News*? My favorite poem is "The Road Not Taken," by Robert Frost.

Parentheses (( ))

Extra Information	Parentheses are curved signs that give extra information or an explanation in a reading.	You use it to access (make use of) hundreds of Web sites.

Semicolon (;)

To Connect Independent Clauses	Use a semicolon to connect two independent clauses when there is no conjunction (such as **and, but, or, nor**).	Some people like country music; some people don't.

Colon (:)

In Time	Use a colon to separate hours from minutes.	10:15 AM 9:33 PM
In Letters	In a business letter, use a colon after the greeting.	Dear Mr. Best:
A List	Use a colon to introduce a list.	Kim enjoys lots of physical activities: hiking, swimming, soccer, and baseball.

○ Italics

- When using a computer, use *italics* in the situations below.
- When using handwriting, use underlining.

For Emphasis	Use italics for words you want to emphasize.	Do you *really* want to go?
Titles of Documents	Use italics for titles of: documents, newspapers, magazines, books, movies.	*The Constitution* *The Sunday News* *Fun Magazine* *The Pearl*
Foreign Words	Use italics for foreign words in an English sentence.	In Turkish, the first two numbers are *bir* and *iki*.

First Word in Sentence	Use a capital letter for the first word in a sentence.	**A** word problem uses words and data.
First Word in a Quoted Sentence	Use a capital letter for a quotation that is a complete sentence. Do not use a capital letter for the second part of a quoted sentence that is interrupted.	He said, "**W**e are leaving at 4:00." "We are leaving," he said, "at 4:00."
Pronoun "I"	The subject pronoun **I** always has a capital letter.	Mario is hungry, but **I** am not.
Proper Nouns	The names of the days and months always begin with capital letters. The names of people and titles always begin with capital letters.	My birthday is **T**uesday, **M**arch 24th. My father's name is **D**r. **I**brahim.
Nationalities, Languages, Academic Courses, Organizations, Holidays, Historical Events, and Special Events	Use capital letters for the names of nationalities, languages, academic courses, organizations, holidays, historical events, and special events.	**A**merican **S**panish **A**lgebra I **T**he **A**merican **R**ed **C**ross **F**ourth of **J**uly **B**attle of **G**ettysburg **W**inter **C**oncert
Specific Places and Geographical Names	Use capital letters for street names. Use capital letters for the names of cities, states, countries. Use capital letters for the names of mountains, rivers, lakes, and oceans.	**F**ifth **A**venue, **E**ast **S**treet **S**acramento, **C**alifornia **U**nited **S**tates the **R**ocky **M**ountains, the **H**udson **R**iver, **L**ake **E**rie, the **P**acific **O**cean
Titles of Works	Capitalize the first word and the important words in the titles of books, magazines, newspapers, works of art, musical compositions.	*Before We Were Free* *Scientific Magazine* *Community Newspaper* *Mona Lisa* "**S**ymphony **N**o. 5"

Editing and Proofreading Symbols

Symbol	Meaning
⌐H	insert a paragraph indent
∽	transpose (move around) letters, words, or sentences
Sp	check spelling
∧	insert word, words, or punctuation mark
ℓ	delete/take out
ˆ⌣	insert a comma
⊙	insert a period
∧ʃ	insert a semicolon
⊙⊙	insert a colon
⟨⟨ ⟩⟩	insert quotation marks
ḛ	make a capital
⧣	make lowercase
#	insert a space
‿	close up the space

Revising and Editing

○ Revising and Editing Checklist

1. Development of Ideas/Content

   a. Did I choose an appropriate form of writing (e.g., personal letter, letter to the editor, review, poem, report, narrative) for my purpose?

   b. Is the purpose of my writing clear?

   c. Is my writing focused on the topic I chose to write about?

   d. Did I support my ideas with details, facts, examples, and explanations?

   e. Did I write appropriately for my audience?

2. Organization

   a. Is my writing clear and logical?

   b. Do I have a strong, interesting beginning that gets the reader's attention?

   c. Did I group related ideas? Did I use transition words correctly?

   d. Did I maintain a consistent focus?

   e. Do my ideas progress logically? Can I improve the progression?

   f. Can I improve the meaning and focus of my writing by adding, deleting, consolidating, clarifying, and rearranging words and sentences?

   g. Do I have a strong ending that summarizes my topic?

3. Sentence Structures

   a. Are my sentences complete? Do they have a subject and a verb?

   b. Did I use declarative, interrogative, imperative, and exclamatory sentences appropriately?

   c. Did I make sure that there are no run-on sentences or fragments?

   d. Did I use different types of sentences—simple, compound, complex, and compound-complex?

   e. Can I revise to connect short, related sentences with appositives, participial phrases, adjectives, adverbs, conjunctions, transitions, and prepositional phrases?

4. Paragraph Structure
Single Paragraph

   a. Does my paragraph have a topic sentence?

   b. Did I support my topic sentence with facts and details?

Multi-Paragraph

   a. Did I provide an introductory paragraph?

   b. Did I establish and support a central idea with a topic sentence at or near the beginning of the first paragraph?

   c. Did I include supporting paragraphs with simple facts, details, and explanations?

   d. Did I provide details and transitional expressions that link one paragraph to another in a clear line of thought?

   e. Did I conclude with a paragraph that summarizes the points?

5. **Grammar and Usage (see pages 430–446)**
   a. Is my writing in the right tense (for example, present or past tense)?
   b. Did I use subject pronouns and object pronouns correctly?
   c. Did I use the pronouns *she*, *her*, or *hers* for women and girls, and *he*, *him*, or *his* for men and boys?
   d. Do my verbs agree with their subjects? Did I use singular verb forms with singular subjects and plural verb forms with plural subjects?
   e. Did I use articles, nouns, adjectives, and compound words correctly?
   f. Did I use correct verb forms (regular and irregular) and appropriate verb tenses?

6. **Word Choice**
   a. Did I choose exact and descriptive words?
   b. Did I use a dictionary, thesaurus, or glossary to help me choose better words?
   c. Did I eliminate extra words so that my writing is not wordy?

7. **Writing Conventions**
   Form
   a. Did I write my name and the date?
   b. Did I write a title and underline it?
   c. Did I leave margins at the top and bottom and on both sides of the paper?
   d. Did I use correct spacing between letters in words and words in a sentence?
   e. Did I indent the first line of each paragraph?
   f. Did I use my best handwriting or, if I used a computer, did I create an attractive presentation?
   g. Did I need to include a bibliography? If so, did I correctly cite my references?

   Spelling (see pages 448–449)
   a. Did I check the spelling of all words I'm not sure about?
   b. If I wrote my paper on a computer, did I use the spell check?

   Punctuation (see pages 452–453)
   a. Did I punctuate each sentence with the right punctuation mark?
   b. For direct speech, did I use quotation marks and commas correctly?
   c. Did I use apostrophes correctly in contractions and possessives?
   d. Did I use parentheses for extra information?
   e. Did I use commas, colons, and semicolons correctly?

   Capitalization (see page 454)
   a. Did I capitalize the pronoun "I" and the names of proper nouns?
   b. Did I start each sentence with a capital letter?

8. **My Own Criteria**
   What are some things you want to look for in your writing?
   a.
   b.
   c.

The Research Process

○ The Research Process

STEP 1 Identify a topic.

Choose a topic that is specific, not general. It is difficult to research and write about a general topic.

General Topic	Specific Topic
Rain Forests	The Climate of the Rain Forests
	Ways to Save the Rain Forests

STEP 2 Frame a central question or questions about your topic.

Your questions guide your research. As you find out information, write new questions and revise your original questions, as necessary.

STEP 3 Use references.

Find out more about your topic by using a variety of reference resources.

Reference	Description	How to Use It
computer catalog	database of all books in the library	Type in keywords to find books and other references related to your topic. Ask the librarian for help, if necessary.
books	books with information related to your topic	Look at the table of contents, preface, appendix, and index to locate content related to your topic. Also look at citations, end notes, and bibliographic entries that provide more information.
encyclopedias	collection of articles on thousands of topics; often include illustrations, photos, charts, and maps	Print encyclopedias: Look up topics in alphabetical order; they often have cross-references to related topics. CD-ROM or online encyclopedias: Type in keywords related to your topic, then click on the articles; links within the articles indicate cross-references.
atlas	collection of maps that show location of places or other features, such as geographic, economic, or political features	Print atlas: Look at the table of contents or index to locate information related to your topic. CD-ROM or online atlas: Type in keywords related to your topic, then click on the links.
almanac	yearly publication that includes lists, tables, and brief articles relating to a topic	Print almanac: Look at the table of contents or index to locate information related to your topic. CD-ROM or online almanac: Type in keywords related to your topic, then click on the links.

Reference	Description	How to Use It
dictionary	list of words in alphabetical order with pronunciation, part of speech, meanings, and often word origins	Print dictionary: Look up the word alphabetically. CD-ROM or online dictionary: Type in the word.
thesaurus	dictionary of synonyms (words with the same or similar meanings); often includes antonyms (words with opposite meanings)	Print thesaurus: Look up the word alphabetically; use the head words (words at the top of the page) to guide you. CD-ROM or online thesaurus: Type in the word.
magazine	a weekly or monthly publication that includes articles, stories, essays, and photos	Use an electronic database at the library to locate magazines with articles about your topic. Use the table of contents of the magazine to find the article. Current issues are usually on display. Older ones will be in the electronic archives.
newspaper	a daily or weekly print paper containing news articles	Use an electronic database at the library to locate articles about your topic. Current issues are usually on display. Older ones will be in the electronic archives.
Internet	a computer network of electronic information	Type keywords into a browser. Scan the links to find sites that seem useful.

STEP 4 Take notes on note cards.

Note cards help you keep track of the information you find and the sources of the information.

Use note cards to organize this information.

a. Follow the format below to record the information that answers your questions.

b. Paraphrase or summarize the information from your source. Use your own words.

c. If you cite words directly from the source, you must use quotation marks.

d. Provide the complete source information. See page 460 for how to cite sources.

TOPIC: _____

Question: _____

(What do you want to know?)

Paraphrase or summarize your source:

OR **"Quote" your source:**

Source:

When citing sources using handwriting, use underlining as shown below.
When using a computer, use *italics*.

Citations for Reference Sources	
reference	**how to cite**
book	Author. Title of Book, City of Publication: Publisher, Year. **Example:** Roper, Edward R. Rain Forest, New York: Omni Publishing, 1998.
encyclopedia	Author of Article, "Title of Article." Title of Book. City of Publication: Publisher, Year. **Example:** Alpert, Louis C. "Inca." Encyclopedia Americana, International Edition. 1999.
magazine or newspaper	Author of Article. "Title of Article." Title of Magazine or Newspaper Date: Page(s). **Example:** Tyler, Dawn. "On the Sands." Hawaii Living February 1998: 20-23.
Internet article	Creator's Name (if given). "Title of Article." Web Page Title. Institution or Organization. Date of access. <URL address>. If you cannot find the information, use the web address as the citation. **Example:** Likakis, Angela. "The World of Science." Science News. Science Resource Center. InfoSci. February 28, 1998. <http://infosci.thinkgroup.com/itweb/boston_massachusetts>

STEP 5 Write your research paper.

a. Organize your note cards in logical sequence.

b. Create an outline from your notes. See page 461 for how to create an outline.

c. Use your outline to draft your paper.

d. Revise and edit your paper. Use the Research Paper Checklist on page 462.

e. Incorporate visuals.

STEP 6 Create a title page, table of contents, and bibliography.

a. The first page should include the title of your research paper, centered on the page. Include your name and the date in the bottom right-hand corner.

b. At the beginning of your research paper, make a "Table of Contents" to show the organization.

c. At the end of your paper, start a new page with the title "Bibliography."

d. In your bibliography, list all your sources. Use the correct citation format. List your sources in alphabetical order.

Research Paper Outline

1. Sort your note cards before you do your outline.
2. Organize topics and subtopics into a logical order.
3. Write a topic or a thesis.
4. List major headings after a Roman numeral and a period.
5. List subtopics after a capital letter and a period.
6. List supporting details and examples after a number and a period.

Title

I. Topic 1 or Thesis
   A. Subtopic 1
      1. Detail/Example
      2. Detail/Example
   B. Subtopic 2
      1. Detail/Example
      2. Detail/Example

II. Topic 2 or Thesis
   A. Subtopic 1
      1. Detail/Example
      2. Detail/Example
   B. Subtopic 2
      1. Detail/Example
      2. Detail/Example

III. Topic 3 or Thesis
   A. Subtopic 1
      1. Detail/Example
      2. Detail/Example
   B. Subtopic 2
      1. Detail/Example
      2. Detail/Example

IV. Topic 4 or Thesis
   A. Subtopic 1
      1. Detail/Example
      2. Detail/Example
   B. Subtopic 2
      1. Detail/Example
      2. Detail/Example

V. Conclusion (restate thesis)

○ Research Paper Checklist

1. **Research**
   a. I framed a central question.
   b. I researched my question using a variety of reference materials.
   c. I took notes with information from these sources.
   d. I revised my research questions and added new ones as needed.
   e. I organized my information in an outline.
   f. I used at least three sources.

2. **Reference Materials**
   a. I evaluated each reference source for credibility.
   b. I did not plagiarize. I summarized and paraphrased, or I quoted my sources.
   c. I documented sources for all information that is not my own opinion.
   d. When I used exact words from a source, I put them in quotation marks and cited where they came from.

3. **Organization**
   a. I stated my thesis clearly in the introduction.
   b. I stayed focused on my topic and thesis.
   c. I combined short, related sentences with appositives, participial phrases, adjectives, adverbs, and prepositional phrases.
   d. I used transitional words between paragraphs.
   e. I summarized and answered my thesis question in the conclusion.

4. **Writing**
   a. I checked my spelling with a dictionary or with the computer's spell check.
   b. I checked my punctuation in every sentence.
   c. I checked my choice of words.
   d. I checked my verb tenses and subject-verb agreement.

5. **Form**
   a. I wrote an interesting title that reflects the subject.
   b. I wrote my name and date.
   c. I used correct margins on each page.
   d. I used double spacing on the computer.
   e. I indented each paragraph.
   f. I used correct capitalization and punctuation.
   g. I cited my sources correctly.

6. **Evaluation**
   a. I thought about how well I answered my research questions.
   b. I thought about questions for further research.

Technology Guide

◯ The Computer

You can use a computer to help you work. You can also use a computer to help you find information. A computer is made up of **hardware** and **software.** Hardware is the part of the computer that you can touch. Software is the instructions that make the computer work.

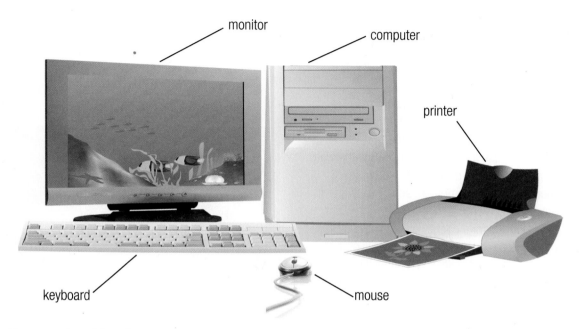

monitor   computer   printer

keyboard   mouse

Computer Hardware

1. The most important part of a computer is the box that contains the computer's memory. Your information is stored in the computer's memory.
2. You give information to the computer by typing on a keyboard or by clicking a mouse.
3. You see the information on the monitor. The monitor looks like a television screen.
4. You can use a printer to print the information on paper.

Computer Software

Software is made to do a special kind of job. For example, there is software that helps you write and edit your writing (word processing). There is software that makes it easy to create presentations. Other software lets you find information on the Internet. These pieces of software are also called **programs** or **applications.**

○ Word Processing

A word processing program is a tool for writing. You can use it to:
- correct mistakes, move text around, and add or delete text.
- do spelling and grammar checks to help you find and correct errors.
- find synonyms by using a thesaurus in the program.
- create visuals.
- choose text features such as **boldface type** and *italic type*.

How to Create a Document

Anything that you write in a word processing program is called a **document.**

1. Make sure that the computer is on.
2. Find the **icon** (the little picture) for your word processing program on the screen.
3. Use the mouse to move the arrow onto the word processing icon and click on the program to open it. Different computers do this in different ways. Ask someone to help you.
4. When the program opens, you can start typing.
5. You can learn how to use special keys on the keyboard. For example, if you press the key marked **Tab** when you are at the beginning of a line, the computer will make a paragraph indent. The **Shift** keys make capital letters.
6. Look at the icons in this illustration. You can click on these icons with the mouse to make special effects such as **bold** or *italic* type. (The icons on your program might be different from these.)
7. VERY IMPORTANT: The computer will not "remember" your work by itself. You have to save it to the computer's memory. There is a Save icon that will make the computer do this. When you click on the Save icon the first time, the computer will ask you to name your document. As you write, save your work often.
8. When you have finished your first draft, use the spelling and grammar checks to find and fix errors. You can add text features and visuals if you like. Print your work or send it to someone by e-mail.

tab—makes a paragraph indentation

shift—makes capital letters

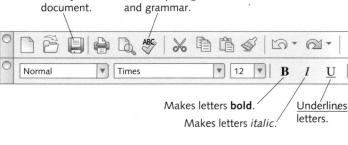

Saves your document.

Checks spelling and grammar.

Normal | Times | 12 | **B** *I* U̲

Makes letters **bold**.

Makes letters *italic.*

Underlines letters.

○ Technology Presentations

Using media such as video, graphics, and slides on a computer can make your oral presentations clearer and more interesting.

STEP 1 Plan the media parts of your presentation.

1. Plan, organize, and prepare your presentation. Take notes on how technology could help make your points.
   a. Is there a video that would help show your idea? Could you make one?
   b. Would music add to your presentation? What kind? Where can you get it?
   c. Should you show charts and visuals on the computer?
2. Make note cards. Use one card for what you will say and another card for the technology parts. Put the cards in order.

Card 1 My speech	Card 2 Media	Card 3 My speech
Sports Important in our community Most people like some kind of sport. Introduce video.	Play video of sports scenes in town.	Sports are fun. Teamwork Healthy

STEP 2 Prepare the media parts of your presentation.

1. Find or create the images and sounds that you want to use.
   Look in the "Clip Art" section of your software or scan art or photos into your program.
2. If available, use the presentation software on your computer to organize the images and sounds.

STEP 3 Practice your presentation.

1. Practice your technology presentation out loud.
2. Ask a partner to watch your presentation and give suggestions for improvement.

STEP 4 Give your technology presentation to your audience.

1. Set up your equipment early to be sure that everything is working.
2. After your presentation, ask the audience to evaluate your presentation.

How to Use the Internet

Key Definitions

Internet	millions of computers connected together to exchange information
Web sites	locations on the Internet
browser	software that lets you see Web sites
keywords	words typed into a search engine to find information on a certain topic
link	takes you to another Web site or to another place on the same Web site when you click your mouse on it

address bar—
Type Web
addresses here.

search box—
Type your
keywords here.

Click here
to start
your search.

Do Research on the Internet

1. Open your browser. Ask your teacher or a classmate how to do this.
2. Type keywords for your topic in the "search" box. Click on the button that says "go" (or "start" or "search").
3. Look at the list of Web sites that comes up on the screen. Choose one of the sites that seems interesting and click on it.
4. On a Web site, there are pages of information. Sometimes there are links to take you to other Web sites.
5. If you already know the exact address of a Web site, you can type it into the address bar. For example, http://visions.heinle.com.

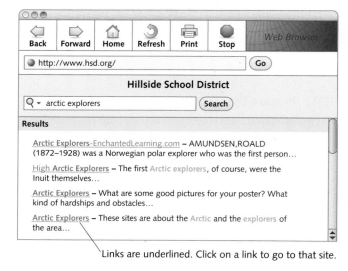

Links are underlined. Click on a link to go to that site.

Use Information from the Internet

Many Web sites have good information. Others may have mistakes, or they may tell only one side of an issue. You must evaluate the information that you find on the Internet. Ask your teacher or another adult for suggestions of sites that you can trust. Use other resources to check the information you find on the Internet.

◯ How to Use E-Mail

Key Definitions

e-mail	software that lets you type a message and send it to someone else who has e-mail
e-mail address	where the e-mail system sends the message
inbox	a list of who sent you messages and what the messages are about

Read an E-Mail Message

1. Open the e-mail program. Ask your teacher or a classmate how to do this. See if there are any new messages in your inbox.
2. Open a message. Programs do this differently. Usually you double click the mouse on the message.
3. Read the message.
4. If you want to keep the message, do not do anything. The computer will save it in your inbox. If you want to discard the message, click on the "delete" button on the toolbar.
5. To send an answer back, click on the "reply" button. Write your message and click "send."

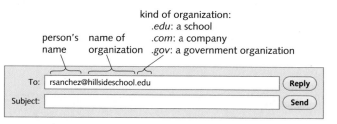

kind of organization:
.edu: a school
.com: a company
.gov: a government organization

person's name   name of organization

To: rsanchez@hillsideschool.edu   Reply
Subject: Send

Send an E-Mail Message

1. Open your e-mail program.
2. On the toolbar, click on the "new message" button.
3. Type in the address of the person you are writing to.
4. Type in a subject that tells what the message is about.
5. Type your message.
6. Click on the "send" button.

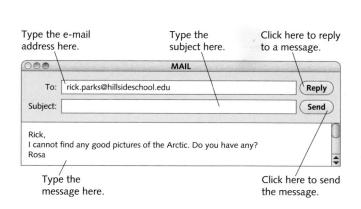

Type the e-mail address here.   Type the subject here.   Click here to reply to a message.

MAIL

To: rick.parks@hillsideschool.edu   Reply
Subject: Send

Rick,
I cannot find any good pictures of the Arctic. Do you have any?
Rosa

Type the message here.   Click here to send the message.

○ **Print Letters**

○ Cursive Letters

Glossary
Key Vocabulary, Academic Vocabulary, Literary/Text Element Terms

The definitions included in this Glossary represent how the words are used in this student book. Many words have multiple meanings. These additional meanings can be found in a dictionary.

Glossary Pronunciation Key

- The pronunciation of each listing is shown in parentheses after the listing.
- The words below are examples of how each letter and sign is pronounced.
- The symbol (′) appears after a syllable with heavy stress.
- The symbol (′) appears after a syllable with light stress.

  For example: **pronunciation** (prə nun′sē ā′shən)

a	map, flag	k	keys, sink	ᴛʜ	the, mother
ā	gate, play	l	library, animal	u	run, son
ä	art, barn	m	math, room	ü	school, rude
â	fare, scared	n	nice, green	u̇	could, pull
b	book, tub	ng	sing, hang	v	value, weave
ch	chair, teacher	o	hot, closet	w	watch, shower
d	desk, bald	ō	motive, polar	y	yes, employer
e	net, pen	ô	war, story	z	zip, stanza
ē	heal, scene	ȯ	fall, cause	zh	visual, conclusion
ėr	nurse, germ	oi	soil, annoy	ə	**a** in ability
f	fact, sofa	ou	proud, brown		**e** in liberty
g	go, bag	p	pillow, lamp		**i** in pencil
h	helmet, holiday	r	ruler, hair		**o** in dictionary
i	miss, image	s	sunny, class		**u** in injury
ī	wise, rhyme	t	time, weight		
j	jacket, subject	th	theme, truth		

How to Use the Glossary

The **entry** shows how the word is spelled.

- A yellow dot indicates a **Key Vocabulary Word.**
- A purple dot indicates an **Academic Vocabulary Word.**
- A green dot indicates a **Literary/Text Element Term.**

The **pronunciation** shows how the word is pronounced and how it is broken into syllables.

The **definition** gives the meaning(s) of the word (as used in this student book).

- **age** (āj) *noun* a time period in life
- **distinguish** (dis ting′gwish) *verb* to see or understand differences
- **interview** (in′tər vyü) *noun* conversation in which one person asks questions, and another person answers

The **part of speech** shows how the word is used.

A

- **abolish** (ə bol′ish) *verb* to end something

- **accomplish** (ə kom′plish) *verb* to finish or achieve

- **achievement** (ə chēv′mənt) *noun* success; accomplishment

- **acknowledge** (ak nol′ij) *verb* to respond; to admit

- **activist** (ak′ti vist) *noun* a person who works at changing something, especially in politics

- **advocate** (ad′və kāt) *verb* to propose or support an idea

- **affect** (ə fekt′) *verb* to influence or have an impact on someone or something

- **age** (āj) *noun* a time period in life

- **analyze** (an′ ə līz) *verb* to examine something so as to understand what it is and means; to study

- **anxious** (angk′shəs) *adjective* worried; nervously fearful

- **approach** (ə prōch′) *verb* to move toward

- **argument** (är′gyə mənt) *noun* a reason given in order to persuade

- **arrangement** (ə rānj′mənt) *noun* something made by putting things together

- **assembly** (ə sem′blē) *noun* a grouping of people; a gathering

- **assume** (ə süm′) *verb* to believe something is true without knowing for sure

- **attitude** (at′ə tüd) *noun* an opinion or way of thinking

- **audience** (ȯ′dē əns) *noun* the group of readers an author is writing for

- **audition** (ȯ dish′ən) *noun* a performance as a tryout

- **autobiographical short story** (ȯ′tə bī əg ra′fi kəl shôrt stôr′ē) *noun* a short piece of fiction that comes from an author's experiences

B

- **ban** (ban) *verb* to block or prohibit

- **boxed item** (bokst ī′təm) *noun* a comment or activity that relates to but is separate from the main text; it often appears to the side of the main reading

- **boycott** (boi′kot) *noun* a refusal for political reasons to buy certain products or do business with a certain store

- **brochure** (brō shər′) *noun* a brief public document that communicates specific information

- **bullet** (bùl′it) *noun* a dot or small symbol used to create a list

C

- **cause** (kȯz) *noun* an event or action that produces a result

- **ceremony** (ser′ə mō′nē) *noun* a formal event, usually with rituals (customary words and actions done many times before)

- **challenge** (chal′ənj) *noun* a difficult task

- **character** (kar′ik tər) *noun* a person in a story

- **cherish** (cher′ish) *verb* to hold dear in one's mind

- **chronological order** (kron′ə lo′ji kəl ôr′dər) *noun* the order in which events happen

- **classify** (klas′ə fī) *verb* to divide things into groups so that similar things are in the same group

- **climax** (klī′maks) *noun* the turning point of a story, when the decisions or actions of the main character come together

- **coherence** (kȯ hîr′əns) *noun* clarity of order; having every sentence, paragraph, and section in an order that helps a reader to understand the subject

- **companion** (kəm pan′yən) *noun* a person who goes with another person

- **comprehend** (kom′pri hend′) *verb* to understand the meaning of something
- **complexity** (kəm plex′sə tē) *noun* a situation or condition with many difficult parts to it
- **concept** (kon′sept) *noun* a general idea that usually includes other related ideas
- **conclusion** (kən klü′zhən) *noun* something you decide is true after thinking about it carefully
- **conflict** (kon′flikt) *noun* a struggle between two opposing forces
- **connotative meaning** (kòn′ə tā′tiv mē′ning) *noun* the images or feelings we attach to a word
- **consist** (kən sist′) *verb* to be made up of; to be composed of
- **context** (kon′tekst) *noun* the information surrounding a word or phrase that determines exactly how it is meant
- **contrast** (kən trast′) *verb* to compare two things as a way to show their differences
- **contribution** (kon′trə byü′shən) *noun* a giving of money, one's time, etc.; a donation
- **convince** (kən vins′) *verb* to cause someone to believe that something is true or worth doing; to persuade
- **corps** (kôr) *noun* an organized and often highly trained group
- **courageous** (kə rā′jes) *adjective* brave; able to face and overcome danger and/or difficulties
- **crisis** (krī′sis) *noun* an emergency
- **current event** (kėr′ənt i vent′) *noun* an activity happening at the present time
- **curriculum** (kėr ik′yə ləm) *noun* the courses offered at an educational institution

D

- **date** (dāt) *noun* an important day, month, and year
- **debt** (det) *noun* a sum of money owed to another
- **deduce** (di düs′) *verb* to reach a conclusion by reasoning
- **define** (di fīn′) *verb* to give the meaning of
- **definition** (def′i ni′shən) *noun* the explanation of a word or phrase
- **denotative meaning** (dē′nō tā′tiv mē′ning) *noun* a word's actual meaning
- **depressed** (di prest′) *adjective* saddened; in low spirits
- **derivative** (di riv′ə tiv) *noun* a word that comes from another word, sometimes in a different language
- **description** (di skrip′shən) *noun* vivid details that add interest to a narrative
- **destination** (des′tə nā′shən) *noun* a place where someone is going or something is sent
- **determination** (di tėr′mə nā′shən) *noun* strong will, conviction, or drive
- **device** (di vīs′) *noun* an electrical or mechanical machine; a tool or implement
- **dialogue** (dī′ə lòg) *noun* conversation between characters
- **dictionary** (dik′shə ner′ē) *noun* a book or computer program that provides definitions of words; most dictionaries also provide other information, such as a word's part of speech, pronunciation, and etymology (word origin)
- **difference** (dif′ər əns) *noun* something that distinguishes one thing from another
- **discouraged** (dis kėr′ijd) *adjective* feeling a loss of confidence or hope
- **disgrace** (dis grās′) *verb* to dishonor or bring shame to

> - A yellow dot indicates a **Key Vocabulary Word.**
> - A purple dot indicates an **Academic Vocabulary Word.**
> - A green dot indicates a **Literary/Text Element Term.**

- **disheveled** (di shev′əld) *adjective* to have one's appearance (hair, clothes, etc.) in disorder
- **distinguish** (dis ting′gwish) *verb* to see or understand differences
- **distribute** (dis trib′yüt) *verb* to give out
- **droplet** (drop′lit) *noun* a small drop

E

- **effect** (ə fekt′) *noun* a result produced by a cause
- **embarrassed** (em bar′əst) *adjective* ashamed, self-conscious, ill at ease, uncomfortable
- **emphasize** (em′fə sīz) *verb* to place importance on
- **enforce** (en fôrs′) *verb* to make people obey (laws, rules, etc.)
- **engage** (en gāj′) *verb* to get and hold the attention of
- **enhance** (en hans′) *verb* to improve, add to
- **enlightening** (en līt′n ing) *adjective* giving greater knowledge
- **enrich** (en rich′) *verb* to add good things to
- **entangled** (en tang′gəld) *adjective* mixed in and caught by something else
- **enunciate** (i nun′sē āt) *verb* to speak clearly
- **equally** (ē′kwəl lē) *adverb* the same
- **equation** (i kwā′zhən) *noun* a mathematical statement that two amounts are equal
- **equivalent** (i kwiv′ə lənt) *adjective* equal; the same
- **escort** (es′kôrt) *noun* someone who goes with another as a guide, guard, or companion
- **establish** (e stab′lish) *verb* to found, create
- **etiquette** (et′ə ket) *noun* the correct and expected way to behave
- **event** (i vent′) *noun* a specific happening, particularly an important one

- **evidence** (ev′ə dəns) *noun* words, objects, or facts that help someone find the truth
- **evolve** (i volv′) *verb* to develop, change
- **exhausted** (eg zȯ′stid) *adjective* extremely tired
- **experiment** (ek sper′ə mənt) *noun* a test done to see if something works or happens
- **expert opinion** (ek′spėrt′ ə pin′yən) *noun* the opinion or belief of a person who knows a lot about a particular subject
- **export** (ek′spôrt) *verb* to ship from one country to another
- **expository text** (ik spoz′i tôr′ē tekst) *noun* a reading in which the author's goal is to inform or to describe

F

- **fact** (fakt) *noun* something that can be proven
- **factor** (fak′tər) *noun* someone or something that actively contributes to a result
- **fine-tune** (fīn tün′) *verb* to adjust slightly for a higher level of performance
- **first-person narrative** (fėrst′ pėr′sən nar′ə tiv) *noun* a story that is told by the main character who uses the first-person pronoun "I" to refer to himself or herself
- **figurative language** (fig′yər ə tiv lang′gwij) *noun* language that goes beyond the literal meaning of words in order to help the reader see an idea or subject in a new way
- **fluid** (flü′id) *adjective* smooth, graceful
- **formal style** (fȯr′məl stīl) *noun* a serious tone
- **framework** (frām′wėrk) *noun* a structure used to support other things
- **free-verse poetry** (frē vėrs pō′e trē) *noun* poetry that may have rhyming words, lines with different numbers of words, and stanzas with different numbers of lines

G

- **garbled** (gär′bəld) *adjective* hard to understand
- **generosity** (jen′ə ros′ə tē) *noun* readiness to give
- **glisten** (glis′n) *verb* to shine, glitter, or sparkle, often as if from wetness
- **global** (glō′bəl) *adjective* relating to the whole world; worldwide
- **graduate** (graj′ü āt) *verb* to receive a degree from an academic institution
- **guarantee** (gar′ən tē′) *verb* to give a promise to do or provide something

H

- **heading** (hed′ing) *noun* a boldfaced word or phrase used to introduce or organize material into sections
- **historical detail** (hi stôr′ ə kəl di′tāl) *noun* an aspect of life in another time period, such as the way people lived, how they behaved, and what they wore
- **hum** (hum) *verb* to sing with the mouth closed
- **hyperbole** (hī pûr′bə lē) *noun* extreme exaggeration (figurative language)

I

- **identify** (ī den′tə fī) *verb* to recognize something and be able to say what it is
- **idiom** (id′ē əm) *noun* an expression or phrase that does not have the same meaning as its individual words
- **ignorant** (ig′nər ənt) *adjective* unknowing; uninformed
- **image** (im′ij) *noun* a mental picture of someone or something
- **immense** (i mens′) *adjective* huge
- **impose** (im pōz′) *verb* to place upon

- **impression** (im presh′ən) *noun* a feeling about someone or something
- **incentive** (in sen′tiv) *noun* something that makes someone work harder; motivation
- **incident** (in′sə dənt) *noun* an event or occurrence
- **indicate** (in′də kāt) *verb* to show or suggest that something else is true
- **infer** (in fûr′) *verb* to make a guess about something that is unknown using some information that is known
- **influence** (in′flü əns) *verb* to change someone's mind or to have an effect on something
- **innate** (i nāt′) *adjective* part of someone from birth; natural
- **intention** (in ten′shən) *noun* purpose, plan
- **interact** (in′tər akt′) *verb* to communicate with someone through words or actions
- **internal dialogue** (in tėr′nl dī′ə lóg) *noun* the thoughts of the narrator revealed to the reader
- **interview** (in′tər vyü) *noun* conversation in which one person asks questions and another person answers them
- **introduction** (in′trə duk′shən) *noun* the part of a story where the characters, the setting, and the main problem are presented
- **invest** (in vest′) *verb* to put effort (time, money, energy, etc.) into something

J

- **jazz** (jaz) *noun* a form of American popular music
- **judge** (juj) *verb* to consider something and then give an official decision
- **justify** (jus′tə fī) *verb* to give a reason for an action

---

- A yellow dot indicates a **Key Vocabulary Word.**
- A purple dot indicates an **Academic Vocabulary Word.**
- A green dot indicates a **Literary/Text Element Term.**

L

- **launch** (lȯnch) *verb* to start; to put into operation
- **lesson** (les′n) *noun* information to be learned with activities
- **locate** (lō′kāt) *verb* to find
- **logical** (loj′ə kəl) *adjective* showing good sense or reason

M

- **magazine article** (mag′ə zēn′ är′tə kəl) *noun* an informational text that presents nonfiction writing
- **main idea** (mān ī dē′ə) *noun* the most important, or central, message
- **measure** (mezh′ər) *verb* to find the size, speed, weight, etc., of something
- **memoir** (mem′wär′) *noun* a story from the life of an author
- **metaphor** (met′ə fôr) *noun* a comparison made by describing one thing as if it is another thing (figurative language)
- **mission** (mish′ən) *noun* the purpose of the business that a person or organization conducts
- **monologue** (mon′l ȯg) *noun* a long talk by only one person, usually in drama
- **mood** (müd) *noun* the feeling an author wants a reader to experience while reading scenes or moments in a piece of writing
- **moral** (môr′əl) *noun* a lesson based on ideas about what is right or wrong
- **mortal** (môr′tl) *adjective* human; subject to death
- **motivate** (mō′tə vāt′) *verb* to give someone a reason to do something

N

- **narrator** (nar āt′ ər) *noun* the character or voice that tells a story
- **negotiate** (ni gō′shē āt) *verb* to reach an agreement through discussion

- **notation** (nō tā′shən) *noun* a set of symbols used to represent musical notes, numbers, etc.

O

- **obvious** (ob′vē əs) *adjective* easy to see or understand; clear
- **old-fashioned** (ōld′fash′ənd) *adjective* no longer in common use; out-of-date
- **onomatopoeia** (on′ə mat′ə pē′ə) *noun* words such as "buzz" or "hiss" that sound like their meanings
- **opinion** (ə pin′yən) *noun* a personal view or idea
- **organization** (ôr′gə nə zā′shən) *noun* the order, or structure, of the material presented in an article
- **outcome** (out′kum′) *noun* an end result or effect
- **outshine** (out shīn′) *verb* to perform better than someone else

P

- **pace** (pās) *noun* speed; the tempo of an activity
- **panel** (pan′l) *noun* a group of people chosen for a project or a discussion of issues
- **participate** (pär tis′ə pāt) *verb* to take part or have a role in an activity or event
- **particle** (pär′tə kəl) *noun* a very small piece of something
- **personification** (pər son′ə fi kā′shən) *noun* giving human traits and abilities to non-human things
- **place name** (plās nām) *noun* name of a location where an important event happened
- **plot** (plot) *noun* events in a story that happen in a certain order
- **possess** (pə zes′) *verb* to have; to own
- **predict** (pri dikt′) *verb* to say what will happen in the future

prestige (pre stēzh′) *noun* qualities, such as excellent reputation, wealth, and power, that bring admiration or honor

primary source (prī′mər′ē sôrs) *noun* a document created at the time of an event or quotations from a person who lived at that time

process (pros′es) *noun* a series of actions taken to get a specific result

progress (prog′res) *noun* advancement; movement toward a goal

promote (prə mōt′) *verb* to support; to contribute to the progress or growth of

promotion (prə mō′shən) *noun* movement to a new and better job

proof (prüf) *noun* evidence that shows something is true

propose (prə pōz′) *verb* to suggest or recommend

proverb (prov′ĕrb′) *noun* a saying that expresses a common truth

purpose (pėr′pəs) *noun* the goal an author has for writing

pursue (pər sü′) *verb* to chase; to go after someone to capture

Q

quarrelsome (kwôr′əl səm) *adjective* always ready to fight about something

quote (kwōt) *noun* an exact statement made by a person

R

random (ran′dəm) *adjective* happening at any time; unplanned

range (rānj) *noun* a variety of things, ideas, or products

rather (raŦH′ər) *adverb* preferably

real-life example (rēl līf eg zam′pl) *noun* a true experience that proves a point or provides a model for learning

reflect (ri flekt′) *verb* to think deeply about

reform (ri form′) *verb* to improve something that exists, especially government

relate (ri lāt′) *verb* to connect

reluctant (ri luk′ tənt) *adjective* concerned, afraid, or hesitant

repetition (rep′ə tish′ən) *noun* using a word or phrase two or more times to make a point or to create a sense of rhythm

reputation (rep′ yə tā′shən) *noun* an opinion about the quality of something, such as a person's character

resolve (ri zolv′) *verb* to find a solution to a problem

resolution (rez′ə lü′shən) *noun* the conclusion or final result of the story

resource (ri sôrs′ or rē′ sôrs) *noun* a supply of support, money, knowledge, or anything needed

restate (rē stāt′) *verb* to say something again

restriction (ri strik′shən) *noun* a rule that limits something

reveal (ri vēl′) *verb* to uncover something that is hidden or secret

rhyme (rīm) *noun* words ending with a similar sound

rhyming poetry (rīm′ing pō′i trē) *noun* poetry that uses rhyming words, with the same number of words or syllables in each line, and the same number of lines in each stanza

rhythm (riŦH′əm) *noun* a regular beat within a line of poetry

rising action (rī′zing ak′shən) *noun* the events that lead up to the climax of a story

root (rüt) *noun* the basic part of a word

rupture (rup′chər) *noun* a break or split in something

- A yellow dot indicates a **Key Vocabulary Word**.
- A purple dot indicates an **Academic Vocabulary Word**.
- A green dot indicates a **Literary/Text Element Term**.

S

- **sacrifice** (sak′rə fīs) *verb* to suffer loss, pain, or injury in order to achieve a goal
- **scientific experiments** (sī′ən tif′ik ek sper′ə mənts) *noun* tests done to see a result
- **select** (si lekt′) *verb* to pick or make a very careful choice
- **sequence** (sē′kwəns) *noun* a connected series of events or items, one following the other
- **setting** (set′ing) *noun* the time and place where the events of a story take place
- **shelter** (shel′tər) *noun* any building or covering (tree branches, a cave, etc.) that gives physical protection
- **simile** (sim′ə lē) *noun* a comparison of two different things by using like or as (figurative language)
- **slew** (slü) *noun* a lot; a large amount of something
- **slim** (slim) *adjective* thin or slender
- **snare** (snâr) *verb* to get or catch
- **solution** (sə lü′shən) *noun* an answer to a problem or a way to solve a problem
- **spectacle** (spek′tə kəl) *noun* a strange or amazing sight
- **speech** (spēch) *noun* a formal or informal presentation made by one person before an audience of any size
- **stalk** (stók) *noun* the stem of a plant
- **standard** (stan′dərd) *noun* something against which other things or ideas are measured
- **stanza** (stan′zə) *noun* group of lines in a poem or song that share a subject or a theme
- **stomp** (stomp) *verb* to step down strongly with the foot
- **stroll** (strōl) *verb* to walk in an unhurried and relaxed way

- **structure** (struk′chər) *noun* the way that the parts of something are put together or organized
- **stunned** (stund) *adjective* surprised or shocked; made speechless
- **suffix** (suf′iks) *noun* a word part that is added to the end of a word
- **summarize** (sum′ə rīz) *verb* to make a summary or a brief account of a reading
- **summary** (sum′ə rē) *noun* a brief statement that covers the most important features of a reading selection
- **summon** (sum′ən) *verb* to call or send for
- **support** (sə port′) *verb* to agree with or advocate; to back up with information
- **supporting detail** (sə pôr′ting dē′tāl) *noun* any information that relates to the main idea and helps you understand it
- **supporting material** (sə pôr′ting mə tir′ ē əl) *noun* evidence that proves statements are correct
- **symbolize** (sim′bə līz) *verb* to represent, stand for, or suggest something else

T

- **template** (tem′plit) *noun* a guide with codes, symbols, etc.
- **testimonial** (tes′tə mō′nē əl) *noun* a direct quote from consumers or participants who share positive experiences with a company or its product
- **theme** (thēm) *noun* the main message or point that an author wants a reader to take from a story
- **thesaurus** (thi sôr′əs) *noun* a reference book that provides synonyms, or words that are the same or similar in meaning
- **timid** (tim′id) *adjective* easily frightened; shy; hesitant
- **tireless** (tīr′lis) *adjective* dedicated

- **tone** (tōn) *noun* an author's overall attitude toward the reader or the subject he or she is writing about
- **tournament** (tėr′nə mənt) *noun* a competition with a series of events leading to a winner or winners
- **tradition** (trə dish′ən) *noun* a custom or belief that is passed on from one generation to another
- **transform** (trans fôrm′) *verb* to change from one shape or appearance to another
- **trek** (trek) *noun* a long, difficult journey
- **trigger** (trig′ər) *verb* to cause something to start

U

- **unity** (yü′nə tē) *noun* the sense that all of the material in an article is related or connected in some way

- **universal** (yü′nə vėr′səl) *adjective* found or practiced everywhere

V

- **valid** (val′id) *adjective* based on sensible reasoning
- **vapor** (vāp′ər) *noun* a gas, mist, haze, or fog that is barely visible
- **vast** (vast) *adjective* wide in area
- **violate** (vī′ə lāt) *verb* to break or disregard, as in a rule or a law
- **visual aid** (vizh′ü əl ād) *noun* a picture, drawing, or a chart that helps you understand what you are reading
- **vocabulary** (vō kab′yə ler′ē) *noun* a group of words, often related by subject matter
- **voice** (vois) *noun* characteristics of a narrator

- A yellow dot indicates a **Key Vocabulary Word.**
- A purple dot indicates an **Academic Vocabulary Word.**
- A green dot indicates a **Literary/Text Element Term.**

Index of Skills

Grammar, Usage, Mechanics, and Spelling

Literary/Text Elements and Features

Reading

Independent Reading

Meet the Author

Meet the Founders

Reading Fluency

Readings

Reading Strategies

Writing

Penmanship

Writing Applications

Writing Conventions

Writing Strategies

Text Credits

Illustrator Credits

Photo Credits